The Metaphysics of Love

Studies in Renaissance love poetry
from Dante to Milton

A. J. SMITH

Professor of English
University of Southampton

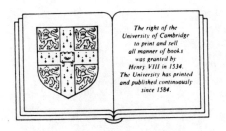

The right of the
University of Cambridge
to print and sell
all manner of books
was granted by
Henry VIII in 1534.
The University has printed
and published continuously
since 1584.

CAMBRIDGE UNIVERSITY PRESS

Cambridge
New York   New Rochelle
Melbourne   Sydney

Published by the Press Syndicate of the University of Cambridge
The Pitt Building, Trumpington Street, Cambridge CB2 1RP
32 East 57th Street, New York, NY 10022, USA
10 Stamford Road, Oakleigh, Melbourne 3166, Australia

First published 1985
Reprinted 1987, 1988 (twice)

Printed in Great Britain by the
Athenaeum Press Ltd, Newcastle upon Tyne

Library of Congress catalogue card number: 84-14945

British Library cataloguing in publication data

Smith, A.J. (Albert James)
The metaphysics of love.
1. Love poetry — History and criticism
I. Title
809.1'9354   PN1076

ISBN 0 521 25908 8

PP

The Metaphysics of Love

And Nature, seeing the beauty of the form of God, smiled with insatiate love of Man, showing the reflection of that most beautiful form in the water, and its shadow on the earth. And he, seeing this form, a form like to his own, in earth and water, loved it, and willed to dwell there. And the deed followed close on the design; and he took up his abode in matter devoid of reason. And Nature, when she had got him with whom she was in love, wrapped him in her clasp, and they were mingled in one; for they were in love with one another.

And that is why man, unlike all other living creatures upon earth, is twofold. He is mortal by reason of his body; he is immortal by reason of the man of eternal substance. He is immortal, and has all things in his power; yet he suffers the lot of a mortal, being subject to Destiny. He is exalted above the structure of the heavens; yet he is born a slave of Destiny. He is bisexual, as his Father is bisexual, and sleepless, as his Father is sleepless; yet he is mastered by carnal desire and by oblivion.

Corpus Hermeticum, Pimander, Libellus i, 14–15

Contents

Contents

Acknowledgments

This book owes much to the help of friends and colleagues, notably Dominic Baker-Smith, J. J. Lawlor, W. A. Craik, J. A. Berthoud, A. Palmer. The author acknowledges with gratitude the support he has received from the following bodies: the Leverhulme Trust, the British Academy, the English Speaking Union, the Folger Shakespeare Library, the Huntington Library, the British Council, the University of Southampton, the University of Keele, the University College of Swansea.

Versions of material in this book first appeared in *The Review of English Studies*, n.s., IX, 1958; *The Anglo-Welsh Review*, Spring, 1967; *Stratford-upon-Avon Studies*, XI, 1970; *Essays and Studies*, 1973; *Poetry Wales*, Autumn, 1975; *Thames Poetry*, Winter, 1976; *An English Miscellany Presented to W. S. Mackie*, ed. B. S. Lee, Cape Town, 1977; *John Donne Journal*, I, 1983. I am grateful for permission to draw on this earlier work.

Preamble:
The Lineage of Love

The studies in this book follow the conduct of a prolonged debate about the spiritual worth of love. They mark some proving points in a trial of humane values, posing unlike possibilities of love which set each other off the more sharply when we find them realised in great works of art. Love looms so large in spiritual regard from the twelfth century to the seventeenth century because it challenged men's rage for a fulfilment beyond change, bringing home to us human creatures our thraldom to time and circumstance, the contradictions of our nature, the alienness of our environment, the incongruity of our designs with the universe we encounter. Is love strong as death? Or does it betray us to corruption? Seventeenth-century love poets seem peculiarly prone to be caught in two minds because the times made a metaphysical predicament of the frailty of sexual passion in the world as we have it, which was felt most acutely when love itself offered the means to deliver us from ourselves. Donne and Milton, no less than Shakespeare and the Jacobean dramatists, show us lovers whose commitment to their end brings them to an extremity of their entire being.[1]

The attempt to find spiritual value in sexual love becomes urgent when the love of a fellow being is taken to redeem our nature in a corrupted world, or when sexual fulfilment itself is felt to give meaning to life. European writers from Dante to Milton share a concern with the status of love and our sexual nature which impels them to seek metaphysical reassurance in the prospect of a human bond that is not wholly subject to time, of qualities beyond flesh and blood in a fellow creature, of a providence in our chance conjunctures. A conceit which tries temporal circumstances in the order of final truth quite properly 'affects the Metaphysicks', whose categories inform the language of love while love is taken to engage our spirit and our senses together, however individual the vision and whatever the alteration of times.

Dante and Milton were heirs to a platonic tradition of intellectual love and beauty. Yet they drew more directly upon the work of

Christian metaphysicians who developed the impulse of the Canticles and the Gospels into a universal doctrine of love. These ardent saints and doctors found a common need to regulate spiritual passion; and they sponsored a cult of love which dramatised devotional life. Devotees of divine love diverged chiefly in the way they sought to reconcile themselves with God, some inviting grace through a right understanding of his nature and his works, some by the sheer intensity of their longing for him. Intelligence and feeling began to move apart.

Life in the world posed a harder choice when men's secular concerns were taken for distractions from final truth, or corrupting allurements in themselves. How may our worldly attachments bear upon the love of God? If we consummate our being in the union with our Creator then the love which binds fellow-creatures stands in question, not least sexual love. A man who looks to the beauty of another human being to redeem him from carnal desire, and further the needs of his spirit, makes a large demand upon reason as well as his own nature. Over some four centuries European love poets asked themselves how far our amorous urges simply commit us to change and the frailty of sense. Some of them looked for other ways of approaching God through the love of his creation. None could be indifferent to the metaphysical consequences of their commitment to love.

The present inquiry seeks to follow out a crisis of our European engagement with love by contrasting some writings in which love acutely poses such issues as the relation of the body to the mind and the spirit, the bearing of sexual passion upon spiritual devotion, the consonance of natural life with supernatural being, the prospect of permanence in a universe of flux, the ultimate worth of experience in time. Its particular concern is to mark some shifts of response to these extremities over several centuries, and to see what qualities and character each body of writing owes to its author's individual management of love. All these writers entered the area of a traditional discussion of love, and might draw upon a range of prescribed attitudes to our sexual nature. To track their ideas to the sources would not much illuminate the encounter. Yet the writings discriminate themselves partly by the scope they allow to certain animating conceptions which were formulated in antiquity, in the prime Christian texts, and in the early Renaissance.

All the writings considered here are shaped by the momentous assumption that human love in some way rehearses a universal condition. This conceit seized the earliest European metaphysicians, in a debate whose terms still haunted English love poetry in the seventeenth century. Heraclitus of Ephesus (flourished 500 BC) issued a challenge which prompted a cosmology of love. He envisaged a cosmos of atoms in perpetual flux, in which everything that occurs comes about by chance collision. Change and opposition necessarily make up our existence. Things come into being by the death of other things; and this continual tension between becoming and dissolving imposes a kind of equilibrium in which the overall bulk of each form of matter remains the same, even though the particular manifestations of it are continually changing.

Empedocles of Akragas (flourished 460 BC) transformed this stark cosmology when he identified the forces of becoming and dissolving as love and strife. He supposed that the cosmos renews itself by the continual alternation of opposite processes, a drawing together of unlike elements in love followed by their fragmenting themselves again in strife. The mingling of an immortal force of love with mortal matter produces a mixed condition, in which the tension of opposite impulses generates new and wonderful life. Change is perpetual, yet amounts to no more than an unceasing transformation of substance in which nothing is ultimately lost. Behind the appearance of flux the universe continues in eternal stasis. Empedocles adds that the cosmic process simply enlarges the fruitful alternation of impulses we know in our own bodies, between love which draws us to a union of unlikes and strife which elements us again. Yet the stasis he predicates lies beyond our realisation. Neither he nor Heraclitus leave scope in their atomism for our final self-fulfilment in a love beyond change.

In the *Timaeus* Plato (c. 429–347 BC) takes up from Empedocles the bold conceit of a fusion in a single nature of mortal matter and immortal being. But he altogether transforms pre-Socratic thinking when he proposes that the constant pull between these diverse elements may be resolved if they are brought into accord in a single pursuit of ideal form, that intelligible idea of perfection which exists beyond appearances and partakes of the eternal and divine. The myth of a universal work of love has been decisively redefined when love is taken for an attraction to beauty, and beauty itself for a reflection of unchanging idea. Not the least of Plato's legacies to Renaissance thinkers is that he discovers an intellectual quality in physical beauty, and gives a spiritual direction to the ideal representation of the body itself. The sheer spiritual purposefulness of the quest for universal beauty is far removed from the fluctuating state which his predecessors prescribe for mankind and all other phenomena:

And now, Socrates, there bursts upon him that wondrous vision which is the very soul of the beauty he has toiled so long for. It is an everlasting loveliness which neither comes nor goes, which neither flowers nor fades; for such beauty is the same on every hand, the same then as now, here as there, this way as that way, the same to every worshipper as it is to every other.

Nor will his vision of the beautiful take the form of a face, or of hands, or of anything that is of the flesh; it will be neither words, nor knowledge, nor a something that exists in something else such as a living creature, or the earth, or the heavens, or anything that is, but subsisting of itself and by itself in an eternal oneness; while every lovely thing partakes of it in such sort that, however much the parts may wax and wane, it will be neither more nor less, but still the same inviolable whole.

Symposium 210E–211B[2]

Diotima's doctrine of love, as Socrates recounts it in *Symposium* 201D–212D, is no mere intellectualising of physical attraction. It links in a hierarchy of qualities the particular perceptions of our senses with a universal order of ideal forms, such as pure intellect alone may apprehend. Diotima pictures the lover's ascent up a scale of being, marking out a progress which starts in the perception of the beauty of particular objects, passes to an appreciation of moral and intellectual beauty in general, and is perfected beyond the reach of mere mortality in the vision of ideal beauty itself:

But if it were given to man to gaze on beauty's very self – unsullied, unalloyed, and freed from the mortal taint that haunts the frailer loveliness of flesh and blood – if, I say, it were given to man to see the heavenly beauty face to face, would you call *his* ... an unenviable life, whose eyes had been opened to the vision, and who had gazed upon it in true contemplation until it had become his own for ever? And remember ... that it is only when he discerns beauty itself through what makes it visible that a man will be quickened with the true, and not the seeming, virtue – for it is virtue's self that quickens him, not virtue's semblance. And when he has brought forth and reared this perfect virtue, he shall be called the friend of God; and if ever it is given to man to put on immortality, it shall be given to him.

Symposium 211E–212A

Each state marks an advance to a higher condition of love and leaves the earlier stages behind, so that a lover could no longer be wholly content with the beauty of an individual body once he had glimpsed a superior beauty. Nonetheless physical beauty is still truly beauty, and there is certainly no despising of the flesh in itself in

Diotima's vision, much less a repudiation of bodily grace. All beauty partakes of the universal form of beauty, and draws from the same source. We may love at a lower level or a higher, as we apprehend beauty through the senses or with the mind. Yet the decisive first step is the impulse to love beauty at all; and there is no moral gulf between those who stay at the beauty of the body and those who move beyond the body in pursuit of spiritual beauty.

Aristotle (384–322 BC), Plato's pupil, offers a quite different expectation of love; in fact the two fourth-century academicians open the gap between the ideal and the natural which would continue to perplex love poets. In his *De Anima* Aristotle simply undercuts Plato's scale of transcendence with the formal argument that activities and functions are logically prior to faculties, by which he means that the faculties we ascribe to our nature exist only in what they do (II, 4). Intellect itself has being only when it thinks. The soul, or spirit, is not a separate element but a logical entity only, in the sense that it is nothing more than the name we give to the animating principle of the organism. The soul is what moves the body (II, 2); it is the actuality of a particular body, the realisation in function of that body's potential capacities. The dispositions which we call the attributes of the soul, such as anger, courage, love, are all conjoined with body and attended by some particular affection of the body. Soul neither acts nor is acted upon apart from the body, indeed thought itself cannot be independent of body. In common with all the other processes of thought, love is a function not of the thinking faculty alone but of the entire organism. We must think of it as an attribute of the possessor, not of one particular faculty (I, 4).

Aristotle brings Diotima's endeavour back to earth when he accounts for actions by looking to their biological causes rather than to voluntary ends, as if a moral election simply expresses the needs of the particular organism. He speaks of the very differences between man and man as different responses to the same stimuli, which may be attributed to their unlike bodily constitutions (I, 1). The actions of particular organisms simply give effect to appetites, in as far as they serve the impulse of all living beings to perform their natural functions. In his analytic account of the powers of the soul (II, 2–12) Aristotle indicates the part love plays in the economy of organic nature. He says that the most natural function of all living things is to reproduce their own species, 'animal producing animal and plant plant, in order that they may, so far as they can, share in the eternal and the divine. For it is that which all things yearn after, and that is the final cause of their natural activity' (II, 4, 415a, 26–62).[3] Individual beings are incapable of sharing continuously in the eternal and divine because nothing in the world of perishables can abide numerically one and the same. So they partake in the eternal and divine in the only way they can. Each persists in a representative rather than in itself, seeking to renew itself in something which is specifically yet not numerically one with it. Love serves the biological need to perpetuate ourselves in our kin (II, 4).

The aristotelean urge to value an activity by the extent to which it realises the capacities of the whole organism continued to challenge Platonist lovers who found a moral imperative in the order of creation itself. Christian teaching made room for both dispositions. Christians supposed that we inhabit a creation of love, to which a partial or perverse response is a dire self-impoverishment or worse. Their understanding of love followed Christ's categorical injunctions that we must first love God entirely, and then love our neighbour as ourselves. Love sums up the witness of a master who told his disciples that they must love their enemies as they loved one another, and made it the final proof of love that a man lay down his life for his friends. Christ's teaching does not set sexual love apart from the general love which should link all God's creatures. His estimation of it simply follows out his embodiment of a humanity that reconciles and binds, his disavowal of what divides or excludes. Man and wife are one flesh, joined in inseparable union by God himself. Adultery and whoredom are undoubtedly to be repented and renounced; yet such sins of human kindness better merit forgiving compassion than sins of self-regard:

Neither do I condemn thee: go, and sin no more.

John 8: 11

Her sins, which are many, are forgiven; for she loved much; but to whom little is forgiven, the same loveth little.

Luke 7: 47

Christ's followers took up his revolutionary testimony of our oneness in God's love and found in love the indispensable saving virtue – 'the greatest of these is charity' (Corinthians 1: 13). Love brings us nearest to God just because it allows us to partake of God's very nature and essence, which he manifested when he gave his only son to die for us, or died for us himself: 'He that loveth not knoweth not God; for God is love' (1 John 4:8). God dwells in us, and his love is perfected in us when we love one another; we must love our brother before we can love God. The evidence of the Epistles of St John is that their very vocation of unworldly love soon drew Christians together in a fellowship which set them apart from the world.

For St Paul right love may save us by grace through faith. Yet love avails us only if it detaches us altogether from life without Christ, impelling us to abjure such commitments in the world as divert us from the true object of our devotion. The rigour of St Paul's own repudiation of his secular career is reflected in his separation of worldly attachments from the love of Christ, sexual love from devotion to God. Virginity is a better state than marriage; marriage has the advantage over lust though it must still distract from pure spiritual love; and indulgence of the senses is simply death.

Holy Writ itself seems to offer other attitudes to sexual love, notably the sustained outpouring of sensual passion which interposes so startlingly in the Old Testament between Ecclesiastes and Isaiah under the style of The Song of Solomon:

How fair and how pleasant art thou, O love, for delights! This thy stature is like to a palm tree, and thy breasts to clusters of grapes. I said, I will go up to the palm tree, I will take hold of the boughs thereof: now also thy breasts shall be as clusters of the vine, and the smell of thy nose like apples; And the roof of thy mouth like the best wine for my beloved, that goeth down sweetly, causing the lips of those that are asleep to speak. I am my beloved's, and his desire is toward me.

The Song of Solomon 7: 6–10

On the face of it the Canticles rehearse a dialogue of love, which catches one up in the sheer ecstatic ardour of a sexual awakening:

I sleep, but my heart waketh: it is the voice of my beloved that knocketh, saying, Open to me, my sister, my love, my dove, my undefiled: for my head is filled with dew, and my locks with the drops of the night. I have put off my coat, how shall I put it on? I have washed my feet; how shall I defile them? My beloved put in his hand by the hole of the door, and my bowels were moved for him. I rose up to open to my beloved; and my hands dropped with myrrh, and my fingers with sweet smelling myrrh, upon the handles of the lock.

5: 2–5

Such a ravishing avowal of unrestrained bodily rapture does not self-evidently chime with St Paul's admonitions against our attachments in the world and indulgence of the senses. The staid orthodox gloss still incites us to take a quite unascetic view of devotional life – 'The church's love to Christ', 'The mutual love of Christ and his

7

church.' St Bernard is arrestingly bolder than that. In his sermons on the Canticles he allows full scope to the erotic intensity of the writing, taking the lovers' exchanges for reciprocal expressions of yearning and wooing between the soul and Christ. The way was opened to a theology of love which need not exclude sensual passion.

Opponents of such devotional excesses looked to St Augustine as much as to St Paul. St Augustine of Hippo (354–450 AD), like St Paul a sensualist turned ascetic, formalised the Pauline division of man's nature, positing two warring elements in our make-up which were and ought still to be in harmonious union. He denies that the body is worthless in itself. On the contrary, God is to be praised for creating even in the least fly an animal nature which wondrously and stupendously combines corporeal and incorporeal elements, so that in due proportion flesh mingles with spirit, sense with intelligence, appetite with reason (*De Civitate Dei* xxii, 24). Our human constitution remains wholly praiseworthy while it keeps its right order, which it has when body is subject to spirit and appetite subject to reason, as when man's reason rules woman's sexual nature (*Confessions* XIII, xxxii; *de Genesi contra Manichaeos* ii, 15). In our right state the harmonious equality of mind, love and knowledge corresponds to the order of the Trinity (*De Trinitate* IX, i, iv, 4–5).

In *De Civitate Dei* xiv–xv Augustine categorically distinguishes the unfallen condition of humanity from the fallen condition. He supposes that man's body and spirit were at one before the Fall, and that paradise was for the good of both parts of our nature. Adam's flesh and his mind alike wholly obeyed his will; lust was not necessary to procreation or pain to childbirth, and the human pair felt no shame in coupling. The Fall not only put man's nature at odds with itself but perverted it, so that the carnal state precedes the spiritual state. The effects of a man's corrupted nature must now be evil and carnal at first, and may become good and spiritual only when he is regenerated by Christ. Will and desire work so counter to each other that the flesh will not respond to the wish. Lust is the spur to procreation, and turns to shame the moment it is gratified. A man is constantly racked by the discord between his spiritual will and his carnal will, his soul and his lust.

The *Confessions* makes example of St Augustine's own carnal conflict. He sets out the character of his profligate youth, discovering the evidence of our general perversion in that bondage to sensual appetite which corrupted friendship in concupiscence, and turned his pursuit of beauty into a preoccupation with a mere formal symmetry such as lures a man's senses to their own destruction. He takes his youthful state for a compound of all sins since it comprehended in itself the fatal impulses of the Fall, which he distinguishes by their perversion of the several elements of our nature as a commitment to the pleasure of the flesh, self-loving pride, and intellectual curiosity. All these are forms of perverse love, even the last one amounting to a concupiscence of eyes and mind which kindles our lust for vain knowledge; and they must be accounted the primal sins just because they most engrossingly divert us from the love of God.

Augustine looks beyond his own carnal will for the promptings which awakened him to his condition. He tells how he was drawn to struggle upwards from body to soul, sense to intelligence, self to God, a travail which was concluded in a moment by that providential reading of St Paul – 'Tolle, lege'. Romans 13:13 opens his eyes to the stark contradiction between the life of sense and the love of Christ. His abrupt conversion from delight in sensible allurements to the wholehearted love of God implies an absolute commitment to an unchanging spiritual beauty which altogether transcends all other beauties:

Too late came I to love thee, O thou Beauty both so ancient and so fresh, yea too late came I to love thee. And behold, thou wert within me, and I out of myself, where I made search for thee: I ugly rushed headlong upon those beautiful things thou hast made. Thou indeed wert with me; but I was not with thee: these beauties kept me far enough from thee: even those, which unless they were in thee, should not be at all. Thou calledst and criedst unto me, yea thou even breakedst open my deafness: thou discoveredst thy beams and shinedst unto me, and didst chase away my blindness: thou didst most fragrantly blow upon me, and I drew in my breath and I pant after thee; I tasted thee, and now do hunger and thirst after thee; thou didst touch me, and I even burn again to enjoy thy peace . . .

When I shall once attain to be united unto thee in every part of me, then shall I no more feel either sorrow or labour: yea, then shall my life truly be alive, every way full of thee.

Confessions x, xxvii–xxviii†

Loving God alone, we unify our nature in single constancy; God himself kindles a love that burns but never consumes.

For St Augustine, as for St Paul, right love is the absolute condition of right order in our nature, and it must now be won out of dire struggle with the perverse love which engrosses us in the world. Yet it draws us providentially to its source. Love kindles us to move upward from the earth as by the force of a superior gravitational pull, and ascend towards God in stages (*De Civitate Dei* xi, 28). Regenerate love expresses our natural appetite to fulfil our own nature in our due place, drawing us to search through all creation for the marks of God's image, which is our true image also. We move upward towards him as to the object and cause of our love; and in finding him we find ourselves.

What part love may play in the encounters of secular society was a question to which the mediaeval followers of St Augustine returned a bleak answer. St Francis and his adherents practised love in the world, but in the catholic manner of Christ's own ministry. The Humanists of the fourteenth century and fifteenth century mark a turn towards our modern concern with sexual motives. They sponsored a drastic reappraisal of love when they shifted attention from the contemplative ideal of retired piety to the idea of a life of active virtue in the world. The leading Humanists were not theologians but state officials and scholars, such as Petrarch, Salutati, Bruni, Alberti, Poliziano, men who stood close to power in the Curia or the Councils of their own States. Their prime concern was the conduct of government and of civil life; and their revived interest in classical writers as historical figures coincided with, or partly prompted, the rediscovery of ancient codices which themselves called for relative evaluation.

The need to place antique writings historically sharpened men's perception of historical change. History no longer presented itself as a simple continuum of events or a series of absolute gestures, but began to be taken for an evolving process in which a pattern might be discerned. In the sixteenth century Guicciardini, Machiavelli, and Vasari assume the working of a natural law of growth and decline by which entire civil cultures, as well as the virile powers of those who make them, flourish and fail in time.

Organic change implies ripeness, however brief. Humanists cited the civil cultures of Periclean Athens and of Augustan Rome to bear out their assumption that a civilisation consummates itself in a moment of perfect maturity, whose proof is a perfecting of the arts and the language itself. In this succession of ripening and decaying history simply enlarges the order of individual lives, exemplifying in political attitudes the same natural processes of change in time to which all human impulses are subject, not least love. It follows that a man's attitudes and manners cannot be judged absolutely but must be referred to his particular circumstances at a phase of his life, of an attachment, of the social order which partly defines him. Sexual love presents a moral crux just because it offers such a telling instance of our ever-shifting struggle to reconcile ourselves to our predicament and our fellow-beings.

Plato's dialogues emerged as a revelation to the Humanists who succeeded Petrarch, opening up a fresh vision of our nature and a new vista of human possibility. Yet Plato was not wholly unknown in the Middle Ages, nor did he simply supersede Aristotle as the mentor of writers about love. Art continued to be engendered in the tension between unlike accounts of our condition. In a Christian era the quarrel between men's animal nature and their spiritual aspirations uneasily assumed the terms proposed by Plato and by Aristotle, growing still sharper when it defined itself as an issue which divided the fathers of Western European thought. It also divided a de Meun from a Cavalcanti; and we need to remind ourselves how far love poets from their time on were able to draw upon platonic and aristotelean ideas.

The body of Aristotle's work on logic and natural science was well known in mediaeval Europe. Many of the major texts were studied, and formed the basis of university teaching; indeed some of the sharpest divergences between scholastic thinkers simply followed out differences of emphasis in the reading of Aristotle. Aquinas wrote a commentary on *De Anima*, c. 1271, as well as undertaking that massive synthesis of aristotelean thought with Christian dogma which caught the entire creation in a rational system. What may not always be allowed for is that aristotelean teaching continued to flourish in Renaissance universities, often in deliberate opposition to neoplatonic speculations. The University of Padua, which traditionally favoured the natural sciences and investigative medicine, became a notorious centre of opposition to neoplatonic Florence, producing a healthy succession of sceptical logicians and empirical inquirers. In Protestant Europe Peter Ramus's reform of Aristotle's logic, which attracted such a following in the 1580s and 1590s, amounted to a reordering and simplifying of the aristotelean categories of reason.

Plato, by contrast, could not be directly studied in the West until the first half of the fifteenth century. Some idea of the character of his thinking reached mediaeval Western thinkers from Byzantium, from the Arab philosophers, and through such confirmed platonisers as St Augustine, Boethius, and pseudo-Dionysius. Yet the only authentic text which was even available to mediaeval universities was the

Timaeus, in partial translation. Plato's conceit of intelligible beauty must have come home to the Tuscan poets of the thirteenth century, not least Dante. Nonetheless Petrarch (1304–74) is the earliest Western scholar who is known to have owned a manuscript of a Plato text in the original (it was the *Phaedo*); and he could not read Greek. Somewhat later in the fourteenth century authentic texts of Plato's major dialogues did become available to the few scholars who then knew the language; and these writings gained a wider audience when Bruni and other Humanists translated them in the early fifteenth century. Ficino, the leading scholar of the so-called Platonic Academy in Florence, translated all the dialogues of Plato into Latin in 1468, and devoted his career to the translation and exposition of platonic and hermetic texts. Ficino's commentary on the *Symposium* (published 1484), together with Pico della Mirandola's platonic commentary on some love poems by Benivieni (published 1495), transformed the discussion of love in sixteenth-century Europe. This humane rendering of Plato's ideas gained general currency when Castiglione made such effective play with it in *Il Cortegiano* (1528), the supreme Humanist idealising of civil manners.

The Florentine Platonists revalued human nature and secular existence. They celebrated the possible dignity of our ambiguous state, and found spiritual worth in love between friends, taking the beauty of Christ's manhood to justify their assumption that noble and virtuous action in the world might itself incarnate eternal values. Christ realised Plato's intuition that our secular attachments are capable of their own grace, and of reconciling sense and mind in the apprehension of the timeless in time. Love may discover the divine presence in natural events. Nonetheless the prospect which Christian Platonism opens to our nature is fearful as well as sublime, making us more painfully aware of the bestial and demonic elements in ourselves which pull us quite another way. The legacy of the Humanists to writers of love was moral and practical in that they took love for a pattern of our struggle to live well in the world, and assumed a mutual commitment which makes the lovers one flesh. Yet they also invited the recognition that our passion for a fellow-creature may catch us in a metaphysical dilemma, being compounded of a heavenly yearning and an urge to self-destruction. It was because this dilemma epitomises the paradox of our condition that love so urgently engaged the writers whose work is studied here.

I

Sense and Innocence

For this lust doth sway in the whole body, moving the whole man, without, and within, with such commixtion of mentall affect, and carnall appetite, that hence is the highest bodily pleasure of all produced: So that in the very moment of the consummation, it over-whelmeth almost all the light, and power of cogitation.

St Augustine, *Of The City Of God* xiv, 16,
translated J. Healey, 1610, p. 518

Therfore *Hippocrates* sayd that carnal copulation was a little *Epilepsy*, or falling sicknes. *Architas* the Tarentine to shew the plague of pleasure, bad one to imagine some man in the greatest height of pleasure that might be: and averred that none would doubt him to bee voyd of all the functions of soule, and reason as long as delight lasted.

J. L. Vives, commentary on the above, p. 519

Therefore man lived in Paradise as hee desired, whilest he desired but what God commanded, he inioyed God, from whence was his good ... And can wee not in all this happinesse suppose that they might beget their children without lust, and moove those members without concupiscentiall affect, the man being laid in his wives lap without corruption of integrity? ... For as their child birth should not have been fore-run by paine, but by maturity, which should open a way for the childe without torment: so should their copulation have beene performed without lust full appetite, onely by voluntary use.

Of The City Of God xiv, 26, pp. 528–9

In *Joabs* treachery, in *Judas* treason, is the kisse defamed, and in the carnall and licentious abuse of it, it is every day depraved. They mistake the matter much, that think all adultery is below the girdle: A man darts out an adultery with his eye, in a wanton look; and he wraps up adultery with his fingers, in a wanton letter; and he breaths in an adultery with his lips, in a wanton kisse. But though this act of love, be so defamed both wayes, by treachery, by licentiousnes, yet God chooses this Metaphore, he bids us *kisse the Sonne* ... In this kisse, where *Righteousness and peace have kissed each other*, In this person, where the Divine and the humane nature have kissed each other, In this Christian Church, where Grace and Sacraments, visible and invisible meanes of salvation, have kissed each other, *Love is as strong as death*; my soule is united to my Saviour, now in my life, as in my death, and I am already made *one spirit with him*: and whatsoever death can doe, this kisse, this union can doe, that is, give me a present, an immediate possession of the kingdom of heaven.

Donne, *Sermons* III, pp. 318–21[1]

Sense and Innocence

i. *Contrasting kisses: Inferno* and Eden

It is usefully disconcerting to put side by side two celebrated portrayals of sexual love which were written some four hundred years apart and span a European tradition of love poetry. Both passages describe a kiss that leads on to sexual coupling, and has a consequence beyond the physical consummation, but in most other respects they are as dissimilar as any two truly sublime pieces of writing may be. Dante and Milton write so unlike each other that they must have had very different ideas of poetic style; and yet that contrast of styles only expresses such deeper disaccord as appears in their finding opposite dispositions in a kiss. For there is no doubt that something separates the two poets here which matters to our understanding of European love poetry and of love itself. Comparison of the two passages may show us what the disagreement between Dante and Milton amounts to, and where it takes us. Here are the passages:

(a)
> Noi leggevamo un giorno per diletto
> di Lancialotto come amor lo strinse:
> soli eravamo e sanza alcun sospetto.
> Per piú fiate li occhi ci sospinse
> quella lettura, e scolorocci il viso;
> ma solo un punto fu quel che ci vinse.
> Quando leggemmo il disiato riso
> esser baciato da cotanto amante,
> questi, che mai da me non fia diviso,
> la bocca mi baciò tutto tremante.
> Galeotto fu il libro e chi lo scrisse:
> quel giorno piú non vi leggemmo avante.

One day we read for pastime of Launcelot, and how love prevailed upon him; we were alone, and without any suspicion. Time and again that story drew our eyes to meet, and flushed our faces; but there was just one moment of it which overcame us. When we read how the desirous smile was kissed by such a lover this one, who can never be divided from me, kissed my mouth all trembling. The book was a pandar, and he who wrote it: that day we read no further in it.

Dante, Inferno v, 127–38

(b)
> So spake our general Mother, and with eyes
> Of conjugal attraction unreprov'd,
> And meek surrender, half imbracing leand
> On our first Father, half her swelling Brest
> Naked met his under the flowing Gold
> Of her loose tresses hid: hee in delight
> Both of her Beauty and submissive Charms

14

Smil'd with superior Love, as *Jupiter*
On *Juno* smiles, when he impregns the Clouds
That shed *May* Flowers; and pressd her Matron lip
With kisses pure: aside the Devil turnd
For envie, yet with jealous leer maligne
Ey'd them askance, and to himself thus plaind.
 Sight hateful, sight tormenting! thus these two
Imparadis't in one anothers arms
The happier *Eden*, shall enjoy thir fill
Of bliss on bliss, while I to Hell am thrust,
Where neither joy nor love, but fierce desire,
Among our other torments not the least,
Still unfulfilld with pain of longing pines

Milton, *Paradise Lost* iv, 492–511

The lines from the *Divina Commedia* are some of the first words spoken to Dante in hell by a damned soul and it matters that they are the confessions of a lover. Dante and Virgil here confront the shades of Paolo Malatesta and Francesca da Polenta, who are no mere allegorical abstractions but people well known in Dante's time as members of the ruling families of the Marche, and remembered for the horror of their end; any contemporary reader would have recognised them for a pair of adulterous lovers, who had been caught in the act and butchered by Francesca's husband at the castle of Gradara in 1285. The meeting takes place in the second circle of hell, where Dante and Virgil have just descended to be at once assailed by wailing, blaspheming and dolorous lament. They find themselves in a black place of contrarious blasts which incessantly buffet the souls of the damned. Dante's fifteenth-century commentator Landino says that the wind 'signifies no other than the continual instability and inconstancy and sudden change in lovers; for ... in love are all these things'.[2] This then is the place of carnal sinners, those 'who subordinated reason to sensual desire' (*Inf.* v, 38–9) and are punished now by being hurled about ceaselessly, lashed forever in the tempest of their own passions without hope of rest or relief of pain. Dante puts these people before us for characters of history, whose present state only fulfils their human existence and figures by dreadful contrary the true direction of love. Queen Semiramis epitomises vicious lust, as one who killed off her lovers and legalised incest to extenuate her lechery with her own son. Virgil next points out Dido, 'she who killed herself for love, and broke faith with the ashes of Sichaeus' (*Inf.* v, 61–2); and many other carnal lovers follow, wanton

15

Cleopatra, Helen of Troy, Achilles, Paris, Tristan, and 'more than a thousand shades ... whom love had parted from our life' (*Inf.* v, 67–9). This throng of the victims of passion, who are lumped together so curiously just because they had all once played a like part in human affairs, affects Dante powerfully. 'When I heard my mentor name the ladies and knights of old pity overcame me and I was as a man lost to himself' (*Inf.* v, 70–2). Pity, and some sense of human involvement in the fate of lovers, carries the poet over into the set confrontation of the canto. In effect, Paolo and Francesca are summoned by the force of his compassion.

Anyone who has read the *Inferno* through up to this point must be struck by the drastic change of tone as Dante singles out from the same troop as Dido – from among the lovers rather than the lechers – the two 'who go together, and seem so light upon the wind' (*Inf.* v, 74–5). The writing at once lifts us beyond the visions of horror to a strange melancholy beauty:

> e tu allor li priega
> per quello amor che i mena, ed ei verranno

and you then entreat them by that love which leads them, and they will come

Inferno v, 77–8

> O anime affanate,
> venite a noi parlar

O distressed souls, come and speak with us

80–1

> Quali colombe dal disio chiamate
> con l'ali alzate e ferme al dolce nido
> Vegnon per l'aere, dal voler portate

As doves called by desire, with raised and steady wings come through the air to the sweet nest, borne by their will

82–4

Here is Dante's sweet style at its most limpid, than which no human utterance could be more ravishing, and it is remarkable to find him lavishing it on an account of the damned. This Virgilian simile of the doves is as beautiful as anything in Dante, even if the doves are really emblems of *lussurio* as some early commentators say,[3] or the spirits respond so in sympathy with the voice of Dante's own passion, as Vellutello thought.[4] Hardly less striking is the formal courtliness of

16

Francesca's address, whose dignity seems so touchingly ironic in that place:

> O animal grazioso e benigno
> ... se fosse amico il re de l'universo
> noi pregheremmo lui de la tua pace
> poi c'hai pietà del nostro mal perverso

O gracious and benign being ... if the ruler of the universe were our friend we would pray his peace upon you, because you have pity on our unnatural suffering

Inferno v, 88–93

'Come può esser che in Inferno sia cortesia?' asked Tasso, tartly censuring a breach of decorum here.[5] But there is more to it than a rule of rhetoric. This is the ravishing manner of the love poets of the 'sweet new style', Dante's sometime associates, to which he at once unforcedly responds in kind:

> Ma dimmi: al tempo de' dolci sospiri,
> A che e come concedette Amore
> Che conosceste i dubbiosi desiri?

But tell me: at the time of sweet sighs, by what means and how did love permit you to acknowledge your doubtful desires?

Inferno v, 118–20

Indeed Dante here reminds us of his own early love poetry.[6]

The lines which answer him are put into the mouth of one of the damned lovers, the woman as it happens, whom the compassionate poet has thus invited to tell the 'first root' of their love, how love passed from 'sweet sighs' in solitude to mutual avowals. Her reply is an act of courtesy to one whom it especially 'pleases to hear and to speak of love', as Benvenuto da Imola pointed out in his commentary;[7] and the gain of having the woman speak it is the all-out commitment of passion she makes, and the pity and compassion her telling elicits.[8] She singles out the very moment of that fatal transition, which is evidently of consequence for Dante's poem, and prepares us to hear an impassioned account of it – 'I will tell you as one who weeps and speaks' (*Inf.* v, 126).

In fact it is the naked intensity of her speech we remark, as though at times feeling is only just held in check by the formal order of the verse itself. 'Ma solo un punto fu quel che ci vinse' – the simple, weighed words and lucid syntax, caught up in that exquisitely natural fall of the cadence, seem to put nothing between us and the swell of the speaker's passions. So strong are the natural rhythms indeed that a slight disturbance of them, even a momentary check, tautens the voice with feeling. The whole twelve-line speech is held together quite formally in a single dramatic impulse by the delicately pointed phrasing of the terza rima pattern, each three-line stanza framing its own little drama yet each sweeping us on to that breathtaking break across the stanza pattern at the moment which changed everything irredeemably. Dante has her throw in almost as an aside, loading the fatal act with its consequences before it even arrives, the momentous ambiguity of their eternal union: 'che mai da me non fia diviso'. Lovers touchingly inseparable even in hell? Or as Boccaccio and Gelli assumed, damned souls who must confront forever, without hope of fulfilment, the occasion of their ruin?[9]

The climactic moment is singled out by the phrasing, which holds the sense unresolved over the three-line stanza and piles it up on the first line following, so that the whole sweep of the movement is abruptly arrested and the voice held back in quivering tension. The experience is powerfully rendered. Dante mimes Francesca's supreme moment for us there in the line as though he lived it; and one cannot but wonder at such tenderness, so close an imaginative involvement with an impulse he himself condemns to hell. But then these mimetic textures involve the reader too, compelling us to realise the sensations physically in our own lips, tongue, and throat:

la bocca mi baciò tutto tremante

It is all vividly there in the lingered-over labials, the sudden sharp arrest at 'baciò', the pause in the voice; and then the whispered drawn-out throbbing of 'tutto tremante', so tellingly picking up the 'amante' of line 134. Reading this with dramatic sympathy you feel the passion in your vocal cords. Without any striving for emotional fervour Dante comes as close here as a poet can get to the creation of sensuous passion in words. So the two discrete lines that follow fall almost as quick throwaway observations after the lingering climax. But they are far from thrown away. It must matter that Francesca's outburst against the book breaks into the uncompleted story and precedes the simple massive reticence of her final words, which is so dignified and moving in itself. 'Galeotto fu il libro e chi lo scrisse'. Bursting sibilantly off the tongue the line savagely turns back on her own tender recollection and on the compassion it may have elicited. What follows needs no drawing out, partly because it is already settled by that first fatal contact of sense.

The poet's close involvement in the writing is evident in the sheer intensity of feeling released here. Dante presents himself in character as the wayfarer through hell who sympathetically shares these lovers' passions, intensely reliving with them the trembling moment of discovered love, weeping at the grief of their memory of past happiness, swooning at the hopelessness of their present state. His commentators had reason for supposing that he felt the experience so keenly because he had been such a sensual lover himself, or even because he was licentious by nature.[10]

A feature of the telling is the way that Francesca is made to re-enact for us the artless ambiguities of her motives, resolving them only at the end when artlessness gives place to wilful misprision. The striking anaphora of her first speech insists upon a certain *imperium* of love:

> Amor, ch'al cor gentil ratto s'apprende,
>   prese costui

Love, which quickly seizes the gentle heart, took him

100–1

> Amor, ch'a nullo amato amar perdona
>   mi prese del costui piacer si forte

Love, which pardons no one who is loved from loving in return took me so strongly with pleasure in him

103–4

> Amor condusse noi ad una morte

Love led us to one death

106

da Imola noticed how Francesca excuses herself by this repetition of 'Amor'.[11] Love has its dire compulsions, as well as its pleasure and terrors. Francesca attributes the fate of lovers to a dark god of sense who seizes them and hurries them away with him, as the damned souls are hurried now by the punishing wind.

Her own case is more inwardly apprehended than that. She and Paolo read together 'for amusement' of Launcelot's affair with Guinevere, and particularly of how 'amor lo strinse', how love beset and constrained that pattern of chivalric adultery. They were alone, and 'sanza alcun sospetto'. Not suspecting what will ensue, they have as yet no fear of interruption or the suspicion of others; as though the peril lay in the situation rather than in themselves. The simple inversion in the sentence describing their mutually arrested eyes, which holds back the subject to the following line, picks out 'quella lettura' as the surprising agent of their first timorous exchanges. It was the writing, the story itself, which made them stay their eyes as one, and go pale; though we are left to ask whether that was because they amazedly recognised their own case there, or because the love story itself had some hidden force in it to make people love. 'Ci vinse' suggests that they were not just overcome by the desire the story described and kindled (who would not be ravished at such beauty as Dante renders for us here!), but subjugated by it as to a power beyond their own will. Landino tartly comments that these lovers represent the perversion of love because they have foregone the superior light of reason, and so put their desire before the love of God.[12]

Francesca's speech is a continual self-disclosure, in the typical manner of a poem which places people quite precisely by the way they use words. We see her hovering between the ecstatic memory of a first recognition of love, such as circumstances had prompted, and the plea that they had been betrayed into fatal love by a force beyond themselves which had just put the circumstances in their way. The 'Galeotto' outburst settles all that, laying the whole error on others. Both book and writer were pandars in bringing these lovers to their ruinous kiss, just as Galhault in the Old French Romance played the pandar when he persuaded Guinevere to kiss the timorous Launcelot.[13] She condemns the passion which has brought such fearful consequences, while wilfully laying the fault of it at somebody else's door. Yet she can still close with that simple line of understated recollection: 'quel giorno piú non vi leggemmo avante'. Her classic reticence has such effect here because it puts the mind to what has not been said at all, the bliss with which she is not crowned: 'Nec ultra volui legere'.[14] The wistful echoes of fatal passion – Dido and Aeneas, Launcelot and Guinevere – are answered with the uncompromising testimony of discovered truth. 'Nam in omni adversitate fortunae infelicissimum est genus infortunii fuisse felicem.'[15]

> Nessun maggior dolore
> che recordarsi del tempo felice
> ne la miseria

121–3

The trouble with these lovers is that their minds have nowhere to go beyond the memory of their 'tempo felice' of sensuous bliss, and their present experience of hell.

Milton's lines offer us a gravely beautiful picture, Dante's an impassioned drama. After Dante's manner of naked involvement with his subject Milton's magisterial detachment, which gives his writing its monumentality, may seem chill. Such weighty locutions as 'So spake our general Mother' distance the actions they relate by keeping the reader's mind on general ideas, and making him aware that something huge is being defined here. Dante's art really is to make art seem nature, as though word is feeling and syntax a plot of passions. Milton's artifice is on show, at least in that his sense partly depends upon our appraisal of the unexpected order in which he disposes his words. His writing gets much of its excitement from a continual play of syntactical artifice across the formal movement of the verse, so that we are surprised with purposeful inversions, dislocations, suspensions, extreme ellipses and so on. Moreover the diction itself has a marked intellectual life in the way it continually presents the simple gestures it describes in the character of general ideas. In fact Milton's words never just describe. They are always developing ideas and attitudes, and working to suggest a coherence between things.

The passage from *Paradise Lost* Book iv does not so much tell a story as present a situation. But the scene is dramatically realised, for we know of Satan's lurking presence within earshot of the human pair, and our view of the garden and of them is punctuated by his avowals of destructive malevolence. The irony of our first seeing Eden and human innocence over Satan's shoulder shows up Satan's squalor without diminishing them; and there is nothing that calls for our pity in the picture of Adam and Eve which Milton offers us here, even though we know they will shortly fall and lose the delights they rehearse. The lovers themselves remain quite unaware that they are being spied on or have any cause for anxiety. There is no tension in their exchanges, which amount to a series of defining gestures such as must take on absolute value in a universe not yet subject to time. What their comportment defines here is right human love.

A little dramatic retrospect leads us into the lines describing the kiss. Eve has just told of her first encounter with Adam, and how her early barren attachment to her own image, the one human thing she had then seen, was turned to yielding love and admiration of him. Everything in the passage that follows is controlled by the picture of attraction and surrender given us in its first three lines, and especially by the way this is put. The terms of Milton's depiction, such as 'with eyes/Of conjugal attraction unreprov'd', have a massive impersonalness not usually associated with loving glances; but they work rather to define and distance the affection than to mime it, and evidently what mattered for Milton was that they should be just. Eve's eyes draw Adam to her in undesigning conjugal love, blamelessly then because this is true married love, a 'meek surrender' of herself and not a mere use of sex or a self-indulgent abandonment. 'Conjugal attraction' singles out this sexual impulse from all others, such as wisdom must reprove; and in insisting that Adam and Eve were married it also implies a comment on the true nature of that bond.

The striking feature of the passage, though, is the way that everything that happens in it turns about the verb 'leand' in line 494, which the phrasing picks out and draws vividly across the line-end to 'our first Father'. All that precedes this verb qualifies Eve's leaning, and what follows describes its outcome. The simple act is thus invested with a meaning which we read partly in Eve's attitude and partly by what comes of it. This constant interweaving of sense and intelligence, act and its import, is one reason why actions which might seem voluptuous in themselves are yet so tenderly cool as Milton describes them. Even in the moment when the two bodies close thus unselfconsciously, Eve nakedly caressing Adam in sensuous pleasure, the little tag-phrase 'On our first Father' slips in to remind us that the end of these embraces is fruit, offspring, *us*; and that our existence is what justifies them.

Plainly the difference between the effect of this passage and of Dante's has to do with the distance Milton keeps from his characters and their attitudes. He does not involve us in intimate enactments of passion, but keeps the sense of archetypal events before us. Yet his writing is far from frigidly remote. One of the features of the passage is the way it balances majesty and human intimacy, which it could not do at closer quarters, or without that curious alternation of latinate and native diction whose impact so immediately suggests that the elevated and the familiar are at one here.

The beautiful description of their embrace seems pointedly placed to show us how much sense matters in human love. No one might suppose from these terms that the writer has been reputed an ascetic; less delicately controlled, it is a voluptuary sensibility they would display. Where decorous generalities would have been easy, though a mere apology for their sexual lovemaking in effect, Milton firmly insists on the physical actuality and its pleasure. In the sudden intimacy of 'half her swelling Brest/Naked met his', that most sensuous 'swelling' not only describes the mature breast but suggests its movement against him. The soft nakedness of the encounter is carefully qualified, but not played down, by its concealment 'under the flowing Gold/Of her loose tresses'. Their unconsidered natural modesty here is different indeed from the modesty shame induces in them after their fall.

That description of Eve's hair strikingly shows how the diction of this poem evokes ideas as well as images, how far mind interpenetrates sense in Milton's writing. For 'flowing Gold 024 ... loose tresses' does much more than tell us that Eve's hair was long, loose, and fair. 'Flowing Gold', for one thing, distinguishes this living wealth and sumptuous natural beauty from the barren stuff Mammon hoards and values. But these phrases also link Eve's beauty with the beauty of the garden, in which the reader has already encountered the 'vegetable Gold' of the fruits on the trees (iv, 219–20), and the 'crisped Brooks,/Rowling on Orient Pearl and sands of Gold' (iv, 237–8). That distanced brightness of pure natural life, sensuous without stirring sense, images true beauty and true wealth for us, and implies a oneness in the natural cycle by which beauty is fruitful through love. The passage tells us that the end of beauty is not admiring contemplation but active love, and fruit; and 'loose tresses' just hints that pure beauty needs the regulation of something beyond itself even so.

Adam responds to Eve's half-embrace in delight rather than desire, not indulging his own sensations but drawn by her 'Beauty and submissive Charms'. Delight in beauty is as carefully distinguished from passive admiration as from sexual arousal. In Book iv altogether Milton shows us a creation delighting in its own right activity, as if delight itself is the active spirit in which nature works, and the natural accompaniment of its proper functioning:

> The Birds thir quire apply; aires, vernal aires,
> Breathing the smell of field and grove, attune
> The trembling leaves, while Universal *Pan*
> Knit with the *Graces* and the *Hours* in dance
> Led on th'Eternal Spring.

iv, 264–8

Adam's delight in Eve intimates a kind of pleased sharing in a general process of nature, which we must take for a more active and

23

simply more human self-surrender than the admiring contemplation neoplatonists speak of.

Yet the focus of everything that happens in this sentence (497–502) is 'Smil'd with superior Love', an action whose calm magisterial grandeur itself affirms a placing of sense. Formally, all the account of Adam's response to Eve's sensuous gesture is regulated by the idea of love, and of superior love at that, where 'superior' implies among other things the elevation of this loving impulse we might now expect such an embrace to enkindle. Of course it is open to us to understand other kinds of superiority, such as that Adam's is a kind of love which fitted him to be the leading partner in their lovemaking, or that his is a higher love than hers because he comprehends love better, or even that his body leaned over hers as for the natural act of lovemaking. All these senses have place in the poem, and the literal sense is a discreet pointer to the natural consummation of their human love which will shortly follow.

Lines 499b–502a work a curious sleight of syntax. We have the Ovidean simile coming in as a parenthetical parallel to Adam's superior love, but then suddenly cut off as the main sentence resumes with the co-ordinate action, 'and pressd ...'; so that syntactically Adam's kiss frames the cosmic fertility of Jupiter's delight in Juno: 'Smil'd ... and pressd her Matron lip.' In fact the only indication that we are to revert to the main drive of the sentence after '*May* Flowers' is the change of tense. The simile moves us into a universal present – 'smiles .... impregns .... shed' – from which we are abruptly switched back into the past of Adam's actions – 'and pressd'. Such witty artifice is the life of Milton's blank verse, but this is a particularly pointed little switch. It reminds us that all this action of superior love is in the past, gone and irrecoverable; whereas the universal processes continue, though we are no longer in tune with them as Adam was. The jar in syntax is a jar in sense too, bringing out a fundamental meaning of the passage and the poem as it happens.

Another formal feature which shapes the way we read this sentence is the quite different stressing, and placing, of the two co-ordinate phrases which describe Adam's action:

> Smil'd with superior Love ...
> ... and pressd her Matron lip
> With kisses pure

The first phrase is quite sharply singled out, driven home, and emphatically cut off; whereas the second has a more even emphasis and is drawn out as a coda, moving with a series of firm pressures rather than the incisive weight of the first. The effect of the two actions becomes pointedly unequal. That smile of superior love leads all the rest; and the kisses themselves are subordinate to it in effect, coming almost as a natural afterthought or consequence which needs no such decisive emphasis. When Milton calls them 'kisses pure' we already understand that these are not trembling climaxes of passion but the innocent accompaniment of love, manifesting the universal spirit of delight and fruitfulness.

Yet the simile of Jupiter's smiling upon Juno, which slips in so naturally here, does more than embellish Milton's strikingly beautiful picture of human lovemaking. One effect of the elegant transition to myth, just at this point, is to enlarge the human impulse into a universal process without making it impersonal or losing its spirit of delight. It shows Adam's connubial love as the human repetition of the lifegiving interplay of the elements themselves, in a universe impelled to generation by love and joy. The image of aether impregnating the clouds and begetting spring flowers is sexual without being erotic, and delicately points us to the true end of those human embraces before we come to their consummation. Even the Botticelli-like downpour of flowers suggests insemination and fertility, being most like Botticelli in the way it transforms biological process into myth, graceful yet pregnant. Milton's figure is boldly ambiguous. Do the impregnated clouds literally rain down flowers, as if giving birth to them? Or is it by metonymy that they are said to 'shed *May* Flowers' in that they effuse the cause of the flowers, those seminal rains of April which quicken the dormant earth? Both senses, the sexually direct myth and the bold rendering of spring growth in sexual terms, come back upon the human lovers whose mutual exchanges prompted this parallel. By such graceful means, and without the slightest indecorum, Milton shows us quite particularly what he takes to be the right end of love between human beings.

Part of the point of this little episode, though, is that for Adam and Eve it is more than a casual passage of their day which we happen to observe via Satan. Their lovemaking, as everything they do, has its fit time and place, so that a kiss is not a dramatic turning point for them, or a spur to copulation. Yet they are still human lovers, whose embraces might strike us as staidly rendered by such a description as 'pressd her Matron lip/With kisses pure', which empties the kisses of passion. That is surely Milton's point however. He needed a relatively neutral action, one that implies sensuous union, and sensuous communion in pleasure as well, without passionate desire. The terms distinguish the act and the relationship here in fact – 'pressd', 'Matron', 'kisses pure'. They tell us that there is no compulsive demand in these kisses; indeed Eve is presented as passive under them, simply receiving Adam's imprints of love. This is a delight of sense which must be distinguished absolutely from erotic contacts such as stir up feeling, or release the pent-up force of illicit (and perilous) desire. In the full understanding which Milton has presented, it is a natural part of a natural process whose only motives are delight and love.

As Milton describes it, Satan's torment of unappeasable frustration is worse than the suffering of Paolo and Francesca in hell. For at least they have lost all desire, which is externalised as the harassing wind that impels them, and keep only the perpetual double guilt of each other's presence, so reminded at once of the sin and of their having drawn each other into it. Yet there is nothing in their state that Satan might envy; and his jealous emparadising of the embrace of Adam and Eve, in that neologism whose grammatical boldness suggests the force of his jangling passions, sharply points the contrast between Dante's placing of his lovers and Milton's. The enactment of the love of Paolo and Francesca hurls them about in a hell of perpetual unfulfilment, as well as perpetual self-reproach. But Adam and Eve are most truly fulfilled in each other's arms, and in sexual fruition. That is their sum of bliss, the consummation of their human state and their happier Eden.

It is true that Adam and Eve are innocents in an unfallen world at this stage, and that once they have fallen they become much more like Paolo and Francesca in their guilty play. They too will burn with desire, mastered by the peremptory demands of sense. Yet they are redeemable even then, if only because they never commit themselves wholly to the sensual sin as do Dante's lovers, or lose the idea of a happier condition than appetite can allow them. A remark of Blake's to Crabb Robinson so exactly misrepresents the poem as to sharpen our sense of what Milton is really showing us here: 'I saw Milton in imagination and he told me to beware of being misled by his *Paradise Lost*. In particular he wished me to show the falsehood of his doctrine that the pleasures of sex arose from the Fall. The Fall could not produce any pleasure.'[16] No; but then the doctrine of *Paradise Lost* is that the true pleasures of sex arise from nothing else than love.

The contrast between the two portrayals of love seems extreme. Dante offers us an adulterous affair to stand for sexual love and passion altogether, and he represents it as damned by the first contact of sense. Milton shows us a connubial love whose natural expression and sealing human bliss is physical fruition; and he takes it for our original created state in Eden, emparadising the lovers in itself. With all due qualification there does seem a critical difference of understanding here which the two poems make absolute as they develop, the *Divina Commedia* allowing no licit place to any senses save sight and hearing, and moving to transcend even these, *Paradise Lost* positively affirming the value of all the senses when they are properly subordinate to love and reason. Plainly there is more in this divergence than a local disaccord between Dante and Milton. The two poets are separated by unlike expectations of sexual love, and of sensuous delight in the world altogether. The shift from the *Divina Commedia* to *Paradise Lost* marks a changed understanding of ourselves.

Comparison of the two passages raises a more limited question. What are we to make of the paradox that it is Dante who puts his lovers in hell for their kiss, despite the fierce imaginative involvement with them his poetry betrays, while Milton gravely distances and depassions Adam and Eve and yet represents their embrace as a paradise in itself? How to reconcile the inner truth of the poetry with Dante's formal judgment on his lovers! For Dante does put his readers in a quandary here, which it harms the poem to ignore.

As de Sanctis pointed out long ago Dante's early commentators reverse the natural sympathies of a modern reader.[17] They find no difficulty in Dante's assigning to hell such lustful lovers, whose passion he thus distinguishes from the true love we should have for divine things. One of the sagest of them, Dante's son Pietro, finds that the lovers are damned precisely because they follow a mode of love prescribed by Andreas Capellanus.[18] What disturbs these precisians is the compassion the writing displays. Landino puts the episode in an artistic perspective such as the Medici circle habitually sought. He takes Dante's involvement with the lovers' fate for a manifestation of the poet's own sensuality at this point, whose impropriety reason must bring home to his understanding and ours.[19] Vellutello puts it more brutally: 'Dante, understood as the *parte sensitiva*, has compassion on these afflicted ones; but Virgil, that is the reasonable part, considering them justly punished removes them from such consideration.'[20]

Sixteenth-century commentators seem to have found it harder to arrive at a whole view of the poem, or to work up much interest in the idea of a self-transcendence. Moralists and rhetoricians almost to a man, they seek the reason of our pity for Paolo and Francesca in the nature of the sin itself, which Vellutello tells us has more of frailty than of malice in it.[21] Gelli takes a still more indulgent view of them: 'This is a sin which is not born of a malignity of mind or savagery of spirit ... but is born of a humanity, and if one may say so, of a certain benignity and sweetness of nature and of blood.'[22] Gelli pleasantly observes that we often see how carnal men altogether lack avarice, brutishness and malignity, and are much more liberal, loving, and discreet than others; such people are victims of moral improvidence at worst: 'Whoever loves with this lascivious love is usually blind within.'[23]

When Dante's confrontation with sensual passion is taken just to point a moral character then a metaphysic of love is scarcely in prospect. Sixteenth-century poets found a sufficient map of love in Petrarch's anguished self-searchings. Michelangelo is singular both in his devotion to Dante, and in his continual striving for the universal idea in particular objects of sense. Yet Dante's emblem of the perils of sense continued to be taken for a dismissal of the flesh altogether while love poets went on assuming that sense and spirit necessarily pull opposite ways in love. Donne, and then Milton, take their stand against the assumption of centuries. One reason why it is worth our following out the difference between Dante's attempt to transcend sense in love, and Milton's vision of a love which finds its spiritual consummation through the mutual delights of sense, is that these attitudes define so much of European love poetry for us.

ii. *Courtly ardours:* in quest of the secret rose

But the lovers of these carnall delightes them-selves cannot have this affect at their wills, either in nuptiall coniunctions, or wicked impurities: The motion wilbe sometimes importunate, agaynst the will, and some-times immoveable when it is desired: And beeing fervent in the minde, yet wilbe frozen in the bodye: Thus wondrously doth this lust fayle man, both in honest desire of generation, and in lascivious concupiscence: Some-times resisting the restraynt of the whole minde, and some-times opposing it selfe, which beeing wholly in the minde, and no way in the body at the same time.

St Augustine, *Of The City Of God* xiv, 16, p. 519

The integrity of Dante's concern with Paolo and Francesca comes out strikingly if we turn from his lines to Boccaccio's commentary on them, c. 1373, which handles the story of the murdered lovers in a very different way.[24] Writing more than a lifetime after the events Boccaccio claims to have the true circumstances of that squalid little domestic tangle, which nobody seems to have chronicled in its own day, even though it embroiled the leading families of the Marche. All we know for certain is that it amounted to nothing more in itself than an affair between a middle-aged family man and his brother's wife, herself the mother of an adolescent daughter, which ended in the destruction of both of them when the husband caught them in bed together. Boccaccio works the circumstances into a realistic little novella with courtly trappings, drawing out for us what Dante pointedly omits.

In Boccaccio's version the handsome Paolo Malatesta is passed off on Francesca da Polenta as her future husband, having been pointed out to her as such from a window, when really she will be married for dynastic reasons to his elder brother the deformed Gianciotto. She at once falls completely in love with Paolo, and does not realise the imposture until 'the morning following the nuptials when she sees Gianciotto getting up from beside her'. She and Paolo find some way of declaring their love for each other, and as soon as Gianciotto goes away on business for a while they become lovers; but a servant of Gianciotto's betrays them to his master, who returns secretly to Rimini in high rage. When Paolo goes again to Francesca's room Gianciotto is fetched at once, and puts his shoulder to the barred door, shouting for Francesca. As Francesca moves to unbar the door Paolo jumps through a sluice which gives into the sewers below, but unluckily gets a fold of his shirt (*coretto*) caught on an iron projection, and is held there defenceless as Gianciotto rushes in with raised rapier. Francesca tries to ward off Gianciotto's pass at Paolo, but is herself accidentally run through, whereupon Gianciotto goes berserk with loving anguish and kills his brother Paolo too. 'Leaving both dead Gianciotto at once set out and returned to his duties; and on the following morning, amidst much weeping, the two lovers were buried in the same tomb.'

Boccaccio's casual mastery of his craft gives graphic life to a mere cliché of courtly romance. In his version the elements conform to type. The contrived marriage only makes imperative the demands of love, and prescribes their fatal progression. The passion conceived at a window, and then deceived by the substitution in bed, leads inevitably on to their adulterous affair and its cruel outcome, which at least unites them in death. Of the familiar company of the drama of illicit love only the go-between is lacking, and that just because Boccaccio will not credit Dante's detail of the pandering book of *Galeotto*, saying that there is no knowing how the lovers came together. He tells the story against Dante's treatment of it, leaving us to gather that a marriage for dynastic expediency rather than love is liable to beget the violence it deserves.

It is a commonplace that mediaeval writers do not always treat adultery so brusquely. People who married their children by prearranged contract, and disposed of a daughter as a property, took it for granted that the heart is one thing and marriage quite another. Andreas Capellanus reports a judgment of the Lady Mengarda of Narbonne, who resolved the question whether there is greater affection between lovers or between married people with the judgment that 'marital affection and the true love of lovers are quite different, and arise from entirely different impulses'. For this lady love is simply 'a desire to receive a secret and hidden embrace' such as 'cannot be in marriage'. Capellanus tells us that Queen Eleanor herself settled a love suit which came before her by ruling that since 'love can have no force between husband and wife a lady should not refuse her lover on the ground that she is married' (*De Amore* II, vii, ix and II, vii, xvii, ed. S. Battaglia, Rome, 1947, pp. 322 and 332). *Causa coniugii ab amore non est excusatio recta*, matrimony excuses no one from loving, is the very first of the thirty-one rules of love which the Breton knight of Arthur's Court finds written on the card he takes from the hawk's perch.

de Meun suggests that a lady might well prefer to keep love separate from a marriage in which she could never be her husband's equal, much less his ennobling goddess:

> Por ce revoit l'en ensement,
> de touz ceus qui prumierement
> par amors amer s'entreseulent,
> quant puis espouser s'entreveulent,
> enviz peut entr'eus avenir
> que ja s'i puisse amors tenir...

For this same reason we see that all those who at first are accustomed to love each other *par amour* may find that love can scarcely ever hold them once they wish to marry each other; for when he loved *par amour* he would call himself her servant, and she was used to being his mistress; now he calls himself lord and master over her whom he called his lady when she was loved *par amour*.

G. de Lorris et J. de Meun, *Le Roman de la Rose*, ed. F. Lecoy, Paris, 1966, lines 9413–24

The elaborate codes of love drawn up in mediaeval Courts, and the courtly fictions themselves, projected the daydreams or regulated the manners of people whose situation disposed them to equate sexual passion with illicit love. Since Christian teaching had also to be respected, not to say the seigneurial rights of husbands, it is not surprising that the attitudes of literary love were fraught with anxiety. The extreme formalising of love into a ritual progression through a series of well-charted stages at least offered lovers some kind of sanction in a very perilous enterprise; and it refined the brute impulse into a ceremony which paralleled the stages of chivalric quest. Nonetheless the end of this particular quest was no spiritual vision but the mutual appeasement of desire, or the frustration of desire just short of the fatal contact of sense.

On 7 March 1277 Bishop Etienne Tempier of Paris formally condemned as 'Errors in Philosophy' two hundred and nineteen Averroistic opinions of Siger de Brabant and Boetius of Dacia taught in the University of Paris, among them some propositions advanced in 'The book ... *De amore* or *De Deo amoris* which opens: *Cogit me multum, etc*; and concludes: *Cave igitur, Galtere, amoris exercere mandata, etc.*' Tempier's brief preamble to the list of errors couples the treatise on love with books on geomancy and necromancy, and visits excommunication and other heavy penalties on those who teach or listen to the views advanced in these writings.[25] Capellanus's work stands condemned not because it advocates love outside marriage but specifically because it supports such abhorrent propositions as follow; namely, that pleasure in the venereal act does not impede intellectual activity (172); that continence is not an essential virtue (168); that perfect abstinence from sexual acts enfeebles virility and the species (169); that chastity is no greater good than perfect abstinence (181); that natural fornication, since it is freely done on either part, is not a sin (183). These propositions are condemned as intellectual errors, and they appear towards the end of the list in the midst of other false opinions which had presumably been argued in the University, such as that Christian doctrine contains fictions and falsehoods as any other teaching, and that happiness is to be found in this life or not at all.[26] The issue which looms large in mediaeval writings of love goes beyond illicit sex. What these writers put in question is the place of sense in love of whatever kind.

Plainly there was a substantial predicament here which confronted writers with the need to choose between opposite impulses, and frequently left them in unresolvable dilemma or baffled equivocalness. It is dramatised in the *Roman de la Rose* as a debate between Reason and the lover, in which the lover argues for carnal love and Reason shows the inadequacy of a love rooted in sense, when you compare it to more stable kinds of love, such as the love of one's own kin and kind, and the love of God (lines 4199–598). In this poem however the direct outcome of the debate is not equivocal. The choice is for carnal pleasure; and de Lorris offers us a straight celebration of the delights of sense, in provocative defiance of the claims of other kinds of love:

> Les queroles ja remenoient,
> car tuit li plusor s'en aloient
> o lor amies ombroier
> soz ces arbres por donoier.
> Dex! com menoient bone vie!
> Fox est qui n'a de tel envie!
> Qui autel vie avoir porroit,
> de meillor bien se soufreroit,
> qu'il n'est nus graindres paradis
> d'avoir amie a son devis

They were already ceasing their carols, for most of them were going off with their mistresses under the shade of the trees so as to make love. God! what a good life they led! Anyone who does not envy it is a fool. He who might have such a life may need no better bliss for there is no greater paradise than to have one's mistress at one's desire.

1289–98

In de Meun's completion of the poem the consummation of the long and hazardous quest for the rosebud is simply orgasm, given grace by its allegorical trim, and some piquancy by the ironic paralleling of the worship of sex and the worship of God. The lover reverently approaches the shrine, which is a small aperture between two columns, with his staff and sack at the ready; he worships, kisses, contemplates the shrine; then he begins his final attempt to gain entrance. The poem briskly describes his struggle to break the barrier, his thrusts into the breach, the scattering and mingling of the seed as the rosebush widens and lengthens; and then at once follows the abrupt awakening from the dream, that customary con- clusion of the dream-vision which de Meun here transforms into a piece of sharp erotic psychology.

We cannot be sure if this sudden awakening really is the wormseed on the tail, a brief irony that calls in question the whole vast commit- ment to the quest of the rose of love. de Meun is artist enough to leave it there unglossed for his reader to weigh, without ever sug- gesting that the lover should really have devoted himself all the time to a love which does not fail at the moment of its consummation. *Post coitum triste* seems less of a moral turn about than a naturalistic acknowledgment of the inherent irony of carnal love.

Capellanus himself is a cruder and more puzzling case than this, whether or not one takes him as seriously as the Church and C. S. Lewis seem to have done. His long and ingenious codification of the etiquette of love ends with a total recantation. Nearly half of the book is taken up with a series of model dialogues which purport to prescribe the relations between lovers of different social orders; but even these comically formal exchanges do assume a defined doctrine of love, and a devotion to amorous manners that plays off at all points against spiritual life. We hear of the omnipotence and ubiquitousness of love; of the general obligation to love, from which marriage does not excuse us; of the chivalric search for the *via diritta* of love; of the paradise, purgatory, and hell of love, and the need of prayer for those in hell and purgatory; and above all, of the *arcana* of love which can be managed, in absolute secrecy, only by the initiate few who win their way to love's inmost shrine. But there is nothing like the specific direction to coitus of the *Roman de la Rose*; and for all the talk of possession, and of 'secret and hidden embraces', it often seems that for Capellanus the manners of the game of love are their own end. The elaborate artificiality of the rite mirrors, as it seeks to regulate, the tense complexity of the court life out of which it grew.

For the fact is that Capellanus writes as a jurist of love, not a lover. He makes of love a chivalric ritual with its own code and etiquette, in which secrecy is a prime article, and the highest end is the ennob- ling of the lover's passions in faithful service. He prescribes for the amorous life in a body of law based upon the ten (or so) command- ments of love, which is to be interpreted in a Court of Love presided over by the Queen and her companions. His treatise sketches out the orthodox drama of courtly love in which a passion taken at a sudden glance might work so as to involve as many as seven or eight people, drawing into their set roles not only the two lovers but a go-between, a confidante apiece, some spies or slanderers, and the jealous husband.

Above all, the *De Arte Honeste Amandi* exemplifies that stark turn about which marked the inability of courtly lovers to reconcile their passion for a worldly object with the desire for eternal bliss. In the last section of the book Capellanus turns back absolutely on the entire system he has elaborated, and rejects love altogether: 'for many reasons the wise man is bound to shun the promptings of love and always oppose its mandates' (III, iii, pp. 362–4). The reasons he gives, priestly commonplaces as they are, tell us more about the true end of his rite of love than all the elaborate rules. He says that all criminal excesses follow from love; that love produces bodily weakness; that mutual love is impossible since women cannot love properly, and are in any case a bad lot through and through; and in sum, that fornication is a sin and a crime. The celibate cleric reverts to type. His final advice to his young correspondent Gualteri, who had 'avidly asked me to set out the art of loving', is that he should flee such delights of the flesh as the treatise has shown him how to obtain, and await the one true marriage with Christ.

It is not only Christian writers who find small spiritual increment in sexual love. A treatise of love by the eleventh-century Moorish writer Ibn Hazm parallels Capellanus closely enough in its account of the etiquette of love to make comparison illuminating.[27] Hazm musters all the elements of the courtly drama, the go-between, the reproachful friend, the spy, the talebearer, the hazard of the enterprise which compels concealment and secrecy. Moreover he precisely foreshadows some of the familiar attitudes of Renaissance love poetry when he seeks metaphors for the oneness of mutual lovers, distinguishes the situations in which a sleeping lover may be visited by the apparition of his mistress, and speaks of mutual lovers as respectively the eastern and western extremities of their world, whom the sun makes one in its daily passage.[28] This is no superficial lending of conceits but good evidence of the continuity in Europe of a distinctive attitude to love.

Unlike Capellanus, Hazm writes as an experienced lover and finds no barrier between soul and sense in love. Love for him is a mutual consummation and never a solitary attitude of adoration; indeed he defines it formally as a reciprocal passion, which brings about a merging of souls such as physical intercourse must activate and complete.[29] Nor is there any suggestion that the union of lovers is to be adulterous. In fact Hazm's exemplars are often an unattached man and a slave girl, and he is particularly fierce against any attachment that violates the sanctity of the harem. Nonetheless he too advises against love in the end, and counsels continence as a greater virtue. His reason has force. It is that a devotion to love leaves us at the mercy of the violent impulses of our sexual instinct and gives us at best only an uncertain control over ourselves and our fate, putting our lives in unpredictable hazard. In the end the eschewal of passion is best, in respect both of a man's self-possession and of his eternal well-being.[30]

There is nothing Augustinian about Hazm, and it is clearly no priestly animus which leads him to resolve at last that sexual love works against reason and jeopardises our souls. He expresses a more intimate recognition that sexual desire may be an unpredictable and uncontrollable monster, something within ourselves which usurps or escapes our considered will; and he fears its power to control our lives against our better judgment.

The deep equivocalness towards love which these mediaeval commentators express shapes troubadour poetry. Some of the finest songs of the troubadours show us a lover who is fixed in an attitude of hopeless pleading against his mistress's invincible chastity, and turns back upon himself to refine in devoted service both his sufferings and his already gentle heart. Respectful honour is the subject of their story:

> Tan am midons e la tenh car,
> E tan la dopt'e la reblan,
> C'anc de me no.lh auzei parlar,
> Ni re no.lh quer ni re no.lh man.
> Pero ilh sap mo mal e ma dolor,
> E can li plai, mi fai ben et onor,
> E can li plai, eu m'en sofert ab mens,
> Per so c'a leis non avenha blastens.

So much do I love my lady and hold her dear, and so much do I fear and respect her that I never dared speak to her of myself, nor do I seek or ask anything of her. Yet she knows of my sickness and grief, and when she pleases she succours and honours me, and when she pleases I am content with less than that so that no dishonour come to her.

Bernard de Ventadour, 'Can l'erba fresch'e.lh
folha par'

As in the Stuart masques, poetic attitudes quite patently follow out the ruling myths of Court:

> Bel semblan n'ai en parvenssa,
> Que gen m'acuoill e.m. razona . . .

She shows me outward favour for she receives me and speaks with me graciously; but she allows me no more, nor is it right that I should aim so high or that such rich joys should befall me as would befit an emperor. She does enough when she just speaks to me with grace and suffers me to love her . . .

My life is well assured of great worth if this lady ennobles me, by whom all merit increases and grows fine; and he knows little who teaches me that any other lady should ever sustain me. There never was so fair a mother's daughter in Adam's line, not by as much as the sky rains and thunders.

Peire d'Auvergne, 'Ab fina joia comenssa'

Devoted service and moral elevation appropriately accompany a love that earns the poet protection from the bleak blasts outside:

> Tot jorn meillur et esmeri,
> Car la gensor serv e coli
> El mon – so.us dic en apert.
> Sieus sui del pe tro q'en cima,
> E, si tot venta.ill freid'aura,
> L'amors q'inz el cor mi plou
> Mi ten chaut on plus inverna.

Every day I grow better and purer, for I serve and worship the most noble being in the world; I may tell you this openly. I am hers from foot to head, and however cold the wind blows the love that rains in my heart keeps me warm in the worst of winter.

Arnaut Daniel, 'En cest sonet coind'e leri'

Yet the virtues these poets ascribe to love are more than a gloss upon the beneficence of a lordly patron. However expediently, they express a chivalric ideal which finds merit in heroic sufferance:

> Car qui ama de cor non vol garir
> Del mal d'Amor, tant es dolz per sofrir.
> Ancaras trob mais de ben en Amor,
> Qe.l vil fai car, e.l nesci gen-parlan,
> E l'escars larc, e leial lo truan,
> E.l fol savi, e.l pec conoissedor.
> E l'orgoillos domesg'et homelia,
> E fai de dos cors un, tant ferm los lia.

For he who loves wholeheartedly does not wish to be cured of the sickness of love, so sweet it is to suffer.

I find still more good in love, for it makes low things precious, the dullard speak fair, the miser generous, and the turncoat loyal, the fool wise and the ignorant learned. It tames and humbles the proud, and makes two hearts one, so firmly does it bind them.

Aimeric de Peguilhan, 'Cel qui s'irais ni
guerreia ab Amor'

This love thus characterised is quite self-frustratingly ambiguous, caught between awe and fervour. Such studied lovers well recognise that the benefits they ascribe to their unrequited devotion would be lost if the lady should return their passion:

> Qan plus creis, dompna, .l desiriers
> Don languisc, quar no.m faitz amor,
> De lauzar vostre pretz ausor
> Creis plus mos cors, car jois entiers
> No.m pot ges vinir, amija,
> De vos, si.l pretz s'en destrija;
> Q'aitan car teing vostre fin pretz valen
> Com am ni voill vostre cors car e gen . . .
> Q'amar non pot nuls cavaliers
> Sa dompna ses cor trichador,
> S'engal lei non ama sa honor . . .

Lady, the more the longing grows of which I languish because you show me no love, the more my heart swells to praise your highest worth; for I can never have entire joy from you, my love, if your virtue is thereby destroyed, since I hold your rich and lofty virtue as dear as I love and desire your precious and beautiful body . . .

For a knight cannot love his lady without deceitful heart if he does not love her honour as much as he loves her . . .

Sordello

The characteristic stance of static supplication which Valency so luminously describes[31] no doubt figures a professional relationship. But it also brings out the perpetual dilemma of the troubadour love poet, whose lady's chaste beauty kindles him at once to admiration and desire; so that his zeal in celebrating her virtues struggles with his hunger for a sexual consummation which would destroy the very object of desire, and desire itself. This inner self-contradiction continued to characterise courtly poetry in Europe down to the late sixteenth century, and is particularly intractable in those writers who adopt the extreme troubadour posture of humble supplication before a mistress of unattainable loftiness. Court poets as far removed in every way as Serafino and Sidney took it as faith that a noble love is agonisingly irreconcilable with the desire to gratify sense. Few could manage the careless naturalism of an Il Magnifico, who brushed the dilemma aside by flatly announcing that a pure and chaste love may easily come to sexual fruition without diminishing or destroying itself, and that this fruition is the true end of love in fact:

It seems to me that little blame attaches to what is natural. Nothing is more natural than the impulse to unite oneself with something beautiful, and this impulse was ordained in men by nature for human propagation, an end most necessary to the conservation of human kind. And this is the true reason that we ought to be moved not by nobility of blood, or hope of possessions or riches or of any other goods, but solely by natural election, not forced or occupied with any other regard, but moved only by a certain conformity and proportion which the beloved and the lover have in common to the end of the propagation of the human species. And so those people deserve high blame who are moved by their appetite to love most of all such objects as fall outside this natural order and true end which we have proposed; and they are to be praised who, pursuing this end, love one object only, day in and day out, with firm and constant faith.[32]

For Renaissance commentators Petrarch's three hundred and sixty five poetic celebrations of his unresponding Laura represented the sum of sexual love. The *Canzoniere* was taken to be a compendium of every possible aspect of the passion, 'to which nothing can or should be compared in respect of amorous affections'.[33] It is a 'true example of the most faithful and perfect love',[34] a 'most abundant fountain opened to each one of us, from which infinite rivulets may be drawn by our poets'.[35] Their commentaries confirm the petrarchan attitude of petitioning, which at bottom expresses the self-contradictoriness of a love rooted in sense, however the lover may seek to elevate and idealise it. The idea that sexual love is inherently self-defeating emerges sharply in a poem by Dante's contemporary Giraut Riquier, the self-styled last of the troubadours. Riquier's verse epistle 'Als subtils aprimatz' is a commentary on a *canso* by Riquier's forerunner Giraut Calanson, 'A leis cui am de cor e de saber'.[36] This *canso*, which Calanson addresses to the lady who is at once his 'Domn' e seignor et amic' amounts to a definition of love in itself by way of an orthodox little allegory of a courtly lover's progress towards a life of joy in the palace of love. Calanson says that there are three orders of love, four very slippery steps that lead up to the palace of love, and five successive doors that take the lover into the palace, as well as other hazards on the way in, such as a game of chess with fragile glass pawns; yet the palace is even harder to get out of than to enter. Though his professed concern is the lowest order of love, Calanson's allegory amounts to a moral regimen. It figures a *via mystica*, a progressive refinement of manners and understanding, which comes hard at first but gets easier later as the apt few who survive the test draw near their perpetual bliss. The nature of the bliss is not in doubt. Indeed the question Calanson poses is whether he himself will get there.

Riquier's long recension quietly undermines Calanson's simple faith in a sexual elysium, while glossing its terms. Riquier makes a formal hierarchy of love with carnal love at the bottom, natural love in the middle, and celestial love at the top. Carnal love is the lowest kind because it powerfully directs people's will against reason, and knows no rule. It has a false semblance too, offering lovers pleasure at first but soon turning their joy to torment, anguish, ills. The four slippery steps to the palace are honour, secrecy, service, and patient suffering. The fragile glass pawns are mirrors. The first two doors to the palace, the most difficult ones to pass according to Calanson, are the disclosure of desire by amorous demeanour or words, and humble petition. The third door is discreet devotion and service; the fourth is the kiss; and the last one is 'le faitz, per que mor/l'amore ...'[37] In this reading the critical move becomes the passage from the fourth door to the fifth, since a lover might stay at the kiss and behave 'so that love would not grow less or die'; but doing is the death of love, 'for a man holds that door dear in his heart until he has passed through it'.

Riquier plainly is not seeking to arrest love at the stage before coitus, in a familiar troubadour attitude of willing self-frustration. His allegory points the self-contradictoriness of carnal love itself, for the lover will inevitably proceed from the fourth door to the fifth, from the kiss to sexual coupling, and so destroy his love. Hence the condition of carnal love must be momentariness, total instability, since it dies at the moment of its consummation. The lover may escape his dilemma only when he turns from fleshly love to heavenly love. He must leave altogether his self-defeating pursuit of sense and devote himself to the one true and abiding love, which is the love of God – 'L'amor celestial/Del verai dieu'. Then he will win entry to quite another palace than the one he had so fruitlessly gained by carnal love:

> Si quel palais aussor,
> On es patz senes fi
> E amors ses tot si
> E complitz bes ses dan
> E soiorns ses afan
> E plazer ses pezar

E gaug ses dezirar
Nos fassa possezir
E lauzar e grazir
Lo sieu san nom ben dig,
Aissi co es escrig:
Amen, amen, si fassa!

So that he may bring us to possess the loftier palace where there is peace without end, and love without any let, and perfect well-being without harm, and rest without trouble, and pleasure without sadness, and enjoyment without longing; and cause us to praise and hallow his holy felicitous name; thus it is written: Amen, amen, so be it.

908–19

Riquier's dismissal of love emerges naturally enough from his gloss on Calanson's allegory, though it marks the failure of a troubadour faith. Indeed that quiet return upon himself scarcely annuls the careful elaboration of the courtly ritual which makes up most of the poem, and it is not easy to say where Riquier stands at last. So nice a balance between the impulse to refine the code, and the need to reject sexual delight, suggests the radical equivocalness of a man who feels himself deeply committed to opposite causes at once. What Riquier's poem vividly brings out is the conviction he shares with Capellanus, that carnal love and divine love cannot be reconciled.

iii. *Gleams of glory:* New Style and New Life

it is only when he discerns beauty itself through what makes it visible that a man will be quickened with the true, and not the seeming, virtue – for it is virtue's self that quickens him, not virtue's semblance.

Plato, *The Symposium* 212A

Dante's associates, the poets of the *dolce stil novo*, sought precisely to find ways of loving a beautiful woman without losing sight of eternal love and beauty. Their love poems are the most exquisite metaphysical lyrics we have, luminously graceful and quite without strain, yet attempting by the power of their own vision to bridge the distance between sense and spirit, earthly life and heavenly being:

Vedut'ho la lucente stella diana,
ch'apare anzi ch'l giorno rend'albore,
c'ha preso forma di figura umana;
sovr'ogn'altra me par che dea splendore:

40

I have seen the bright morning star, which appears even before day brings the first light, and has taken the form of a human figure. It seems to me that she shines as a goddess, beyond all others.

Guinizelli[38]

This characteristic attitude of ecstatic admiration shifts the emphasis of love poetry from the poet's sufferings to the lady's beauty, making the poet's first task the search for terms to express the degree of her elevation, and of her power to elevate:

> Io voglio del ver la mia donna laudare
> ed asembrarli la rosa e lo giglio:
> più che stella diana splende e pare,
> e ciò ch'è lassù bello a lei somiglio.

I wish to praise my lady truthfully, and resemble her to the rose and the lily. She shines and shows more clearly than the morning star, and that which is beautiful up there I liken to her.

Guinizelli

> E qual con devozion lei s'umilia,
> che più languisce, più n'ha di conforto:
> li'nfermi sana e' domon' caccia via
> e gli occhi orbati fa vedere scorto.
>
> Sana'n publico loco gran langori;
> con reverenza la gente la 'nchina;
> di luminara l'adornan di fori.

And of such as humble themselves to her in devotion, whoever most languishes receives most comfort from her. She heals the infirm, and drives ill spirits away, and makes blind eyes see clearly.

She heals great ailments in the public place; the people bow to her in reverence; they set candles about her to adorn her.

Cavalcanti, 'Una figura della Donna mia',
5–11

> Quest'altissima stella, che si vede
> col su' bel lume, ma' non m'abandona:
> costei mi die' chi del su' ciel mi dona
> quanto di grazia 'l mi' 'ntelletto chiede.

This most lofty star, which is seen by its own beautiful light, never abandons me. It yields me her who, from her heaven, endows me with as much of grace as my mind asks.

Dino Frescobaldi

The terms matter, not only because they have to convey the sweet rarity of an experience which is a *dolce stil novo* of loving as well as of writing, but because the poet is always trying to keep both heaven and earth in view at once, and suggest the eternal verity in the temporal image. These rarefied praises are not meant for mere hyperbole:

> Angelica figura movamente
> di ciel venuta a spander tua salute,
> tutta la sua vertute
> ha in te locata l'alto dio d'amore.

Angelic figure, newly come from heaven to spread your saving courtesy, the high god of love has placed all his virtue in you.

Lapo Gianni

The task these poets set themselves was to praise a living beauty which is nonetheless to be apprehended by intelligence rather than by sense, or by intelligence through the eyes only, since sight is the purest of the senses. Their poems often begin with the passing of love from the eyes to the mind:

> Donna, da gli occhi tuoi par che si mova
> un lume che mi passa entro la mente;
> e quando egli è con lei, par che sovente
> si metta nel disio che i si trova.

Lady, from your eyes seems to move a light that passes into my mind; and when it is lodged there, it seems often to give rise to the desire that I find in myself.

Dino Frescobaldi

No sensible warm motion of the flesh, or of the poet's own passions, is allowed to disturb the sublime vision. The lady, if there was one, is etherealised into an intelligible beauty whom they figure as a lofty star, an angel, an aspect of divinity itself, and love by an effort of intellectual apprehension. The very fulfilment they envisage is an admiring contemplation of the object of their love; as the blessed spirits seek no other felicity than their nearness to love's source:

> Poi che saziar non posso gli occhi miei
> di guardare a madonna suo bel viso,
> mirerol tanto fiso,
> che diverrò beato lei guardando . . .

Because my eyes can never be satisfied with gazing on the beautiful face of my lady, I will behold it so fixedly that I shall become blessed by looking upon her.

As an angel which by its nature stands so high that it becomes blessed just by seeing God, so, being a human creature, gazing upon the form of that lady who holds my heart, I may become blessed here on earth. Such is her virtue, which spreads and reaches out to us, that no one perceives it save him who honours her even in his desire for her.

Cino da Pistoia

The refined manner of the *dolce stil* poets expresses the endeavour
to purge love of sense, and experience it as pure contemplation of a
beauty which raises the mind to heaven and figures our salvation.
They sublime into the mark of an exclusive experience of love the
very terms by which the troubadours signalled their noble devotion,
and their peculiar aptness to receive a lady's favours: 'cor gentil',
'cor ... asletto, pur, gentile', 'gentil valore', 'gentilezza', 'degno in
fede', 'servitore', 'mercede', 'bella donna cortese', 'cortesia',
'grazia'. Like the troubadours before them they dismiss as 'uomini
vili', 'spiriti bassi', the mass of men who are not capable of courteous love, but they direct their contempt to the earthbound spirits
who do not rise above carnal desire in their response to a woman's
beauty. That impulse they distinguish from an altogether different
experience, a transcendent admiration which is possible only to the
few elect spirits who can already glimpse the world of intelligence in
the world of sense, and love an eternal beauty in the beauty of their
lady:

> Come potèo d'umana natura
> nascer nel mondo figure si bella
> com sete voi? Maravigliar mi fate!
> Dico, guardando a la vostra beltate:
> 'Questa non è terrena creatura;
> Dio la mandò da ciel, tant'è novella'

How may it be that of human nature is born into the world a figure as beautiful as
you are? You make me marvel. I say, gazing upon your beauty, 'This is no earthly
creature; God sent her from heaven, so remarkable she is'

Cino da Pistoia, 'Li vostri occhi gentili e pien
d'amore', 9–14

Dante's companions of the *dolce stil novo* show us that his
singleness of vision was hard won. They aimed at it themselves,
which is why they keep insisting that a true lover needs rare nobility
and understanding – *intelletto d'amore* – and perhaps why their own
poetry seems so rarefied. We see them struggling to rise beyond the
inner turmoil of their double allegiance to love, which is at once an
earthly enterprise and a divine, tentatively trying out the powerful
idea that the beauty of a particular creature in the world might itself
have something spiritual in it, and be celebrated as a particle of
heaven's beauty. Indeed they prove themselves by the degree of their
. willingness to give the idea scope. Frescobaldi and Guinizelli hover

ambiguously between complimentary similitude and hyperbolic assertion – a woman is like a star o24 a woman is a star. Frescobaldi:

> un'alta stella di nova bellezza,
> che del sol ci to'l'ombra la sua luce . . .

A high star of miraculous beauty, whose light takes away the sun's shadow, shines in the heaven of love with such potency that its brilliance makes me love it . . . And as a woman, this new star lets it be seen that my existence displeases her, so that she has ascended thus high in disdain. Love, which speaks to me in my mind, makes arrows of her light, and uses my meagre life as his target.

Guinizelli:

> così lo cor ch'è fatto da natura
> asletto, pur, gentile,
> donna a guisa di stella lo 'nnamora.

To the heart which nature has made elect, pure gentle, a woman like a star brings love.

'Al cor gentil rempaira sempre amore', 18–20

Cavalcanti takes the decisive step:

> veder mi par de la sua labbia uscire
> una sì bella donna, che la mente
>   comprender no la può, che 'mmantenente
> ne nasce un'altra di bellezza nova,
> da la qual par ch'una stella si move
> e dica: 'La salute tue è apparita.'

It seems to me that there issues from her lips a lady so beautiful that the mind cannot comprehend it, and from this at once is born another of marvellous beauty, from which it seems that a star issues and says 'Your blessedness stands before you.'

'Veggio negli occhi de la donna mia', 7–12

At their best these poets marvellously create in their verse the beauty they celebrate, and the awe it inspires in them:

> Chi è questa che vèn, ch'ogn'om la mira,
> che fa tremar di chiaritate l'âre . . .?

Who is this who comes, that every man gazes upon her – who makes the air tremble with brightness . . .?

Cavalcanti

To realise thus simply so sublime a conception of love is an incomparable achievement, which we in no way diminish when we remind ourselves that for these poets the poetic vision was something other than the life of flesh and blood. Dante himself urged

Cino da Pistoia to bring his wayward fancies more into line with his poetic professions 'so that your actions may accord with your sweet words' ('Io mi credea del tutto esser partito'); yet he evidently found his lifelong devotion to Beatrice no impediment to family life. The writing has its truth in the poet's hold on human nature and experience.

Dante shares with his friends of the *dolce stil* a vision of elevated love which only the utmost grace of style can render:

> I' fui del cielo, e tornerovvi ancora
> per dar de la mia luce altrui diletto;
> e chi me vede e non se ne innamora
> d'amor non avera mai intelletto,

I was of heaven, and will return there again to give others the joy of my light; and whoever sees me and is not struck with love for me will never have an understanding of love.

'I' mi son pargoletta', 3–6

> Ne li occhi porta la mia donna Amore,
> per che si fa gentil ciò ch'ella mira;
> ov'ella passa, ogn'om ver lei si gira,
> e cui saluta fa tremar lo core,

My lady carries love in her eyes, by which she makes gentle everything she looks upon. Wherever she passes every man turns towards her, and whomever she acknowledges, she makes his heart tremble.

Vita Nuova xxi

Yet even Dante's minor lyrics record an altogether more painful struggle to hold on to a sense of the spirituality of his lady than those other poets express, in which that endeavour must stand the trial of real sexual passion:

> Tu, Violetta, in forma più che umana,
> foco mettesti dentro in la mia mente
> col tuo piacer ch'io vidi . . .

You, Violetta, in a way which was more than human, kindled fire in my mind with the delight I beheld in you; then with the power of an ardent spirit you created hope, which in part heals me there where you smile at me.

Ah, do not wonder at me because I trust in that hope, but direct your eyes to the great desire that burns me; for a thousand women in times past have been brought by their response to feel the pain of another's grief.

Dante's lyric poems, and the *Vita Nuova* itself, are largely a record of the sufferings love causes in one in whom the life of passion seems to have been unusually intense:

Ahi angiosca e dispietat lima
che sordamente la mia vita scemi,
    perchè non ti ritemi
sì di rodermi il core a scorza a scorza,
com'io di dire altrui chi ti dà forza? ...

E m'ha percosso in terra e stammi sopra
con quella spada ond'elli ancise Dido,
    Amore, a cui io grido
merze chiamando e umilmente il priego;
ed el d'ogni merze par messo al niego.

Oh agonising and pitiless file that dumbly abrades my life, why do you not hold
back from gnawing away my heart shred by shred, as I hold back from telling
others who gives you the power to do it? ...

He has struck me to the earth, and stands above me with that sword with which
he killed Dido – Love, to whom I cry, asking mercy and humbly beseeching him;
and he seems to deny me all mercy.

Dante's difficulty, as his intellectual superiority, lies in his absolute
refusal to compromise either his exalted vision or the human
response to a beautiful woman which seems to contradict it. He is no
more willing to ignore the body altogether than he is to despise it,
but strives to find that grace in sense which may point beyond itself
to something higher:

Doglia mi reca ne lo cor ardire
a voler ch'è di veritate amico;
    però, donne, s'io dico
parole quasi contra a tutta gente,
    non vi maravigliate,

ma conoscete il vil vostro disire;
che la beltà ch'Amore in voi consente,
    a vertù solamente
formata fu dal suo decreto antico,
    contra 'l qual voi fallate.

Grief causes me to burn in my heart for a wish that is the friend of truth; so, ladies,
if I speak words that seem counter to all other people do not marvel at it but
recognise your base desire. For beauty, which Love conceded you, was formed for
virtue alone by his ancient decree, which you offend against.

I tell those of you who are in love that if virtue were assigned to us, and beauty
to you, and to him the power to make one thing of two, you would not be able to
love but would have to cover up as much of beauty as is given to you, because
there would be no virtue in it, which is its sign.

Alas, what have I been brought to say! I say that it would show a fine disdain in
a woman, applauded by reason, to sever herself from her beauty by her own
abjuring of it.

He often fails to find what he seeks:

> Lo doloroso amor, che mi conduce
> a fin di morte per piacer di quella
> che lo mio cor solea tener gioiso,
> m'ha tolto e toglie ciascun dì la luce
> che avean li occhi miei di tale stella,
> che no credea di lei mai star doglioso . . .

The dolorous love that leads me to death in the end, at the pleasure of her who used to hold my heart in joy has taken from me, and takes from me each single day, the light that my eyes received from such a star that they never believed that she might ever leave them in sorrow.

And the blow it has given me, which I have borne in secret, now discovers itself by its overmastering pain, born of that fire which has so bereft me of happiness that I never more expect anything but ill; and my being, even to the point of death, sighs and says: 'I die for her whose name is Beatrice.'

The oppressively intractable dilemma of the sonnets and *canzoni* gives way to the providential pattern of the *Vita Nuova*, in which the pains of love have purpose, and even transform themselves into mysterious beauty:

> Già eran quasi che atterzate l'ore
> del tempo che onne stella n'è lucente,
> quando m'apparve Amor subitamente
> cui essenza membrar mi dà orrore.
> Allegro mi sembrava Amor tenendo
> meo core in mano, e ne le braccia avea
> madonna involta in un drappo dormendo.
> Poi la svegliava, e d'esto core ardendo
> lei paventosa umilmente pascea:
> appresso gir lo ne vedea piangendo.

Already there had passed nearly a third of the hours of the time in which every star is shining when Love suddenly appeared to me, whose nature it gives me horror to remember.

Love seemed jocund to me, holding my heart in his hand, and in his arms he had my lady, wrapped in a drape asleep.

Then he woke her up, and fearfully and humble she fed upon his burning heart. Soon afterwards I saw him go his way weeping.

Vita Nuova iii, 'A ciascun' alma presa
e gentil core', 5–14

In marvelling retrospect the poet recognises his first sight of Beatrice when he was nine years old for the beginning of a new life, a *vita nova* in several symbolic senses; and he personifies his early love for her as the visitation of a chastening force, which is at one moment a tyrant god and at another the radiant glance of the lady herself:

> Sì lungiamente m'ha tenuto Amore
> e costumato a la sua segnoria,
> che sì com'elli m'era forte in pria,
> così mi sta soave ora nel core.
> Però quando mi tolle si 'l valore,
> che li spiriti par che fuggan via,
> allor sente la frale anima mia
> tanta dolcezza, che 'l viso ne smore,
> poi prende Amore in me tanta vertute,
> che fa li miei spiriti gir parlando,
> ed escon for chiamando
> la donna mia, per darmi più salute.
> Questo m'avenne ovunque ella mi vede,
> e sì è cosa umil, che nol si crede.

So long has Love held me and accustomed me to his rule that even as he was rough with me at first, so he now dwells sweetly in my heart. Thus when he so robs me of strength that my spirits seem to fly away, then my frail soul feels such sweetness that my face pales with it. Then Love assumes such power over me that he makes my sighs go about speaking; and they issue forth calling on my lady to give me more of her grace. This happens to me whenever she looks upon me, and is so humble an effect that it passes belief.

Vita Nuova xxxvii

These poems vividly dramatise the conflict of sense with a perception of love beyond sense, living out an issue which the neoplatonist theorists would too easily reduce to dry bones. It is a struggle for a metaphysical vision which the continuous equivocalness of the language keeps before us. Such leading terms as 'salute', 'Beatrice', 'nova', 'anima', 'intelletto', hold several seemingly distinct orders of being in prospect at once and invite the poet to see that these orders are one, that Bicce Portinari in thirteeth-century Florence is at one and the same time Beatrice, a blessed spirit in the order of grace.

That struggle passes into the more drastic disturbance of loss by death. At the heart of the *Vita Nuova* is a series of nightmare premonitions and deaths, which shows the poet through grief the inevitable frailty of mere attachments of sense, and brings him to a clearer understanding of the true end of love. The death of Beatrice herself, though the whole work turns upon it, falls almost incidentally after the harsh foreshadowings of ruin because by then the poet is resigned to its inevitability, and has understood that his love for her need no more depend upon her physical presence than her beauty depends upon its physical embodiment. This last detachment of his mind from sense commits him finally and wholly to the proper object of his love:

> Quantunque volte, lasso!, mi rimembra
> ch'io non debbo già mai
> veder la donna ond'io vo sì dolente,
> tanto dolore in torno 'l cor m'assembra
> la dolorosa mente,
> ch'io dico: 'Anima mia, che non ten vai?
> chè li tormenti che tu porterai
> nel secol, che t' è gia tanto noioso,
> mi fan pensoso di paura forte.'
> Ond'io chiamo la Morte,
> come soave e dolce mio riposo;
> e dico: 'Vieni a me' con tanto amore,
> che sono astioso di chiunque more...

Alas, however often I remember that I may nevermore see the lady for whom I go in such grief, so much pain does my grieving mind gather within my heart that I say: My soul, why do you not depart? For the torments you will have to bear in a world which has already become so irksome to you fill my thoughts with strong fear; so that I call upon Death as my soft and sweet rest, and say: 'Come to me', with such love that I am envious of anyone who dies.

It gathers my sighs into a sound of lamentation, which goes forth continually calling on Death. To him turned all my desires when my lady was assailed by his cruelty; for the pleasure of her beauty, withdrawing itself from our view, became a great spiritual loveliness, which sheds through heaven a light of love that glorifies the angels and makes their high and fine intelligence marvel, so gentle it is.

Vita Nuova xxxiii

It is no paradox for him that the death of his lady confirms his new life, bringing him from suffering to self-acceptance and tranquil hope. The very last verses of the work offer a sublimely resolved image of the ascent beyond the highest sphere of the universe of the love which started in his heart, and issues as understanding:

> Oltre la spera che più larga gira
> passa 'l sospiro ch'esce del mio core:
> intelligenza nova, che l'Amore
> piangendo mette in lui, pur su lo tira.
> Quand'elli è giunto là dove disira,
> vede una donna, che riceve onore,
> e luce sì, che per lo suo splendore
> lo peregrino spirito la mira.

Beyond the sphere which circles widest passes the sigh that issues from my heart; a new understanding which love implants in it draws it ever upwards.

When it has arrived there where it wishes to be, it sees a lady who receives honour, and shines so brightly that the pilgrim spirit admires her by the light of her own radiance.

Vita Nuova xli

What remains to him then is just the hope 'of saying of her that which was never said of anyone', and the prayer that his soul may see for itself the blessedness of its lady 'who gloriously gazes upon the face of him *qui est per omnia secula benedictus*'.

Dante's sublime vision consummates, and in a sense makes intelligible the aspirations of his school, which were otherwise mere hyperbole to us:

> Se quanto infino a qui di lei si dice
> fosse conchiuso tutto in una loda,
> poco sarebbe a fornir questa vice ...

If that which is said of her even up to the highest heaven were all consummated in one act of praise it would be too little to answer the present need. The beauty that I saw transcends all other, and not only what we on earth call beauty; but certainly I believe that only its maker enjoys it completely ... From the first day that I saw her face in this life, even up until this present sight of it, my song has never been diverted from following her ... She spoke again: 'We have moved out beyond the greater universe to the heaven which is pure light, intellectual light full of love, love of true good, full of delight, delight which transcends every sweetness.'

Paradiso xxx, 16–21, 28–30, 38–42

In the end, the beauty of the young girl in Florence is not disjoined from the beauty of the blessed spirit who gazes in glory on the face of God, and mirrors its radiance. The *Vita Nuova* tells how the poet is brought to that understanding of a love which fits him for the universal enterprise of the *Divina Commedia*.

iv. *Earthly Paradise:* the crown of the *Purgatorio*

Man being placed in earthly Paradise had great ioy corporally, but farre greater spiritually: for without this, the bodies were painefull rather then pleasing: The mind is the fountaine of delight, which being sad, what ioy hath man in anything.

J. L. Vives, commentary on St Augustine, *Of The City of God* xiv, 11, p. 513

The imaginative attempt to recover our lost divinity takes Dante, as Milton, to the Garden of Eden.[39] Human kind must regain the Earthly Paradise, and regenerate itself, before it may pass beyond the natural state of reason and attain the vision of beauty transfigured. Dante reaches the Garden at the end of his long ascent of the purgatorial mount, when it emerges quite suddenly before the three poets along their way simply as an unanticipated stage in a progress.

Dante renders the Garden as radiant emblem rather than dramatic scene, in a strange passage of sustained beauty:

> Vago già di cercar dentro e dintorno
> la divina foresta spessa e viva,
> ch'alli occhi temperava il novo giorno,
> sanza più aspettar, lasciai la riva,
> prendendo la campagna lento lento
> su per lo suol che d'ogni parte auliva ...

Eager now to search within and around the divine forest, thick and living, which tempered the new day to my eyes, without waiting longer I left the brow, taking the plain very slowly along the ground that gave fragrance on every side. A sweet air which did not alter in itself was striking my brow, not with force but as a gentle wind by which the trembling leaves all readily bent towards the part where the holy mountain cast its first shadow ... and now a stream prevented me from going forward, whose little currents bent leftwards the grass that sprang along its bank. All the waters that are clearest here [i.e. in our world] would seem to have some impurity in them beside that, which conceals nothing even though it moves very darkly under the perpetual shade, which never lets sun or even moon shine there.

Purgatorio xxviii, 1–12, and 25–33

Dante here encounters Eden as it has remained since the expulsion. There is nothing in it to generate tension or recall the drama of the Fall. What he sees is a lady, dancing and gathering flowers:

> Coi piè ristetti e con li occhi passai
> di là dal fiumicello, per mirare
> la gran variazion di freschi mai;
> e là m'apparve, sì com'elli appare
> subitamente cosa che disvia
> per maraviglia tutto altro pensare,
> une donna soletta che si gìa
> cantando e scegliendo fior da fiore
> ond'era pinta tutta la sua via.

I arrested my pace, and cast my eyes beyond the streamlet to wonder at the great variety of fresh blossoms; and on that side there appeared to me, as something that emerges so suddenly that it drives out every other thought for wonder, a solitary lady who went singing and choosing flower from flower with which all her way was embellished.

34–42

Dante addresses her in an attitude of wondering reverence, which the entire passage sustains:

> 'Deh, bella donna, che a' raggi d'amore
> ti scaldi ...'

'Ah, fair lady, who warm yourself in the rays of love (if I may believe the looks which are wont to be the testimony of the heart), may it please your will to draw further forward towards this stream', I said to her, 'near enough to let me understand what you sing. You bring to my mind where and what Proserpina was at the time when her mother lost her, and she lost the spring!'

43–51

Her beauty as she approaches radiates a love which transcends sexual lure:

> Come si volge con le piante strette
> a terra ed intra sè donna che balli,
> e piede innanzi piede a pena mette,
> volsesi in su i vermigli ed in su i gialli
> fioretti verso me non altrimenti
> che vergine che li occhi onesti avvalli ...

As a woman who dances turns with her feet close to the ground and to each other, and scarcely puts one foot before the other, she turned herself towards me upon the red and the yellow flowerets as a virgin who lowers her modest eyes; and she satisfied my entreaties, drawing so near that the sweet sound carried its sense to me. As soon as she reached the place where the grass was newly washed by the waves of the fair river she did me the favour to lift her eyes: I do not believe that such light shone beneath the brows of Venus when she was transfixed by her son, against all his canons. She smiled straight at me from the other bank, arranging in her hands many colours which that exalted earth puts forth without seed.

52–69

The scene is called up very simply in images of light, colour, movement, sound, but the ravishing fall of the lines conveys above all the wayfarer's own astonished apprehension of the beauty which confronts him. We cannot think of this as word painting or sensuous evocation, for it would scarcely be possible to render to the eye an effect which is created in the texture of the words themselves and so intimately fuses image and meaning. As it happens the properties of the scene are quite formally emblematic, presenting qualities which work as much to define as to delineate. They tell us that the place is totally free from vicissitude; that life looks to its proper source there without diminishing itself in doing so; that the Garden is free of sublunary turbulence, although it does not stand in

the eternal sun, because the plateau it occupies is shielded by the
shadow of the holy mountain which rises free of the natural disturbance of land and sea. The clear pure waters of the place conceal nothing, and are constant in their flow, since their source
is God's will; yet they are shaded because they are not celestial.
The breeze, so exquisitely described, is caused by the communicated movement of the Primum Mobile, and scatters abroad seeds
of *virtù* with which the plants it smites impregnate the air, so that
living things in other places bring forth good according to their
natures. The image is notable because it describes the implanting
of timeless virtues in the world of time, and shows how such a
general penetration of temporal being by the pure good of the
eternal order yet produces diverse effects.

The lady herself, whom Beatrice will call Matelda, is no spirit.
Indeed her actions are the embodiment of natural grace, as if
Dante celebrates the qualities of a real woman who had
companioned Beatrice in the Florence of his youth. Matelda
emerges out of Dante's exquisitely recounted dream of Leah in
the previous canto:

> Nell'ora, credo, che dell 'oriente
> prima raggiò nel monte Citerea,
> che di foco d'amor par sempre ardente,
> giovane e bella in sogno mi parea
> donna vedere andar per una landa
> cogliendo fiori; e cantando dicea:
> 'Sappia qualunque il mio nome dimanda
> ch' i' mi son Lia, e vo movendo intorno
> le belle mani a farmi una ghirlanda ...'

I believe it was in the hour when Cytherea, who seems always burning with
the fire of love, first shone upon the mountain from the east, that I seemed to
see in a dream a beautiful young woman going through a field gathering
flowers; and she said, singing: 'know, whoever asks my name, that I am Leah,
and I go thus interweaving my fair hands to make myself a garland'.

xxvii, 94–102

Leah distinguishes her own nature from that of her sister Rachel
– 'She is satisfied with seeing, as I with doing.' The dream of
Leah thus realised in Matelda is a vision of active bodily life at its
height; and within a few lines of it Virgil brings Dante to what
he takes for the limit of the faculty of reason, and bids him
farewell:

'Il temporal foco e l'etterno
veduto hai, figlio; e se' venuto in parte
dov'io per me più oltre non discerno . . .'

My son, you have seen the temporal fire and the eternal; and you have come to a
part where I by myself can discern nothing further. I have drawn you here with
wit and with art; you must now take your own pleasure for guide: you are beyond
the steep ways, beyond the scope of art. See the sun that shines on your brow; see
the grass, the flowers, and the copses which the earth brings forth of itself here.
Until the beautiful eyes appear in joy which, weeping, made me come to you, you
may sit and you may wander among these. Expect no further word or sign from
me: your will is free, right, and whole, and it would be a fault not to act by its
direction: therefore I crown and mitre you over yourself.

127–42

Thus doubly empowered over himself Dante no longer needs
Emperor or Pope; and reason alone can get him no further. He
approaches the Garden with restored nature, free, right, and sound
in will.

A central passage of the *De Monarchia* helps us place this strange
rendering of the Garden. In *De Monarchia* iii, xiv Dante says that the
Earthly Paradise typifies man's bliss in this earthly life 'which consists in the exercise of his own powers'. The earthly Paradise
presents the type of right life in the world and represents our final
goal as body; so that its bliss is finite and corruptible. But because
man's nature is double and made up of body and soul, he exists for a
double purpose, and alone among created beings dwells in two final
orders, having one goal as corruptible being and a different goal as
incorruptible being. So the bliss of body is to be put alongside the
bliss of soul, that eternal well-being which consists in the enjoyment
of the divine vision, and is accessible to us only when we are aided by
divine light. This incorruptible and eternal state is made intelligible
by the celestial paradise. In the *De Monarchia* Dante educes the
function of Empire and Church from the doubleness of man's nature
and objectives, the end of temporal rule being to bring men to the
final bliss of the body, the perfection of natural life, while the purpose of the Church is to bring men to the final bliss of the soul, the
eternal contemplation of the celestial vision.[40]

Figuring humanity unfallen or restored, Matelda shows that the
condition of human innocence was nothing other than the perfect
fulfilment of the active life of the body. This is the state apprehensible to reason alone, and actually dreamed of by the pagan poets
when they spoke of a golden age, as Matelda herself perfects the

mythic images of Proserpina, Venus, Hero, and amends the fall of Eve. This state needs no dramatic realisation here, for it has nothing in it of sexuality or sexual love. It is the perfection not of sense but of active reason, whose chief mark is a sound will or judgment such as is capable of choosing freely and justly without external prop or guide. But it fulfils one part of our nature only, and the other part seeks a different end which is figured by Rachel and realised in Beatrice, seeing not doing. In the *De Monarchia* the two perfections are paralleled as if they might be independently sought, or as though the pursuit of one of them would exclude the other.

The very arrangement of *La Divina Commedia* suggests a more profound relationship of the two ends. The stream which at first cuts Dante off from Matelda marks something still needing to be done before he is fit even to recover the state of innocence. Yet the *Purgatorio* still has five cantos to run at this point; and in those cantos Dante's understanding passes beyond the active and corruptible life of body to the contemplative and eternal life of soul, exchanging the order of nature for the order of grace, reason for pure spiritual intelligence. That this transition takes place within the Garden only shows us how the life of grace grows out of the life of reason, and itself depends upon a free and innocent will.

The last cantos of the *Purgatorio* figure the total transformation of sense and reason in spiritual vision. One entire canto, xxix, is devoted to images of mystery and revelation drawn from Exodus, Isaiah, Revelations, and other places in the Gospels. The poet has to face east to see these mystic figures, which pass before him in radiant pageant. He marks in succession the candlestick with seven lights; the twenty-four elders; the reflection in Lethe of the worst part of himself; the four winged creatures about the car, symbolising the Evangelists; the triumphal car of the Church; the three ladies who dance at one side of the car, figuring the evangelical virtues of faith, hope and love; and the four ladies who dance at the other side, figuring the cardinal virtues; the two old men, Luke and Paul; the writers of the General Epistles; St John; the New Testament writers; and so on. The visitor from the world of time is made discomfortingly aware of his former distance from absolute truth.

Only at this point of revelatory recognition is Dante moved to comment on our loss of the Garden; and he simply blames Eve's wilfulness for it. Where all else obeyed, she did not suffer to stay under any restraint. If she had been submissive the poet might have tasted these delights before and for longer, and he would not have needed to have his own worst part thus shown to him before the memory of it can be removed. There is particular point in this mingling of references to the Fall, and its consequences, with the instruments of amendment and revealed truth. Here is the very process in the fallen world of the redemption of earthly life, and the entry upon revealed truth and mystery.

The simultaneous return of Beatrice and departure of Virgil, at the height of the pageant, is one of the great turning points of the poem and precisely marks the replacement of reason by a higher intelligence, the direct intervention of grace into human life as yet not fully redeemed:

> così dentro una nuvola di fiori
> che dalle mani angeliche saliva
> a ricadeva in giù dentro e di fori,
> sovra candido vel cinta d'uliva
> donna m'apparve, sotto verde manto
> vestita di color di fiamma viva ...

So within a cloud of flowers which rose from the angelic hands and fell down again within and without, a lady appeared to me, her white veil encircled with olive, vested under a green mantle the colour of living flame. And my spirit, which had now lacked her presence for so long, trembling with dismayed awe, felt the great power of enduring love without the help of my eyes, by the hidden virtue that radiated from her. As soon as my sight was struck by that high virtue which had already transfixed me before I was out of my childhood, I turned to the left with the trust with which a little child runs to its mother when it is afraid or in distress, so as to say to Virgil: 'No drop of blood remains to me that does not tremble: I acknowledge the power of old fire.' But Virgil had bereft us of himself, Virgil sweetest father, Virgil in whose hands I put my salvation; nor did all that the ancient mother lost serve to keep from bitterness the dew that washed my cheeks as I wept.

Purgatorio xxx, 28–54

The passage defines a powerfully mixed response in which intellectual awe struggles with an earthier passion, and all that feeling for Beatrice is suddenly caught up in the human grief of the loss of Virgil. The poet's physical agitation is put so like the passions of Paolo and Francesca as to imply a transmutation of their impulse of sense; yet his intense fellow-feeling is still sensible, purely human, and itself to be left behind in a spiritual love, as it has already left behind the cupiditous self-gratification which Paolo and Francesca took as their end. Impassioned attachment to kind will be subsumed in intelligent understanding.

Dante's hold upon human fellow feeling makes his transcendentalism convincing, and it is never so movingly evident as in these lines; yet Beatrice reproves him for this natural human grief as if it is out of place here:

> 'Dante, perchè Virgilio se ne vada,
>   non pianger anco, non piangere ancora;
>   che pianger ti conven per altra spada.'

'Dante, because Virgil has gone do not weep yet, do not weep yet, for it behoves you to weep for another wound.'

55–7

The departure of Virgil marks not only the term of the usefulness of mere reason but the severance of the last attachment of the heart. Her first addresses to the poet severely upbraid his human failings – 'How do you deign to approach this mountain? Do you not know that here man is happy?'; and he receives them like a chidden schoolboy, with such shame that the accompanying spirits themselves take compassion on him. The episode is central to the poem, and to our understanding of Dante's love poetry altogether:

> Non pur per ovra delle rote magne,
>   che drizzan ciascun seme ad alcun fine
>   secondo che le stelle son compagne,
> ma per larghezza di grazie divine,
>   che sì alti vapori hanno a lor piova
>   che nostre viste là non van vicine,
> questi fu tal nella sua vita nova
>   virtualmente, ch'ogni abito destro
>   fatto averebbe in lui mirabil prova . . .

Not just by the working of the great wheels that direct each seed to some end according to the favour of the stars, but by amplitude of divine graces, which rain down from such high vapours that our sight cannot approach them, this man was potentially such in his regenerated life that every right disposition would have come to marvellous proof in him.

But the better the natural vigour of the soil, the more harmful and wild it becomes with bad seed and lack of cultivation. For some time I sustained him with my countenance; showing him my youthful eyes I led him with me in the right direction. As soon as I was on the threshold of my second age and I changed my life, he detached himself from me and gave himself elsewhere. When I had risen from flesh to spirit, and beauty and virtue had increased in me, I was less clear to him and less pleasing; and he turned his steps along an erroneous way, following false images of good which fulfil no promise. Nor did it avail me to seek means of prompting him, by which in dreams and in other ways I called him back to me; so little did it matter to him. He fell so low that all persuasions to his salvation now fell short, save to show him the damned people.

For this I visited the threshold of the dead, and my weeping prayers were carried to him who has led him up here. God's high decree would be broken if one were to pass Lethe, and taste such sustenance, without some charge of penitence such as prompts tears.

109–45

The passage makes explicit the great personal myth on which Dante has founded his entire poetic career. It takes in the promise of the early life – his *vita nuova* – and the sustaining power of his first devotion to Beatrice, telling us how his running to wild disorder after her death, and forgetfulness of her in his pursuit of other women, led to the confrontation with the damned in hell which she herself brought about at the behest of the Virgin and St Lucy. Its immediate effect, however, is to transform Dante's tears for Virgil into tears for himself, to supplant the expression of the natural bond with a bitter self-recognition which will put away such human weakness.

Once Dante has acknowledged, and condemned, the great error of his life then Beatrice can show him what the love of flesh and sense is worth in respect of right love:

> Mai non t'appresentò natura o arte
> piacer, quanto le belle membra in ch' io
> rinchiusa fui, e sono in terra sparte;
> e se 'l sommo piacer sì ti fallìo
> per la mia morte, qual cosa mortale
> dovea poi trarre te nel suo disio? . . .

Never did nature or art present you with pleasure as great as that you took in the fair members which housed me, and they are scattered in dust; and if the highest pleasure so failed you by my death, what mortal thing should then have drawn you to desire it? At the first prick of frail things you ought indeed to have raised your mind aloft after me, who was no longer so. Neither young girl nor other shortlived vanity should have weighed your wings down to earth, to await more assaults.

xxxi, 49–60

Matelda draws him through Lethe and inducts him into the dance of the four cardinal virtues, and the higher order of the three contemplative virtues; and Beatrice unveils her smiling eyes to give him a glimpse of the mystery of the divine nature itself: 'O isplendor di viva luce etterna' (139). When all recollection of his sins has been thus blotted out he sees the stripped tree of Adam resume its foliage, figuring the restoration of just order in earthly life; and he walks out with Beatrice from the shade into the noonday sun, exchanging the world of relative values for the absolute and unchanging state. He

58

has lost even the memory of his estrangement from her, and she helps him to free himself from fear and shame, imprinting his brain with her love as a seal stamps the blank wax. The final lines of the *Purgatorio* complete the account of his purification. He drinks the waters of Eunoe and comes from them remade and renewed, 'puro e disposto a salire alle stelle' (xxxiii, 145).

'Neither creator nor creature was ever without love' (*Purg.* xvii, 91–2). *La Divina Commedia* unfolds a vision of creation in which love is the animating and cohesive principle of the entire universe, as well as its moral centre. Love is 'the seed in you of every virtue, and of every deed that merits punishment' (*Purg.* xvii, 104–6). Sin and evil are simply misdirections or perversions of a love which only fails to produce general good because different natures receive it differently, making unlike things of it and directing it to dissimilar ends. Some natures are altogether unapt for good love, as bad wax spoils the impression of the stamp or poor soil spoils the seeds (xviii, 34–9).

In essence human love expresses the longing of the soul to return freely to its source, and to reunite itself with that sum of beneficence which created it in love and breathed it out without intermediary, so enamouring it of himself at its birth that it eternally desires him (*Convivio* iv, xxviii, 2–3 and 7–8;[41] *Paradiso* vii, 142–4). This unappeasable yearning is the reason that the soul continually attempts to unite itself with an object of loving desire, and needs to be curbed and guided by judgment if it is to follow its true end, not just licensed to run like a child after every trifling and beguiling good:

> Esce di mano a lui che la vagheggia
> prima che sia, a guisa di fanciulla
> che piangendo e ridendo pargoleggia,
> l'anima semplicetta che sa nulla,
> salvo che, mossa da lieto fattore,
> volentier torna a ciò che la trastulla ...

The little simple soul issues from his hand who delights in it even before it has being, as a young girl who childishly weeps and laughs, knowing nothing save that moved by a joyful maker it spontaneously turns to what pleases it. At first it tastes the savour of some slight good; it deludes itself there and runs after it, unless guide or curb redirect its love. Hence it was fitting that law should be set as a curb ... You may clearly see that it is ill-guidance which has made the world bad, rather than that nature is corrupt in you.

Purgatorio xvi, 85–94, 103–6

In *Purgatorio* xvii, 90–125, Virgil distinguishes between two kinds of love, natural love and the love of the mind. He says that the natural love of plants and the like cannot err, whereas the love proper to rational creatures may err by its choice of an ill object, or by excess of defect of vigour. We cannot choose but love, love being an appetite which is in us 'as the desire of the bees to make honey' (xviii, 58–60). But we may elect our end in love, choosing objects which are fit or unfit, right or wrong, just in as far as they lead us towards or away from the final object and source of love. *De Monarchia* i, xii, distinguishes an arbitrary election from true freedom (*Tutte Le Opere*, p. 347). There Dante argues that right love is appetite controlled by judgment. Lacking judgment, the lower animals are not morally free; yet it is not the mere power of choice which makes us free, for the blessed spirits, whose wills are fixed, nonetheless retain and exercise perfect freedom of judgment in that they wholly assent to the inerrancy of their will. In *Purgatorio* xviii, 46–75, Virgil adds that a misguided choice of love is a constraint of freedom to the extent of its error, which is remediable when the will itself gives assent to the remedy. We are truly free only when we use our judgment to will a fit end of love.

Right judgment of love follows right understanding. Virgil takes Dante as far as reason may go in the understanding of human love when he explains how the mind, 'created quick to love', is so seized by an impression from an outside object that it enters into desire, moving upwards like fire in a spiritual impulse which never comes to rest until the loved object makes it rejoice (*Purg.* viii, 19–39). Then beyond the reach of reason, Beatrice's intensifying beauty accompanies a progressive opening of the poet's understanding and of his desire to be one with its source, the sum of love itself.

v. *Stairway to God:* St Augustine, and the itinerary of love

without order [all things] are restless; restored to order they are at rest. My weight is my love; by it I am borne wherever I am borne. Thy gift kindles us and carries us upwards; we burn and go onwards, we ascend thy stairs in our heart and sing a song of degrees.

St Augustine, *Confessions* XIII, ix

Love is the weight of the soul, as gravity the body.

St Augustine, *Ad Inquisitiones Januarii* 2, LV, 18, in Donne's rendering, *Sermons* I, p. 204

The first act of will is love, says the School; for till the will love, till it would have something, it is not a will. But then, *amare nisi nota non possumus*; it is impossible to love anything till we know it. First our understanding must present it as *verum*, as a known truth, and then our will embraces it as *bonum*, as good, and worthy to be loved. Therefore the philosopher concludes easily, as a thing that admits no contradiction, that naturally all men desire to know, that they may love.

Donne, *Sermons* VIII, 9, p. 222

Dante's vast conceit of universal love transforms into personal vision a systematic metaphysic of love, which was developed in his own age from ideas in St Augustine by just those doctors of the Church whom he calls up to expound love to him high in the ranks of the blessed. The mystical ardour of St Bernard's sermons on the Canticles kindled Richard of St Victor and St Bonaventura to an account of an amorous way to truth which strikingly diverged from the analytic discipline of the schools, and continued to affect European thinking about love until well into the seventeenth century. Dante did not know the *Symposium* or the *Phaedrus*. His understanding of love draws on St Augustine's conception of a universe of qualities which love orders and moves, and is shaped by the contemplative systematising of the amorous pursuit which brings the mind to God.

St Augustine posits that every created thing has its specific kind of love in that it loves according to its proper nature, and is impelled by that love to seek its own place:

If we were stones or waves or wind or flame or something of this sort we should indeed have no sense of life, but we should nonetheless not lack a certain impulse towards our fit place and order.

De Civitate Dei xi, 28

Dante strikingly develops this idea in *Convivio* iii, ii and iii, iii. He says that simple bodies possess a love which has innate affinity to their proper place, 'and so earth always descends to the centre' whereas fire loves with an impulse that takes it upwards. Primary compound bodies, such as minerals, love the place where their generation is ordained, which makes a magnet pull towards the source of its power. Primary animated bodies, such as plants, love to grow in one place rather than another as their constitution requires. Sensitive creatures, which lack understanding, love and find their first place by instinct, as birds, beasts, fishes and every brute kind. Nonetheless we see that the love of brute animals is superior to that of plants and minerals, not only in that they have a more manifest love for their place but because 'we see that they love one another' (iii, iii, 5).

In this universal impulse of things to seek their proper place by love all creation partakes of divine will, in greater or lesser measure. Every form possesses the divine nature by participating in it, and the more noble the form the more it retains of this nature. The human soul, which is the noblest form of all those generated beneath heaven, receives more of the divine nature than any other and therefore wills and desires to be united with God. Man's own specific love is for all perfect and noble things, those beings which themselves partake most directly of God's nature. But his very superiority to the other natures lies partly in his having something of each of them within himself, so that he comprehends in himself all kinds of love, or all kinds of possible loves: 'And because ... by his nobility he has in himself the nature of all these things, he may have all these loves and he has them all' (iii, iii, 5).

St Augustine thinks of human love as a dynamic condition. He equates love with weight, and supposes that man's nature is drawn several ways by the weight of its love:

For this force of their own weight which impels all bodies, whether downwards if they are heavy or upwards if they are light, is no other than their love. For the body is impelled by weight as the soul is impelled by love to move whichever way it does move.

De Civitate Dei xi, 28

Augustine takes our election of love to determine the fate of the body as well as the soul,[42] for love may pull us downward to earth as gravity or draw us upwards as fire or magnetism:

And I did not wait to enjoy my God but was ravished to thee by thy beauty [*decore*], and yet I was soon dragged from thee by my own weight and sank down sighing into these lower things; and this weight was carnal custom.

Confessions VII, xvii

In thy gift we rest: in this we enjoy thee. Our rest is our place. Love lifts us there, and the goodness of thy spirit exalts our humbleness beyond the gates of death. In good will is our peace. The body is pulled by its weight towards its place. The weight does not pull it towards the lowest extreme but towards its own place. The fire tends upwards, the stone downwards.

XIII, ix

Dante adds that sense, the love of simple bodies, pulls man downwards away from God; and in virtue of simple body, which innately predominates in the subject, 'he naturally loves to go downward, and so when he moves his body upwards he finds it a greater labour.'[43]

Augustine pictures our state of amorous unrest in which we run through all things under us and all creation seeking our own likeness, the marks of the creator's image and of God's essence, so as to return to him from whom we fell (*De Civitate Dei* xi, 28). Having freedom of choice we may mistake or misapprehend our bliss of love, but we cannot then find the proper satisfaction of our own nature and so come to rest. All things move by their weight to their own place, fire upwards, stone downward, oil above, water below:

without order they are restless; restored to order they are at rest. My weight is my love; by it I am borne wherever I am borne. Thy gift kindles us and carries us upwards; we burn and go onwards, we ascend thy stairs in our heart and sing a song of degrees.

Confessions XIII, ix

The character of right love, or of a right choice of love, is that it impels the lover to find his own fit place in the universal order and leaves him at rest there in the perfect fulfilment of his own nature.

Love kindles the soul to yearning and leaves it restless with desire, perpetually unsatisfied until it can unite in bliss with the source of love:

The love is the cause of the seeking; the seeking is the fruit and the proof of love.[44]

St Bernard of Clairvaux found a model of devout life in the Song of Songs. His *Sermones in Cantica Canticorum* and *De Diligendo Deo* inspired a theology of love which gave prominence to the naked intensity of our ardour for God, 'Hinc zelus, hinc ardor iste quaerendi quem diligit anima tua':[45]

Such a love is zealous; it befits the friend of the bridegroom; that faithful and prudent servant must burn with it to whom the Lord gives charge over his household. It fills, it scalds, it boils over, it resolutely spreads itself, gushing forth and erupting ... For love is the plenitude of the law and the heart, and fulfils them both. Then God himself is love, and nothing that exists may satisfy the creature who is made in the likeness of God, save God who is love, who alone is greater than all these.[46]

St Bernard's magnificent rhetoric suggested to his many devotees that the sheer force of amorous desire may suffice to carry the soul through the veil of sense and worldliness which separates us from spiritual apprehension:

the capacity of any man's soul is measured by the amount of love he has, so that he who has much love is great, he who has a little is small, he who has nothing at all is nothing . . . you may try to take the kingdom of love by force, until by this holy onslaught you succeed in possessing it even to its utmost limits.[47]

Yet St Bernard himself had a more deliberate progress in view which takes us by degrees from sensual to spiritual love:

Nevertheless because we are carnal, and born of the concupiscence of the flesh, it must follow that our desire or love begins in the flesh; which if it is directed by right order, advancing by its several degrees led on by grace, will at last be consummated in spirit.[48]

It was this understanding of an amorous progress which the Victorines formalised into a contemplative way to truth. Richard of St Victor follows St Bernard in making our will to love the instrument which raised us to God:

I exclaim O how good, how benign, O how soft, how sweet, O how loving, how deeply embracing, how wholly admirable, how completely desirable! O blessed who loves! O happy, whose love is judged worthy! Happy me if I may enjoy it; blessed me if I may aspire to possess it.[49]

But for Richard the process that takes us up through the darkness of sense and forgetfulness which veils God's light from the soul is as much a kindling of the intelligence as the heart. His anonymous fourteenth-century epitomiser precisely catches his drift:

For it fals to a perfite saule [both] to be enflawmede with the fire of luf in the affeccion, and also to be illumynde with lyght of knawing in the reson.[50]

As well as the ecstasy of love – 'O quam suavis!' – there is the elaborate intellectual discipline which enables us to rise to spiritual apprehension by means of the senses:

By the sight of things visible we rise to the cognition of things invisible, just in as far as we can draw a likeness between the one and the other.[51]

Richard is deeply sceptical about the easy assumption that our desire for Christ alone will serve to bring us to him, and has a sharp eye for the ways in which unrestrained fervour may mislead the intelligence. He says that even if you have been taken up into the high mountain, and think you see Christ transfigured, you must not be too ready to believe anything you see in him or hear from him but need to confirm the vision with the word of the Scriptures.[52]

These are the ideas which St Bonaventura developed into a full-blown metaphysics of love.[53] Bonaventura's mystical theology grows from the premise that creation is sustained and animated by

love just because it is an analogue of its creator, who is love itself.[54]
Bonaventura speaks of love as the universal vitalising force which
works on creatures most directly through the most spiritual
elements in our creation, such as the stars, and holds the creation in
coherence about its centre in God's own being.[55] Seventeenth-
century expositors crudified this powerful idea into the conceit of a
universal magnetism of love:

For a lover is nothing but a *load stone*, to drawe the lover to him. *Est magnis magni
magnum amoris amor*. And a load stone (in respect of iron) seems to be nothing,
but (as it were) a lover. For what is that which makes the *loadstone* drawe iron to it,
but *love* ... to the iron, desiring (according to the true and chiefest propertie of
love) to be united and ioyned to it. Now if this be so, tell me where there is greater
love then in *God*, who (as S. John sayes) is *love* it selfe.[56]

Nonetheless Bonaventura is clear that we cannot participate in the
universal reciprocity of love, or have such direct cognition of the
creator in the creatures as we had until the Fall, while we remain
alienated from our first state.[57]

The nearer we get to that loving oneness with the rest of creation
which was Adam's state in Eden, the better we are able to read the
Book of Creation as Adam did.[58] 'The entire universe presents one
mirror full of the light of divine wisdom.'[59] Like Richard of St
Victor, St Bonaventura supposes that the creation mirrors or repro-
duces its creator in the precise sense that it offers us a series of signs
or analogues of God, a vast system of divine hieroglyphs whose key
is Scripture. By love and grace we may so use Scripture as to open up
the book which creation presents to us; our wit subtilises itself to
find divine truths in sensible objects, the Creator in the creatures.[60]
He describes the steps or itinerary by which the mind proceeds from
sensible love of particular things, through an inward image of being
itself, to cognition of the first created reason of all things.[61]

St Bonaventura allows that his regimen of witty love is not the
only way to God. He thinks that we approach God in three distinct
stages, the purgative, the illuminative, and the perfective, and may
securely set out by the common way of discursive reasoning which
he terms the way of knowing. But the mystic and occult way of love,
the way of contemplating, is superior to any other because by grace
it yields us in one instantaneous perception that apprehension of
God which is true wisdom.[62]

Yet Bonaventura sees a danger in the use of the creatures, which
leads him to discriminate between the kinds of knowledge the

creation may yield us.[63] We must categorically distinguish between the sensible Book of Nature and the intelligible Book of Nature. To read the sensible Book is to occupy ourselves with things as they appear to our senses, physical properties only, and this knowledge may become its own end so that our minds are distracted from the intelligible Book altogether. Bonaventura remarks that it was just such a distraction from intelligible to sensible knowledge which caused the Fall. He disjoins altogether the knowledge of worldly things which our senses give us from the reading of the intelligible world which leads us to God. Sense does not lead us to God, and may indeed damningly distract us from him.

Bonaventura supposes that we may apprehend God through his creation just in as far as we love him. We know love by love.[64] He does not dismiss even cold logic as a way of arriving at intelligible truth, though he holds it inferior to the way of ardour, which we take when we fervently yearn to become one with the animating spirit of love in the universe. When he says that a loving desire for oneness with Christ and God prompts our search for truth he is far from opposing the heart to the head, or assuming that ardour is incompatible with intellectual rigour.[65] St Bernard himself allows that our knowledge of the world of sense need not impede spiritual apprehension.[66] The great doctors of love of the twelfth and thirteenth centuries agree that man's will may be purged of its devotion to sense and the world by a regimen which illuminates understanding as it increases desire.

vi. *Towards the heart of light:* the *Paradiso*

But if it were given to man to gaze on beauty's very self, unsullied, unalloyed, and freed from the mortal taint that haunts the frailer loveliness of flesh and blood – if … it were given to man to see the heavenly beauty face to face, would you call his … an unenviable life whose eyes had been opened to the vision, and who had gazed upon it in true contemplation until it had become his own for ever?

Plato, *The Symposium* 211E–212A

We love aright to the extent that our differing capacities and natures inform our understanding. In *Convivio* iii, ii Dante says that our animal (or sensitive) nature impels us to love like a beast, according to sensible appearance; and in this kind of love we most need regulation because of its overmastering operation, especially in the delight of taste and touch. When unresponsive material causes the creature to deviate from the path it should take then the consequence is an adverse movement of love – 'the prime impulse, distorted by false pleasure, moves to earth' (*Par.* i, 109–42). But the highest part of our nature is truly human, or even angelic, because it is rational; and by this we love truth and virtue, and from this springs true and perfect friendship drawn from honesty.

Love draws the soul to seek its fit place in the providential order according to its nature, 'and this is the motive force in immortal creatures which binds earth together and makes for one' (*Par.* i, 117). The loving quest for union with Beatrice takes us beyond sense and the world:

So we should lift the veil of our worldly affairs and turn to God with all our heart and understanding so that we reach that part in all sweetness and perfect peace.

Convivio iv, xxviii, 3, 11, pp. 351–2

The *Purgatorio* presents a progressive purifying of the willing soul from the weight of sense and worldly affairs, so that it may ascend in pure intelligible love to the place fit for its own nature, which will be its particular blessedness:

E io più lieve che per l'altre foci
m'andava, sì che sanz' alcun labore
seguiva in su li spiriti veloci,

And I was going on lighter than at the other pathways, so that I followed the swift spirits up without any labour.

Purgatorio xxii, 7–9

Damnation is simply that state of being fixed in aberrant love which cannot be purged because it is set in the limited course it has willed, and weighs as gravity against the movement of right love in the creation. In the *Paradiso* Dante, and then Beatrice, follow St Bonaventura in identifying this aberration of love as *cupidigia*, cupidity, thus turning to love of self the sin of covetousness marked out by St Paul (Colossians 3:5; Thessalonians 4:5). They speak of cupidity as a willed depravity which makes time work for evil instead of good, and denies and reverses the whole purpose of creation. Cupidity is a melting oneself into ill will instead of the benign will, the state of being fixed upon a false end of love, and thus wilfully alienating oneself from that universal reciprocity of love which fulfils both the providential design and one's own nature (*Par.* xv, 1–33).

Beatrice blames *cupidigia* for turning love to bad ends in the world and corrupting innocence (*Par.* xxvii, 121–48). She lets us see why the *Divina Commedia* needs no arch-adversary to bring about a lapse from right love, and why even the Adam and Eve we meet in the poem do not involve a tempter in their fall. The poem presents a creation qualitatively ordered by kinds and degrees of love, in which people define their places just so far as they grasp love's true end, or stop short of understanding, or wilfully misdirect love. The one absolute distinction Dante makes is that between irredeemable and redeemable aberrations of love, between *cupidigia* and such frailities as an unwitting attachment to sense. Redeemed love itself is blessedness, the state of pure intellectual apprehension of love to the extent that one's own nature allows.

The damned themselves may be pitiable when they recognisably suffer for their attachment to others. Yet Dante's structural paralleling of three victims of forced marriage puts the damnable and the redeemable states of love in clear perspective. Francesca da Rimini in *Inferno* v stands against La Pia in *Purgatorio* v, 130–6, and Piccarda de Donati in *Paradiso* iii, 43–123. La Pia, far from being stuck in a worldly attachment, gives no thought to the harsh fate she suffered at the hands of a murderous husband, and her one concern is that the poet should pray for her soul when he returns to the world. To our understanding Piccarda has reason to lament the forced violation of her vow of chastity which has caused her to be set so low in the order of blessedness; but she joyously tells Dante that she wishes no other station in Paradise than the one she has, because her will and desire are wholly satisfied there where they are at one with God's will:

> 'Frate, la nostra volontà quieta
> virtù di carità, che fa volerne
> sol quel ch'avemo, e d'altro non ci asseta . . .'

'Brother, the power of charity quietens our will and makes us will only what we have and thirst for nothing else. If we desired to be placed higher our desires would not accord with the will of him who appoints us here; which you will see cannot happen in these circles, if it is necessary to be in charity here, and if you well consider the nature of the place. Indeed, it is the essence of this blessed state to hold oneself within the divine will, so that our wills themselves make one will; thus our placing from grade to grade throughout this kingdom pleases the whole kingdom, as it pleases the king who involves our will with his. And in his will is our peace: it is that sea to which everything moves, both that which it creates and what nature makes.'

It was clear to me then how everywhere in heaven is paradise, even though the grace of the supreme good does not pour down everywhere in like manner.

Paradiso iii, 70–90

Dante beautifully rounds off her discourse with the apt Augustinian image for it. She 'vanished singing, as a heavy thing through deep water', moving by the weight of her own love to her fit place in the universal equilibrium.

Blessedness is an ardour of the intelligence, and consists as much in knowing and understanding as in the satisfaction of will and desire. 'And you must know that all have delight just so far as their sight profounds itself in the truth which stills every intellect. From which you can see that blessedness is founded in the act of vision and not in that which loves, which follows after it' (*Par.* xxviii, 106–14). Dante mingles metaphysics with mystical vision because he does not oppose love to knowledge, ardour to intellect, but sees even knowledge of the world as a help towards our salvation. This is why he insists from the first on the 'intelletto d'amore' (*Vita Nuova* xix and *Par.* i, 120), and why Beatrice is 'she who imparadises my mind' (*Par.* xxviii, 3). Right love is inseparable from understanding because it is an impulse of the mind towards an intelligible idea of perfection; and the end of our exercise of mind 'is to see God, who is the supreme object of the intellect' (*Convivio* iv, xxii, 13–14, II, p. 283). Indeed, 'in the Angels an intensity of knowledge is love' as Colet finely said,[67] for only to recognise such an idea is to desire and love its accomplishment.[68] Understanding gives us our 'liberty of intelligent creatures' (*Par.* v, 22–3) by showing us the right end of love, which we cannot fail to choose when we see it.

When the eternal light shines in the mind we must love it, for 'the mind of everyone who discerns truth is bound to that essence by love' (*Par.* xxvi, 25–69). Once seen, it 'solely and always kindles love'; and any other light we may choose to follow in love is merely a vestige of that, ill-understood if it does not lead back to the source (*Par.* v. 1–12). We are drawn willingly upwards in the spiral of grace described by St Augustine, knowledge increasing love and love intensifying the desire to understand.[69] The end of the ascent will be total love and total comprehension together to the full extent of our nature, a condition which is not the assuagement of love and desire but a perfect equilibrium of desire and understanding, not an abandonment of self in the Divine Will but the greatest possible enhancement and fulfilment of particular being:

Così la mente mia, tutta sospesa,
mirava fissa, immobile e attenta,
e sempre di mirar facìesi accesa.
A quella luce cotal si diventa,
che volgersi da lei per altro aspetto
è impossibil che mai si consenta;
però che'l ben, ch'è del volere obietto,
tutto s'accoglie in lei, e fuor di quella
è defettivo ciò çh'e lì perfetto

So my mind, wholly held in suspense, was gazing fixedly, still and intent, and ever kindling itself with gazing. At that light one becomes such that it is impossible ever to consent to turn from it to some other form; for the good which is the object of the will is wholly gathered up in it, and whatever is set apart from it would be defective, which there is perfect.

Paradiso xxxiii, 97–105

In its movement towards true understanding our intelligence has the support of providence and grace. Dante shows grace working directly for his good through St Lucy, Virgil, Beatrice, St Peter Damian:

'Giù per li gradi della scala santa
discesi tanto sol per farti festa
col dire e con la luce che mi ammanta;
nè più amor mi fece esser più presta;
chè più e tanto amor quinci su ferve,
sì come il fiammeggiar ti manifesta . . .'

'I have come so far down along the grades of the holy stairway only to welcome you with speech, and with the light that enwraps me; nor was it greater love that made me more swift, for love as much and more burns up there, as its flaming shows you. But the high love that makes us prompt to serve the counsel that governs the world assigns us here as you see.'

'I well see, holy lantern,' I said, 'how in this court free love suffices to let you follow eternal providence.'

xxi, 64–75

But grace also works indirectly in the creation itself, which everywhere affords to our intelligence the signs of its Creator, and traces of eternal love. 'The prime and ineffable power so ordered everything which turns in mind and in place that he who looks upon it cannot but taste of him' (*Par.* x, 1–15). In the *Convivio* Dante shows how man must use creatures to ascend to a God who transcends his own creation. Indeed our wish to unite ourselves with objects as they appear to us most perfect expresses our soul's desire for union with God, which is its ultimate well-being and perfection. Some things manifest more of the divine love than others, according to the good of their own natures. Hence the soul reveals its own state and quality by the objects of love it proposes, the things which it deems most perfect and nearest God's perfection. Human beauty apprehended in the mind through the eyes is the temporal condition which most nearly approaches God's perfection, leading us through love towards its source.[70] Dante pointedly distinguishes between the love we entertain in other parts of our nature, and that intellectual love which is the desire to unite ourselves spiritually with such things as more nearly approach God's perfection. He says of his own love that it is 'the union of my soul with the gentle lady in whom so much of the divine was revealed to me', and declares that it spoke to him in his mind, 'giving birth to sustained thoughts by reason of my gazing and pondering upon the worth of this lady who was spiritually made one thing with my soul'.[71]

Such intelligible beauties as Dante appraises in Beatrice are the 'teeth with which love bites us' (*Par.* xxvi, 25–69), the 'bites', 'baits', and 'nooses' of grace to draw our minds to God, of which she herself is the supreme example (*Par.* xxvii, 88–141; *Par.* xxviii, 3, and 11–12). But the mind does not receive these promptings passively. On the contrary, 'Your perception takes from outward reality an impression, and unfolds it within you so that it makes the mind turn to it; and if the mind so turned inclines to it, that inclination is love' (*Purg.* xviii, 22–7). The mind must seek the divine trace in the temporal appearance, abstracting the form from the substance to make an idea of beauty; and it is better able to do this where 'hot love' has disposed and imprinted 'the clear vision of the prime virtù', so that the beauty of its subject already shows more of the divine light (*Par.* xiii, 52–81).

The austere imaginative attempt to find in a finite creature an idea of the absolute beauty of the source of love put upon the poets who attempted it a more than human refinement of style and life. The celebrated encounter with Guinizelli and Daniel in *Purg.* xxvi, at the approach to the Earthly Paradise, precisely brings home to Dante the cost of purer vision – 'consiros vei la passada folor' (line 143) – as Velutello renders it, 'In questo rosso guado la passata follia.'[72] The sixteenth-century commentator Bernardino Daniello points out that Daniel, 'gran maestro damor', is a type of Dante's own previous career as a love poet, and stands here for all those who had written the great Romances of love.[73] The two poets welcome the fire which refines them of just such impassioned sensuousness as a love poet might cultivate, willing their liberation from the life of nature.

To pass from the life of nature to the life of grace is to rise beyond mere humanity altogether – *trasumanar*, as Dante pungently puts it (*Par.* i, 70). Until the final judgment, that is to disjoin sensible being from intelligible being, to leave sense behind and become pure intelligence, for the body has no place in Paradise meanwhile. 'Why do you dazzle yourself to see something which has no place here? My body is earth in earth, and will be there among the others until our number makes up the eternal purpose' (St John in *Par.* xxv, 122–6). To transcend nature so completely is also to see how little our world and men's history count for in respect of final truth (*Par.* xxii, 133–5, and xxxiii, 94–6).

Yet Dante crucially will not dissever life in the world from spiritual being, or exclude from the order of intelligible existence all such human knowledge as depends upon sensible appearance in time. On the contrary, he supposes that time is continuous with eternity and may even be a mode of eternal being. Events in time are leaves of a tree that has its roots in the eternal centre (*Par.* xxvii, 118–20), and time itself takes its measure from the Divine Mind (*Par.* xxvii, 115–17). It is because the entire *Divinia Commedia* enacts this understanding that its Renaissance defenders go so wrong with it when they try to moralise Beatrice into a personification of theology or Grace or whatever, not grasping that the poet is at once speaking of the sensible incarnation – a real woman – and of an intelligible spirit:

> Molti costei d'eterna beltate
> La chiaman donna; ma il tuo dolce Dante,
> In suo poema, fra l'alme beate
>
> Beatrice la chiama sì raggiante,
> E chi Teologia per altro nome.
> Vottene dire quel che n'e costante . . .
>
> O Beatrice, o vuoi dir Teologia,
> Nomi le sono sinonimi, ed uno
> Subietto è solo a vera fantasia.[74]

Many of them call eternal beauty a woman; but your sweet Dante calls her Beatrice in his poem where she is set so radiantly among the blessed souls, and some know her as Theology by another name. I want to speak to you of her as that which is unchanging ... You may choose to speak of Beatrice, or of Theology; the names are synonymous, and afford one single object of true conceit.

Such a commentator might have attended to Dante's own explanation of the fourfold meaning of his poem in his letter to Can Grande, which clearly assumes that secular events have final consequences and part in an eternal pattern. Christ's incarnation governs Dante's thinking as it does Milton's, substantiating a movement of history which begins with Adam and Eve and ends in the heart of light.[75]

Dante's poetry gets its distinction from his vision of the co-presence of the final order with the contingent order. It is precisely this understanding of the relation of our life to eternal being which makes him a metaphysical poet, and not an ascetic or agnostic. His poetry enacts the search for an intelligible order of love which interpenetrates the order of sense, acclaiming a providential design in human history itself. This is the ideal aspiration of the *dolce stil novo* which Cavalcanti is the only other poet to realise so rigorously, the vision which St Bernard completes when he replaces Beatrice high in Paradise. The very homeliness which the sixteenth-century commentators censured in Dante for a gross breach of decorum marks his sense of the presence of spiritual being in natural life, annulling our arbitrary categories of experience. It is a metaphysical vision which calls for no dramatic break with the world, or yearning to flee from it, but must be imaginatively lived out with some degree of heroism just the same.

One of the distinctions of Dante's metaphysical vision is that he enacts without tension the transformation of sense into intelligence, and renders a spiritual state with such luminous serenity by the sensible means of art:

> Come'n peschiera ch'è tranquilla e pura
> traggonsi i pesci a ciò che vien di fori
> per modo che lo stimin lor pastura,
> sì vid'io ben più di mille splendori
> trarsi ver noi, ed in ciascun s'udìa:
> 'Ecco chi crescerà li nostri amori'
> E sì come ciascuno a noi venia,
> vedeasi l'ombra piena di letizia
> nel fulgor chiaro che di lei uscia.

As in a fishpool which is tranquil and clear the fishes draw towards that which comes there from outside, taking it to be their food, so I clearly saw more than a thousand splendours draw towards us, and in each one might hear 'Here is one who will increase our loves.' And as each of them approached us one might see by the clear refulgence it gave out from it that its spirit was full of delight.

Paradiso v, 100–8

To complain that the domestic image of the eager fish moving in together in the clear water is indecorously used of blessed spirits, would be to impose that barrier between sense and intelligence which the poetry is working to abolish when it shows us sense itself transformed in disembodied luminosity. The rhetorical cavilling of Dante's sixteenth-century censurers is not mere pedantry, for their objections evidently assume an unbridgeable difference in kind between the categories of being. Yet it is precisely in such continual interweaving of homely and sublime images of light, sound, human feeling, that the order of Dante's universe is established.

In *Paradiso* xiv and xv Dante first of all parallels the everchanging coruscation of light which surrounds the cross as it moves towards him with the play of light on motes of dust in sunbeams shining through shutters. Then as the lights gather into audible harmonies he speaks of the effect of many-stringed instruments tuned in temper, which make a 'dolce tintinno' even to one who does not understand the tune, so that 'I was moved to such love that until then nothing had bound me with chains so sweet.' That climax does not quite complete the vision however, for Dante now suddenly introduces his ancestor Cacciaguida with the amazing image of a swift spurt of fiery light along the cross, 'fire behind alabaster', which he at once beautifully familiarises for us with the simile of a shooting star that suddenly startles the complacent eye on a serene evening. Then that intense impulse of light very movingly transforms itself into human love: 'So piously the shade of Anchises reached out, if our greatest poet merits belief, when he recognised his son in Elysium' (*Par.* xiv, 13–27).

Dante controls his exposition of intelligible love through the key images of fire and light, elements which he depicts throughout the poem as varying in kind and degree according to the condition of love at each stage. The fire which the damned feel as torment, and the penitent as purging pain, inflames and transfigures the blessed. Light, which hell lacks, is intellectual illumination as well as the radiance of beauty, so that the exposition of doctrine is a natural part of each enlargement of vision. 'The world used to believe in its peril that the fair Cyprian rayed forth mad love' (*Par.* viii, 1–15). Erotic desire transforms itself into pure intellectual ardour. The condition of the Blessed Spirits is love – 'Here is one who will increase our loves' (*Par.* v, 105); and love draws towards its source as iron moves to the universal loadstone, or soars upwards as flame which burns more intensely the more it is fed from the centre by 'the ray of grace, which kindles true love, and which then grows by loving' (*Par.* x, 83–4). St James acknowledges 'The love with which I continually burn' (*Par.* xxv, 83–5); St Peter Damian assures the poet that his own love is not singular, 'for love as much and more burns up there, as its flaming shows you' (*Par.* xxi, 67–9); St Bonaventura speaks of 'The love which makes me beautiful' (*Par.* xii, 31); St Bernard says that he burns 'entire love' for the Queen of Heaven (*Par.* xxxi, 100–1). The poetry suggests that all such desire is intellectual by fusing images of deepening intellectual beauty with doctrine and exposition, so that the lines at once illuminate the nature of transcendent love and express the intensity of its effects. The great doctors of love all come before us as ardent lovers, blessed spirits who expound love as the state of blessedness they experience and comprehend. Scholastic theologians and mystical visionaries support and complement each other.

Dante sees in Beatrice herself an 'intellectual light full of love'. Her intensifying beauty, 'which flames the more as it rises higher up the stairs of the eternal palace' (*Par.* xxi, 7–8) presents itself as brightening light which is tempered to his growing understanding, and would destroy him if it were not so tempered. It gathers into her eyes, which are both instruments and mirrors of the Paradise which surrounds them: 'For paradise is not only in my eyes' (*Par.* xviii, 20–1). She weans him from her particular beauty to the universal beauty which she shares.

Paradiso xxiii, one of the most powerfully sustained imaginative impulses in European art, shows the complexity and scope of Dante's apprehension of love. The canto opens in quiet beauty with an extended simile of a dawn watch. As a bird eagerly awaits the light that will let her see and nourish her 'dolce nati' again, so Beatrice looks for the radiance of the approaching hosts of Christ's Church. The images show us vivid light suddenly breaking upon darkness:

> Ma poco fu tra uno e altro quando,
> del mio attender, dico, e del vedere
> lo ciel venir più e più rischiarando.

But the time was brief between the one and the other, between my first attending, I say, and my seeing heaven grow more and more refulgent.

Paradiso xxiii, 16–18

Beatrice's face is all aflame as she points out the splendour of the 'hosts of Christ's triumph' which wheel about them, transfigured spirits whom Dante sees as the stars attending a full moon, and as fire breaking from a cloud.

Here a great climax of the poet's devotion to Beatrice momentarily interrupts the cosmic pageant. Dante bursts out in passionately tender praise of her for bringing him to such a vision, 'Oh Beatrice dolce guida e cara!'; and she responds with a momentous invitation – 'Open your eyes and look at me as I am: you have seen things which give you the power to sustain my smile.' He describes the effect of the smile upon him in some of the most intense writing in the entire poem:

> Io era come quei che si risente
>   di visione oblita e che s'ingegna
>   indarno di ridurlasi alla mente,
> quand'io udi' questa proferta, degna
>   di tanto grato, che mai non si stingue
>   del libro che'l preterito rassegna.
> Se mo sonasser tutte quelle lingue
>   che Polimnia con le suore fero
>   del latte lor dolcissimo più pingue,
> per aiutarmi, al millesmo del vero
>   non si verrìa, cantando il santo riso
>   e quanto il santo aspetto facea mero;
> e così, figurando il paradiso,
>   convien saltar lo sacrato poema,
>   come chi trova suo cammin riciso.

I was as one who comes to himself from a lost vision and puzzles in vain to recall it to his mind when I heard this offer, worthy of such gratitude that it may never be expunged from the book that registers the past. If there were now to sound, in my aid, all those tongues which Polyhymnia and her proud sisters have most enriched with their sweetest milk, they would not reach a thousandth part of the truth in singing the holy smile, and how resplendent it made the holy face. And so, figuring Paradise, it befits the sacred poem to jump like one who finds his path cut off.

49–63

But the revelation does not end there. Its object is to pass him on to a still greater power of beauty: 'Why does my face so enamour you that you do not turn to the beautiful garden which flowers under the rays of Christ?' The light beyond them increases. As a field of flowers is lit up by the sun's rays streaming through broken cloud, so he sees a host of splendours irradiated from above by burning rays whose source is hidden. A flaming torch takes the shape of a crown and wheels about the central figure, surrounding it with light in which he recognises the Virgin Mary herself.

Now he hears the music which the hosts make as they move, the imagery merging sound into light as it reaches for an intensity of rapture beyond anything we can know. 'Whatever melody is most sweetly played here below, and most draws the soul to itself, would seem a cloud that belches thunder compared with the sound of that lyre which crowned the beautiful sapphire by which heaven is most brightly ensapphired.' The song which reaches him is the very voice of joyous love: 'I am angelic love who encircle the supreme joy which breathes from the womb that was the inn of our desire.'

The climax of the canto directs our imagination upwards and outwards to cover the entire cosmos, and yet at once bring it back to a homely human intimacy:

> Lo real manto di tutti i volumi
>   del mondo, che più ferve e più s'avviva
>   nell'alito di Dio e nei costumi,
> avea sopra di noi l'interna riva
>   tanto distante, che la sua parvenza,
>   là dov'io era, ancor non appariva . . .

The royal mantle of all the spheres of the world, which most burns and is most quickened in the breath of God and in his working, had its inner shore so distant above us that no sight of it yet appeared there where I was placed, so that my eyes did not have the power to follow the crowned flame that rose after her seed. And like an infant that stretches out its arms towards its mother after it has taken the milk, because its spirit flames out openly, each of those refulgences reached up with its flame so that the high affection they had for Mary was clear to me. Then they remained there in my view singing 'Regina coeli' so sweetly that the delight never left me.

112–29

Dante comprehends in one evolving movement a tellingly diverse order of events, the tenderness of the waiting bird, the solicitude of Beatrice, the fervent joy of the heavenly hosts, Mary's crowning, the beauty of the spheres, the child reaching for the mother who feeds it, the radiance of the spirits. Weaving all these elements into one imaginative texture of passion, the canto implicitly persuades us that the texture of love is indivisible throughout the creation. The loving bird and the instinctively loving infant are one in their love with the blessed spirits, the angels, the spheres, and with Mary and Christ themselves.

Dante's progress in love becomes an intensification of his perception of beauty, which is also an enlargement of understanding. He passes from Beatrice veiled to Beatrice as she really is – 'riguarda qual son io' (*Par.* xxiii, 46) and then to the wider harmony about and beyond her. As they move higher, 'sì presso all'ultima salute' (*Par.* xxii, 125), Beatrice more and more directs his strengthened vision away from herself to the love and harmony of which her beauty is part. She points out the turning spheres far below among which our globe, 'the threshing floor that makes us so fierce' (*Par.* xxii, 151), cuts too ludicrously mean a figure for the passions enacted there to perturb the general order. Then she herself draws the vision together into a vast defining image of universal harmony, showing him how the entire universe, bound in by eternal providence, moves about the divine intelligence in a continual reciprocity of love and *virtù*, sustained from that centre which is also the source of time itself. 'Light and love enclose it in a circle, as it does the others ... and how time should have its roots in that vessel and its leaves in the others may now be plain to you' (*Par.* xxvii, 106–20).

The vision confirms Dante's own recognition that every particular thing we may prize is to be valued for what it manifests of its Creator. We love God's creature for the love he bestows upon it. To heavenly acclaim Dante acknowledges that it is not Beatrice alone who has saved him but that our very being, and all human existence, have come together with the particular evidences of God's love for us, and of our salvation, to draw him from perverse to right love (*Par.* xxvi, 55–66):

> Le fronde onde s'infronda tutto l'orto
> dell'ortolano etterno, am'io cotanto
> quanto da lui a lor di bene è porto.

The leaves which enleaf all the garden of the eternal gardener I love to the extent of the good which is carried from him to them.

Par. xxvi, 64–6

The increase of light this vital recognition gains him immediately shows him Adam, whom he will shortly see again placed as high in glory as St Peter, at the side of the Queen of Heaven itself. Dante has passed from his post-purgatorial witness of regenerate humanity to the proof of a humanity finally redeemed and transfigured in glory. Yet in this heaven of love Adam himself does not come before us as a lover, even one who has exchanged perverse love for right love;

while Eve herself has long vanished from the poet's mind in the waters of Eunoe (*Purg.* xxix and xxxiii). Adam remains a prime example of wilful disobedience which grace has transformed to good. He shows us that a nature which was created pure, good and at one with its maker, may be restored to blessedness even though 'by its own act ... [it] was banished from Paradise because it turned away from the way of truth and from its own life' (*Par.* vii, 25–45). Indeed we are told that it was not even his tasting the fruit of the tree which in itself cost Adam his long exile, for he was punished solely because the act signified his 'going beyond the mark' which God had set for him (*Par.* xxvi, 115–17). Adam appears now in glory as the realised testimony of God's love for us which the *Paradiso* has long announced: 'It pleased the Word of God to descend where the nature that was separated from its maker he united with himself in his own person by supreme act of his Eternal Love' (*Par.* vii, 25–45). The contrast with Milton's commitment to Adam is acute. There is no place in Dante's vision for the paradise of another's arms. Beatrice herself has never been other to her lover than an intelligible bliss, 'she who imparadises my mind' (*Par.* xxviii, 3).

Successive transformations of his understanding enable the poet to sustain an increasingly intense degree of beauty and love. In the Empyrean, having gazed at last on Beatrice's unveiled beauty which would have destroyed him earlier, he prepares himself to go beyond even that sweet smile of the woman whom he has pursued from the first day he saw her in this life right up to his present vision. 'Now it is fitting that my pursuit desists from following behind her beauty, poetising, as every artist at the limit of his power' (*Par.* xxx, 31–3). She takes him on into 'the heaven which is pure light – intellectual light, full of love; love of true good, full of joy; joy which transcends all sweetness' (*Par.* xxx, 38–42). Then they pass to the vision of the concord of heaven, which succeeds and completes her great image of the cosmic harmony.

Dante visualises the Church Triumphant in the extended image of a rose, a living organism of the company of the blessed which gathers itself into one order in petals of light and rank, and wholly rejoices. Beatrice draws him 'into the yellow of the sempiternal rose that expands and orders itself and exhales odours of praise to the sun which makes perpetual spring' (*Par.* xxx, 124–9); and he sees the whole extent of the flower in one instant, breadth, height, and distance, neither adding nor losing anything, because 'natural law has

no effect where God governs without intermediary' (*Par.* xxx
118–26). *La Divina Commedia* thus pointedly offers itself to us as a
dream-allegory whose climax is a vision of the rose. But in Dante's
great love poem the gaining of the rose is not the consummation of
the lover's pursuit of his lady. On the contrary, the vision requires a
relinquishing of such single commitment, the transforming of a
lifelong devotion into wider understanding. The rose of the *Paradiso*, which enacts the supreme transfiguration into one vital order
of those who entered the realm of grace while they were still in this
world, invites the lover to find his fruition in self-forgetful
admiration.

Dante's mind grows by degrees to comprehend the Church
Triumphant. He first takes in the harmonious reciprocity of the life
of the organism, whose elements are continually engaged in drawing
vital love from its source so that they may fulfil themselves in the
wider order of beauty:

> In forma dunque di candida rosa
> mi si mostrava la milizia santa
> che nel suo sangue Cristo fece sposa . . .

So in form of a white rose was shown me the holy host which Christ espoused
with his own blood. But the other host, which as it flies sees and sings the glory of
him who enamours them, and the bounty that made them such, like a swarm of
bees that at one moment enflowers itself and at another returns where its toil
turns to sweetness [i.e. it moves between the flower and the honeycomb],
descended into the great flower that adorns itself with so many petals, and thence
reascended there where its love forever abides ... Their faces were all of living
flame and their wings of gold, and the rest was so white that no snow could reach
that purity. When they descended into the flower, rank upon rank, they gave it of
the peace and ardour that they had taken in as they flew freely ['ventilando il
fianco'].

Paradiso xxxi, 1–18

We may see here why Dante is so fleetingly occupied with Adam's
state. This rose, and not the Garden of Eden, is his defining image of
the harmony of all creation in which active and contemplative being
are simultaneously consummated. In the *Divina Commedia* the state
of innocent incarnation is as nothing compared to the state of
blessedness. The harmonious life of men and women upon earth
concerns us only as it offers a means to our final end.

When Dante turns to question Beatrice he finds an old man in her
place; and then he sees Beatrice beyond them, smiling at him as he
acknowledges for the last time her gracious power over him before

she turns back to her own bliss, 'all'etterna fontana', and disappears from the poem altogether (*Par.* xxxi, 93). The jolt to Dante's expectation, and the reader's, marks the last transformation of love. Devotion to a beautiful object is subsumed in universal love itself, spiritualised sexuality transforms itself to pure unmediated ardour. St Bernard of Clairvaux, 'sent by prayer and divine love', replaces Beatrice appropriately here both as ardent adept of love and as the great celebrant of the Virgin, whom he will shortly point out to Dante at the heart of the mystic Rose. But specifically the lines name him as the living justification of the pursuit of a divine presence in earthly being, in that he actually experienced the final order within the order of time. He was one 'who in this world by power of contemplation tasted of that peace' (109–11).

The second stage of the vision of the Rose prepares Dante intellectually for the Beatific Vision itself by clearing his mind about the ordering of the mystic hierarchy of love which makes up the Church Triumphant. We are swept majestically into St Bernard's careful distinctions by the sheer vitality of an image that intimates in working energy of light an unimaginable degree of love and joy, and warrants the astonished awe which the writing itself imputes to the wayfarer:

> Io levai li occhi; e come da mattina
> la parte oriental dell'orizzonte
> soverchia quella dove'l sol declina,
> così, quasi di valle andando a monte
> con li occhi, vidi parte nello stremo
> vincer di lume tutta l'altra fronte . . .

I raised my eyes; and as in the morning the eastern part of the horizon rules over that where the sun declines, so as if climbing with my eyes from valley to mountain, I saw a region in the extremity conquer with its light all the other front. And as that point most enflames itself where the shaft that mis-guided Phaeton is awaited, and on this side and on that the light diminishes, so that pacific oriflamme brightened itself in the middle, and on each side the flame diminished equally.

And at that midpoint I saw more than a thousand festive angels with wings spread, each distinct in refulgence and skill. I saw there smiling at their games and their songs a beauty which was joy in the eyes of all the other saints. And if I were as rich in speech as in imagination I would not dare to attempt the least part of her delight.

Bernard, as he saw my eyes fixed and intent upon the fire that warmed him, turned his own to her with such affection that he made mine more ardent to continue their gazing.

Paradiso xxxi, 118–42

In the long exposition that follows, the lucid intensity of the writing quite marvellously fuses doctrine and passionate vision. St Bernard takes Dante into the heart of the rose, pointing out to him the prophets on one side and the saints on the other, with the great exponents of divine love high among them, and then displaying Mary herself at the centre. Mary does not sit unaccompanied however, for she has Adam on one side of her and St Peter on the other, 'as it were the two roots of this rose'. The root of humanity and the root of the Church of Christ now take equal place in glory, as once in human frailty (*Par.* xxxii, 85–126).

In one vital way Dante gives regenerate and redeemed humanity a more secure seat in glory than unfallen innocence itself. Only some innocent beings have access to paradise, and the rest are 'held down below there' (*Par.* xxxii, 84). The Holy Innocents themselves, whom Dante sees here in the Rose, have their place among the elect not by their own desert but by the merit of others, 'since they were released from the body before they had true power of choice' (*Par.* xxxii, 40–84). Not having willed their commitment to the love which is perfect freedom they are admitted to the Church Triumphant only by a special dispensation of grace, because their parents submitted them to such formal rites of entry to the true church as the age understood. Innocence, far from making choice possible, removes the power of choice altogether. But it does not make us blessed in that state (as Henry Vaughan supposed that it must).[76] It merely puts the responsibility for our eternal condition on the choice others make for us, since the one indispensable condition of bliss is right choice itself.

Dante has been drawn by love up the spiral of grace. He has passed from experience to understanding, from doctrine to reality, from reflected refulgence to direct radiance, from Beatrice to Mary. What remains is the heart of light itself, the source of all the love and beauty and knowledge he has sought. 'One God, alone and eternal, himself unmoved, moves all heaven with love and desire' (*Par.* xxiv, 130–2). The centre of the creation is the divine mind, kindling love and raining it down. St Bernard takes Dante on to the culminating grace, the beautific vision of the primal love itself. Dante presents this supreme experience as an instant of total absorption, and total comprehension, in which the several ends of intellect and will are fulfilled together and brought into one transcendent order. All the particularities of being which are spread through the universe, all purely human events, and human history itself, are resolved into a single light; and all the good which is the object of the will is gathered in there, so that any other end must fall defectively short of it:

> O abbondante grazia ond'io presunsi
> ficcar lo viso per la luce etterna,
> tanto che la veduta vi consunsi!
> Nel suo profondo vidi che s'interna,
> legato con amore in un volume,
> ciò che per l'universo si squaderna;
> sustanze e accidenti e lor costume,
> quasi conflati insieme, per tal modo
> che ciò ch' i' dico è un semplice lume.

O abounding grace by which I dared fix my gaze on the eternal light so intensely that the view consumed my sight! I saw that it enclosed in its depth, bound by love in one volume, that which is fragmented through the universe, substances and accidents and their operation as it were merged together in such a way that what I speak of is a simple light.

Paradiso xxxiii, 82–90

As in the vision the 'tre giri/di tre colori' are 'd'una contenenza' and yet remain three, so the final end and fulfilment of all seeking is that equilibrium of pure contemplation which brings will and desire wholly into one with the universal impulse of love, and yet leaves them wholly themselves. 'The love that moves the sun and the other stars already turned my desire and will as a wheel that is moved equally' (*Par.* xxxiii, 143–5). Pure love is at once pure selflessness and pure self-fulfilment, willing and desiring only what accords with the love which impels all creation. We turn the wheel by which we are turned.

La Divina Commedia thus figures the transcendence of sensual passion in an impulse of intellectual love which finally defines itself as the will and desire to return to the fount of beauty, and to rest there in pure contemplative bliss, wholly at one with the force that moves the universe. We are attracted upwards through particular beauties to the one source of beauty, sustained and moved by God's love for us towards the fulfilment of our being in the universal harmony. Dante thinks of love as a universal loadstone which draws creation into perfect equilibrium, and makes that willing harmony in which all impulses are exactly reconciled; and beauty is the attractive power itself, the outward pledge of love.

Such an exalted understanding of love has its logical ground. We may find it in Aristotle's distinction between the object of desire and the object of intellectual apprehension, which Albertus Magnus rendered as a flat opposition between the *appetibile bonum* and the *intelligibile bonum*, that which pleases our appetite through the senses, and that which satisfies our intellect.[77] Albertus says that our *appetibile bonum* can delude. But the *intelligibile bonum* stirs the understanding without check and intermediary; for there is no need that it should first announce itself as good through the senses, which move the appetite, nor is there any holding back on the part of the receiving intellect, since the thing loved is good in itself and immediately received, and vanquishes the whole desire of him into whom it flows. Thus sensible appetite may impede intellect, and should be resisted then.

The *Divina Commedia* places people precisely as they have put the good of appetite before the good of intellect, or have striven to prefer intellectual good. Dante told Can Grande that 'the purpose of whole and part is to remove from the state of wretchedness those who are living this life, and to lead them to the state of blessedness',[78] an intention which Filippo Villani acutely glossed, c. 1400, when he remarked that the anagogical sense of the poem shows how the holy soul escapes from the slavery of corruption to the liberty of eternal glory by putting off its flesh.[79] The poem takes us through the process of recognition by which sensual appetite gets transformed into reason, and then sense itself is transcended altogether in pure intelligence. We see how the natural state may be subsumed in the spiritual state when we exchange our human condition in the world for the absolute and eternal condition of love, pure intellectual apprehension of the sum of good, pure delight in the source of love and participation in that universal impulse. The body will be reunited with the soul at the last judgment; but it will not then be a body of sense at all:

> 'Perchè t'abbagli
> per veder cosa che qui non ha loco?
> In terra terra è 'l mio corpo, e saràgli
> tanto con li altri, che 'l numero nostro
> con l'etterno proposito s'agguagli . . .'

'Why do you dazzle yourself to see something which has no place here? My body is earth in earth, and will be there as long as others until our number makes up the eternal purpose . . .'

Paradiso xxv, 122–6

In *La Divina Commedia*, as in the *Roman de la Rose*, right sexual love has no reference to marriage. But Dante's regard for Beatrice goes beyond sense altogether, so that his desire may be sublimated into a pure intellectual admiration of ideal beauty, which is ultimately weaned from its devotion even to the most spiritual particular beauty and taken up into universal love. A passion which remains essentially sensuous must be a damning impediment to right love, putting the *appetibile bonum* before intellectual contemplation of universal beauty and altogether distracting from that end. Such a commitment defines itself as the opposite of right love, for it has a particular object, and its end is active, finite, centred in self.

Paolo and Francesca condemn themselves not only by their adultery but by the very nature of their love, their commitment to that particular end. In the final sense of the poem they are scarcely lovers at all but wilful creatures of passion. Velutello aptly finds them guilty of denying the good of intellect when he comments that 'Every sin principally consists in the appetite, or rather in the will.'[80] Landino says that they sinned in following blind desire instead of reason and so putting their perverse love before the love of God, a state which is incapable of satisfaction because it consists in unappeasable appetite.[81] In committing themselves to the sexual enjoyment of each other, wholly neglecting the *intelligibile bonum* for the *appetibile bonum*, Paolo and Francesca lock themselves in their own hell. Arrested in sense, and in the consequences of their commitment to sense, they stand as the countertypes of a love which will disclose its true nature only in the realm of spirit.

Dante's tacit irony is to make the bliss of the *Roman de la Rose* the hell of his *Divina Commedia*. The two great quests for the rose of love map extremes of erotic experience, posing as exclusive alternatives that desire whose whole end is the satisfaction of sense in sexual climax, and the devotion which finds its consummate joy in pure spiritual contemplation. These love poets have at least this much in common, that they suppose that love imposes an election between unlike elements in our nature, and allows no final accommodation between sense and spirit.

Dante's magnificent imaginative synthesis closes for the poem a distance which already separated the thinkers who enlighten him, and continued to divide the dialecticians from the seekers of mystical illumination. They all had to ask themselves how our experience in this world may contribute to eternal life at all if our nature is so much at odds with itself that sense perverts intelligence, and enchains spirit. What has a love of the creatures to do with love of their creator, or with the love entertained by the blessed spirits in the state beyond this? Is it not enough to save us that we simply spurn the world and love Christ?

Dante's treatment of the unfortunate lovers has its place in a pattern of encounters which call forth the wayfarer's fellow-feeling only to show him what he must transcend in his own nature. This is decisively not a dismissal of human love but a placing of carnal passion, sense unredeemed by intelligence. Dante does not disjoin our love of a fellow-being from our love of God, or oppose the admiration of a woman's beauty to the desire for eternal beauty:

> E come il tempo tegna in cotal testo
> le sue radici e ne li altri le fronde,
> omai a te può esser manifesto.

And how time might keep its roots in such a pot and its leaves in the other elements may now be clear to you.

Paradiso xxvii, 118–20

Time has its roots in eternity, love and right understanding in the world follow out the eternal love and truth. The vision of the *Divina Commedia* grows out of the understanding that the intelligible and spiritual order interpenetrates the order of sense and is co-present with it, accessible to idealising intellect. The beauty of an earthly object may itself be a spiritual quality, a ray of the divine beauty which the elevated intelligence perceives for what it is, and abstracts from its vesture of sense to contemplate in itself as pure idea.

Ardour is not distinct from intelligence. On the contrary, love follows understanding and comprehends the relationships of sense which make up our knowledge of the world. It is repeatedly brought home to the poet as his awareness deepens that an exact understanding of that love which holds the creation in coherence is as necessary to the beatific vision as an ardent longing to be one with love's source. Aristotelean distinctions order and explicate the testimonies of the ecstatics. Virgil, Aquinas, St John the Divine, St Bernard, St Bonaventura, Richard of St Victor all present themselves as Dante's equal mentors in his ascent through the orders of the blessed, just because passion and logic sustain each other in the approach to the consummating vision.

In bringing these diverse testimonies into one order Dante draws on, and transforms, Aquinas's dictum that 'the essence of happiness consists in an act of understanding' which makes love contingent upon knowledge:

Love ranks above knowledge in moving, but knowledge goes before love in attaining; nothing is loved but what is known.[82]

When Dante has Beatrice refer to Dionysius's discrimination of the angelic orders (*Par.* xxviii, 130–2) he is effectively resolving a question which Aquinas had raised when he drew out Dionysius's distinction between the ardour of the Seraphim and the ardour of the Cherubim, blessedness which is all fire and bliss which is pure light. Aquinas himself thinks that the difference between the two modes of beatitude is no more than a matter of emphasis. Right love will be both ardent and illuminative, for love must attend upon understanding in any case.[83] In Colet's neat formula, the Seraphim are wise loves while the Cherubim are lovers of wisdom – 'amores sapientes . . . sapientiae amantes'.[84]

Dante quite pointedly refuses to discriminate even so far between the orders of love. In the crystalline sphere Seraphim and Cherubim turn together in the circle closest to the point of radiating light from which hang the heavens and all nature, and follow their course most swiftly 'because of the burning love which impels it' (*Par.* xxviii, 45); their striving to move faster, so as to be more like the point about which they turn, is satisfied just in so far as their vision is exalted, 'e posson quanto a veder son sublimi' (*Par.* xxviii, 102). Beatrice directs us to the heart of Dante's understanding of love:

E dei saper che tutti hanno diletto
quanto la sua veduta si profonda
nel vero in che si queta ogni intelletto.

Quinci si può veder come si fonda
l'esser beato nell'atto che vede,
non in quel ch'ama, che poscia seconda;

e del vedere è misura mercede,
che grazia partorisce e buona voglia:
così di grado in grado si procede.

And it must be understood that all have delight to the extent that their vision reaches further into the truth which stills every intellect. So it may be seen how blessedness is founded in the act which sees and not in that which loves, which follows upon it; and merit [mercede], which grace and good will beget, is the measure of seeing. So it proceeds from grade to grade.

Paradiso xxviii, 107–14

The vision of the heart of light comes as a moment of total illumination which is itself pure love, and comprehends the entire creation.

> La forma universal di questo nodo
> credo ch' i' vidi, perchè più di largo,
> dicendo questo, mi sento ch' i' godo.

I believe that I saw the universal form of this knot, for in speaking of it I feel my joy increase.

xxxii, 91–3

Love and understanding are the same thing.

vii. *Spiritual ardours:* St Bernard, and the suitors of Christ

I sleep, but my heart waketh: it is the voice of my beloved that knocketh, saying, Open to me, my sister, my love, my dove, my undefiled: for my head is filled with dew, and my locks with the drops of the night ... Many waters cannot quench love, neither can the floods drown it: if a man would give all the substance of his house for love, it would utterly be contemned.

The Song of Solomon 5: 2 and 8: 7

love is of God; and every one that loveth, is born of God, and knoweth God. He that loveth not, knoweth not God, for God is love.

1 John 4: 7–8

though I had the gift of prophecie, and knew all secrets, and all knowledge, yea, if I had all faith, so that I could remove mountaines, and had not love, I were nothing ... now abideth faith, hope and love, even these three: but the chiefest of these is love.

1 Corinthians 13: 2 (Geneva text)

It was not within the scope of many adepts of spiritual love to comprehend in a single vision both ardour of passion and intellectual illumination. As some sought to work up in themselves a fervour of love for Christ which is scarcely distinguishable from erotic passion, so others devoted themselves to the cool contemplation of spiritual beauty. Mystical and intellectual activity come to be flatly opposed to each other, and even to exclude each other;[85] so that the question is posed whether we are distracted from right love by our passions, or by our reasoning minds.

Devotees of the way of pure ardour looked to St Bernard of Clairvaux. When St Bernard speaks of the 'scientia mundi, quae docet vanitatem', and proclaims that the only true learning is the cross of Christ,[86] he implies that our understanding of the world will not in itself bring us to eternal life. Sensible knowledge and discursive reasoning offer us no such means to final truth as mystical illumination and pious fervour. St Bernard insists upon the ardour of divine love because he supposes that we may reach God by the intensity of our loving desire, to which our logical discriminations and our attachments to worldly objects are in the end superfluous. As Dom David Knowles summarises him, the mystical union is to be achieved not by knowledge but by love and unity of will.[87]

In his *Soliloquium De Arrha Animae* Hugh of St Victor advises the soul that it may love by the sheer force of its desire that which it cannot see or know:

Man... You have a bridegroom but you do not know him. His beauty is everything to you but you do not see his face ... you have a true love for him who visits you but he comes invisibly, he comes hidden, he comes incomprehensibly. He comes and touches you, without your seeing him; he comes and admonishes you, without your comprehending him; he comes not so much wholly pouring out himself as offering himself to your taste ... And this is the utmost pledge of betrothal which befits you, that as in future he will give himself to your sight and your perpetual possession, so now he sometimes – however sweet the recognition – offers himself to your taste. Love him, love him for himself, love him for his gift of himself. Love him and enjoy him, love him who loves you ... This is pure and chaste love which has nothing sordid about it, nothing bitter, nothing transitory, but has a decorous chasteness, a joyful sweetness, eternal steadfastness. *The Soul*. Your discourse inflames me, I perceive its ardour and apprehend its heat[88]

Richard of St Victor, who was not generally hostile to secular learning and science, nonetheless speaks of a darkness of sense which veils God's light from the soul, as if love must kindle the will to take us up through the barrier of forgetfulness interposed between lovers by the mind's concern with the world.[89] In a Bernardine devotional treatise called the *Stimulus Amoris*, which was long thought to have been written by St Bonaventura himself but is now attributed to one Jacobus Mediolanensis, Christ's love is said to be an intoxicating and attractive power which draws the willing soul to itself and requires a return of naked erotic passion. The seventeenth-century translator well catches the mode:

that heart which is not drawen to love, by this lover, or this loadstone, (call it which you will, I mean *Christ* in his Passion), is colder and harder than any iron in the world.[90]

The love-drunk soul is fervently urged to meditate Christ's sufferings on the cross so that it apprehends them as its own, and comes to savour the unimaginable delight of union with Christ; it may then enjoy in amorous prospect the delicate and delicious pleasures of pining away, melting with desire, being consumed with kisses and absorbed into the embraces of the spouse, entering in at Christ's wounds.[91] Contemplated sensation is now to save us from sense.

The fire of divine love is an ardour which consumes everything save the love of God, as the celebrated prayer of St Francis powerfully suggests:

Detach my mind, Lord, from all that is under heaven, by the fiery and sweet power of your love; so that I may die for love of your love, who deigned to die for love of my love.[92]

St Francis of Assissi can scarcely be held to have separated the love of the creatures from the love of God; yet he adjured his followers not to seek after 'the sort of learning that brings pride', and opposed learning to virtue, predicting that 'the corrupting influence of learning' would be the ruin of the Order.[93] 'Scientia inflat, karitas autem hedificat.'[94] The simple unworldliness of the Franciscans confirmed the opposition between love and logic, and opened a mystic way of pure ascetic fervour such as cold intellect could only obstruct. Unrestrained love for Christ is all in all; and experiencing it, the devotee dies to the sinful world and longs only for a blissful consummation in heaven:

> Amor de caritate, – perché m'hai si ferito?
> lo cor tutt'ho partito – ed arde per amore.
> Arde ed incende, nullo trova loco,
> non può fugir però ched è legato,
> si se consuma como cera a foco . . .

Love of loves why have you so wounded me? I have wholly parted with my heart, and it burns for love. It burns and flames, and finds no resting place, yet it cannot escape because it is bound, so that it consumes itself as wax in the fire. It dies a living death, it languishes in fever, it asks for power to escape for a little, and finds itself placed in a furnace . . .

Love, love, Jesus full of longing, I want to die for love in your embrace; love, love, Jesus my sweet spouse, love, love, I ask you for death; love, love, Jesus so delightful, I surrender myself to you and transform myself into you, consider that I go about in agony for you; Love, I no longer know what I am, Jesus, my hope, bury me in love!

Jacopone da Todi, *Lauda* xc[95]

The soul cannot live without love but must always love something, because she is made of love, since I created her by and for love. And this is why I told you that affection moves the understanding, as it were saying: I want to love, for the food which nourishes me is love. Then the understanding, feeling itself awakened by affection, rises as though it says: If you wish to love I will indeed give you what you may love.

St Catherine of Siena, *Libro della Divina
Dottrina (Dialogo della Divina Providenza)*,
ch. LI[96]

Then drown yourself in the blood of Christ crucified, and bathe yourself in the blood, and make yourself drunk with the blood, and satiate yourself with the blood, and clothe yourself with the blood. And if you have been unfaithful, baptise yourself again in the blood; if the demon has clouded the eye of your understanding, wash the eye with the blood; if you have fallen into the ingratitude of unacknowledged gifts, be grateful in the blood; if you have been an unworthy pastor and without the rod of justice, tempered with prudence and mercy, draw it from the blood; and with the eye of understanding, see it in the blood, and take it with the hand of love, and grasp it with panting desire.

St Catherine of Siena, letter to Frate
Raimondo da Capua[97]

The opposing attitudes to divine love declare themselves with uncompromising explicitness in the work of two fourteenth-century English mystical writers, Walter Hilton and Richard Rolle. Hilton devotes several chapters of his *Scala Perfectionis* to 'the fire of love', telling us how the love of God 'burneth and wasteth all sin out of the soul and maketh it clean, as fire maketh clean all manner metal'. But he speaks scathingly of those 'lovers of God that make themselves for to love God as it were by their own might; for they strain themselves through great violence, and pant so strongly that they burst into bodily fervours as they would draw down God from heaven to them, and they say in their hearts and with their mouth, "Ah, Lord, I love Thee, and will love Thee. I would for thy love suffer death."' The 'gift of love' which God offers us does not come in this way. Sometimes the soul receives it 'without any fervour outward shewed, and the less it thinketh that it loveth or seeth God, the nearer it nigheth for to perceive the gift of the blessed love'. For Hilton, as for Aquinas and for Dante, God is not won by ardour alone and intellectual understanding precedes love: 'for love cometh out of knowing and not knowing out of love, therefore it is said that in knowing and in sight principally of God with love is the bliss of a soul, and the more he is known the better is he loved.'[98] To think otherwise is to deceive oneself dangerously, for mindless passion is as dangerous as knowledge unwarmed by desire:

For wyte thou wele that a nakyd mynde or a nakyd ymagynacion of Ihesu or of any gastly thynge, with-outyn swetenes of lufe in affeccyon, or with-outyn lyghte of knowynge in reseone, it is bot a blyndenes, and a say to disceyte, if a man halde it in hys awen syghte mare than it is. Therfor I halde it sekyr that he be meke in his awen felynge, and halde this mynde in regarde nought til he may be custome and usynge of this mynde fele the fyre of lufe in hys affeccion, and the lyght of knawynge in hys resone ... it suffys to me forto lyfe in trouthe principlay, and nought in felynge.[99]

The one caveat Hilton puts in is that the soul may not know or love God, who is love itself. In that luminous phrase of Juliana of Norwich, the love is the ground of our beseeching, and until we bring home to our understanding its nature and extent we cannot respond with our love:

What, woldest thou wytt thy lordes menyng in this thyng? Wytt it wele, love was his menyng. Who shewyth it the? Love. (What shewid he the? Love.) Wherfore shewyth he it the? For love. Holde the therin, thou shalt wytt more in the same. But thou schalt nevyr witt therin other withoutyn ende.[100]

Richard Rolle's ardour for God's love leaves him with as little regard for the intellect as for the world:

Yet carnal love will flourish and perish like some flower of the field in summer, and its joy and being will seem to last no more than a day, so sure is it to last for a brief while and then decline in sorrow; and beyond doubt this will be the bitter lot of those who love vanity. Their pride, their playing with false beauty, will be flung down in filth in their eternal lot. This will never pass away, unlike their false happiness and joy in shining beauty, which have now passed into nothingness, and all that they delighted in has swiftly vanished.

God gives men and women beauty, not indeed that they should burn in love for one another and despise their creator, as nearly everyone now does, but that they should recognise it as a gift of God their Lord, so that they glorify him with their whole heart, and love him without cease; and so that they should constantly yearn for that unending beauty compared with which all worldly beauty and glory is nothing. For if a lovely form appears in the servants of the world, what will be the beauty of the sons of God set in heaven?[101]

Rolle categorically separates our love of human kind from our love of God, and distinguishes the beauty of the creatures from the beauty of spiritual things. His understanding allows no prospect that our admiration of our own kind might itself celebrate our creator. The working of the mind, and our desire for knowledge, can only dampen ardour; theology itself is frivolous if it does not heighten love:

So let us rather make sure that the love of Christ burns within us than that we pursue useless disputation. For when we preoccupy ourselves with extravagant inquiries we do not feel the truly sweet savour of eternity. Thus many now burn so hotly for knowledge rather than love that they scarcely know what love is, or how it tastes. Yet all their study should have looked to no further end than that they might burn with divine love. For shame, that an old woman may be more expert in the love of God and less set on worldly indulgence than the theologian, whose study is vain ... who deserves to be reputed a fool rather than learned.[102]

Followers of St Bernard who commit themselves to spiritual ardour tend to turn from the world and deny the intellect any part in love. St John of the Cross categorically lays it down that the way of love is devotional, and entangles the participants in nice points of metaphysics only when it is thwarted, 'For this way does not consist in the understanding which philosophers call active, whose operation is in the forms and fantasies and apprehensions of the bodily powers.'[103] St John regularly speaks of devotional life as a state of fierce desire, and of piety as a fire of love which grows more intense as the lover approaches God. In the *Subida del Monte Carmelo* and the *Noche Oscura* he sets out the steps of a 'mystical ladder of divine love according to St Bernard and St Thomas';[104] and he still more zealously emulates St Bernard in his *El Cantico Espiritual*, which amounts to a mystical reading of the Canticles by way of an exposition of his own poems on them. As in St Bernard's own sermons and commentaries, the amorous ardour of the Canticles is simply taken for an image of the living fire of love which carries the soul to God. The lover burns in his own fire, at first purgatively then sweetly, the intensity of his desire gradually increasing until his soul is wholly consumed in the ecstatic union with God which is pure love. He experiences that 'total transformation in the beloved in which both sides give themselves up to each other in complete possession, with a certain consummation of the union of love...Very much as when the light of the star or candle is joined and made one with that of the sun.'[105]

In the progress of love which St John's poetry powerfully describes, the lover's hardest but most vital task is to shatter by the sheer violence of his yearning the veil of sense and web of worldly preoccupations. He must break through that curtain which hides God from us, 'which curtain it is that impedes so great an enterprise, for it is an easy thing to reach to God once the impediments are removed and the curtains are broken which hold back the union between the soul and God'.[106] St John says that there are three curtains which must be broken so that the soul may approach and possess God perfectly. They are the temporal understanding, 'which comprehends all creatures'; the natural understanding, 'which comprehends purely natural operations and inclinations'; and the sensitive understanding, 'which comprehends only the union of the soul with the body, which is sensitive and animal life'. The first two curtains have to be broken in a spiritual purgation when the flame of love is keen, 'so that we may attain to this possession of union with God in which all the things of the world stand denied and renounced, and all the appetites and natural affections are mortified, and the operations of the soul turned from natural to divine'. But in the final encounter the flame is 'already so very subtle and delicate and spiritualised from this union with God' that it no longer assails the curtain rigorously but burns us delightfully and sweetly, 'which is why the soul here speaks of the flame as a *sweet encounter*, which is the more sweet and pleasant the more it seems to break the curtain of life'.

St John's poetry renders the sweetness of the final encounter of love, rather than the struggle to break through the curtain:

> Oh llama de amor viva,
> que tiernamente hieres
> de mi alma en el más profundo centro!;
> pues ya no eres esquiva,
> acaba ya, si quieres;
> rompe la tela de este dulce encuentro . . .

O living flame of love, that tenderly wounds my soul in its inmost centre, since you no longer disdain me, please finish your work now and break the veil of this sweet encounter.

O gentle cautery! O delicate wound! O soft hand! O tender touch, that knows eternal life and clears all debts! By killing you have transformed death into eternal life.

> *Llama de Amor Viva. Canciones Que Hace El*
> *Alma En La Intima Union En Dios Su Esposo*
> *Amado*, stanzas 1 and 2[107]

The lover speaks as one who would die to natural being, and passionately savours the delightful pains of love which must accompany unimpeded union. His lines enact the perfecting of an inner condition, which he measures by the extremity of a sweetness and joy he has already discovered. The proof of his spiritual gain is the intensity of his passion.

viii. *The lure of beauty:* Florentine neoplatonism

For the integrity depends upon the minde.

> J. L. Vives, commentary on St Augustine, *Of*
> *The City Of God*, xiv, 26, p. 530

And when he has brought forth and reared this perfect virtue, he shall be called the friend of God: and if it is ever given to man to put on immortality, it shall be given to him.

> Plato, *The Symposium* 212A

When the soul is being drawn towards a body in this first protraction of itself it begins to experience a tumultuous influx of matter rushing upon it. This is what Plato alludes to when he speaks in the *Phaedo* of a soul suddenly staggering as if drunk as it is being drawn into the body; he wishes to imply the recent draught of onrushing matter by which the soul, defiled or weighted down, is pressed earthwards . . .

Now if souls were to bring with them to their bodies a memory of the divine order of which they were conscious in the sky, there would be no disagreement among men in regard to divinity; but, indeed, all of them in their descent drink of forgetfulness, some more, some less . . . Truth is more accessible to those who drink less of forgetfulness because they more easily recall what they previously knew above. That is why in Greek the word for reading *Anagnorisis* means 'knowledge regained': when we are learning the truth we are relearning those things that we naturally knew before the influx of matter intoxicated our souls as they approached their bodies.

> Macrobius, *Commentarii in Somnium Scipionis*
> xii, 7–11, ed. W. H. Stahl, New York, 1952,
> p. 135

The neoplatonic Humanists of the late fifteenth century are the heirs of the poets of the *dolce stil novo* in a recognisably Florentine tradition of transcendental love, which takes love to be an aspiration of intelligence rather than a rage of desire. Ficino and Mirandola prescribe a way of love in which the lover freely chooses to pass from sensible appearance to intelligible reality, as he learns to recognise the only true object of his love.[108] But Ficino decisively goes beyond Dante in altogether separating the life and end of mind from the life and end of sense.[109] Sense limits understanding and distracts the mind from its proper end, which is rest and contemplation. Sense is committed to action and its condition is change; seeking only contingent and relative ends it inevitably weighs us downwards towards total instability, whereas the mind aspires to ultimate stasis in pure contemplation of a reality which is absolute, universal, unchanging. The resurrection of the body will not be the raising of the body of sense but a celestial and immortal garbing of the soul.

Florentine neoplatonism emerged out of the idealist synthesising that went on around Il Magnifico at San Marco and Careggi, and accommodated the *Commedia* to Diotima's soaring vision, as it were assimilating both Plato and Dante to the mystical platonism of Dionysius Areopagus and the Plotinians. Yet Ficino and Mirandola have not Dante's grasp of the world or his comprehensive vision of love. They make love the moving force in a transcendental religion of beauty. Beauty reflects the divine splendour, and love is its attractive power which 'quasi hamo trahi sursum ut Deus evadat':

The splendour of the highest good shines in individual things, and where it shines more fittingly, there it especially allures him who contemplates it, excites him who looks at it, enraptures and takes possession of him who approaches it ... There it is apparent that the soul is inflamed by the divine splendour, glowing in the beautiful person as in a mirror, and secretly lifted up by it as if by a hook in order to become God.[110]

Our love of beauty, which so mysteriously elevates the soul, works in us as a desire for union with the beloved. But union is stasis, for the pattern of consummated love is the change from movement to rest. So the end of love is the state of contemplation, which is perfectly stable and hence quite beyond sense, wholly intellectual.[111] The final object of love is God alone, who draws us thus to union with him and the contemplation of his beauty:

Hence the light and beauty of God, which is wholly pure, and free of every condition, is without doubt infinite beauty. Infinite beauty calls for infinite love. Hence I implore you ... that you love the creatures with a definite limit and end. But you must love the Creator with infinite love. And take as much care as you can that in loving God you observe no limit or measure whatever.[112]

Any lesser love than this is necessarily imperfect, and will indeed frustrate the true end of love if it is not already committed to the ascent from matter to form:

The eye alone, then, enjoys [fruitur] bodily beauty. And as love is a desire to enjoy [fruendae] beauty, and one perceives beauty only by one's eyes, the lover of the body is satisfied just to see the bodily aspect of the loved one.[113]

The vision is both dynamic and qualitative for it supposes that the whole contingent creation is in progressive movement, either upwards towards final stasis or downwards towards total flux and chaos. Men may will their course according to the quality of their election in love, the one motive power, which 'causes some to fall as far as bodily touch and others to rise as far as the vision of God'.[114] So that love is moral choice; and the doctrine gets its characteristic moral impetus from the way it discriminates between our contingent loves, disposing them as lower or higher forms of the desire for union with the beloved according as they impede or tend towards the final end of love. Mirandola posits three distinct orders of amorous union, as there are three types of men. Voluptuous men seek only animal copulation, practical men seek human love, and contemplative men seek celestial love. Animal copulation, the lowest order, is not really love at all. Its end is the mere conjunction of material objects, so that it remains wholly subject to the conditions of the world of matter such as momentariness or change; and it is governed by touch, seeking only the satisfaction of that sense:

> I say that sense judges that this beauty has its origin in the body, and therefore the end of all animal love is coitus. But reason, by opposite judgment, recognises that this material body not only is not the fount and principle of beauty, but is wholly diverse from that and corruptive of it; and it recognises that the more one separates beauty from the body and considers it in itself, the more it has of its own nature and proper dignity and presence.[115]

Such a state of slavery to matter cannot be transformed, for it does not aspire beyond itself; there is only the choice, to settle for it and forgo one's humanity, or to renounce it altogether.

Human love, the realm of the earthly Venus in Mirandola's myth, has a middle status and nature, being a mixture in varying degrees of animal copulation and intellectual contemplation. It is governed by the highest of the senses, sight, and by our specific human faculty of reason. But it leaves us still pulled either way, and obliged to choose one course or the other. Pico says that most men occupy themselves with these two orders of love and aspire no further.[116]

Celestial love, which belongs in the realm of the Celestial Venus, is possible only to men 'whose intellect is purified by philosophical study so that they recognise sensible beauty for a mere image of a more perfect beauty; and having abandoned the love of sensible beauty they begin to desire the sight of celestial beauty'.[117] Ficino puts that process more drily as a matter of a progressive abstraction of contingent qualities. Taking away matter and place the lover sees the beauty of soul; taking away time he sees the beauty of angelic mind; taking away multiplicity he arrives at the One pure light which is the beauty of God himself.[118] So the end this love proposes is the final goal of all creatures which set out up the long stairway from material chaos to formal order. It is nothing less than the pure spiritual contemplation of Ideal Form itself, static, immutable, absolute.[119]

As a structure of deduced hypothesis the system has an elegant self-sufficiency, and it opens an inspiring prospect. The account of the amorous life which Mirandola projects from it is positively enraptured. He says that love in the lover is the exalted pursuit of ideal beauty up 'the ladder of amorous stages'[120] towards the source of all beauty. Glimpsing a gleam of it in another human being the lover elects the amatory life, which is our only escape from the bondage of body and matter. He commits himself to a heroic way of transcendence, a kind of epistemological pilgrim's progress in effect, passing by a process of successive abstraction and idealisation from lower senses to higher, sensible qualities to intelligible, sight to contemplation, participated apprehension to direct, particular physical beauties to the one pure form of beauty, and lastly to universal form itself.[121] At each stage he leaves his former state behind, drawn by an ever more powerful desire to see again that beauty which his soul glimpsed 'before it was immersed in the body',[122] until he raises himself beyond the human state altogether, and dies as man to be born again 'as if purged by the fire of love to the form of an angel'.[123]

This is the one way open to the man of philosophical mind who finds himself loving a worldly object; and it cannot start in touch or seek its satisfaction there, for 'the libidousness of touch is not part of love or an impulse of the lover'[124] and does not point upwards beyond itself. On the contrary, 'adulterated love is a ruinous descent from sight to touch'.[125] So Ficino finds the highest and best form of a purely human love in a union in which sight and mind are all and touch cannot licitly enter, that between an older man and a handsome youth, founded as it must be in the disinterested admiration of beauty:

Finally the lovers exchange beauty for beauty. The older man enjoys with his eyes the beauty of the younger; and the younger man enjoys with his mind the beauty of the older. And the one, who is beautiful in body alone, by this habit becomes beautiful in soul; and the other, who is beautiful only in his mind, fills his eyes with bodily beauty. This is a marvellous exchange for the one and the other, honest, useful, delightful.[126]

This may strike us as a rarefied notion of love, beautiful but scarcely human, and a paradoxical way of asserting the essential dignity of man against such as Savonarola. For however much Ficino may urge that a person so loved has the duty of returning love,[127] the end cannot be a mutual regard between human beings. At last the lover leaves particular objects of enjoyment behind altogether and recognises then that the beauty he loved was within himself; he acknowledges that his soul has endowed an external object with its own intrinsic power of beauty, which is a function of universal beauty.[128] In the end the lover's striving for oneness with the beloved, his wish that he might die to himself and live again in another being, is consummated as the universal process of fruition is consummated in the union with God; for 'the fount of all beauty is God. God is the fount of all love':[129]

Whoever in the present time gives himself with charity wholly to God will finally recover himself in God. For he will return to his own Idea, by which he was created . . . But joined then by love to our own idea, we shall become whole again; in such a way that it will appear that we first loved God in things so as then to love things in him; and that we honour things in God so as to recover ourselves above all. And loving God, we have loved our own selves.[130]

The lover loses himself, only to find himself completely for the first time.

Ficino's account of physical coupling exemplifies the invincibly teleological habit of the neoplatonic school. He says that bodily union is an absolute impediment to right love for 'The appetite for coitus and the appetite for love are not only not the same impulses but show themselves to be contraries.'[131] Yet this appetite may be allowed when it is not itself the end that is sought, so that the begetting of children in marriage is not blameworthy because the end is the begetting, and not the mere gratification of sense. However, the desire to achieve that end has nothing to do with love.[132]

Il Magnifico himself speaks as a practical lover when he demurs from so coldly schematic a resolution on the ground that it runs counter to nature and the conservation of the species.[133] For Lorenzo the good lovers are those who in gratifying the appetite to couple with their beloved yet 'love one sole thing perpetually both with firm constancy and with faith'. Much later in the *Comento* he speaks of the 'sweet death' he himself hopes for when he transforms himself into his beloved, this being 'that sweetness which human concupiscence can achieve'. He awaits this, he says, 'as the true end of all my desires and my own saving remedy'.[134]

Lorenzo's practical commonsense shows up the uncompromising idealism of a system which valued ends and norms before experience. Dante had not laid himself open to the charge of confusing a metaphysical ideal with the domestic practicalities, which the Florentine neoplatonists conspicuously invited in their attempts to live out their studied ideals as a circle of loving brothers around the Medici. The celibate Ficino, judging amorous behaviour simply as it furthers or hinders an end already defined *a priori*, looks just to deductive logic to resolve the moral exigencies of love, and no brute imperatives of sexual life must resist his wish to impose it upon them. So we have the central paradox of the entire neoplatonic doctrine of love, the persuasion that love is more truly itself as it purges itself of sense, of passion, even of regard for a particular human object, and rises free of historical placing and circumstance to an absolute stasis beyond time:

Hence it comes about that the vehemence of the lover is not quenched by any touch or aspect of body; for he desires not this body or that one: but he desires the splendour of the supernal majesty shining in bodies, and it is this that he marvels at.[135]

Between that and Donne's figure of ecstasy there is a human world of difference.

We come to live aright as we better understand the true end of love, and learn to discriminate it more sharply from all inferior objects of love. This Florentine circle gives a distinctive place to reason and election. It follows Dante in supposing that reason gives us a choice of ends and may be vanquished by sensual passion; but it offers man's reason the key to the universal hierarchy of qualities, allowing the soul to mediate between intelligible and corporeal natures and elect its own state of being. Man alone can pass through all the qualities of the universe because he is related to them all, and comprehends all created kinds in his own nature. He becomes the microcosm of a dynamic creation in which qualities constantly tend downwards or upwards, pulling towards the condition of the basest matter, or aspiring to the condition of the purest spirit. Yet all other things resolve their ultimate place by their own nature, as material bodies which refine themselves to the higher forms of matter, or return to dust:

> *Plants* in the *root* with Earth do most Comply.
>   Their *Leafs* with water, and humiditie,
>   The *Flowres* to air draw neer, and subtiltie,
> And *seeds* a kinred fire have with the sky.
>
> All have their *keyes*, and set *ascents*; but man
>   Though he knows these, and hath more of his own,
>   Sleeps at the ladders foot

Vaughan, 'The Tempest' lines 33–9

Man's possession of reason frees him to range the created hierarchy at will; and comprehending all nature in himself he focuses the universal contest in his own will. Men nowhere define their natures so categorically as in their election of love.

Mirandola speaks of 'our chameleon nature' and has God directly allow Adam his unique prerogative of reason, which gives him freedom of choice over himself and the universe.[136] Man's freedom is the ground of his dignity. It is characteristic of the Humanist to insist on what we may make of ourselves. Petrarch says nothing new when he argues that a man must know himself before he can know anything else,[137] but the reason he gives is that we have far more profit in our own minds than from anything which lies beyond us;[138] and this attitude precisely marks the distance between the poet of the *Canzoniere*, whom love submits to half a lifetime of moral self-questioning, and the poet of the *Vita Nuova* for whom love is an instantaneous spiritual awakening. J. L. Vives's *Fabula de homine* (c. 1518) represents man as the central actor on the stage of the universe, who is rewarded for performing well with a seat near to Jupiter among the gods.[139]

A renewed concern with the conduct of civil life and the establishment of a just commonwealth followed out the persuasion that men may voluntarily elect to live in justice and dignity, and that this moral freedom itself attests the inherent nobility of our nature. Man's freedom of will makes civil justice possible, and permits a good life in human society on earth, which would reproduce here so much of the condition of the city of God as our erected wit might conceive. Valla tackled a central difficulty of Christian Humanists and neoplatonists alike when he sought to reconcile God's foreknowledge with man's free will so as to vindicate our freedom of moral choice (*De libero arbitrio*). The superiority of man's mind over unredeemed sense emerges never so directly as when we freely choose to love a spiritual quality in temporal beauty:

> Non vider gli occhi miei cosa mortale
> allor ch' ne' bei vostri intera pace
> ͺtrovai, ma dentro, ov'ogni mal dispiace,
> chi d'amor l'alma a sè simil m'assale . . .

It was no mortal thing my eyes saw when in your beautiful eyes they discovered perfect peace; but within, where every evil is abhorrrent, I saw him who in love fashions the soul in the likeness of his own divinity. And if the soul were not created equal to God it would not seek to go beyond the external beauty which pleases the eyes; but because that is so frail, the soul transcends it in Universal Form.

I say that what dies cannot satisfy the desire of living souls; nor does it seem that eternity waits upon time, which changes people's skins.

Sense is not love but unbridled will, which kills the soul; whereas our love perfects friends here, but still more by death in heaven.

Michelangelo Buonarroti

The attitudes of the Protestant Reformers paid no less regard to human nature but were critically at odds with Humanist confidence in man. A tension grew between opposed ideas of ourselves, which shows itself in individual writers, and gets notable expression in *Astrophil and Stella* and *Hamlet* to say no more. Where the Humanists had emphasised man's dignity, reforming sects insisted on the inherent depravity of human nature, and on the vanity of our illusion of freedom. The unhappy example of Spenser's first two *Hymnes*, in which a powerful poetic imagination struggles to redeem intellectual incoherence, shows the profound effect of conflicting ideas of human nature upon committed Protestant writers who still sought to find a metaphysics in sexual love. Milton remains the one Protestant Humanist who saw how to have it both ways. In his imaginative vision the idea of man's inherent dignity is not in conflict with the persuasion that man's nature is depraved. He set out to demonstrate that the intercourse of sense need not damningly confirm the Fall, but may be a partial recovery of innocence, and a means to true wisdom.

ix. *Love the magician:* hermeticists and alchemists

Accordingly, since Mind emanates from the Supreme God and Soul from Mind; and Mind, indeed, forms and suffuses all below with life; and since this is the one splendour lighting up everything and visible in all, like a countenance reflected in many mirrors arranged in a row; and since all follow on in continuous succession, degenerating step by step in their downward course; the close observer will find that from the Supreme God, even to the bottomest dregs of the universe, there is one tie, binding every link and never broken.

Macrobius, *Comentarii in Somnium Scipionis*
xii, 15, p. 145

But why do we deem love a magician? Because all the power of magic is to be found in love. The work of magic is the attraction of one thing by another in virtue of their natural affinity. Now the elements of this world, which are as members of one sole being, all depending upon one creator, are bound to each other by the communion of a single nature. For just as in our constitution the head, the lungs, the liver and the other members interwork between themselves, give mutual help to each other, and share in the suffering of any one of them, so the members of this great animal, that is, all the elements of the world linked together by their common purpose, give and take each other's natures by turns and are affected together. From their common bond is born a common love, and from love a common attraction. This, indeed, is the true magic.

Ficino, *De Amore*, ii, p. 1348

When Ficino published his translation into Latin of Codex A of the Hermetic Writings in 1471 he commended the *Pimander* to Cosimo de' Medici as the work of Mercurius Trismegistus, a contemporary of

Moses and high priest of 'una priscae theologiae' whose spiritual heir is Plato, 'divi Platonis nostri praeceptor'.[140] The inversion of the true intellectual descent may have helped his own attempted fusion of platonic and hermetic ideas; and it undoubtedly gave rise to a powerfully influential metaphysics of love which held good for some two hundred years. The supposed recovery of primitive wisdom enshrined in Hermes and Plato was exploited in the sixteenth century and the seventeenth century by writers on spiritual magic and alchemy, as well as in works on hieroglyphics, and in some spiritual regimens.[141]

The conceit which sustains this thinking comes straight from the Hermetic Writings themselves. It predicates that the creation is alive, and spiritually animated:

Now this whole Kosmos, – which is a great god, and an image of Him who is greater, and is united with Him, and maintains its order in accordance with the Father's will, – is one mass of life; and there is not anything in the Kosmos, nor has been through all time from the first foundation of the universe, neither in the whole nor among the several things contained in it, that is not alive . . . For it was the Father's will that the Kosmos, as long as it exists, would be a living being; and therefore it must needs be a god also.[142]

No part of this cosmic life may ever cease. 'There is not, and has never been, and never will be in the Kosmos anything that is dead.' What we take for death is no more than change: 'Dissolution is not death; it is only the separation of things which were combined; and they undergo dissolution, not to perish, but to be made new.'[143]

Nor is this condition of change at all random or mechanical, for it is everywhere controlled by mind. Natural life itself compounds two distinct elements of being, moving mind and moved bodies. In the cosmos, 'The celestial souls send forth their virtues to the celestial bodies, which then transmit them to this sensible world. For the virtues of the terrene orb proceed from no other cause.'[144] Agrippa sets out the system of universal dependency which subjects the entire creation to the power of the ardent intellect:

We must know therefore that every superior moves its next inferior, in its degree, and order, not only in bodies, but also in spirits. So the universall soul moves the particular soul; and the rational soul acts upon the sensual, and that upon the vegetable; and every part of the world acts upon another, and every part is apt to be moved by another; and every part of this inferior world suffers from the heavens according to their nature, and aptitude, as one part of the Animall body suffers from another. And the superior intellectuall world moves all things below itself, and after a manner contains all the same beings from the first to the last, which are in the inferior world. Celestiall bodyes therefore move the body of the elementary world, compounded, generable, sensible, from the circumference to the center, by superior, perpetual, and spirituall essences, depending on the primary intellect, which is the acting intellect; but upon the vertue put in by the word of God, which word the wise Chaldeans of *Babylon* call the cause of causes, because from it are produced all beings.[145]

The creation is made up of elements as diverse as spirit and matter, which generate the forms of innumerable distinct kinds; yet all these creatures become reconciled in their right operation and end, and make up one living organism:

This whole then, which is made up of all things, or is all things, consists, as you have heard me say before, of soul and corporeal substance. Soul and corporeal substance together are embraced by nature, and are by nature's working kept in movement; and by this movement, the manifold qualities of all things that take shape are made to differ among themselves, in such sort that there come into existence individual things of infinitely numerous forms, by reasons of the differences of their qualities, and yet all individuals are united to the whole; so that we see that the whole is one, and of the one are all things. The elements through which all matter has been indued with form are four in number, – fire, water, earth, and air; but matter is one, soul is one, and God is one.[146]

We must have in mind not a mechanical conjunction of atoms but an animate being, which is quickened and made one by the spirit of love. The world is 'the living statue, image, temple of God in which he has depicted his acts and written his conceits';[147] or it is God's very being, which holds all things in pure love; and love is stronger than death:

It is a truth to be accepted as sure and evident above all other truths, that by God, the Master of all generative power, has been devised and bestowed upon all creatures this sacrament of eternal reproduction, with all the affection, all the joy and gladness, all the yearning and the heavenly love that are inherent in its being.[148]

In his fragmentary poem on nature Empedocles speaks of the bond of love which links creation; but he supposes that the cosmos is continually pulled between the impulse to loving order and the chaotic hatred engendered by strife (*Fragments* 16–36). Sixteenth-century cosmologists replaced that idea of a mechanical alternation of order and chaos with the image of a right functioning organism, whose elements are linked in one harmonious whole by the 'influence and bond of love'. Love is the force that holds the entire universe in cohesion:

For the parts of this huge world, like the limbs and members of one living creature, do all depend upon one Author, and are knit together by the bond of one Nature: therefore as in us, the brain, the lights, the heart, the liver, and other parts of us do receive and draw mutual benefit from each other, so that when one part suffers, the rest also suffer with it; even so the parts and members of this huge creature the World, I mean all the bodies that are in it, do in good neighbourhood as it were, lend and borrow each others Nature; for by reason that they are linked in one common bond, therefore they have love in common; and by force of this common love, there is amongst them a common attraction or tilling of one of them to the other. And this indeed is Magick.[149]

The idea that the cosmos is sustained and moved by a magnetic force of love goes back at least to Dante, and emerges strikingly among the followers of St Francis. The fourteenth-century Catalan Franciscan John of Rupescissa was a practising alchemist, who founded his art in 'that influence and bond of love between the celestial bodies and the things that correspond to them on earth'. He finds his proof of the power of the bond in the behaviour of the compass-needle:

Consider and see how those sailing the sea affixing a needle with the stone adamant make it turn against the polar star. Whence has the needle this property that it always unfailingly turns against that star and does not turn to any other place? Without doubt this is because both iron and adamant by order and command of God are generated on earth by the influence of that star and have in them the nature and influence and property of the star. And therefore the needle always turns to it as to its like.[150]

Gilbert's *De Magnete* itself shows how firm was the conviction that magnetism is a spiritual force. In this outrider of modern physics, first published in 1601, Gilbert shrewdly suggested that polar attraction might account for magnetic effects; yet he still assumes that magnetism itself is to be taken for the natural observable evidence of God's providential love.[151]

Magnetism looms large in theories of magic, as in protophysics, because investigators of nature assumed in common that the play of universal forces of attraction and repulsion accounts for physical events. Hermeticists supposed that the spiritual force which draws natural objects together is sympathy, that special attraction which holds between like and like:

the exploits of sympathy, and also those of antipathy in every thing, are effected by a magneticall power, which is both to expell by an irascible or odible expulsion, and allure and draw unto it by a concupisible attraction.[152]

Creatures lacking reason respond instinctively to the power which holds them in their fit course. A man may feel the power of sympathy, not to say control it, only when he clears his spiritual apprehension of its cloud of sense and grossness, and is not misled by his corrupted reason. The elder Pliny authorised the idea which Plutarch confirmed, that the natural creation may actually be superior to corrupted man in its instinctive following out of its appointed purpose:

As for all other living creatures, there is not one, but by a secret instinct of nature knoweth his own good, and wherto he is made able ... man only knoweth nothing unlesse he be taught ... apt and good at nothing he is naturally, but to pule and cry.[153]

Not every free spirit agreed that animals, plants and stones have a right instinct which man has lost. Campanella was one powerful exponent of spiritual magic who scouted as great folly the idea that reason is itself a corrupting force.[154] Yet he too accepts that the man who seeks control over himself and his world must recover by art that original power of sympathy with the rest of created being.

The condition of the right correspondence of loving sympathy in the creation, as in the human constitution, is harmony. Men have power over the elements just as far as their nature harmoniously corresponds with all that lies beyond it, for 'the Soul answers to the Earth by Sense, to the Water by Imagination, to the Air by Reason, to the Heaven by the Intellect, and the Soul goes out in an Harmony of them according as these are tempered in a mortall body'.[155] Agrippa shows how a grasp of the numerical ordering of the universe is a spiritual achievement in itself, and even a key to the universal work of love, when he remarks that the number five 'is the seale of the Holy Ghost, and the bond that binds all things, and the number of the cross, yea eminent with the principall wounds of Christ' (p. 188); Fludd roundly declares that Christ's Passion is the source of all effective love, 'the band or tie, whereby the discording elements are compelled into a harmonious accord' (p. 22). These writers strikingly develop Macrobius's idea that the effective expression of cosmic harmony is music:

The wise Ancients therefore knowing that the Harmonious dispositions of bodies and souls are divers, according to the diversity of the complexions of men, did not in vain use Musical sounds and singings, as to confirm the health of the body, and restore it being lost, so to bring the minde to wholsome manners, untill they make a man sutable to the Celestial Harmony, and make him wholly Celestial.

Moreover, there is nothing more efficacious to drive away evil spirits then Musicall Harmony (for they being faln from that Celestial Harmony, cannot endure any true consent, as being an enemy to them, but fly from it).[156]

To restore the entire being to health is to go some way towards a recovery of the state Adam forfeited, opening a man's mind to that celestial music which his pure spirit may know only when it has elevated itself altogether beyond this muddy vesture of decay. Campanella says that the world is full of spiritual influences, not only heavenly music but angels, demons and the like, which the opaqueness of our bodies obscures from our understanding and use; nonetheless we shall grasp even the subtlest and purest expressions of this spiritual life when we issue from the dark cave of the body and ascend to the heavens as pure immortal mind.[157]

We natural creatures may find our most direct evidence of the working of pure spiritual intelligences in the splendour of the stars, whose rays transmit secret virtues and powers, and engage with other such spiritual emanations in processes of mutual fruition.[158] The stars receive God's love by way of the angels who are its instruments, and mediate it to the creatures by their radiant virtues:

For we must know ... that the essentiall beams descending from God to the Angels, and from the Angels to the Starrs, and from the Starrs unto the creatures, are continuall because indivisible: For there is no formal Virtue issuing from God, that can be separated from its Fountain.[159]

Agrippa shows how this continuity of love may be used;

The Celestiall souls send forth their vertues to the Celestial bodies, which then transmit them to this sensible world. For the vertues of this terrene orb proceed from no other cause then Celestiall. Hence the Magician that will worke by them, useth a cunning invocation of the superiors, with mysterious words, and a certain kind of ingenious speech, drawing the one to the other, yet by a naturall force through a certain mutuall agreement betwixt them, whereby things follow of their own accord, or sometimes are drawn unwillingly.

Such processes have their strict causal logic, which a man who would draw upon them needs to know:

Hence saith *Aristotle* in the sixth book of his Mysticall Philosophy, that when any one by binding or bewitching doth call upon the Sun or other stars, praying them to be helpfull to the work desired, the Sun and other Stars do not heare his words, but are moved after a certain manner by a certain conjunction, and mutuall series; whereby the parts of the world are mutually subordinate the one to the other, and have a mutuall consent, by reason of their great union: As in mans body one member is moved at the motion of another. So when any one moves any part of the world; other parts are moved by their perceiving the motion of that.

The key to a man's power over spiritual, as material being, is an understanding of the chain of sympathy in the creation:

The knowledge therefore of the dependency of things following one the other, is the foundation of all wonderfull operation, which is necessarily required to the exercising the power of attracting superior vertues ... inferiors, must have respect to their beginning, that it may be strengthened, and illustrated by that, and receive power of acting through each degree from the very first author. Therefore we must be more diligent in contemplating the souls of the Stars then their bodies, and the supercelestiall, and intellectuall world, then the Celestial corporeal, because that is more noble, although also this be excellent, and the way to that; and without which medium the influence of the superior cannot be attained to.[160]

Given the premises, such an account of the working universe is as nice in its observance of cause and effect as any of the cosmological reasoning then current, and it was widely entertained. No less a proto-astronomer than Kepler makes much of the 'harmonious rays which descend from the celestial bodies to Earth', such as have their effects upon the nature of sublunary souls and the human soul; and he insists that a 'geometry in the rays of the stars affects sublunar nature'.[161]

Such a direct commerce between 'the superior, spiritual essences' and man as Thomas Vaughan aspired to[162] needs to be reciprocal, whether it operates through the stars or through the instrumental agency of angels, as Agrippa supposes it might.[163] Some writers take this process for an interchange of voluntary love, by which spirit is not only linked to spirit but bound to matter in one impulse of mutual ardour. Heaven marries earth in the same cosmic process of *discordia concors* as links the soul to the body. The *Pimander* authorises the conceit that man's nature is the outcome of the love of eternal being for its mortal offspring:

And Nature, seeing the beauty of the form of God, smiled with insatiate love of Man, showing the reflection of that most beautiful form in the water, and its shadow on the earth. And he, seeing this form, a form like to his own, in earth and water, loved it, and willed to dwell there. And the deed followed close on the design; and he took up his abode in matter devoid of reason. And Nature, when she had got him with whom she was in love, wrapped him in her clasp, and they were mingled in one; for they were in love with one another.

And that is why man, unlike all other living creatures upon earth, is twofold. He is mortal by reason of his body; he is immortal by reason of the Man of eternal substance.[164]

For the hermetic writers of the sixteenth and seventeenth centuries such a union of opposites was perfected in Christ's own love, which impelled him to take on a double nature of spirit and sense conjoined.

They inferred that the nearer a man approaches to Christ in love the more effective will be his mastery of that 'certain Art by which a particular spirit may be united to the universal',[165] and the greater will be his hold over nature. Neoplatonists among them assumed that he might fully gain this state only when he has left his body behind, and merged back into the one source of all love and all life.

Yet in theories of magic universal love does not at all tend towards the purging of the traits of kind in a disembodied return to the One. On the contrary, 'in the Soul of the world there be as many Seminal forms of things, as *Idea's* in the mind of God'.[166] The essence of created harmony is unity in extreme diversity, in as far as this oneness expresses the bond of love between creatures who are distinctly differentiated one from another by the properties God has stamped upon them. Each created kind has its individual nature and quality, which is not so much an outward aspect of sense as an interior spiritual virtue such as impels it to fulfil the particular purpose God assigned to it. These hidden virtues bear their hidden seal, a signature with which heaven imprints each creature so as to denote its inner nature, and mark God's providential disposition of it. 'There is nothing that nature has not signed in such a way that man may discover its essence.'[167] Yet such talismanic signs may be recognised only by the purified intelligence, a mind 'free from wordly thoughts';[168] and as Agrippa explains at length, the mind which can grasp them acquires power over the virtues they embody:

All Stars have their peculiar Natures, properties and conditions, the Seals and Characters whereof they produce through their rayes even in these inferior things, *viz.* in Elements, in Stones, in Plants, in Animals, and their members, whence every things receives from an harmonious disposition, and from its Star shining upon it, some particular Seal, or Character stampt upon it, which is the significator of that Star, or harmony, conteining in it a peculiar vertue differing from other vertues of the same matter, both generically, specifically, and numerically. Every thing therefore hath its Character pressed upon it by its Star for some peculiar effect, especially by that Star which doth principally govern it: And these Characters contain, and retain in them the peculiar natures, vertues, and roots of their Stars, and produce the like operations upon other things, on which they are reflected, and stir up, and help the influencies of their Stars, whether they be Planets, or fixed Stars, and figures, and Celestiall signes, *viz.* as oft as they shall be made in a fit matter, and in their due, and accustomed times. Which ancient wise men considering, such as laboured much in the finding out of the occult properties of things, did set down in writing the images of the Stars, their figures, Seals, Marks, Characters, such as nature her self did describe by the rayes of the Stars, in these inferiour bodies, some in stones, some in Plants, and joynts and knots of boughs, and some in divers members of Animals.

pp. 65–6

'Man is an epitome of all the world, and he is also the student of this world if he seeks to know God who made it.'[169] 'The world was made after the similitude or Type of God.'[170] To the extent that the aspiring intelligence is able to grasp these signatures of hidden virtues it may read God's mind in his creation, discovering hieroglyphs of spiritual truth in creatures of sense themselves:

The creatures are half lost, if we only employ them, not learn something of them: God is wronged, if his creatures be unregarded; ourselves most of all, if we read his great volume of the creatures, and take out no lesson for our instruction.[171]

St Augustine's conceit of the Book of Nature had been turned to devotional use by Bishop Eucherius of Lyon; it gets a curious new direction when the Book itself is taken for an occult gallery of divine hieroglyphs, such as the ancient Egyptian priests directly perceived in those early times before men's wits decayed so far, and Horapollo transcribed.[172] We find God when our purified wit is capable of apprehending the spiritual work of love in sensible nature, as Robert Boyle assumed.[173] Such discoveries of the providential links between things seemingly unrelated will be directed to the end of deciphering that sublime work of wit which is God's creation, and may need to be expressed hieroglyphically. Hieroglyphic devices embody 'sacred hidden secrets, having in themselves some occult divinity';[174] and their expositors claim no less for them than that they try the utmost cunning of men's minds:

man has imitated God in the devising of *imprese* to the extent that he has been able to draw upon the likeness that all things have with each other.[175]

there is nothing in the world so covered and so hidden that the ingenuity of the human wit cannot discover and divulge it.[176]

Man's special virtue is to know how to discover the likenesses and conformity between things which seem diverse. He stands equally in the midst of all things of whatever kind, and gathers in from that host more powers or less, according to the degree of his difficulty in making them out, and the sharpness and clarity of his wit in penetrating them.[177]

The discovery of the hidden natures of things need not be only an intellectual recognition. Man 'is immortal, and has all things in his power';[178] he 'acteth with all, and hath power on all, even on God

110

himself, by knowing and loving him'.[179] The man who seeks control over nature must bring his own nature into harmony with the spirit of creation by the combined power of his purified spiritual intelligence, and of his sympathy or love:

Whosoever therefore shall know himself, shall know all things in himself; especially he shall know God, according to whose Image he was made; he shall know the world, the resemblance of which he beareth; he shall know all creatures, with which he Symbolizeth; and what comfort he can have and obtain, from Stones, Plants, Animals, Elements, Heavens, from Spirits, Angels, and every thing, and how all things may be fitted for all things, in their time, place, order, measure, proportion and Harmony, and can draw and bring to himself, even as a Loadstone Iron.[180]

Spiritual magic is founded in the capacity of the magus to recognise and control in himself 'this affinity and bond of nature wherewith all natural things are linked to each other'.[181] Love brings him into intimate correspondence with creation and so opens its harmonising virtues to his intelligence, subjecting sense and time to his will and fitting him to follow the supreme magus, Christ himself. All such practice of art is a spiritual achievement because it aims at Christ, as the maguses followed the star to his crib.[182] Christ is the philosopher's stone and the pearl of great price, comprehending in himself the double nature of pure gold and pure spirit, the highest form of material being and the quintessence of mind.[183] The mind filled with true love of Christ shares not only Christ's wisdom, and knowledge, but his power:

Therefore our mind being pure and divine, inflamed with a religious love, adorned with hope, directed by faith, placed in the hight and top of the humane soul, doth attract the truth, and sudainly comprehend it, and beholdeth all the stations, grounds, causes and sciences of things, both natural and immortal in the divine truth it self as it were in a certain glass of Eternity. Hence it comes to pass that we, though Natural, know those things which are above nature, and understand all things below, and as it were by divine Oracles receive the knowledg not only of those things which are, but also of those that are past and to come, presently, and many years hence; Moreover not only in Sciences, Arts and Oracles the Understanding challengeth to it self this divine vertue, but also receiveth this miraculous power in certain things by command to be changed: Hence it comes to pass that though we are framed a natural body, yet we sometimes praedominate over nature, and cause such wonderfull, sodain and difficult operations, as that the evil spirits obey us, the stars are disordered, the heavenly powers compelled, the Elements made obedient.[184]

Hermeticists supposed that a man's power to use the hidden virtues of things may take several directions. He might practise

spiritual alchemy, and seek to mark his progressive spiritual refinement, and recovery of Adam's wisdom, by advancing the
natures of material elements up the scale of being towards the
condition of gold. Or he might turn to Paracelsian medicine,
drawing on the hidden sympathies and vital virtues of organic
nature so as to restore health by the homeopathic powers which
inhere in the creatures themselves. Della Porta says that all such
powers over matter simply draw upon the forces of sympathy and
antipathy which are already inherent in natural life, for 'a diligent
searcher of Natures workes, as he seeth how Nature doth generate
and corrupt all things so doth he also learn to do so'.[185] Fludd
thinks that a heavenly spirit directly instructs men in the use of
hidden virtues in healing.[186] Thomas Vaughan sums up all these
ideas when he speaks of the Atonement itself as the true end of all
experiment, and supreme physic of love.[187]

Yet all these writers agree that the consummate form of
spiritual art is that of the true magus himself, who arduously seeks
the power of mind to marry earth to heaven and control the forces
of sense:

So the Philosopher who is skilful in the stars (for such is properly a Magician)
works by certain bait, as it were, fitly matching earthly and heavenly things
together, and platting them as skilfully one within another as a cunning Hus-
band-man planteth an old grasse into a young stock: nay, he layeth earthly
things under heavenly things, and inferiours so fitly for their superiours everywhere to work upon ... even so the Magician, when once he knows which and
what kinds of matters Nature hath partly framed, and partly Art hath perfected, and gathered together, such as are fit to receive influence from above;
these matters especially doth he prepare and compound together, at such a
time as such an influence raigneth; and by this means doth gain to himself the
vertues and forces of heavenly bodies.[188]

Agrippa indicates how an art which starts in self-knowledge and
aims at self-perfection gives a man control over nature, and at last
exalts him so far in power that he becomes one with God himself:

no man can come to the perfection of this art, who shall not know the
principles of it in himself, but by how much the more every one shall know
himself, by so much he obtaineth the greater power of attracting it, and by so
much operateth greater and more wonderfull things, and will ascend to so
great perfection, that he is made the Son of God, and is transformed into that
Image which is God, and is united with him, which is not graunted to Angels,
the world, or any creature, but to man only, *viz.* to have power to be made the
Son of God, and to be united with him.[189]

Prospero's rough magic scarcely aims so high, being directed to the recovery of an earthly common wealth of love:

> I have bedimm'd
> The noontide sun, call'd forth the mutinous winds,
> And 'twixt the green sea and the azur'd vault
> Set roaring war: to the dread rattling thunder
> Have I given fire, and rifted Jove's stout oák
> With his own bolt; the strong bas'd promontory
> Have I made shake, and by the spurs pluck'd up
> The pine and cedar: graves at my command.
> Have wak'd their sleepers, op'd, and let 'em forth
> By my so potent art.
>
> *The Tempest* V. i, 41–50

The higher the magus aspires, the more rigorously he must refine his understanding and his ardour. A true magus will 'dye to the world, and to the flesh, and all senses, and to the whole man animal'; he will 'exceed the way of the flesh' to become one with the celestial spirits and pure intelligences.[190] He will be born again, resurrected out of the corruption of his former state as if from death and burial, in a figuring of the final resurrection.[191] In their understanding of this regeneration, however, the devotees of Hermes decisively divided. Platonists echoed the *Pimander*'s exalted proclamation that in man's transfigured state, when flesh and sin are finally transcended in pure spirit, the body can have no place.[192] They agreed with Cusanus, that a love which is to be consummated in Christ must lift a man altogether beyond sense and time.[193] Yet the *Asclepius* intimates that man's double nature makes him superior not only to other creatures but to the gods themselves;[194] and no less an authority than Agrippa concluded that an art which requires the perfection of our entire nature might help man to glory:

man being united to God, all things which are in man, are united, especially his minde, then his spirits and animal powers, and vegetative faculty, and the Elements are to the matter, drawing with it self even the body, whose form it hath been, leading it forth into a better condition and an heavenly nature, even untill it be glorified into Immortality.

He puts the seal of Christian Humanism upon the claim in *Asclepius* when he adds that the condition he speaks of 'is the peculiar gift of man, to whom this dignity of the divine image is proper, and common to no other creature'.[195] Henry Vaughan was a hermetic writer who expressly and vehemently took issue with the Platonists. He adduces the manifold authority of Scripture to bear out his conviction that the body itself will ultimately be raised in glory. In that blissful reawakening sense will no longer be a distinct category from intelligence. Body and spirit will be finally reconciled, to make one indivisible whole.[196]

The idea that magic is a mode of love remained intellectually valid for even less time than the cult of the hieroglyph. Ficino put it forward in the preamble of his translation of the *Pimander* in 1471; and it was fatally undercut by Casaubon's demonstration in 1614 that the Hermetic Writings are not the wisdom of the *prisci teologi*. Frances Yates points out that by the 1620s Mersenne was already taking a rationalistic view of supernatural Christianity in the manner of the eighteenth-century divines.[197] In England the issue between a sacramental and a rational understanding of the natural creation was fought out between the devotees of spiritual magic and the pioneers of empirical physics; and it had still not resolved itself by the middle of the seventeenth century, as we see not only by the alchemical activities of a Thomas Vaughan but in the hermetic interests of such leaders of the new science as Boyle and Newton.[198] The Little Gidding community and its sympathisers, George Herbert and Henry Vaughan among them, set store by the spiritual regimen of the Catholic Reformer Juan de Valdes (c. 1500–41). This system seeks to harness the celestial influences through the universal bond of love, so that they help the regenerate spirit draw even nearer that condition of pure love and pure understanding whose consummation is the union with Christ.[199] Its effect lingered on in Vaughan's poetry in the 1650s; but by then a sacramental explanation of the universe of matter had more than Cromwell's partisans against it.

A universe animated by love was the cause for which the brothers Vaughan fought their 'rearguard action ... against a crudely materialistic science and the beginnings of deistical theology'.[200] Their different means of advancing their state, lyric poetry and spiritual alchemy, had more in common than appears in the outcome. How far Milton felt himself embattled in the interest of the universal working of love we may tell by *Paradise Lost*.

x. *The bond of kind: Paradise Lost*

the attributes of the soul are ... as anger and fear, inseparable from the physical matter of the animals to which they belong, and not, like line and surface, separable in thought.

Aristotle, *De Anima* I, I, 403b, 16–19

Their love to God was unmoved, their union sincere, and there upon exceeding delightfull having power to inioy at full what they loved. They were in a peaceable avoydance of sinne, which tranquility kept out all externall annoyance ... Wherefore in Paradise both locall, and spirituall man made God his rule to live by, for it was not a Paradise locall, for the bodies good, and not spirituall for the spirits: nor was it a spirituall for the spirits good, and no locall one for the bodies: Noe, it was both for both.

St Augustine, *Of The City Of God* xiv, 10 and
xiv, 11, p. 512

Milton's vision of embodied beauty and intelligence emerges quite early on in *Paradise Lost*, and comes before us as historical fact:

> Two of farr nobler shape erect and tall,
> Godlike erect, with native Honour clad
> In naked Majestie seemd Lords of all.

iv, 288–90

This first entry of Adam and Eve is a critical moment in the poem, if not in European consciousness. But it is not at all dramatic, for Milton keeps it free of the excitements that surround it, and even of the jar of Satan's presence in the garden. At this calm centre his words work only to describe and define; and the language in which he fleshes his human paragons gives their humanity itself a metaphysical consequence, such as merits the attention of hell and heaven:

> And worthie seemd, for in thir looks Divine
> The image of thir glorious Maker shon,
> Truth, Wisdom, Sanctitude severe and pure,
> Severe, but in true filial freedom plac't;
> Whence true autoritie in men; though both
> Not equal, as thir sex not equal seemd;
> For contemplation hee and valour formd,
> For softness shee and sweet attractive grace,
> Hee for God onely, shee for God in him:
> His fair large Front and Eye sublime declar'd
> Absolute rule; and Hyacinthin Locks
> Round from his parted forelock manly hung
> Clustring, but not beneath his shoulders broad:
> Shee as a vail down to the slender waste
> Her unadorned gold'n tresses wore
> Dissheveld, but in wanton ringlets wav'd
> As the Vine curles her tendrils, which impli'd
> Subjection, but requir'd with gentle sway,
> And by her yeilded, by him best receivd,
> Yeilded with coy submission, modest pride,
> And sweet reluctant amorous delay.

iv, 291–311

There can be no doubt that Milton means this astonishing account for literal truth. The terms are weighed, precise, sublime. Here is an apotheosis of man such as even Mirandola scarcely conceived, but which Christ himself had confirmed by taking our nature in supreme testimony to the native worth and dignity of the human state. Milton shows us what we might be, mingling the terms of moral elevation, physical beauty, and divinity, as though the qualities they mark are inseparable from each other in a whole human character or are aspects of a single embodied grandeur. He attributes to our body and form an inherent beauty which is spiritually sublime in itself and needs no transcendence of the flesh to realise it at full, being most intense when we are most fully human:

> So passd they naked on, nor shunnd the sight
> Of God or Angel, for they thought no ill:
> So hand in hand they passd, the lovliest pair
> That ever since in loves imbraces met,
> *Adam* the goodliest man of men since borne
> His Sons, the fairest of her Daughters *Eve*.

iv, 319–24

To be fully human is not to be given over to sense. It is Satan who chooses to take their bliss for a merely sensual condition – 'Like this fair Paradise, your sense'; and in seeing them so he yet again precisely defines the true state for us by his own palpable perversion of it. Creatures of sense they are, but admirably so for sense is in its place. Their very language shows sense interpenetrated with intelligence, and ordered by a faculty beyond self. 'Sole partner and sole part of all these joyes'. By contrast with Satan's self-entangling rhetoric Adam's *traductio* expresses an act of comprehension, the movement of the mind from a limited to the more inclusive understanding. One control upon their senses is an understanding of the right order of their being, within the larger order of creation; and another regulating power is love.

The portrayal of Adam and Eve quite incomparably affirms the bond between man and woman:

> To whom thus *Eve* repli'd. O thou for whom
> And from whom I was formd flesh of thy flesh
> And without whom am to no end, my Guide
> And Head, what thou hast said is just and right.
> For wee to him indeed all praises owe,
> And daily thanks, I chiefly who enjoy

So farr the happier Lot, enjoying thee
Praeeminent by so much odds, while thou
Like consort to thy self canst no where find.

iv, 440–8

To define their respective natures so carefully is as much a way of showing us their mutual need of each other as of distinguishing between them. The terms link them as one nature, without however suggesting that Adam is not capable of standing alone again as he did before Eve was created, or proposing that their mutualness may ever be more than a reinforcement of their moral freedom:

I from the influence of thy looks receave
Access in every Vertue, in thy sight
More wise, more watchful, stronger, if need were
Of outward strength; while shame, thou looking on,
Shame to be overcome or over-reacht
Would utmost vigor raise, and rais'd unite.

ix, 309–14

The pull of the bond of kind is confirmed in Eve's beautiful account of their first meeting, when she runs away from Adam after falling in love with her own reflection in the pool:

As I bent down to look, just opposite,
A Shape within the watry gleam appeerd
Bending to look on me, I started back,
It started back, but pleasd I soon returnd,
Pleasd it returnd as soon with answering looks
Of sympathie and love; there I had fixt
Mine eyes till now, and pin'd with vain desire,
Had not a voice thus warnd me, What thou seest,
What there thou seest fair Creature is thy self,
With thee it came and goes: but follow me,
And I will bring thee where no shadow staies
Thy coming, and thy soft imbraces, hee
Whose image thou art, him thou shalt enjoy
Inseparablie thine, to him shalt beare
Multitudes like thy self, and thence be calld
Mother of human Race: what could I doe,
But follow strait, invisibly thus led?

iv, 460–76

Milton leaves it open to us to find here the first hint of a fatal female vanity but the incident turns upon Eve's natural response to human beauty, the immediate attraction of like to like. Her brave new world of a recognisable human image more immediately charms her with its beauty than does Adam, whose manly qualities win her only when he woos her with the pledge of their human oneness in the flesh:

> Till I espi'd thee, fair indeed and tall,
> Under a Platan, yet methought less faire,
> Less winning soft, less amiablie milde,
> Then that smooth watry image; back I turnd,
> Thou following cryd'st aloud, Return fair *Eve*
> Whom fli'st thou? whom thou fli'st, of him thou art,
> His flesh, his bone; to give thee being I lent
> Out of my side to thee, neerest my heart
> Substantial Life, to have thee by my side
> Henceforth an individual solace dear;
> Part of my Soul I seek thee, and thee claim
> My other half: with that thy gentle hand
> Seisd mine, I yeilded, and from that time see
> How beauty is excelld by manly grace
> And wisdom, which alone is truly fair.

iv, 477–91

The sustained beauty of the approach to their nuptials prepares a fulfilment which is pointedly not a climax:

> So promisd hee, and *Uriel* to his charge
> Returnd on that bright beam, whose point now raisd
> Bore him slope downward to the Sun now fall'n
> Beneath th'*Azores*; whether the prime Orb,
> Incredible how swift, had thither rowld
> Diurnal, or this less volubil Earth
> By shorter flight to th'East, had left him there
> Arraying with reflected Purple and Gold
> The Clouds that on his Western Throne attend:
> Now came still Eevning on, and Twilight gray
> Had in her sober Liverie all things clad;
> Silence accompanied, for Beast and Bird,
> They to thir grassie Couch, these to thir Nests
> Were slunk, all but the wakeful Nightingale;
> Shee all night long her amorous descant sung;
> Silence was pleas'd; now glowd the Firmament
> With living Saphirs: *Hesperus* that led
> The starrie Host, rode brightest, till the Moon
> Rising in clouded Majestie, at length
> Apparent Queen unvaild her peerless light,
> And ore the dark her Silver Mantle threw.

iv, 589–609

These magnificent descriptions are not just decorative backcloth. They work to show vast cosmic events attending upon human affairs, which are themselves continuous with the life of the entire creation. Milton's universe is intensely alive, as an organism whose rich beauty is the visible sign of its delight in its own interworking: 'now glowd the Firmament o24 With living Saphirs'. The right human state is naturally enacted in the cosmos also, where all created kinds are impelled to harmony by love. The nightingale's amorous descant pleases silence; Hesperus heads the starry host, as Gabriel the angels; the queen–moon unveils herself and throws her silver mantle over the darkness. Such high conceited personifications are far from mere embellishment, for the moon's graceful gesture of concern links the heavenly bodies with the watchful angels, as with human tenderness. We must take Milton's figure for a pointed reversal of effects in the fallen world. A mantle did not then serve to conceal shame or guilt, as Nature wished the snow to cloak the world at Christ's birth,[201] but folded in and set off its charge; for there was no dishonour to hide.

The affairs of Adam and Eve are closely inwoven with the life of a beneficent creation whose beauty lies in the natural performance of function, each part expressing its own nature in fit relation with the whole:

> To whom thus *Eve* with perfet beauty adornd.
> My Author and Disposer, what thou bidst
> Unargu'd I obey; so God ordains,
> God is thy Law, thou mine: to know no more
> Is Womans happiest knowledge and her praise.
> With thee conversing I forget all time,
> All seasons and thir change, all please alike.
> Sweet is the breath of morn, her rising sweet,
> With charm of earliest Birds; pleasant the Sun
> When first on this delightful Land he spreads
> His orient Beams, on herb, tree, fruit, and flour,
> Glistring with dew; fragrant the fertil earth
> After soft showers; and sweet the coming on
> Of grateful Eevning milde, then silent Night
> With this her solemn Bird and this fair Moon,
> And these the Gemms of Heav'n, her starrie train:
> But neither breath of Morn when she ascends
> With charm of earliest Birds, nor rising Sun
> On this delightful land, not herb, fruit, floure,
> Glistring with dew, nor fragrance after showers,
> Nor grateful Eevning milde, nor silent Night
> With this her solemn Bird, nor walk by Moon,
> Or glittering Starr-light without thee is sweet.

iv, 634–56

Their exchanges are not so much a model for fallen beings as the human aspect of the universal order, expressing a relationship between man and woman which holds only while Adam himself stands right towards God and the rest of the creation. Innocence is the state in which they are part of the animating joy of the universe they inhabit and their pleasure, as their beauty, is at full. There is no call here for the exhilaration of the cosmic dance. Milton places the true human pleasure of sex, as of any other innocent function, in the tranquil gratification of the mind through the senses. Adam and Eve walk quietly to their nuptial couch at due time after completing their fit offices, and themselves affirm their sense of having place in a creation whose elements work to perfect each other:

> These have thir course to finish, round the Earth,
> By morrow Eevning, and from Land to Land
> In order, though to Nations yet unborn,
> Ministring light prepar'd, they set and rise;
> Least total darkness should by Night regaine
> Her old possession, and extinguish life
> In Nature and all things, which these soft fires
> Not onely enlight'n, but with kindly heate
> Of various influence foment and warme,
> Temper or nourish, or in part shed down
> Thir stellar vertue on all kinds that grow
> On Earth, made hereby apter to receive
> Perfection from the suns more potent Ray.

iv, 661–73

Milton has them attest for themselves the universal beneficence which surrounds them, showing us that they understand the harmony of which they are part, and acknowledge the bond between the human world and the universe of spirits:

> These then, though unbeheld in deep of night,
> Shine not in vain: nor think, though men were none,
> That Heav'n would want spectators, God want praise;
> Millions of spiritual Creatures walk the Earth
> Unseen, both when we wake, and when we sleep:
> All these with ceasless praise his works behold
> Both day and night: how oft'n from the steep
> Of echoing Hill or Thicket have we heard
> Celestial voices to the midnight air,
> Sole, or responsive each to others note
> Singing thir great Creator: oft in bands
> While they keep watch, or nightly rounding walk,

With Heav'nly touch of instrumental sounds
In full harmonic number joind, thir songs
Divide the night, and lift our thoughts to Heaven.

iv, 674–88

The bond links them to vegetable nature also, as the beautiful flower-passage shows:

Thus talking hand in hand alone they passd
On to thir blissful Bower; it was a place
Chos'n by the sovran Planter, when he fram'd
All things to Mans delightful use; the roofe
Of thickest covert was inwoven shade
Laurel and Mirtle, and what higher grew
Of firm and fragrant leaf; on either side
Acanthus, and each odorous bushie shrub
Fenc'd up the verdant wall; each beauteous flour,
Iris all hues, Roses, and Gessamin
Reard high thir flourisht heads between, and wrought
Mosaic

iv, 689–700

As the firmament, so their nuptial bower itself is a living texture of beauty, wrought as it were voluntarily by the interworking growths with a natural wealth and decorum beyond artifice:

underfoot the Violet,
Crocus, and Hyacinth with rich inlay
Broiderd the ground, more colourd then with stone
Of costliest Emblem

iv, 400–3

In this setting the human couple move towards a completion of their day, seeking not sexual excitement but rest, of which the 'rites 024 Mysterious of connubial love' are a natural part. They approach their couch as a meal with grace before, or as a sacrament, at once winding up the day and preparing for the night with a due recognition that the fulfilment of their bliss is their 'mutual help- 024 And mutual love'. The seal will be their lovemaking, which they turn to so naturally that they do not even need to anticipate it.

Nor do they need to speak more words. Milton's withdrawal from them at this point is an act of reverent decorum, which also allows him to be magnificently explicit in his acclaim of sexual love:

121

nor turnd I weene
Adam from his fair Spouse, not *Eve* the Rites
mysterious of connubial Love refus'd:
Whatever Hypocrits austerely talk
Of puritie and place and innocence,
Defaming as impure what God declares
Pure, and commands to som, leaves free to all.
Our Maker bids increase, who bids abstain
But our Destroyer, foe to God and Man?

iv, 741–9

He marvellously transforms the old yearning for a lost Golden Age of love, in which no tyrant honour inhibited men's attempts to snatch a momentary ecstasy from the jaws of darkness:

Amiam, che non ha tregua
Con gli anni umana vita, e si dilegua.
    Amiam: che'l Sol si muore e poi rinasce;
A noi sua breve luce
S'asconde, e'l sonno eterna notte adduce.

Let us love, for human life has no truce with the years, and melts away. Let us love, for the sun dies and is then reborn; it hides its brief light from us, and sleep brings an eternal night.

Tasso, *Aminta* 1, 2,633–7

The end of this coupling is no brief or contrived excitement but fruit, a crown of constant delight:

Haile wedded Love, mysterious Law, true sourse
Of human ofspring, sole proprietie
In Paradise of all things common else.
By thee adulterous lust was driv'n from men
Among the bestial herds to raunge, by thee
Founded in Reason, Loyal, Just, and Pure,
Relations dear, and all the Charities
Of Father, Son, and Brother first were known.
Farr be it, that I should write thee sin or blame,
Or think thee unbefitting holiest place,
Perpetual Fountain of Domestic sweets,
Whose Bed is undefil'd and chast pronounc't,
Present, or past, as Saints and Patriarchs us'd.

iv, 750–62

Coming out so strongly against the reprovers of bodily pleasure Milton removes the ground of courtly love and transcendental love alike, contemptuously dismissing those who would deny sense, as well as those who put their whole bliss in sense, and those whom sense torments into implacable self-conflict. Love is not the self-rapt

ritual of lament in which poets have dressed their frustrated desires,
but the mutual bond of an Adam and Eve:

> Here Love his gold'n shafts imploies, here lights
> His constant Lamp, and waves his purple wings,
> Reigns here and revels; not in the bought smile
> Of Harlots, loveless, joyless, unindeard,
> Casual fruition, nor in Court Amours,
> Mixt Dance, or wanton Mask, or Midnight Ball,
> Or Serenate, which the starv'd Lover sings
> To his proud fair, best quitted with disdain.
>
> iv, 763–70

Constancy and revel together, this is the essence of right love. Here
Milton does speak outrightly of our experience in the fallen world,
where such truth is paradox because we habitually disjoin ends
which should be one. He implies that conjugal love is our means of
recovering at least some part of the created harmony which Adam
and Eve simply share. But they lie at one in a wholeness of bliss we
cannot recover, blessed by nature, lulled by nightingales, showered
with unfading roses, sanctified by the whole order of creation:

> Sleep on,
> Blest pair; and O yet happiest if ye seek
> No happier state, and know to know no more.
>
> iv, 773–5

Being their heirs, and no such innocent lovers, we can never forget
that they will fall. But those last few words present a fact as well as a
warning. Their bliss in each other's arms, as they themselves apprehend it, is the height of their human state.

How finely done then to turn from human tenderness to the quite
different brilliance of the epic action between Satan and the angels!
This is Milton working at the top of his imaginative powers, and
displaying his intellectual grasp in the way the events flow with
inevitable dramatic logic out of the sense of the whole narrative. The
passage richly opens a new prospect of man's place in the created
order, and of the creation's attendance upon him. Uriel's watch over
paradise, which dramatically offsets Satan's presence throughout
the book, leads on naturally to the deployment of the angelic squad-
rons in their particular office of guardianship. Occupying our minds
with the sense of forces coming together over vast distances of
cosmic space, Milton promises a confrontation which will fulfil a
moral idea. In the clash of adverse principles we may see what

Satan's presence in the garden contributes to the account of created harmony.

The syntax enacts for us the suddenness of that first amazing encounter of opposites – 'So started up in his own shape the Fiend.' Satan is at all points the foil to native love and beauty, the anti-principle of single self who brings out the essential oneness of creation for us by personifying division; and by a like providential paradox he is also the radical testimony to a God in whom love and freedom are the same thing. If the high heroic ritual of vaunt and counter-vaunt seems oddly attributed to an action of angels, yet it does enable Milton to contrast Satan tellingly with Gabriel's hosts at this point. His ugly aspect and gestures, set off against the great beauty of the angels, show the moral bankruptcy of the heroic attitude he strikes and of the traditional valuing of military puissance. He seems dignified and brave but is all self-display, revealing himself as a creature of arrogance and venom, shifty expediency, barren rhetoric. The gesture of defiance is quite empty:

> who more then thou
> Once fawnd, and cring'd, and servilly ador'd
> Heav'ns awful Monarch?

> 958–60

Waldock was fatally half-right.[202] Satan does not fall; he is exposed. In fact he gets fairly burlesqued here.

Yet in this universe of mutual regard, love leaves even its opposite free to be itself; and the confrontation also shows the limit of force, for the angels themselves cannot constrain Satan's will:

> The Fiend lookd up and knew
> His mounted scale aloft: nor more; but fled
> Murmuring, and with him fled the shades of night.

> 1013–15

Superb lines, certainly. The trouble is that an epic action of ethereal beings cannot really admit the possibility of effective physical force, and Milton has already got himself into the difficulty here which disturbs readers of Book vi:

> nor wanted in his graspe
> What seemd both Spear and Shield

> 989–90

Well – was it spear and shield, or was it not? Or why bother with such seeming in an encounter of angels! No doubt this 'seemed' is a signal that we are to take the military array as a metaphor for the terms of a metaphysical event, in the spirit of accommodation that is to govern our understanding of spiritual action in heroic poems – 'Thus measuring things in Heav'n by things on Earth'. But in *Paradise Lost* the embodiment of moral qualities is crucially not a metaphor; and the poet cannot have it literally for Adam and Eve and figuratively for all the rest. The dilemma he never escapes or resolves is how to show Adam and Eve in full dramatic action without suggesting that the supernatural beings who share the stage with them, including God, are engaged in the action on the same terms. Within a hundred lines of the human nuptials the striking contrast between Zephon and Satan wholly depends for its effect upon its physical realisation:

> So spake the Cherube, and his grave rebuke
> Severe in youthful beautie, added grace
> Invincible: abasht the Devil stood,
> And felt how awful goodness is, and saw
> Vertue in her shape how lovly, saw, and pin'd
> His loss; but chiefly to find here observd
> His lustre visibly impar'd; yet seemd
> Undaunted.

844–51

Evidently Milton means to show us that true beauty is no mere intellectual ideal, or an abstraction from particular beauties either, but the manifest expression, as a grace in the flesh, of a personal moral dignity. His difficulty is inherent in his moral understanding, which always looks to incarnate virtues. Here is the mind of the Christian Humanist, for whom Christ's taking flesh is the central fact of our existence if not of all existence.

Milton directly appraises the relationship between man's material being and his spiritual being in a curious passage of Raphael's dialogue with Adam in Book v. The lines have been much called in question, for it is not obvious why Raphael is so pointedly made to share a meal with Adam and Eve, let alone discourse on angelic digestion. Robert Ellrodt shows a welcome sense of the defining centrality of the episode when he assumes that in v, 469–505, Milton traces a neoplatonic continuity of development from flesh to spirit, whereas metaphysical poetry assumes a paradoxical conjunction of elements which are in themselves wholly and sharply distinct:[203]

To whom the winged Hierarch repli'd.
O *Adam*, one Almightie is, from whom
All things proceed, and up to him return,
If not deprav'd from good, created all
Such to perfection, one first matter all,
Indu'd with various forms, various degrees
Of substance, and in things that live, of life;
But more refin'd, more spiritous, and pure,
As neerer to him plac't or neerer tending
Each in thir several active Sphears assignd,
Till body up to spirit work, in bounds
Proportiond to each kind. So from the root
Springs lighter the green stalk, from thence the leaves
More aerie, last the bright consummat floure
Spirits odorous breathes; flours and thir fruit
Mans nourishment, by gradual scale sublim'd
To vital spirits aspire, to animal,
To intellectual, give both life and sense,
Fansie and understanding, whence the Soule
Reason receives, and reason is her being,
Discursive, or Intuitive; discourse
Is oftest yours, the latter most is ours,
Differing but in degree, of kind the same.
Wonder not then, what God for you saw good
If I refuse not, but convert, as you,
To proper substance; time may come when men
With Angels may participate, and find
No inconvenient Diet, nor too light Fare:
And from these corporal nutriments perhaps
Your bodies may at last turn all to spirit,
Improv'd by tract of time, and wingd ascend
Ethereal, as wee, or may at choice
Here or in Heav'nly Paradises dwell;
If ye be found obedient, and retain
Unalterably firm his love entire
Whose progenie you are. Mean while enjoy
Your fill what happiness this happie state
Can comprehend, incapable of more.

v, 468–505

This is scarcely a dispraising of flesh or sense, much less contempt of it. Raphael seems to be positing a graded hierarchy of qualities, from matter to spirit, up which creatures may ascend without interruption in just such an unbroken continuity of progress as Donne envisages for the natures of the virtuous dead (but only for them) in his funeral poems:

> So is her flesh refined by death's cold hand.
> As men of China, after an age's stay
>   Do take up porcelain, where they buried clay;
> So at this grave, her limbeck, which refines
>   The diamonds, rubies, saphires, pearls, and mines,
> Of which this flesh was, her soul shall inspire
>   Flesh of such stuff, as God, when his last fire
> Annuls this world, to recompense it, shall,
>   Make and name then, th' elixir of this all.
>
> *Elegy on the Lady Markham*, lines 20–8

Raphael is saying that created beings differ from each other by contingent qualities rather than in essence, for all things are created of 'one first matter', however they may be 'Indu'd with various forms, various degrees/Of substance, and in things that live, of life'. Things thus inessentially differentiated in their creation are 'more refin'd, more spiritous, and pure' the nearer they are placed to God, and the more they tend towards his nature. Yet the hierarchy of being is not static, for each nature is assigned to 'several active Sphears', and matter itself may work its way up to spirit 'in bounds/ Proportiond to each kind'. We understand that each nature comprehends in itself a range of qualities, in a due proportion of matter to spirit according to its created kind.

The lines about the plant undoubtedly describe a continuous process:

> So from the root
> Springs lighter the green stalk

Raphael follows out a movement that begins from the root in earth, and ascends through the green stalk and the airier leaves, to fulfil itself in the 'bright consummat floure' which 'Spirits odorous breathes'. The flower and its scent are made to exemplify a state of being which is sensible and spiritual at once, just because it is sustained by a vitality that works without break from sense to spirit.

The account of this vital process is curiously carried over to the distinction between man's reason and angelic intuition. Milton strains syntax here to frame a parallel which signifies that discursive reason and intuitive reason differ just as matter and spirit differ, in degree but not in kind:

> flours and thir fruit
> Mans nourishment, by gradual scale sublim'd
> To vital spirits aspire, to animal,
> To intellectual, give both life and sense,

127

> Fansie and understanding, whence the Soule
> Reason receives, and reason is her being,
> Discursive, or Intuitive; discourse
> Is oftest yours, the latter most is ours,
> Differing but in degree, of kind the same.

The sense is elusive because syntax and some of the terms seem indomitably ambiguous. In this context, how are we to take these 'vital spirits'? Are they constituents of our chemical constitution? Or are they the life of our spiritual being?

The lines attempt something bold, to prescribe for an intermingling of sense and spirit in the constitution of men and of angels alike; and Milton's difficulty is that he wants to make the same process define both human nature and the angelic state of being. Indeed, if he had not particularly wished to show how both states of being do share one nature he need not have raised this question at all by having Raphael eat material food and digest it, and by making Adam so pointedly invite an explanation. Far from dropping into inadvertent gaucherie he seems to be settling a question which the poem has powerfully put at issue.

Raphael's description of the life of the flower shows an intermingling of sense and spirit in the processes that sustain our being. Flowers, the most spiritual part of the organism, warrant the fruit which nourishes men; and fruit may itself be sublimed to vital spirit by a gradual progression. So fruit gives life and sense to both animal and intellectual elements of our nature at once, nourishing fancy and understanding from which the soul receives reason. In so tellingly offering Adam an example from organic life Raphael shows him how the same organism, having the powers of both material and spiritual nature within it, may nourish together the sensible and the spiritual constituents of man's being by way of sustaining their vital spirits; and the vital spirits themselves thus have the power to work a physical and a spiritual end at once, because there is no essential difference between the proper life of sense and the life of spirit. The fact that in human nature the vital spirits sustain a life of sense as well as a life of spirit need not cut men off from pure spiritual being; on the contrary, right human nature does not run counter to angelic nature, for the discursive logic by which we arrive at knowledge, and the direct intuition which serves the angels, are simply different modes of reason whose end is the same truth.

Men differ from angels in that God 'saw good' for them their own special state and station, this particular means of nourishing their vital spirits. It is because Raphael differs from Adam in order and degree, rather than kind, that he finds no difficulty in dropping into the mode of men, and accepting food which he can 'convert, as you,/To proper substance'. Moreover, since the same provident process serves him and his human hosts he quite plausibly supposes that a time may come when men will be able to share in the life of angels 'and find/No inconvenient Diet, nor too light Fare'. Men's bodies may then simply wean themselves from their corporal nutriments and

> at last turn all to spirit,
> Improv'd by tract of time, and wingd ascend
> Ethereal, as wee, or may at choice
> Here or in Heav'nly Paradises dwell

Raphael beautifully shows them the door they will not take. He opens the prospect of some future state of refinement in which men might wholly assume the nature of angels and become ethereal, or simply add the angelic nature to their own sensible nature and exist as both men and angels. They would then freely choose whether to remain in the earthly paradise as creatures of sense, or inhabit the heavenly paradise as angelic beings of spirit.

Milton offers these elevating alternatives as Raphael's speculations, which do no more than open up several distinct possibilities for unfallen human kind. But their import is more than hypothetical. Raphael is saying that matter itself is not essentially base and corrupted but was created continuous with spirit, to which it is inferior only in its distance from God and God's own essence. Man is a mixed being, in whom material and spiritual elements intermingle to his good if they are kept in proper order. He has something of animal nature and something of spiritual nature, both elements being sustained at the same sources; so that angels can share man's nature, and in a limited way, through their reason, men may even have part in angelic nature. Angels differ from men in that having no material being they do not need sustaining in animal life as men do, and they understand by immediate intuition rather than by discursive reasoning. Yet even these differences are not absolute while men sustain their animal being by the most spiritual part of organic nature, through the agency of their vital spirits.

A time may come when obedience, and the unalterably firm retention of God's entire love, will win men a spiritual degree still

nearer God. But Raphael is careful to attest that men were not
created in that state, and do not need it for their bliss:

> Mean while enjoy
> Your fill what happiness this happie state
> Can comprehend, incapable of more.

The double sense of 'fill' allows the human pair the full satisfaction
of their present being, animal and intellectual together. For them it
would not be happiness to aspire now beyond the state in which God
created them. Their present being requires the full satisfaction of the
nature they have, in which matter is intermingled with spirit and
understanding interpenetrates sense.

If we wish to call this thinking platonic then we must at least
distinguish Milton from Dante and the Florentine neoplatonists in
the status he gives to animal being and sense in the first created
condition. Milton precisely refuses to separate sense from spirit in
his delineation of innocence. He does not even share Donne's
assumption of a human nature which comprehends within itself two
distinct and separate elements, one given to time and the other
standing altogether beyond time. When he has Raphael join in the
human meal and then discuss with Adam the nature of men and of
angels Milton shows us a natural sacrament, a sharing in the fruits of
creation such as gives to our daily needs and functions a kind of
pristine holiness which we have since quite desecrated. From this
innocent intercourse of sense and spirit follows the need to define
the relation of human nature to pure spiritual being, and to show
how even animal nature had spirituality then because sense and spirit
were not distinct elements. Milton here makes explicit the central
assumption of his portrayal of created nature in *Paradise Lost*, which
is that our separation of the objects of sense from the objects of
intelligence is precisely a consequence of the Fall.

Pure spirit has taken man's nature and put on our body of sense;
Christ entered the world of history which the Fall of Man had
brought about. *Paradise Lost* is ordered by time, as the *Divina
Commedia* is not, because Milton's concern is the contrary working
in human affairs of these two events. We measure our moral distance
from Adam and Eve by a historical degeneration, which only
Christ's sacrifice can help us arrest or reverse. Milton, like Donne in
his *Anniversaries*, invites us to recognise that the determining disorder is our lapse of understanding.

Adam and Eve define themselves for us as creatures whose good, as their freedom, consists in embodied moral intelligence. Comprehending the right relation of things, they know what befits their own nature and are free of the limitations which ignorance would impose upon their choice. In this poem wise reason lies in understanding rather than argument, Raphael's mode not Satan's; and as it happens, argument itself, whether devilish or human, commonly turns out to be special pleading or wantonly specious. Understanding makes Adam a moral agent. Raphael's conversation with him (Books v–viii) attests the reach of man's mind, as well as God's loving concern and the right commerce between the orders of being. An intellectual texture which is so closely woven itself gives understanding a special prominence and interest. Meeting Eve's arguments for their disastrous separation with a true appraisal of their circumstances, Adam forcibly lets us see that he will be well aware of what he is doing when he falls, and what particular distortion of human nature the Fall entails:

> for thou knowst
> What hath bin warnd us, what malicious Foe
> Envying our happiness, and of his own
> Despairing, seeks to work us woe and shame
> By sly assault; and somwhere nigh at hand
> Watches, no doubt, with greedy hope to find
> His wish and best advantage, us asunder,
> Hopeless to circumvent us joind, where each
> To other speedie aide might lend at need;
> Whether his first design be to withdraw
> Our fealtie from God, or to disturb
> Conjugal Love, then which perhaps no bliss
> Enjoyd by us excites his envie more
>
> ix, 252–64

It is Adam, just before the Fall, who brings out the humaneness of human love and shows how that distinction of our being depends upon reason:

> for smiles from Reason flow,
> To brute deni'd, and are of Love the food,
> Love not the lowest end of human life.
> For not to irksome toile, but to delight
> He made us, and delight to Reason joind.
>
> ix, 239–43

Milton puts the case again in his own voice when Adam and Eve fall
to passionate quarrelling, after their fall:

> For Understanding rul'd not, and the Will
> Heard not her lore, both in subjection now
> To sensual Appetite, who from beneath
> Usurping over sovran Reason claimd
> Superior sway

ix, 1127–31

It is at the fatal point of their parting that Milton has Adam define
our moral standing for us, and regulate all the intercourse of human
lovers:

> within himself
> The danger lies, yet lies within his power:
> Against his will he can receave no harme.
> But God left free the Will, for what obeyes
> Reason, is free, and Reason he made right,
> But bid her well beware, and still erect,
> Least by some faire appeering good surpris'd
> She dictate false, and missinform the Will
> To do what God expresly hath forbid.
> Not then mistrust, but tender love enjoines,
> That I should mind thee oft, and mind thou mee.

ix, 348–58

While they are guided by reason Adam and Eve need no self-
control to keep sense from dominating their will, and cannot
succumb to anything so self-regarding as passion. The trouble is that
our reason itself may be corrupted and lose the name of reason,
though never without blame to the lapse of intelligence:

> O much deceav'd, much failing, hapless Eve,
> Of thy presum'd return!

The characteristic Miltonic sleight of syntax offers us the general
statement, immediately calls it back to the particular instance, and
yet allows both senses to stand. Eve plainly is much failing as well as
much deceived, for Satan even tells her, with fearful *double entendre*,
who he is:

> ye shall not Die:
> How should ye? by the Fruit? it gives you Life
> To Knowledge: By the Threatner? look on mee

It is a measure of Milton's Humanism that he makes so great a moral
lapse the consequence of an intellectual outsmarting.

Little in the Fall or in fallen behaviour need surprise us, if only because the terms of human corruption have already been well established in Satan's self-disclosure, and in the account of innocence itself. Moreover, what Milton now turns to show us with excruciating truth to life is just ourselves and our world. Satan's persuasions of Eve corrupt both reason and language in artful rhetoric, politic special pleadings aimed to insinuate the demonic view of creation. Eve's arguments are of little account once she has accepted the subtly offered ethic of emulation, and easily get diverted into frivolous questionings of God's providential ordinance; here, as later, we see how quickly reasonings without reason become no more than a specious gloss upon the will to dominate. Reason and wisdom dwindle to knowledge, and knowledge is corrupted to power, which she aspires to because it promises a godlike supremacy; 'ye shall be as Gods' proposes the ultimate blasphemy for beings whose true excellence is to be wholly themselves.

Once Eve's reason is corrupted she becomes a creature of sense; and her senses are soon debased into the grossest appetites. Milton shows her how her will is dominated by the sound of Satan's words and the sight, smell, touch, taste of the fruit; so that we see her subjecting reason to pitiful exercises of self-gratification. Her unrestrained indulgence in sense when she does get hold of the fruit shocks little less than the neglect of God's injunction, offending so deeply against the dignity of human nature. Yet even here she is never just a creature of sense:

> for *Eve*
> Intent now wholly on her taste, naught else
> Regarded, such delight till then, as seemd,
> In Fruit she never tasted, whether true
> Or fansied so, through expectation high
> Of knowledg, nor was God-head from her thought.
> Greedily she ingorg'd without restraint,
> And knew not eating Death

ix, 785–92

Greed and hubris work together, sensual and intellectual appetite intertwine. This then is no more an indictment of sense as such than of intellect; it simply portrays what happens when both faculties lose the restraint of reason, as Milton has defined it. In the same way the lustful behaviour of Adam and Eve once Adam too has eaten the fruit

133

> hee on *Eve*
> Began to cast lascivious Eyes, shee him
> As wantonly repaid

marks a degeneration of sense into appetite and a debasement of sexual love; and Eve's idolatry before the fatal tree perverts the true reverence for godhead, which had expressed itself so fitly before their nuptials in Book iv.

Milton presents Adam's fall as a tragedy of good perverted to harm, love undone by itself even though it never ceases to be love of a kind. Eve returns to Adam speaking of her new superiority in knowledge which has now become the end of all for her, and thinking of him as a rival who might be made a dependant. Jealousy enters, too, with the thought that if Adam does not share the fruit with her then he may survive her to marry again, her genuine love for him now turning to possessiveness, and even bringing her to contemplate the destruction of its object. Now for the first time we hear of the agony of love, such as she feels in their short separation; and we understand that the pain lovers suffer is self-regarding, being born of possessive envy which gets worse the more fierce the love.

Eve lies to Adam about her reasons for taking the fruit – 'which for thee/Chiefly I sought' – not only to excuse herself but because she now speciously believes that she meant to make them equal, so that they would love each other better. Once the idea of equality has come in she uses their love itself in a kind of calculus of sense and pleasure:

> op'ner mine Eyes,
> Dimm erst, dilated spirits, ampler Heart,
> And growing up to Godhead; which for thee
> Chiefly I sought, without thee can despise.
> For bliss, as thou has part, to mee is bliss,
> Tedious, unshar'd with thee, and odious soon.
> Thou therfore also taste, that equal Lot
> May joine us, equal Joy, as equal Love;
> Least thou not tasting, different degree
> Disjoine us, and I then too late renounce
> Deitie for thee, when Fate will not permit.

ix, 875–85

The beautiful conceit of the dropped and withering flower-garland, which Adam had wreathed in love, signals the way things formerly admirable will now begin to run disastrously awry. Its pathos does not blur the intimation of the coming fall and its effects;

and we see that the emblem of the loving oneness of created things ironically becomes the first sign of the fatal breach between man and nature. Adam's resolve comes at once, with pathetic irony:

> no no, I feel
> The Link of Nature draw me: Flesh of Flesh,
> Bone of my Bone thou art, and from thy State
> Mine never shall be parted, bliss or woe.

ix, 913–16

It is a brave human insight to make the moment of downfall so admirable. This is no pitiable misadventure of a couple of guilty victims, a Paolo and Francesca, but a deliberate resolve to put fellow-feeling first which has its own nobility as far as it goes. As Milton conceives it the tragedy is that our noblest human impulses now undo us. Adam falls because he cannot bring himself to deny his sense of oneness with Eve, or sever the bond of kind. *Amor nil posset amori denegare* runs the twenty-sixth rule of love in Capellanus's treatise, which Adam's words now ironically confirm:

> So forcible within my heart I feel
> The Bond of Nature draw me to my owne,
> My own in thee, for what thou art is mine;
> Our State cannot be severd, we are one,
> One Flesh; to loose thee were to loose my self.

ix, 955–9

Moving as this loyalty to his own kind is, it nonetheless entails a limitation of true love which leads Adam into imaginings of exaltation and superiority even before he has eaten the fruit:

> hee yet lives,
> Lives as thou saide, and gaines to live as Man
> Higher degree of Life, inducement strong
> To us, as likely tasting to attaine
> Proportional ascent, which cannot be
> But to be Gods, or Angels Demi-Gods.

ix, 932–7

Milton does not spare him the irony of the ambiguous appeal to nature, having him take the natural bond in so limited a way when he is just about to break the bond with God. But the lines show the dilemma Adam faces because of Eve's fall, which has dissevered the two objects of his love. Our love of kind and our love of God, once the same and both supremely good, are now at odds and demand a choice. Putting the lesser good first Adam must err; yet he chooses compassionately, and in memorable words:

> How can I live without thee, how forgoe
> Thy sweet Converse and Love so dearly joind,
> To live again in these wilde Woods forlorn?
> Should God create another *Eve*, and I
> Another Rib afford, yet loss of thee
> Would never from my heart

ix, 908–13

The pathetic irony of their dialogue continually mocks their heroic resolve nonetheless, especially Eve's braveries, since she is the one who has already fallen. Adam's 'glorious trial of exceeding Love,/Illustrious evidence, example high!' is pitifully different from Christ's trial of love, which Eve's hyperbole must put in our minds. The irony is the measure of their falling short in love. They sacrifice the human race for the satisfaction of their immediate love of each other, the greater good for the limited self-consolation; whereas absolute love, wholly regardless of self, will sacrifice itself to save human kind. Yet Eve's weeping ecstasies over Adam's decision do repeatedly mingle something fine with her plaintive self-regard, showing us that she still recognises love though she turns it to lovers' lies and vanity. We may be sure that she would not really die herself rather than cause hurt to Adam; and it is patent enough that the proof of his ennoblement by love, which prompts her tender tears of joy, is just his willingness to share her fate. Much worse is that when Adam does eat they turn at once to coarse jocularities and carnal pleasure, soon followed by mutual recriminations, guilty passion succeeding passion. But Milton's insight is that they remain redeemable partly because they never lose the sense of involvement with each other, or turn love back wholly upon self as Satan does. Their sadly perverted attachment is still love.

For the moment though love is debased to appetite, sport, mere appeasement of sense, as Adam's changed language shows:

> For never did thy Beautie since the day
> I saw thee first and wedded thee, adornd
> With all perfections, so enflame my sense
> With ardor to enjoy thee, fairer now
> Then ever, bountie of this vertuous Tree.

ix, 1029–33

Their lovemaking, no longer a natural expression of love in fit place and time, becomes its own end and peremptorily impels them to gratify sense, as Satan had represented it all along. We see the pattern of fallen sexuality when urgent desire extinguishes itself on the instant, and turns to enervate degeneracy and aversion:

> So rose the *Danite* strong
> *Herculean Samson* from the Harlot-lap
> Of *Philistean Dalilah*, and wak'd
> Shorn of his strength, They destitute and bare
> Of all thir vertue

ix, 1059–63

What follows their expense of spirit is worse than shame:

> silent, and in face
> Confounded long they sate, as strook'n mute,
> Till *Adam*, though not less then *Eve* abasht,
> At length gave utterance to these words constraind.
>   O *Eve*, in evil hour thou didst give eare
> To that false Worm, of whomsoever taught
> To counterfet Mans voice, true in our Fall,
> False in our promisd Rising; since our Eyes
> Op'nd we find indeed, and find we know
> Both Good and Evil, Good lost, and Evil got,
> Bad Fruit of Knowledge, if this be to know,
> Which leaves us naked thus, of Honour void,
> Of Innocence, of Faith, of Puritie,
> Our wonted Ornaments now soild and staind,
> And in our Faces evident the signes
> Of foul concupiscence; whence evil store

ix, 1063–78

The disfigurement of the human face divine induces self-disgust, and then repression. Milton makes prudery the child of guilt, and allows it no place in a right attitude to sexual love. In fact the very idea of thwarting one's senses is an unnatural outcome of concupiscent desire.

Their quarrel over whose fault it all was has its diverting side, though it may disturb us to see ourselves thus sharply hit off. Commentators who find them interestingly human only in their bickering do small justice to what Milton is showing us of love by its degeneration. The sated lovers project onto each other the offence they give themselves. 'More and more perceiving his fall'n condition' Adam laments his own lapse, and then curses Eve as Samson curses Dalila, though with much less cause:

> Out of my sight thou Serpent, that name best
> Befits thee with him leagu'd, thy self as false
> And hateful

x, 867–9

He blames her entirely for the way love will run awry in the world – 'Through formal snares' he says at this point; and he makes a grim little muster of marital prospects thereafter, when a man may not find a fit mate at all but be compelled to put up with what he gets by misfortune or mistake, or the woman he wants will perversely reject him for a far worse man, or her parents will prevent her from marrying him, or he will meet the right woman too late, when she is already bound 'to a fell adversary, his hate or shame'. The power of Milton's *argumentum ad misericordium* is that he always appeals to our condition. Adam's prophetic picture of a sexual passion which has thus become an infinite calamity to human life, and a confounding of household peace, stands alongside the former picture of right love inviting our assent, and compelling our acknowledgment of a grievous transposing of good to harm.

Eve weeps, Adam pities her and relents, both of them showing themselves touchingly human still in their capacity to regret their lapse and share each other's suffering for it. It is their still greater need of each other's support that Adam now expresses:

> let us no more contend, nor blame
> Each other, blam'd enough elsewhere, but strive
> In offices of Love, how we may light'n
> Each others burden in our share of woe

X, 958–61

Distinctive human qualities persist, sympathetic love, dignity, and a glimmer of wisdom. There is concern for an end beyond herself even in Eve's desperate suggestion that they should thwart Satan's purpose of ruining mankind through them by refusing to beget, or by killing themselves. Though that would be to fall from sin to sin, and abolish mankind, she speaks with dignified solicitude:

> But if thou judge it hard and difficult,
> Conversing, looking, loving, to abstain
> From Loves due Rites, Nuptial embraces sweet,
> And with desire to languish without hope,
> Before the present object languishing
> With like desire, which would be miserie
> And torment less then none of what we dread,
> Then both our selves and Seed at once to free
> From what we fear for both, let us make short,
> Let us seek Death

X, 992–1001

Adam is able to see the error of her argument even while he still knows nothing of an atonement, and points it out in a passage of reasoned judgment. Yet he justly acknowledges something 'sublime/And excellent' in her words, for the lines Milton gives her are surely fine in their sympathetic understanding of sexual love, a great gain in fellow-feeling upon their self-indulgence just after their lapse. We see a right order reasserting itself in their minds, or as much of a right order as their diminished humanity may recover. It is conspicuous in all these passages of lapsed and corrupted love that Milton shows the pair redeemable just in as far as they retain the capacity for tender concern, regret, and humane understanding of the justice they have brought upon themselves. In this poem, redemptive love itself only perfects the human quality of love.

History is the distance between innocence and us, an interval we call time which Christ's love may redeem. The vision of history which Michael discloses to Adam from the top of the high hill is a bleak one because it shows the distempered state prevailing, and the world running irrecoverably worse awry as time goes on. Disease and death follow debauchery as people put their own sensual pleasure before a 'nobler end/Holy and pure', and 'Unmindful of their Maker', also neglect the godlike dignity they might bear:

> Immediately a place
> Before his eyes appeard, sad, noisom, dark,
> A Lazar-house it seemd, wherein were laid
> Numbers of all diseas'd, all maladies
> Of gastly Spasm, or racking torture, qualmes
> Of heart-sick Agonie, all feavorous kinds,
> Convulsions, Epilepsies, fierce Catarrhs,
> Intestin Stone and Ulcer, Colic pangs . . .
> Dropsies, and Asthma's, and Joint-racking Rheums.
> Dire was the tossing, deep the groans, despair
> Tended the sick busiest from Couch to Couch;
> And over them triumphant Death his Dart
> Shook, but delaid to strike, though oft invok't
> With vows, as thir chief good, and final hope.
> Sight so deform what heart of Rock could long
> Drie-ey'd behold? *Adam* could not, but wept,
> Though not of Woman born; compassion quell'd
> His best of Man, and gave him up to tears
> A space, till firmer thoughts restraind excess,
> And scarce recovering words, his plaint renew.

xi, 477–84, 488–99

The dreadful emblems of the lazar house stand against that first account of Adam and Eve in Book iv as the measure of a self-imposed degradation, a loss of the very sense of human worth, which is no less apparent in the images of violence and debauchery that follow:

> Thir Makers Image, answerd *Michael*, then
> Forsook them, when themselves they villifi'd
> To serve ungovernd appetite, and took
> His Image whom they serv'd, a brutish vice,
> Inductive mainly to the sin of *Eve*.

xi, 515–19

Such a world of willed depravity is beyond amendment. The man who would recover paradise must abandon that fair of vanities, to cultivate loving obedience and the private virtues in solitary retreat:

> onely add
> Deeds to thy knowledge answerable, add Faith,
> Add Vertue, Patience, Temperance, add Love,
> By name to come calld Charitie, the soul
> Of all the rest: then wilt thou not be loath
> To leave this Paradise, but shalt possess
> A paradise within thee, happier farr.

xii, 581–7

We have no vision of re-emparadising embraces to reassure us. Yet the beings who leave the Garden are not the depraved hopeless creatures Masaccio so powerfully depicts in the *Expulsion* of the Capella Brancacci. They go with human responsibility for themselves, guided by Providence, and mutually supporting each other's frailties:

> They hand in hand with wandring steps and slow,
> Through *Eden* took thir solitarie way.

Milton leaves us in the end with the dignity of the human bond, which consoles and supports even if it cannot redeem.

xi. *From Dante to Milton*

For it is the most natural function in all living things, if perfect and not defective or spontaneously generated, to reproduce their species; animal producing animal and plant plant, in order that they may, so far as they can, share in the eternal and the divine. For it is that which all things yearn after, and that is the final cause of all their natural activity.

Aristotle, *De Anima* III, 415a–b

We should not therfore iniure our creator in imputing our vices to our flesh: the flesh is good, but to leave the creator and live according to this created good, is the mischiefe: whether a man do choose to live according to the body or the soule or both, which make full man, who therfore may be called by either of them. For he that makes the soules nature, the greatest good, and the bodies the greatest evill, doth both carnally affect the soule, and carnally avoid the flesh: conceiving of both as humaine vanity, not as divine verity teacheth.

St Augustine, *Of The City of God* xiv, 5, p. 502

Paradise Lost persuades us that we have our right state when we fulfil our own nature, in the body and in our fit place in the created order. We would recover the Fall not by rising above human kind, or denying some part of our nature, but by regaining our full humanity. Recovery calls for a renewal of self rather than a self-transcendence, not so much a denial of our nature as a restoring of lost wisdom, or retreat to a state nearer Eden.

Milton accords the human body its own dignity, even its semblance of divinity, and allows sense itself its proper good in its place. He does not separate the good of appetite and the good of intellect, much less oppose sense to mind. The mind may gain its good through the senses, indeed mind moderates sense in the language which evokes man's created condition. What matters is that reason should order appetite and will, and not simply deny itself by becoming their creature. Moral disorder follows an abdication of right reason, for perverse reasoning corrupts will in self-love, and overcharges sense by allowing appetite more than its due.

What passes between Adam and Eve in their innocence has part in a universal exchange of love which is actively sexual in the natural creation, love replicating God's divine creativity and serving the economy of providence in the joy of seed and fruit. All creatures realise themselves in the work of providence according to the law of their kind, celebrating their creator in acts which reasonable beings can make articulate. Milton transforms the cosmic dance into a cosmic lovemaking, in witness that the universe is nothing else than a living organism of creatures who endlessly fulfil their own being in enjoying each other. Love holds in one harmonious order creatures who everywhere differentiate themselves in nature and kind, bringing complementary capacities into fit and fruitful union. Human love subsists by that mutualness-in-difference which Milton so particularly defines, the reciprocity of natures which makes us whole. We are most truly human when we involve ourselves in our kind; and our humanity perfects itself in reverent conjugal love, of which sexual acts are the natural expression.

Milton's conception of love commits him to a universe of dynamic activity, whereas Dante always looks to the still centre. In Dante's paradise all particular attachments are finally taken up into the one universal love, which moves and perfects all creation. The many return to the One, and satisfy their own natures wholly when they are at one with God in will and desire. *Paradise Lost* takes us back to the individual qualities of things, making a universal harmony of creatures who are truly themselves in the active relationships which distinguish them. Book iv has its intellectual integrity in the way the poetry works throughout to define the several elements of creation, and place them in a mutually provident order. At all points Milton substantiates the image of a created order which it is reasonable and self-fulfilling to observe, and our own undoing to flout. He may even seem to offer us a less accommodating universe than Dante, for in *Paradise Lost* the order of creation is already established and we define ourselves in relation to it, whereas *La Divina Commedia* shows us a creation of which some part is always moving to define its true relation to its creator. Yet for Dante the end of that process is repose, in the fixed contemplation which beatifies each nature to the extent of its capacity for love. Ultimately all that part of creation which is capable of regeneration will rise to its settled station, that in which each will is at one with God's will, in a harmony of love about the centre. In Milton's poem life perfects itself when things are wholly themselves, realising the right order of their own kind in a creation of harmonious diversity, which requires not contemplation but action to perfect it.

In the created order the innocence of Adam and Eve is wholly compatible with understanding and reason. Innocence is simply an absence of the will to self-aggrandisement, and a negation of the very idea of competitive selfhood. The 'knowledge of good and evil' takes in the implanting of that idea of self, and kindling of the will towards personal advantage, from which follow pride, vanity, emulation, the impulses that inhibit love.

Love is inseparable from freedom. The proof of love is that it should respect the will of its objects, even their will to flout the love they are offered and reject their own good. In creating things to be themselves God nonetheless leaves them free to choose whether they will be so or not, and endows them with the means of choosing, the faculty of reason. Human reason is free to the extent that we understand both ourselves and our fit place in the created order, for understanding removes the intellectual blinkers which would otherwise limit our liberty to will our own course. A defeat of informed reason is a wilful lapse, which may need love and grace beyond nature to redeem it.

In the *Divina Commedia* understanding follows grace; it is grace which shapes the poem and controls its movement, from the first spiritual promptings to the final ascent into loving comprehension. In *Paradise Lost* divine grace follows the lapse of human understanding. Grace is central to Milton's vision, as to Dante's; but Milton's poem is shaped by our need to bring home to our degenerate understanding the distance between our lapsed state and the created condition, how far things as they are fall short of things as they might be, and once were. The vision of created love answers the need to define a state which an understanding still capable of judgment must yearn to recover.

A conceit which gives such scope to free understanding in a creation ordered by love inevitably projects into drama the universal contradiction between the ordering principle and its opposite, the being who chooses to embody in himself the counter-principle of self-centred pride; and it sustains the ironic tension of our awareness that Adam and Eve will deny right love in action. Milton's dramatic interweaving of the elements of creation gives Satan peculiar prominence as the impulse to ruin, which insidiously entwines itself with our lives though it cannot usurp our will, and sharpens our sense of what love is by electing to enact its contrary. Christ stands against Satan, pure beneficent self-sacrifice counters self-serving destructive envy; and the human creatures stand between opposite possibilities, being freed by understanding to will their own course, as we stand also whose moral understanding the poem itself helps to free. Paolo and Francesca damn themselves by their wilful commitment to such a gratification of self; Eve fails by her assent to Satan's sophistries; heaven and hell themselves attend upon human choice.

The Fall diminished man and betrayed him to time. Both Dante's poem and Milton's contrast the fallen world of time with the timeless state, and seek to weigh man's history against the unchanging truth. In the *Divina Commedia* history is an inessential mode of eternal being. The poem makes absolute judgements upon historical events and their participants, not distinguishing between times and customs but placing people together by the likeness of their confirmed moral natures, as though they act at every moment in an eternal co-presence of all creation. Even those who die in innocence are differentiated from each other by one historical circumstance only, the world's state of grace at the time in which they lived.

Like Shakespeare's chronicle plays *Paradise Lost* is shaped by a sense of historical evolution, and follows out an organic logic of growth and decline. Events have their fruition, consequences declare themselves in time and disclose the true character of their origin. The poem compels us to take a historical perspective, in that its effect depends upon our continual willingness to measure the disparity between the conditions it describes and the present state of the world. The vision of the worsening course of history in Old Testament times, which Michael shows Adam from the high mount, only makes explicit the condition which the poem has been tacitly bringing home to us all along, our own remoteness from the state of innocence, and enmeshment in a process of time. *Paradise Lost* proposes not only that Adam's lapse initiated the movement of history but that temporal events are determined by their distance from the cataclysm, and exist as mere modes of the times in which they occur. Man's nature and circumstances evolve in time, though not towards a moment of perfect ripeness, or the betterment of the race. The poem invites us to confirm in ourselves a progressive degeneration from the right human state.

In a deteriorating creation, which runs ever faster and further awry, we may gain only relative knowledge of ourselves and the creation around us. We perceive a disintegrating universe with decaying faculties, and must measure the events of history by our own condition, as well as by the condition of the times in which they occur:

Now I recognise all too clearly that the unstable world grows ever worse as it grows older

Sannazaro, *Arcadia* Egloga vi, lines 110–11

It is far more difficult for men to act rightly and be truly heroic now than it was in the early state of the lapsed world. In Milton's day the yearning to recover lost spiritual wisdom, and regenerate decayed virtue, took men to primitive mysteries such as Egyptian hieroglyphics were supposed to enshrine, or to the occult truths which might still be read in the vital processes of innocence nature, or even to alchemical operations. Milton sought the harder way of heroic vision, in inevitable opposition to the times and to human nature as he found it. *Paradise Lost* articulates a conceit of sexual love by which love poets define themselves, to the extent of their understanding.

2

Against Mortality

And why all this longing for propagation? – because this is the one deathless and eternal element in our mortality. And since we have agreed that the lover longs for the good to be his own for ever, it follows that we are bound to long for immortality as well as for the good – which is to say that Love is a longing for immortality ... those whose procreancy is of the body turn to woman as the object of their love, and raise a family, in the blessed hope that by doing so they will keep their memory green 'through time and eternity'. But those whose procreancy is of the spirit rather than of the flesh ... conceive and bear the things of the spirit ...

And so, when his prescribed devotion to boyish beauties has carried our candidate so far that the universal beauty dawns upon his inward sight, he is almost within reach of the final revelation. And this is the way, the only way, he must approach, or be led towards, the sanctuary of Love. Starting from individual beauties, the quest for the universal beauty must find him ever mounting the heavenly ladder, stepping from rung to rung, that is, from one to two, and from two to every lovely body; from bodily beauty to the beauty of institutions; from institutions to learning, and from learning in general to the special lore that pertains to nothing but the beautiful itself; until at last he comes to know what beauty is.

Plato, *Symposium* 206E–207A, 208E–209A, 211B–C

> Since brass, nor stone, nor earth, nor boundless sea,
> But sad mortality o'ersways their power,
> How with this rage shall beautie hold a plea ...?

Shakespeare, Sonnet 65

i. From Petrarch to Shakespeare

Petrarch's *I Trionfi* marks the desolating recognition that men's most impassioned commitments in the world are subject to time and circumstance, which continually change. The evidence of a pattern of growth and decline in antique civilisations disturbed the early Humanists with its revelation that history is process, an evolution of values and customs in which we too are inescapably caught up. To understand what men do and think we must refer their dealings to the times in which they lived; and mere accident determines what remnants of their existence survive, and what is lost altogether.

In the flux of relative cravings which of our objectives may have absolute worth? To what final end serves mortal beauty, and the love it engenders in us? A widening prospect of times and manners intensified the urge to find some enduring order in men's natural lives.

The classic response of the Florentine Platonists is put to a severe test of experience in the poetry of Michelangelo. His struggle to reconcile sense and spirit by art strikingly sets off those rather more familiar attempts which we encounter in *The Faerie Queene*, and in Shakespeare's *Sonnets*, to hold a plea for beauty against the rage of time.

ii. *Outbraving time: I Trionfi*

The sequence of six poems which make up *I Trionfi* urgently alternates hope and despair, checking the poet's faith in the enduring power of love and beauty with the fear that all our human glories may be utterly lost in time. Whatever Petrarch knew of the cast of Plato's thought it matters to his conception of this sequence that even the latest of the poems precedes by a good half century the arrival in Florence of an authentic text of the *Symposium*. E. H. Wilkins conjectures that the six poems were composed in pairs over some twenty-five to thirty years, from the 1340s to the 1370s.[1] As we have them they register a cogent progress in the understanding of love, which is brought about through a succession of victories and defeats.

The pattern quite disconcertingly offsets triumph with reversal. The tyrant Love, by means of the beauty of 'a young woman ... purer by far than a white dove' (*Trionfo d'Amore* iii, line 90), gains power over the hapless poet who joins the throng of Love's noted victims, first as a participant in the triumph of Love in a garden of delights on Venus's island domain, then as an aging captive in Love's prison. Love now moves against Laura herself, cheered on by the poet; but her chastity repels the assault and chastens the tyrant, leaving her supreme among the small troop of divine beings who may celebrate this triumph – 'and the purest of them was the most beautiful' (*Trionfo della Pudicizia*, line 174). Yet even Laura cannot defeat Death, who now strikes her down and claims power over the conquerors of Love himself, those whose words and comportment have been like hers, 'truly not human but divine' (*Trionfo della Morte* i, line 22). Laura allows Death no more than a limited triumph over her body, even so; and she herself nullifies Death's tyranny by appearing to the poet the night after her death to make a quite arrestingly beautiful and moving profession of her enduring love for him in her transformed condition of real life. The poet recognises that her refusal to acknowledge her love while she lived has kept him chaste; and he dedicates himself to limiting Death's triumph even in the world by ensuring that the fame of Laura's virtue will endure here, as the fame of so many great lives has endured.

In the final pair of poems, however, the poet recognises that his hope is vain; for time itself must defeat fame at last, and with it all worldly endeavours. In terms of worldly life the triumph of time is final:

> Passan vostre grandezze e vostre pompe
> passan le signorie, passano i regni ...

Your grandeurs and pomps pass away, as do your empires and kingdoms. Time disrupts every mortal thing ... Greedy Time conquers and snatches away everything; what we call Fame is a second dying, which can no more be fended off than the first; so completely Time triumphs over reputations and the world itself.

Trionfo del Tempo lines 112–14 and 142–45

Yet the final and comprehensive conquest is still to come. In the end time itself is annulled in eternity, the heart finds in God a secure and enduring object of its love. The sixth triumph takes place in heaven, with the promise of a renewal of the world and of those truly worthy of renown, who will rise again 'in their most flourishing and vigorous years and have eternal fame with immortal beauty' (*Trionfo dell'Eternità* lines 133–4). Laura will precede all those who go to be made new, and may even reassume the beauty of her earthly body, since not only the world 'but heaven itself yearns to see her entire' (line 138); and the poet's own felicity will then be complete:

> ché, poi ch' avrà ripreso il suo bel velo,
> se fu beato chi la vide in terra,
> or che fia dunque a rivederla in cielo?

for when she has resumed her beautiful veil, if he was blessesd who saw her on earth, what blessedness may he have to see her again in heaven!

Trionfo dell'Eternità lines 142–4

However guardedly (and the commentators have been uneasily guarded) the lines surely envisage the final reuniting of her soul with her body.[2]

Petrarch's sequence distinguishes six clear stages of an advance from the miserable frailty and inevitable disillusionment of sexual love to eternal bliss. The poet's sensual passion for a woman's beauty is left far behind in the providential progression of defeat and triumph. It is put down by chastity and death, revived by the prospect of Laura's fame, and at last abolished by time which severs every worldly attachment. The moral for sexual lovers is that they will never achieve the fruition they seek, or find any lasting satisfaction in the world. Only love of God gives them a secure expectation of enduring beauty, lasting love and bliss.

Petrarch's love of Laura has in the end afforded him a hope of eternal fulfilment. Yet love rewards him solely because its object was already more truly divine than human, so that her heaven-born virtue rebuffed and quelled his ardours, and itself triumphed over death and time. What looks like a simple progress in the world assumes a different aspect when we view it in the order of eternity, and see that nothing matters but the shift from the love of what is mortal to pure spiritual love, such as Laura invited from the first. The world of contingency to which his senses betrayed the lover is defeated or overcome by the abiding virtue of chastity, exercised in the cause of a love which is of a different kind from his. Incarnate virtue itself cannot save its mortal part from death, or its fame from the whim of history, which itself is prey to time; yet its divine essence endures beyond time in eternity. Laura's refusal while she lived to acknowledge her love for the poet simply follows out the nature of true love. What partakes of eternal being may not commit itself to time.

iii. *Matter into grace:* Michelangelo the love poet

In his middle fifties, when he was still caught up in the 'tragedy of the tomb' of Julius II, and already revolving the Sistine Last Judgment, Michelangelo spent a little of his teeming intelligence in a stream of highly finished drawings for a few intimate friends. He made them, it seems, in whatever material came to hand, and offered trial models of them to their recipients with the characteristic diffidence which shows itself so unexpectedly in an artist of his aggressive originality:

Messer Tommaso, if you don't like this sketch tell Urbino so that I may have time to make another by tomorrow evening as I promised you, and if you do like it and want me to finish it send it back to me.[3]

Even if this particular *schizzo* did not make a finished version it was evidently a good deal more than 'one of those cartoons which you fling into the fire', such as Aretino solicited,[4] and had some meaning for the artist and his confidant which he was urgently concerned to realise between them. The subjects of the masterful 'presentation drawings' for Cavalieri in the royal collection at Windsor suggest that we have there a set of private emblems which mythologise the conflict between the several impulses of our nature: the bacchanal of children, the torment of Tityus, the rape of Ganymede, the fall of Phaeton.

These devices are as boldly conceived as they are executed. de Tolnay was surely right to see an allegory of love in the Phaeton and the two compositions in black chalk that show a man in the power of a huge bird.[5] The drawings show the dangers and the rewards of the attempt to glimpse the divine image through an earthly love. Phaeton's unmastered passions hurl him headlong from the sky; the vulture which tears grovelling Tityus in the organs of sense becomes the eagle which ravishes Ganymede to divine heights.[6] Michelangelo gave such a conceit words in a magnificent sonnet to Cavaliere:[7]

> Non è sempre di colpa aspra e mortale
> d'una immensa bellezza un fero ardore,
> se poi sì lascia liquefatto il core,
> che 'n breve il penetri un divino strale.
>
> Amore isveglia e desta e 'mpenna l'ale,
> né l'alto vol preschive al van furore;
> qual primo grado c'al suo creatore,
> di quel non sazia, l'alma ascende e sale.
>
> L'amor di quel ch'i' parlo in alto aspira;
> donna è dissimil troppo; e mal conviensi
> arder di quella al cor saggio e verile.
>
> L'un tira al cielo, e l'altro in terra tira;
> nell'alma l'un, l'altr'abita ne' sensi,
> e l'arco tira a cose basse e vile.

Fierce desire for an immense beauty is not always a harsh and mortal sin if it so melts the heart that a divine shaft may penetrate there more swiftly. Love wakes and rouses and feathers the wings, and does not prevent vain passion from passing into lofty flight; for the soul finds itself unsatisfied with that first stage, and ascends and soars to its creator.

The love which I speak of aspires to the heights; the love for a woman is all too unlike it, and to burn for that love ill becomes the wise and manly heart.

The one love draws us to heaven, and the other pulls us to earth; the one is in the soul, the other lives in the senses and bends the will to low and vile things.

No one would take such a poem for a petrarchan ritual, or doubt that it shows us a mind which is wrestling with matters of profound consequence, and living out its debate in art. Poetry was one of the four arts represented equally on the catafalque which was raised in homage by the Florentine Academy for those celebrated exequies in San Lorenzo in 1564.[8] The estimation of his contemporaries is worth our heed. They celebrated him as a poet 'because this excellent artist has left to the world the fruits not only of his divine hands, but also of his penetrating intellect, that is, compositions full of gravity and of intelligence. So that he no less merits his place among the poets than he has merited the chief place among artists.'[9] We might gloss the critical currency of the day by proposing that Michelangelo wrote poetry of a commitment, power, and intellectual trenchancy which is not much met with in mid-sixteenth-century Europe, and well merits attention in its own right as a living record of the encounter between sense and intelligence in love. Michelangelo the sculptor of tombs apotheosises the attempt to give substance to a metaphysic. What may we make of Michelangelo the poet?

Even the cold facts are cryptic. Michelangelo Buonarroti lived to the age of eighty-nine and died in 1564. He wrote verses casually from his mid twenties, roughing out versions on the backs of letters, the tails of bills, the corners of cartoons. And though he had no concern at all to retain or publish them, and indeed deliberately destroyed most of what he had written before the age of sixty or so, such was the fame his poetry acquired in its own right during his lifetime that quite exceptional care seems to have been taken to preserve the rude documents on which it was scribbled, and a substantial body of it has come down to us. We may have all the poems he wrote after middle age; though certainly little of the earlier writing remains. These extant pieces are very short. Most are sonnets or madrigals but there are a few *capitoli*, satiric or grotesque, and we have a set of fifty funerary epigrams written as an act of friendship to commemorate a Roman youth lately dead. There are also many fragments. Something around three hundred such poems and bits of poems survive in all.

The output was spasmodic and occasional, the activity private, in that the poems were written for personal satisfaction or for the diversion of the friends to whom they were sent. Only a handful of these poems – some half dozen – were published in Michelangelo's lifetime, and the first collected edition of 1623 was so intimately reworked by the editor, the poet's great-nephew, that it was not until 1863 that the real character of the verse re-emerged, just three hundred years after Michelangelo's death. In that year C. Guasti published a tercentenary edition with a text based, as no other had been, on the autograph collections at Florence and Rome. Michelangelo, in fact, is a classic case of the literary revenant. Nor is it now in question that his poems merit attention in their own right: 'In ogni caso', concludes a modern commentator, 'i maggiori lirici in volgar del Rinascimento.'[10] No small claim.

When Miss Emily Anderson's edition of Beethoven's letters came out a few years ago a reviewer remarked that Beethoven was perhaps the nearest approach to a superman the world has known. He might just as well have cited Michelangelo, and if he had gone as far as deification would scarcely have exceeded the considered praises of the old artist's contemporaries and pupils. Such hyperboles have point if they help us delineate a type, and 'superman' seems right for Michelangelo as Beethoven. There is a like heroic posture; one is struck by the same furious dynamism, the same apparently unbridgeable gulf between the petty – almost squalid – circumstances of the life, and the ideal reach of the art. The same uncompromising self-certainty harshens a personal vehemence, crabbedness, difficulty. These qualities bear on their work but the last is habitual to Michelangelo. In the form of an apparent unconcern with communication it often transmits itself in the man's utterances, particularly when he was speaking chiefly to himself in any case.

Michelangelo is a notoriously difficult poet (some would say an impossibly idiosyncratic one) because the form of his expression itself is frequently enigmatic. A reader is confronted, and may be rebuffed, by a manner elliptical to the point of riddling and little concerned with nicety of grammar, by an aggressive roughness, even crudeness, as if the thoughts have not always been fully blocked out in words. There is no doubt that his impatient privateness of manner gave trouble in his own day even to the friends to whom he sent his poems. We find him asking his literary confidant Luigi del Riccio to abbreviate and smooth out a madrigal before he passes it on to the common friend for whom it is intended, and later answering the complaint of del Riccio himself that a particular poem sent to him was incomprehensible:

Messer Luigi, I pray you send back to me the last madrigal, which you don't understand, so that I may put it right; for my messenger was so quick off the mark that he didn't give me time to look over it.[11]

Moreover, an economy of matter is written large in the incomplete state of so many poems. Fragmentariness was a mark of his temperament, to judge by the number of his sculptural projects launched and laboured on but never fully carried through, conceptions abandoned perhaps in half-formed enigma such as the figures of apostles and slaves emerging from the stone in the *Galleria dell'Accademia*, and the last great *Pietà*. The orthodox canon of Michelangelo's poetry opens with an enigmatic fragment scrawled on a sketch for his monumental David:

> Davide colla fromba
> e io coll'arco.
> Michelagnolo.
> Rott'è l'alta colonna.

That is only a degree or two more puzzling than many pieces in the collection. The way is littered with odd couplets or quatrains which leave us wondering whether it is a fragment of a poem we have or a complete epigram.

The circumstances of the writing may well account for some of this. There is also the brusque impetuousness and shrouded privacy of the man's temperament. But it is not beyond possibility that at least some of these qualities have a positive value in his poetry and may even be cultivated, as they sometimes seem to be in his sculpture. Who could say that the finished St Matthew would have been more powerful than the stone-stranded struggling figure we have! Then there is the paradox that at times Michelangelo was the master of a sublime simplicity of manner.

Nor do we get much help with the verse from the known circumstances of the poet's life, a life which is pretty well documented on both its public and private sides. Browning's lines on the lost poems of Michelangelo's loathed rival have their irony:

> Rafael made a century of sonnets,
> Made and wrote them in a certain volume
> Dinted with the silver-pointed pencil
> Else he only used to draw Madonnas: ...

> You and I would rather read that volume,
> (Taken to his beating bosom by it)
> Lean and list the bosom-beats of Rafael,
> Would we not? than wonder at Madonnas—
>
> 'One Word More'

Would we? The laconic comment of a modern Italian scholar seems more to the point: 'anche Rafaello scrisse versi, che nessuno oggi ricorda'.[12] For Browning must have been very disappointed if he brought that kind of expectation to the reading of Michelangelo. Not that dating the poems is a problem. As it happens we do sometimes know the very occasions on which pieces were blocked out since the poet scribbled versions down on the backs of dated documents. But the unromantic truth is that Michelangelo's is not so much a poetry of events, outward or emotional, as of attitudes; and that in Browning's sense it is no more a mirror of his life than a recorder of his heart beats. At the most obvious level of interest it is only very indirectly that we shall get here any light on Michelangelo's artistic activities or glimpse of his daemon. The manner of his few comments on works of art or their circumstances is not what one expects. 'I'ho già fatto un gozzo in questo stento' – 'this den has already given me a goitre': thus he dismisses his four years' stupendous labour on the Sistine Ceiling. Or there is the verse-letter on Rome itself at this same time:

> Here helms and swords are made of chalices:
> The blood of Christ is sold so much the quart . . .[13]

– an epistle which he inscribed sardonically at the foot, 'Vostro Michelagnolo in Turchia'.

We also have his comments on his poetry for he annotated a set of very moving funeral pieces, scribbling observations on the poems to the friend who commissioned them – and apparently paid for them in good dinners.[14] This is the tenor of the commentary:

Messer Luigi, the last four lines of the octave of the sonnet I sent you yesterday contradict each other; hence I beg you to send them back to me or to put these in place of them to make them less clumsy; or you can re-do them for me yourself . . .

This crude conceit, said thousands of times, for the artichokes. Clumsy pieces; but if you want me to do a thousand of them you've got to take them as they come.

Your trout said this, not me; anyway, if you don't like the lines, don't overlook the pepper next time.

Such confidences afford a momentary glimpse into the artist's workshop. But the expression we catch seems only another mask, baffling us still by its irreverent inappropriateness to the occasion and the spirit of his own work. We look for the soul of the great artist and find only the asides of an artisan.

The central body of Michelangelo's verse, as we have it, comes entirely from the poet's late middle age and old age. It falls into two groups, love poetry (loosely called so), and pious or devotional poetry. If I start with the love poetry it is not because this seems of less consequence than the drama of the fearful soul. We do not always know the circumstances and occasion, or even who is being addressed, but there is no doubt of the crucial importance of these sonnets and madrigals of love in Michelangelo's imaginative life and in European verse. Their number and quality are convincing, as well as the degree of seriousness one feels in the writing:

> La forza d'un bel viso a che mi sprona?
> C'altro non è c'al mondo mi diletti:
> ascender vivo fra gli spirti eletti
> per grazia tal, c'ogni altra par men buona.
>   Se ben col fattor l'opra suo consuona,
> che colpa vuol giustizia ch'io n'aspetti,
> s'i' amo, anz'ardo, e per divin concetti
>   onoro e stimo ogni gentil persona?

To what end am I spurred by the force of a beautiful face? for there is nothing else in the world that delights me. [It spurs me] to ascend alive among the spirits who are so exalted by such grace that every other good seems less.

If the work indeed corresponds to its maker, what blow need I expect from justice if I love, indeed burn with desire, and honour and esteem every gentle person for the divinity I perceive in them?

What seems obvious is that these love poems of Michelangelo's early old age have little to do with the onslaughts or complaints of conventional petrarchising, whatever else they might draw from the Tuscan tradition of the sonnet. Nor do they really invite the kind of interest in the poet's emotional life which we might extend unprompted to a Byron or Matthew Arnold. Why should a man in his sixties and seventies set himself ardently to the composing of love verses at all? Why – as we know to have been the case, even if we only occasionally know in which specific pieces – should the two chief objects of the passion he professes and displays be a young Roman nobleman of notable physical beauty, and a middle-aged and widowed Marchioness living the life of a religious recluse? Tommaso Cavalieri; and the poetess Vittoria Colonna, Marchesa of Pescara: the exact nature of

Michelangelo's relationship to these two, and therefore up to a point the tendency of the poetry he wrote for them, has given trouble.

Michelangelo met Tommaso Cavalieri in Rome in 1532 when he was fifty-seven, and a friendship of unusual intensity, which was to be lifelong, seems to have developed at once. We must reckon with the complimentary manners of the time in such extravagant admiration as Michelangelo expressed in a letter he wrote to Cavalieri in January 1533:

Therefore your lordship, the light of our century without paragon in this world, is unable to be satisfied with the productions of other men, having no match to equal yourself ... it is much the same to wonder at God's working miracles as to marvel at Rome producing divine men. Of this the universe confirms us in our faith.[15]

The sonnets we know to have been addressed to Cavalieri at this time are still more ardent and exalted. We hear of 'intense desire', of tears, sighs, and chains, of two beings made one by love:

> S'un casto amor, s'una pietà superna,
> s'una fortuna infra dua amanti equale,
> s'un'aspra sorte all'un dell'altro cale,
> s'un spirto, s'un voler duo cor governa ...

If a chaste love, if a lofty compassion, if one equal fortune holds between two lovers so that the ill-fate of one befalls the other also, if one spirit and one will govern two hearts ...
    if one soul is made eternal in two bodies, raising both lovers to heaven as if by equal wings; if love inflames and rends the vitals of two breasts with one blow of the same golden arrow;
    if either loves the other rather than himself, with one desire and one pleasure, to such effect that both seek the same end:
    if all these were a thousand more they would not make up a hundredth part of such a knot of love and such a faith; and only disdain can break and untie it.

Magnificent ecstasies transform the conventional protestations of the lover's absolute dependence upon the object of his love:

> Veggio co' be' vostr'occhi un dolce lume
> che co' mie ciechi già veder non posso;
> porto co' vostri piedi un pondo addosso,
> che de' mie zoppi non è già costume ...

With your fair eyes a charming light I see,
For which my own blind eyes would peer in vain,
Stayed by your feet the burden I sustain
Which my lame feet find all too strong for me:
Wingless upon your pinions forth I fly:

Heavenwards your spirit stirreth me to strain . . .
Like to the moon am I, that cannot shine
Alone; for lo! our eyes see naught of heaven
Save what the living sun illumineth.[16]

Oscar Wilde's prosecutors would have known what to make of that; as of Michelangelo's known record of intimate friendship with other youths and men – Febo del Poggio, Andrea Quaratesi, Gherardo Perini, and the servant Urbino who was with him for twenty-six years and whom he lamented most movingly in his letters and verse.

The point is though that his close acquaintances did not take his ardours in that way. The reason I chose those lines, and that we know their recipient, is that the great Florentine rhetorician and moralist Benedetto Varchi used them as the starting point of a public disquisition in 1546. He knew Cavalieri and describes him: 'A young Roman of very noble birth, in whom I recognised while I was staying in Rome not only incomparable beauty but so much elegance of manners, such excellent intelligence, and such graceful behaviour that he well deserved and still deserves to win the more love the better he is known'. The burden of Varchi's oration is that Michelangelo's verses are worthy not only of a skilled poet, the compeer of Dante and Petrarch themselves, but of the 'ripest sage'.[17] That might seem a curious claim to make for a love poet, and in such circumstances. Yet it is justified by the way in which particular experience and universal metaphysics of love are made to validate each other in the other poem to Cavalieri which Varchi cites:

> Non vider gli occhi miei cosa mortale,
> allor che ne' bei vostri intera pace
> trovai, ma dentro, ov'ogni mal dispiace,
> chi d'amor l'alma a se simil m'assale . . .

My eyes saw no mortal thing when they found their entire peace in your beautiful eyes; but within, where every evil thought displeases, they saw Him who invests my soul with a love like himself.

And if it were not created like God it would seek no other than the exterior beauty that pleases the eyes; but because this beauty is a deceit the soul transcends it in the universal form.

I say that the desire of a living being cannot be satisfied with that which dies; nor can what is eternal wait upon time, where the husk decays. Sense is not love but unbridled will, that kills the soul; and our love perfects friendship here below, but still more, through death, in heaven.

There may have been something defensive in Varchi's praise, for not all Michelangelo's contemporaries were so highminded. We know that Pietro Aretino, as adept at blackmail as pornography, spread innuendoes about him after he had failed to reply to an ingratiating request for a masterpiece or so from his hand;[18] and Michelangelo's pupils Vasari and Condivi tread carefully here in their biographies of their master, both going out of their way to stress his extreme sexual continence. 'He delighted in reproducing human beauty in art' (says Vasari) '... but he did not indulge in lascivious thoughts, which he avoided, as he showed by his virtuous life, devoting himself to work when a youth and resting content with a little bread and wine, while he showed himself very temperate as an old man'.[19] What really confused matters was that Michelangelo's first editor, in 1623, painstakingly petrarchised the poems by smoothing them out and redirecting to mistresses those written for men. When the true versions at last became known they embarrassed their late nineteenth-century commmentators into pious evasion.

It is surely clear enough in Michelangelo's painting and sculpture that his attitude to the sexes was not a usual one; the question cannot be avoided whether it is that which is here reflected still more directly. Michelangelo could be a moralist of ascetic severity. Was he also – and self-tormentingly then – an active paederast, as some of his recent apologists seem all too ready to concede?[20] It is worth noting at any rate that Michelangelo himself, in what certainly appear to be private communings, refers often to misunderstanding, misplaced disdain and the like, and keeps insisting on 'un casto amore'. The evidence of the poems seems clear enough, for what poems tell us, and there is no doubt that Varchi's reading of the expressions of love for Cavalieri is the one Michelangelo himself understood and approved. We may learn something from his relationship to the other known object of ardent addresses.

Michelangelo met Vittoria Colonna, Marchesa of Pescara, in Rome in the late 1530s at about the time he was beginning his Last Judgment in the Sistine Chapel. She lived in religious retirement in a convent at Viterbo, and on her visits to Rome was the centre of a little circle, almost an academy, of pious if unorthodox thinkers who met in the Church of San Silvestro on Monte Cavallo. This seems to have been a school of devout ideas congenial to a mind of transcendental cast, such as Michelangelo's; and we know from a contemporary attempt to evoke the spirit of these meetings that this scruffy old artisan was a leading figure among the liberal Cardinals and thinkers of the Italian Reform movement, such as Reginald Pole, who regularly took part in the dialogues.[21] Of his personal attachment to the Marchesa, and of hers to him, contemporary biographers leave us in no doubt. We hear of their exchanging letters, poems, gifts; of Michelangelo's loading her with sculpture and paintings made especially for her; of their going out of their way to meet each other on the rare occasions when meeting was possible. The tone of the poems he wrote for her while she lived – those very few we can be sure of – is ecstatic:

> sì sopra 'l van desio
> mi sprona il suo bel volto,
> ch'i' veggio morte in ogni altra beltate.
> O donna che passate
> per acqua e foco l'alme a' lieti giorni,
> deh, fate c'a me stesso più non torni.

her beautiful face spurs me so far beyond vain desire that I see death in every other beauty. O lady, who brings souls through water and fire to blissful days, pray let me never return to myself.

'Un uomo in una donna, anzi uno dio'

When she lay dying in 1547 the 72-year-old poet went at once to the convent; and Condivi records his poignant recollection, years after, of that last visit:

He so loved her that I recall hearing him say he regretted nothing more than that when he went to visit her at the moment of her death he did not kiss her forehead or her face as he did kiss her hand. Recalling her passing, he often seemed stunned by it, like a man out of his mind.[22]

In verse, though again long after, he was hardly less poignant:

> Quand' el minstro de' sospir mie tanti
> al mondo, agli occhi mei, a sè si tolse,
> natura, che fra noi degnar lo volse,
> restò in vergogna, e chi lo vide in pianti.

When the minister of my many sighs took herself from the world, from my eyes, and from herself, Nature which deigned to allow her among us sank into shame, and whoever had ever seen her lamented.

This was clearly not a conventional amorous relationship. Even Aretino, scraping for ammunition, never dared hint at anything physical here, while Michelangelo's own account of the deathbed scene speaks for itself. If the mode of address in these poems too is more formal than personal there is nothing commonplace in the feeling and dignity they convey. The manner is not cool, or just conventionally impassioned, but gravely urgent. Michelangelo seems deeply concerned to say something which needs the conventional terms of praise yet pushes him beyond mere praise altogether:

> L'anima, l'intelletto intero e sano
> per gli occhi ascende più libero e sciolto
> a l'alta tuo beltà; ma l'ardor molto
> non dà tal previlegio al corp' umano
>   grave e mortal . . .
>   Deh, se tu puo' nel ciel quante tra noi,
> fa' del mie corpo tutto un occhio solo;
> né fie poi parte in me che non ti goda.

The soul, the pure and whole intelligence, ascends free and unbound through the eyes to your high beauty; but great ardour gives no such privilege to the human body, heavy and mortal . . .
   Ah, if you have as much power in heaven as among us turn my whole body into a single eye, so that there may be no part of me which does not enjoy you.

'Ben posson gli occhi mie'

The play on eyes and eyebeams is petrarchan, the attitude draws on a familiar complimentary conceit of unappeasable desire; but the direction is wholly transcendental.

The fact seems to be that there is no such difference in temper as the modern reader might anticipate between Michelangelo's love poetry and his religious poetry. It is rather that the high seriousness one feels in the pieces to Cavalieri and Vittoria Colonna becomes imperative when he turns to Christ. These sonnets of his old age are directly and overwhelmingly devout, expressing over and over again, in imminent expectation of death, a fierce sense of sin and fear of likely damnation:

> Carico d'anni e di peccati pieno . . .

Burdened with years, and full of sins, and with evil ways rooted and strong in me, I see myself draw to the one and the other death; and yet I nourish my heart with poison . . .

A devout and even transcendental note certainly was not new in the secular lyric; nor was Michelangelo by any means the first sonneteer to redirect to pious ends the established devices of profane poetry. Yet the impact of these sonnets is extraordinary. They make up as vehemently pungent a set of devotional poems as we shall find anywhere in Christian writing. If pious poetry is out of fashion with us it may be because our view of the character of a religious literature has shifted. The seventeenth century was perhaps the last time one could unquestioningly accept religious verse as instrumental, or purposive. By the mid nineteenth century the universal drama of lived dogma had gone under to moral design or emotional effervescence. What strikes the twentieth-century reader in such devotional verse as Michelangelo's is the harsh reality, the tangibleness, the felt cosmic drama:

> la terra aperse,
> tremorno i monti e torbide fur l'a acqua.

The earth opened, the mountains shook, the waters were whipped up; the Great Fathers were plucked from the kingdom of darkness, the evil angels plunged further into misery; Man alone rejoiced, who was thus reborn to baptism.

'Non fur men lieti che turbati e tristi'

In the drama of these poems the poet himself is the doomed hero – 'O flesh, O blood, O wooden cross, O extreme agony, justify my sin in which I was born and in which my father was born ... so near to death and so far from God.'[23] 'Sí presso a morte e sí lontan da Dio.' There is a dynamic immediacy, an urgency wholly alien to mere expressions of sentiment. Not that this writing lacks passion. Over and over again it conveys fierce self-disgust, the wish to relinquish the 'importunate and burdensome corpse' of a life now become a hated and imperilling burden. It marks the turn from the world:

> Non è più bassa o vil cosa terrena
> che quel che, senza te, mi sento e sono,

Lord, there is no more base or vile thing on earth than that which without you I feel myself to be, and am.

This is unquestionably a lived motive, charged as well with the fatigue, the withdrawal, of protracted old age as with pressing fear. The poet writes in imminent expectation of – indeed wish for – death; but death brings judgment on the soul which has attached itself to the things of this world. 'Che fien or, s'a duo morte m'avvicino?': 'What are these now if I draw near to two deaths? The one I am certain of, and the other menaces me.'[24]

Such self-trial is worlds away from pious attitudinising. It operates at a level of feeling which is prepared to call a whole life in question, and a life's work as heroically huge as that of any other human being who ever lived. Love, even the means to that rarefied

spiritual love which he had tried to live out, is now the fatally
attractive adversary tempting to destruction:

Love, I have dwelt with you now for many many years; I have nourished my soul
with you, and even in part my body; and miraculously, hopeful desire has made
me good. Now tired, I give my thought wings to rise higher, and spur myself in a
more secure and noble part. What you promised me, in the writings about you
and by your own reputation, was vain; wherefore I weep.

'Di te con teco, Amor, molt'anni sono'

'Giunta è già l'ora strema'. Such writing compels us as incandescent
reflex of a struggle which seems to be waged before our eyes. The
outcome is nothing less than the stark renunciation of the principles
on which the poet had built his whole life, not only the *beltà mortal*
passively worshipped but the *beltà* actively realised. Painting and
sculpture, which had made Michelangelo a god to his contemporaries and were his own way to God, are in the ultimate assay
rejected, represented as at best a likely snare to the artist himself –
'what servitude, what tedium, what false aims and great peril of soul
to sculpture here divine things!'.[25] Or worse, art is ultimately – and
with what sublime irony – only another of the errors into which the
world too easily betrays proud and vain man:

> Onde l'affetuosa fantasia
> che l'arte mi fece idol e monarca
> conosco or ben com' era d'error carca.

Whereby the impassioned fantasy that drove me to idolise and make a king of art,
I now plainly see for what it always was, full of error, like every other transient
object of human desire.

'Giunto è gia'l corso della vita mia'

The last word is brief, quiet, but momentous coming from Michelangelo, who sometimes shows a Dantean genius for resolving
general human experience down to the ultimate simplicity:

> Ne pinger nè scolpir fie più che quieti
> l'anima volta a quell'amor divino
> c' aperse, a prender noi, 'n croce le braccia.

Neither painting nor sculpture now can satisfy the soul, turned to that divine love
which opens its arms on the cross to receive us.

Such poetry does not arise *in vacuo*. It expresses the most fundamental of Christian attitudes to the world; and it comes in its
resolved lucidity almost as a precipitation of a particularly rich
literary tradition. Of the pertinence here of the practical tradition of

the spiritual exercise, the preparation for dying, I think there is no doubt.

Michelangelo was a character of contradictions in many ways. In his temperament and conduct harsh impetuousness and violence alternated with great tenderness, crabbed meanness with extreme generosity, ferocious pride with utter humility, monastic solitariness and secretiveness with a quite pathetic yearning for intimate companionship. His life, as his art, often gives an impression of strain, of pulling opposite ways at once. Indeed it is possible that here in the attitudes these poems present, at the very centre of his artistic character, we come on the deepseated tension of the pull of contrary principles.

We are returned to Michelangelo's youth in Florence, and to the contradiction at the heart of that seminal city in the last decade of the Quattrocento. There is that intriguing and celebrated juxtaposition: on the one hand the Medicean garden of San Marco in which Michelangelo himself perfected his craft; on the other, the Dominican convent and pulpit of San Marco. On the one hand, in those long-vanished gardens and at Careggi, the early Florentine Academy brilliantly flourished its devotion to pagan antiquity and to Plato in chief, proposing as its loftiest conceit the transcendental metaphysic of beauty we call neoplatonic. Beauty is the Divine Essence; all apprehensible beauty derives from God more or less directly. The initiate is led through and beyond the sensuous response to physical beauty to the pure intellectual perception of the inner, spiritual beauty it shadows, and ultimately to the mystical contemplation of the eternal source of that beauty. And then in the pulpit a few hundred yards away the terrifying voice of the fire-raising Dominican Frate Girolamo Savonarola from Ferrara proclaimed the *contemptu mundi* in its most savagely ascetic – and melodramatic – form: violent self-disgust, anguish, crude humiliation of the senses, imminent doom on a city given over to such lewd and pagan frivolities as carnivals, amorous verses, secular paintings, passion-stirring music. On the one side Plato and Plotinus; on the other, Savonarola. Rarely can the flushed aspirant to God's ineffable beauty have been so brutally confronted with His condemnatory frown and terrible wrath.

It is hardly a paradox to say that these teachings are not really so far apart; for at least they have a common impulse in an attitude of otherworldliness and opposition to sense. Certainly there was an easy convertibility even if it was all one way. Notable among the crowds of converts to Savonarola's sackclothed *Piagnoni* were some of the chief apostles of beauty. Marsilio Ficino and Giovanni Pico della Mirandola were early (if irregular) devotees, and Pico and Angelo Poliziano, dying in the same year, both requested burial in San Marco in Dominican habit; Pico's nephew, Giovan-Francesco Pico, became Savonarola's apologist; the painter Baccio della Porta took the cowl as Fra Bartolommeo, and with his own hand consigned his nude studies to the flames of the first *Rogo delle Vanità*, as did Lorenzo di Credi; the Della Robbia were adherents; Sandro Botticelli was an impassioned *Piagnone* who – as Vasari tells us – ultimately abandoned painting for piety; Michelangelo's own elder brother Lionardo gave up the world in 1491 and entered the Dominican order in response to Savonarola's preaching. Michelangelo himself was never formally of the lamenting brotherhood, but we know that he remained devoted throughout his life to the memory of its perfervid head. He was twenty-one when Savonarola perished in Piazza Signoria in the flames he had himself helped to kindle; but nearly sixty years later the old sculptor told his pupil Ascanio Condivi that he had always kept the greatest affection towards Savonarola, still read the Scriptures in the light of his teaching, still retained fresh in his mind the living memory of the monk's voice. In the same breath, to judge by the incoherent paragraphing of this part of Condivi's account, he went on to stress his lifelong devotion to the platonic doctrine of love, the guarantee as it appears of his passions. For he loved with extraordinary feeling, as Condivi reports, 'not only human beauty but universally every beautiful thing ... a beautiful horse, a beautiful dog, a beautiful countryside, a beautiful plant, and so on.'[26]

Michelangelo himself, through Condivi, here gives us the lead we seek. We must recognise that (in a different way from Donne) he is a metaphysical poet. His poetry is metaphysical in the sense that it enacts a constant attempt to push experience to transcendental conclusions, to hold the momentary and temporal against the eternal; it offers us the very effort of the struggle to experience in the terms of a systematic belief. Not that Michelangelo was an intellectual, if that means someone who has the habit of submitting experience to detached analysis and codification. Nor was he a learned man, least of all in the Renaissance sense – at seventy he was still only hoping to learn Latin.[27] But he is *par excellence* the man who strives to live the life of ideas, and who feels his thought too in his own way. What Condivi shows us, or the old master himself through Condivi, is a man of dynamic imagination who was seized in his youth by the two great visions then flaming in Florence, found in them the guarantee of his own experience and sensibility, and thereafter tried to live his life by them however uncomfortably they held together. He enacts in his life the tension of his forced synthesis of Greek and Hebrew ideals – pathetically, tragically, heroically as may be – and in this as in other ways shows us in little the course of the Renaissance itself. In Michelangelo's case the oppositions run deep, well beyond the contrast his contemporaries noted between the grandeur of his imagination and the crabbed mode of his personal life. It is the inherent contradiction of an extreme sensuous susceptibility and an ascetic conviction; of a response to physical beauty so overwhelming that to deny it would have been a self-annihilation, coupled with a conviction of the final worthlessness of the world and the corruptness of the senses.

That this inner contradiction issued in art rather than in a wholly self-stultifying inner war may be due in part to Plato, or to his Florentine disciple Marsilio Ficino. Here at least we may immediately locate the high seriousness of the love sonnets and madrigals to the handsome youth and the pious widow. Michelangelo is far from using verse as a confessional, or a catharsis either. He is striving to live an idea, to act out his demonstration of a metaphysical truth, reconciling – as Ficino had showed him he might – his own irresistible response to physical beauty with his no less compulsive Savonarolean – or Augustinian – other worldliness. He celebrates beauties, illicit beauties in the worldly sense; but they are beauties, he assures himself, which reflect the Divine and in whose contemplation he can feel almost palpably the breathtaking radiance of God's very essence:

> Gli occhi mie vaghi delle cose belle
> e l'alma insieme della suo salute
> non hanno altra virtute
> c'ascenda al ciel, che mirar tutte quelle.

My eyes, eager for beautiful things, and my soul also, seeking its own salvation, have no other virtue which ascends to heaven than to admire all these.

Yet in an important sense Michelangelo's concern here is not private at all. The idea that a chaste love has power to purify and ennoble was an old *motif* in the Tuscan love lyric, going back at least to Guinizelli in the thirteenth century – 'Al cor gentile ripara sempre amor'. It is the burden of Dante's *Vita Nuova*, and the residue of Petrarch's long preoccupation with Laura. Such a sense is often explicit in Michelangelo's love poetry too – 'Love is a conceit of beauty, imagined or seen within the heart, friend of virtue and gentleness.'[28] It lurks oddly behind the magnificent 'Se'l mie rozzo martello', where the poet develops the strange conceit that his mistress is a hammer, better able to chasten him with blows now that she is lifted aloft to heaven. But what he commonly shows is the way late fifteenth-century Florentines platonised their own lyric tradition, elaborating and exalting a loosely defined moral influence into a transcendental 'philosophy'. The devotee was offered a formally organised metaphysical regimen, a mystical way denied to 'occhi infermi', which demanded of its novices a self-denying devotion to spiritual beauty, 'che muove/e porta al cielo ogni intelletto sano.'[29]

This is the doctrine which was bandied about Europe thereafter in more or less garbled form. It appears in the English sonnet, notably in the sequences of Sidney and Spenser, as the metaphysical trimmings of what is still essentially an old moral line – noble and chaste love refines one into a better man. Michelangelo is singular among six-teenth-century poets in taking both the Tuscan moral tradition and the neoplatonic metaphysics in deadly earnest, in attempting to harmonise them and interpret his own experience in terms of them. He presses experience through to cosmic conclusions. Sidney is high-minded, Tasso mellifluously platonic; Michelangelo's note is exaltation, sublimity, sustaining a transcendental aspiration beyond moral concern. He attempts an altogether rare coincidence between sensibility and belief. When he takes up a neoplatonic notion – when he says for example that the soul transcends external and particular beauties in the Universal Form of beauty – he is doing more than entertain a high conceit. There is no doubt that he expects to be taken literally.

If we look back to the pieces to Cavalieri and Colonna we may see that in sonnet after sonnet the poet-artist is striving to place all the objects of his admiration in the same perspective:

> Per fido esempio alla mia vocazione
> nel parto mi fu data la bellezza
> che d'ambo l'arti m'è lucerna e specchio . . .

Beauty, which is lantern and mirror of both arts, was given to me at my birth as sign of my vocation. If anyone thinks otherwise he is wrong. This alone carries the eye to that sublime height which prepares me to paint and sculpture here. If bold and foolish judgments attribute to sense that beauty which transports to heaven every sane intellect one can only say that infirm eyes cannot ascend from the mortal to the divine, and must remain fixed there were it would be vain to think of ascending without special grace.

Art and love are cognate intellectual activities having the same origin, moving to the same end and manifesting the same special grace; they are alike at the opposite pole from sense, transcendental while that remains earthbound:

> Passa per gli occhi al core in un momento
> qualunche obbietto di beltà lor sia,
> e per sì larga e sì capace via
> c'a mille non si chiude, non c'a cento,
>   d'ogni età, d'ogni sesso; ond'io pavento,
> carco d'affanni, e più di gelosia;
> né fra sì vari volti so qual sia
> c'anzi morte mi die 'ntero contento.
>   S'un ardente desir mortal bellezza
> ferma del tutto, non discese insieme
> dal ciel con l'alma; è dunche umana voglia.
>   Ma se pass'oltre, Amor, tuo nome sprezza,
> c'altro die cerca; e di quel più non teme
> c'a lato vien contr'a sì bassa spoglia.

In one moment there passes through the eyes to the heart whatever they deem beautiful, and by so broad and capacious a way that it is open not just to a hundred but to a thousand beauties of every age, of either sex; wherefore I fear for myself, burdened with anxieties and still more with jealousy, nor do I know among such different faces which of them might give me entire content before my death.

If an ardent desire remains wholly fixed on mortal beauty then it did not descend from heaven with the soul, and is therefore human will. But if it passes beyond this then, Love, it scorns your name, for it seeks other gods and a timeless state, and no longer fears then what assails so base a husk.

It is an attempt which we can only call heroic at putting a personal difficulty in a cosmic setting. Nothing less is in view than the reconciliation of the whole sensuous basis of art with a transcendental and otherworldly doctrine behind which lay the force of the mediaeval contempt of the world; but at the centre is the poet's titanic struggle to reach a truce between his innate and mastering response to sense-experience and what he consciously believed – between his deepest sensibility, and convictions received but profoundly held. It is a possibility hardly glimpsed by other sixteenth-century celebrants of beauty, whose inability to press beyond moral regeneration led them to locate the crux of their difficulty in a naked conflict between the ideal and the senses. Did even the spiritual hero really achieve his

peace, outside the ideal reach of his art? The poems themselves turn
upon an unresolvable personal dilemma:

> La tuo beltà non è cosa mortale,
> ma fatta su dal ciel fra noi divina;
> ond'io perdendo ardendo mi conforto,
> c'appresso a te non esser posso tale.

Your beauty is no mortal thing but was divinely framed to come among us;
whence I comfort myself in my despairing passion that in your presence I cannot
sustain such a state.

'Dal dolce pianto al dolorosa riso'

And you cannot read Michelangelo anywhere on his own work –
poems, letters, tabletalk – without feeling that constant rage of
self-dissatisfaction which all his biographers describe. Is it idle to
suggest that its root may have been here, in a transcendental imagination betrayed by his own sensibility, and by the necessary medium
of his art itself?

In fact he could not – or did not – sustain the effort. Old age, and
then extreme old age, beat him. Perhaps it was the felt imminence of
death and judgment, sharpened by the discomforting belief that the
longer one lives the harder and unlikelier the attainment of salvation: 'For I am undone if I don't die soon.' Perhaps it was the
inevitable slackening of vitality, and of interest in his world and his
own past attainments. 'Non può, Signor mie car,' – 'My dear Lord,
the fresh and green age cannot feel anything of how in the ultimate
straits one changes taste, love, desires, and thoughts. The world's
loss is the soul's gain; Art and death do not go well together; what
matters at all outside your hope of me?'

'L'arte e la morte non va bene insieme.' Here in sum Savonarola
claimed him whole after sixty years as he had always threatened to
do, and as he had claimed his brother long before. The old artist
turns to address himself to Christ, his pen charged with the
imminent dread of judgment and weighted with the self-disgust,
world-weariness, that signified he has fought, and lost, his last battle
with himself. 'Chiunche nasce a morte arriva.' These late writings
show a spirit engrossed in the contemplation of night and death,
which had always been the food of his imagination. As sculptor he
gave himself over to the mysterious shrouded piety of those last
strange *Pietà*, and as poet to that incomparable series of devout
sonnets, half-meditation half-vehement prayer, in which he enacts in
his own person the cosmic drama he had hurled onto the altar-wall

of the Sistine Chapel, the struggle of a man's soul caught between the death it merits and the salvation it might attain through Christ. We find a series of urgent pleas for that true humbleness of spirit which must precede grace, and for the grace which precedes redemption. The posture is at once rhetorical and meditative. He is at the same time petitioning God and engaging in a vehement assault on his own unregenerated spirit; the practical end is that self-chastening of the will which alone can fit the spirit to receive grace:

> Vorrei voler, Signor, quel ch 'io non voglio:

I would will Lord what I do not wish; between your fire and my heart a veil of ice conceals itself which kills your heat; whereby the pen doesn't correspond with what it writes, and the paper is made a liar. I love you with my tongue and then lament that love doesn't reach down to my heart; nor do I well know how to open the door to grace, which buries itself in the heart and drives out all impious pride:

> Squarcia'l vel tu, Signor, rompi quel muro
> che con la suo durezza ne ritarda
> il sol della tuo luce, al mondo spenta!

Shatter the veil, Lord; break down that wall which with its obduracy keeps back the sun of your light from the spent world! Send your light promised for the future to us now, to your fair bride, so that my heart kindles without holding back, and feels only you.

The words Savonarola himself is said to have written on a book-cover for his gaoler while awaiting his third trial supply a context:

Virtuous living depends wholly on grace; wherefore we must strive to attain grace, and having won, to increase it. To examine our sins, to meditate on the vanity of earthly things, are means towards grace ... Certainly it is a free gift of God, but when we have a strong contempt for the world, a strong desire to turn us to spiritual things, then we may say that even if grace be not yet in us, it is assuredly drawing nigh.[30]

It was Savonarola, too, who had counselled the use of pictures as an aid to meditation, as in a celebrated sermon on the art of dying preached on 2 November 1496. But Michelangelo's poems, mediaeval in temper, have something of the Counter Reformation in their manner and effect. They are among the earliest literary works to demonstrate in action Loyola's meditative exercise of a focusing of all the faculties on the attributes of the crucified Christ to the end of absorption into Christ's redeeming sufferings.[31] In intention at least such writing is purposive rather than expressive. The essence of this explosive rhetoric is that it seeks to act out the turn from the world, to achieve that inner realisation of the sinner's true state as he nakedly confronts his crucified Christ which, paradoxically, is his only bulwark against the deadly sin of despair:

> Le spine e' chiodi e l'una e l'altra palma
> col tuo benigno, umil pietoso volto
> prometton grazia di pentirsi molto
> e speme di salute a la trist' alma.

The thorns, the nails, and the one and the other palm, with your benign and pitying face, promise much grace to repent and hope of health to my miserable soul. Do not let your holy eyes dwell on my past with justice, nor your offended ear cause you to stretch your chastening arm against me: your blood alone laves and erodes my sins ... let it be more abundant as I am older – of prompt help and entire pardon.

'Scarco d'un' importuna e greve salma'

What is the special character of this writing – what parallels does it suggest? In English only Donne and Hopkins compare, such poetasters as Alabaster apart; and in the light of the Jesuitical connections of both these poets (and Alabaster too, for that matter) the comparison may be more than a dilettante exercise. A religious poem such as Herbert's 'The Collar' is dramatic:

> I struck the board, and cry'd, No more,
> I will abroad.

Yet fine as this certainly is it offers itself to us as a vivid narration of a past event which relies for its force on consummate literary artifice. To turn back to Michelangelo is to see what he gains by those compelling present tenses and vehement imperatives:

> stende ver' me le tuo pietose braccia,
> tomm' a me stesso e famm' un che ti piaccia.

Extend your pitying arms towards me; take me from myself and make me whatever pleases you best.

'Per qual mordace lima'

Here is no cold literary narrative or merely re-enacted excitement. Michelangelo's urgent immediacy takes us into the heart of the drama and makes us witnesses of the ultimate struggle itself. The power of these sonnets comes from the force of Michelangelo's cosmic imagination, the absolute necessity he seems to have felt to weigh this world against eternity, to push everything to the transcendental proving-point. But we must appraise them as conscious creations of art. Michelangelo was one of the earliest of the Counter Reformation poets to see that the petrarchan sonnet itself, with its concentrated focus and urgent invocations, might serve a devout end. Here the formal Jesuitical discipline of meditation seems to have been the shaping force. One condition of the individuality and splendour of these pieces is that they are part of and formally sustained by a tradition; and the point about this tradition is that it is only incidentally literary, or even verbal.

Is it just the grandeur of such attitudes, finally, which raises Michelangelo above the swarming ruck of sixteenth-century sonneteers – the reflex of his vast genius, better realised elsewhere? Fine as these are, what seizes one when one reads Michelangelo's poems is something more specifically poetic, the authentic power of a definitive utterance. Michelangelo the poet hardly answers to Coleridge's demand for a wide range of imaginative experience, a variety of felt invention. He is not a poet of continual renewals whose verse reflects the play of a thousand moods and tempers. Moreover, he remained to the end a conceited writer in the petrarchan manner. To this extent he may be as much of an acquired taste as any other sixteenth-century poet of the Italian lyric tradition (such as Sidney), and in his seemingly wanton difficulty an expensive taste at that.

Yet notwithstanding all this, and although he used only the minor forms of poetry, reading him remains a major experience for even in single lines and brief effects he catches and compels the imagination over and over again:

> In me la morte, in te la vita mia;
> tu distingui e concedi e parti el tempo;
> quante vuo', breve e lungo e'l viver mio.
> Felice son nella tuo cortesia.
> Beata l'alma, ove non corre tempo,
> per te s'è fatta a contemplare Dio.

'Beata l'alma, ove non còrre tempo.' 'Blessed the soul where time has ceased to run.' Michelangelo's writing has this clean-chiselled epigrammatic quality which again and again defines some quintessential human experience or posture. We know that he loved Petrarch but revered Dante. At his coolest it is always Dante's manner he reminds us of, the marmoreal weight and marble cleanness of the diction, the dignified simplicity, the resolved lucidity of the thought. He addressed to Dante himself a sonnet of grave beauty:

> Dal ciel discese, e col mortal suo, poi
> che visto ebbe l'inferno guisto e'l pio,
> ritorno vivo a contemplare Dio,
> per dar di tutto il vero lume a noi.

He descended from heaven, and in his mortal body, when he had seen the hell of justice and that of mercy, returned alive to contemplate God, to give to us the true light of all things. Would I were he, who, born to such bitter fortune would not exchange harsh exile with virtue for the happiest state in the world.

Finely conceived and monumentally phrased, it seems a sublimely ingenuous revelation of the naked thought itself, unadorned and untainted by literary artifice.

Michelangelo's brevity is often the condition of this chiselled weight, language cut down cleanly to the bone as the poet strives for an ultimate condensation of felt thought with so little concern to be easy or smooth. Here is the opening of a magnificent sonnet as a recent translator rendered it in a kind of English:

> O make me see you, Lord, in every place!
> If mortal beauty burns me with its flame,
> My fire is ember when at yours I aim,
> And in your love I shall be still ablaze.[32]

This is accurate and in its way pleasing but it translates Michelangelo into a romantic rhetoric of smooth grace and flowing raptured elegance. Here is the original:

> Deh fammiti vedere in ogni loco!
> Se da mortal bellezza arder mi sento,
> appresso al tuo mi sarà foco ispento,
> e io nel tuo sarò, com' ero, in foco.

The lines resist one, whether by rough artlessness or design; this is the half-hewn block rather than the polished product. Yet this resistance itself has great expressive force. What the obstructed texture creates is the mood of the utterance, which the translation waters into mellifluous raptures – effort, struggle, the plea bursting out in the teeth of his own recalcitrance. Moreover, however rough hewn it is certainly not crude; there is a rhetoric at work at least as subtle and calculated as the translator's, though directed to quite a different end. A very little attention to the arrangement of clauses will show how carefully the syntax has been managed to catch not merely the balances and emphases but the cadences, nuances, pitch of the mood.

Such writing does not come by chance, and there are like effects everywhere in this poet. They have evidently been worked at, hard and subtly. If Michelangelo's writing often assaults and savages the reader with its sudden vehemence, the thoughts struggling half-formulated in heroic agony like the Laocöon to which he was strangely devoted, this is as much because it is what he was after as because of the clumsy inexperience he affected when his friends taxed him with unnecessary difficulty. Michelangelo is a true poet – and he is surely that – not only by side-product of the dynamic and heroic temperament which sets him altogether apart as an artist but because in his poetry his creative energy takes on the proper character of verbal expression. Within this restricted range we meet the same loftiness of thought and heroic grandeur of the will to experience, only it is assimilated fully by a poetic imagination into the idiom of rhythm, phrasing, diction, image, attack.

Indeed in one way, if only one, his poetry illuminates his painting and goes beyond it. The visual medium is not well suited to the complication of ideas. Could even a Michelangelo convey through visual effects alone just what it means, as well as how it feels, to seek to transcend sense in universal form? The presentation drawings for Cavalieri need a literary explanation of their platonic metaphors, and we surely apprehend their drift the more particularly for the poems:

> Veggio nel tuo bel viso, signor mio,
> quel che narrar mal puossi in questa vita:
> l'anima, della carne ancor vestita,
> con esso è già più volte ascesa a Dio . . .

I see in your beautiful face, my lord, that which can scarcely be grasped in this life: the soul, still dressed in flesh, has by this beauty already ascended to God many times.

And though the malicious herd commonly attributes to others its own folly and evil, that does not make the intense will less worthy – the love, the faith, the honest desire.

To those who apprehend it every beauty we see here resembles more than any other thing that divine origin whence we all issue. Nor do we have on earth any other evidence or other fruits of heaven; and who loves with faith transcends to God and makes death sweet.

In this sense alone Michelangelo's poetry is a running gloss on his art, almost a pointing of it. Possibly some part of the poetic impulse lay here, in the obscurely felt inadequacy of the visual medium to explain its own significance. At all events the sheer magnificence of the vision and the attempt everywhere imparts its own luminous character to his writing, whose absolute distinction I take to be a matching heroism of temper and of thought, even when a thought is 'not his own' as we judge these matters. This is the quality which in kind at least puts him with Dante, and Milton, and Beethoven, and separates him from almost everybody else.

Yet finally the return to Beethoven may remind us that there is more in Michelangelo than grandiloquence, more human warmth than – say – Milton's verse displays. Oddly, what comes through often enough in the cadence and texture of the voice is pathos; as when he replies with a sonnet to the repeated invitation of an old friend, the Archbishop of Ragusa:

> Ond'io con esso son sempre con voi,
> e piango e parlo del mio morto Urbino,
> che vivo or forse saria costà meco,
>   com' ebbi già in pensier. Sua morte poi
> m'affretta e tira per altro cammino,
> dove m'aspetta ad albergar con seco.

So that I am always with you in spirit, and I weep and talk of my dead Urbino who if he had lived would perhaps even now be visiting you with me, as I once thought to do. But now his death hastens me and draws me by another road, where he awaits me, to lodge with him once more.

'Per croce e grazia e per diverse pene'

The picture of Michelangelo which stays in the mind when we read these last poems is that strange nightpiece Vasari and Condivi show us, the two biographer–pupils, friends of his old age. It is the image of a fettered Titan lingering on year after reluctant year, radically out of sympathy with the times and believing himself less certain of salvation the longer he lived. Behind the formidable front of the artist there is the man who saw his political hopes disappear in the chaos of mid cinquecento Italy, his family hopes disappear in deaths and barrenness, his personal aspirations as finally betraying him, tending only to his own peril of soul. As Vasari pictures him for us he is the very type of the superannuated man, still working ferociously on in the small hours in unregarded squalor, a candle in his artisan's paper hat for light, year after year, to placate some personal daemon, nobody else at all, utterly uncaring of the renown and reward his art had won him, or of the fruits of his life's labours. But it is his own private writing – the letters and poems – which truly brings home to us the pathetic *humanity* of the old superman, this solitary with a craving for companionship, whose few intimates were all long dead – who had no care to satisfy anybody else – and who cannot keep the note of private lamentation for human transience out of his voice even when the matter is the common petrarchan *motif* of the farewell to love:

> Tornami al tempo, allor che lenta e sciolta
> al cieco ardor m' era la briglia e'l freno;
> rendimi il volto angelico e sereno
> onde fu seco ogni virtù sepolta ...

'Torna 'l tempo' – as another manuscript verse has it: 'Bring back the time' ... 'Give back to me that angelic and serene face, in whose burial all good was lost to us.'

Paradoxes to the end. For all Michelangelo's distaste for self-confession humanity is very much the spirit of his writings, and his poetry has a human interest of a rare depth and warmth. While it is not at all the purport of his last poems personal feeling does break through; as Beethoven's heroic pathos, transmuted into impersonal art in the late quartets, emerges almost despite him in his letters. But the real importance of these poems is that the small body of Michelangelo's verse, in its prodigious struggle to realise an idea of love beyond the alterations of sense, makes a unique contribution to European literature and consciousness.

iv. *Fruits of nature: The Faerie Queene*

Spenser's images of the lover's enslavement to sense and time owe more to Tasso than to Florentine platonising:

> So passeth, in the passing of a day,
> Of mortall life the leafe, the bud, the flowre,
> Ne more doth flourish after first decay ...
> Gather the Rose of love, whilest yet is time

> *The Faerie Queene* II, xii, stanza lxxv

But then the Bower of Bliss itself is far from the whole story. Spenser develops his account of love in *The Faerie Queene* by counterposing emblems of sexual behaviour across the entire poem, so that metaphors which seem pointedly like one another have opposite tendencies and effects. Implicitly inviting us to explore the differences between these contesting representations, he engages us in a running debate which is not finally resolved until the Mutability Cantos themselves.

A ready key to the character of the Bower of Bliss is its porter Genius. We must contrast him with the porter of the same name who stands at the gate of the Garden of Adonis, and figures the celestial power of life and generation. This guardian of the Bower is a demonic creature, an enemy to life who envies people's good and brings about their fall through 'guileful semblaunts'. He shows us that we are to take the Bower itself for a total deception, a place full of fair enticement which is created by an artifice that perverts nature. The Bower undoubtedly presents an alluring lotusland of delights. But its lush revel of sense offers itself in images of enervating sexual activity, devitalising satiety, unfulfilled expectation, just because the pleasures it promises are turned back upon themselves and can never be truly realised so. Spenser strikingly brings out the sheer urgency of this snatching at love in the garden of our natural lives, but the process to which such a compulsion commits its victims is centred in self-gratification, and completed in the cycle of the single life. They must seize the brief moment of their maturity, 'gather the Rose of love, whilest yet is time'; and yet the debasement of their minds in sense will not fulfil them as men, however it may satisfy hogs. There is no consolation to be found in this particular version of the expense of spirit in a garden.

Venus, Adonis, and Cupid seem curious emblems of right and fruitful love, especially when we have only just encountered them at Castle Joyous presiding so prominently over a day and night revel of erotic titillation, between squires and damsels who swim 'deep in sensuall desires' (III, i, stanza xxxix, line 8). The formal ritual of stolen love they sponsor there grotesquely parodies the progress of the *Roman de la Rose* and all its offshoots. But then Spenser's very conception of love requires him to distinguish crucially between modes of behaviour which tend to be all too easily confused.

The Garden of Adonis boldly takes up from the Bower of Bliss an organic metaphor of love and fruition, so as to bring out that fruitful sexual activity which realises a right understanding of love. In this garden all life increases and multiplies as God commanded it, by its own volition and accord, without other help. This is a state of stability whose condition is not fixity but change, an endless process of generation and regeneration. Organic change never ceases, so that things are continually caught up in the cycle of maturation and decline; yet they never lose their being, but are continually renewed in their essential nature. As in Empedocles's cosmology, the forms change yet the substance remains.

Time is at work in this garden, but it operates as the sole marring element which lays waste and destroys the growth, and must itself be destroyed before the place can become a true and final paradise. Here lovers enjoy each other as naturally as the living processes which go on around them, and Venus and Adonis in their midst set the mode of mutual joy. Adonis exemplifies the very process of duration in change, being himself 'eterne in mutability'. Enjoying his goddess in eternal bliss he no longer need fear the boar of self-destructive desire which gored him when he remained unfulfilled. Once Venus returns Adonis's love she ineffectualises that boar finally. Cupid enlarges the emblem of mutual love in his perpetual enjoyment of Psyche, whose fruit is a child called Pleasure. So slight a mythic grace confirms a bold conception of love, as of human nature. This mutual enjoyment of physical coupling consummates in pleasure as in offspring the perpetual union of lovers; and it also figures the harmonious fulfilment of our whole nature, sense profiting by its interplay with mind instead of seeking its own blind way of self-indulgence.

A book which opens with erotic fun at Castle Joyous, and has the Garden of Adonis at its centre, concludes with the Masque of Cupid at Busirane's Castle. The Masque itself comes as a pointed reversion to the self-destructive tyranny of disorderly love. The chase after sexual gratification for its own sake lands this particular troop of sensualists in the old sad sequence of frailty and change, reproaches and recriminations. As the climax of the show the display of Amoret's captivity and exposure of her heart do at least suggest that Amoret's still unconsummated passion for Scudamour has put her in the clutches of the monstrous tyrant whom Cupid now presents. Yet her public humiliation here is simply the reward of her fidelity, which causes her such suffering in this unnatural separation from her lover. The stanzas Spenser cancelled in 1596, one hopes for no other reason than to keep the story of Amoret and Scudamour going, do point the grisly exhibition of Amoret as a hapless martyr of faithful love. In the 1590 publication of the first three books of the poem the canto ends with the reuniting of Amoret and Scudamour, who run to embrace each other:

> Lightly he clipt her twixt his armes twaine,
> And streightly did embrace her body bright,
> Her body, late the prison of sad paine,
> Now the sweet lodge of love and deare delight:
> But she faire Lady overcommen quight
> Of huge affection, did in pleasure melt,
> And in sweete ravishment pourd out her spright:
> No word they spake, nor earthly thing they felt,
> But like two senceless stocks in long embracement dwelt.

Had ye them seene, ye would have surely thought,
That they had beene that faire *Hermaphrodite*,
Which that rich *Romane* of white marble wrought,
And in his costly Bath causd to bee site:
So seemd those two, as growne together quite,
That *Britomart* halfe envying their blesse,
Was much empassiond in her gentle sprite,
And to her selfe oft wisht like happinesse,
In vaine she wisht, that fate n'ould let her yet possesse.
Thus doe those lovers with sweet countervayle,
Each other of loves bitter fruit despoile

1590 edition III, xii, stanzas xlv, xlvi, and xlvii lines 1–2

Their mutual consolations melt into a physical union so complete that
they make up just one bisexual creature between them, the celebrated
hermaphrodite of love; and they turn love's fruits into sweets by their
mutual acts of pleasure, 'sweet countervayle' of love. Britomart's
half-envy of the bliss of lovers who suddenly find themselves empar-
adised in each other's arms, and the feeling which their embraces
arouse in her, have nothing in common with the Satanic response to
the lovemaking of Adam and Eve. On the contrary, her passion confirms the natural rightness of theirs, for she simply yearns to find such
blissful release of pain in an ultimate union with the man she secretly
loves.

In the 1590 version of the first three books the story of Amoret and
Scudamour quite pointedly confirms at the level of connubial union
the regenerative myth of the Garden of Adonis. Such unselfregarding
mutualness in itself renews and regenerates the world which self-
centred love decays, and stands against change and time. When the
rest of the poem appeared in 1596 the Mutability Cantos crucially
tested the conceit of a continual opposition between a force of
stability and a force of change. Nature's verdict in VII, vii, stanzas lvii
and lvix, finally rebuts the claim that mutability is the law of the entire
universe, and confirms in the vision of a natural apocalypse the providential purposefulness of change itself. Mutability is not the destructive and reductive enemy to life it seems to be. On the contrary, what
we call change is simply the process by which things dilate their being,
and work their own perfection:

Then over them Change doth not rule and raigne;
But they raign over change, and doe their states maintaine.

VII, vii, stanza lviii

Indeed the stage will be reached when things have so far realised
their own natures that time and change themselves must simply

179

cease to operate. In his last bold sketch of a millennium which will be brought about by the natural evolution of qualities towards their perfected state Spenser finds no occasion to revert to means. But book III altogether leaves no doubt that for him fruitful sexual love fulfils the human part in the process.

In *The Faerie Queene* Spenser offers us an emblematic scheme of love rather than a human embodiment of it. He does not here seek to prove an experience, as do Petrarch, Michelangelo, and Shakespeare. Hence such passages as those cited seem not so much lived through as thought out. Yet the account of love they render is arrestingly different from anything in the Florentine tradition, not least the theories of the Florentine neoplatonists which Spenser is supposed to have favoured. In truth he takes us forward to Shakespeare, Donne, and Milton, rather than back to Pico and Ficino. The essence of his understanding is that the creation is a living organism moved by love, in which human love fulfils an organic need. What then distinguishes love from mere appetite, and makes human life itself more than a brief vegetable process? Spenser distinguishes between fruitful fulfilment of the organic impulse in mutual love, and a self-defeating indulgence of it in mere sexual gratification. Mutual love between the sexes is the means by which human kind participates with delight in the endless process of regeneration and renewal that sustains the entire creation. Who seeks only his own titillation in sex will find no more than momentary pleasure, and may forfeit his humanity if not his eternal life. At the threshold of the new century Spenser's brave attempt to humanise a naturalistic version of love's motives quite strikingly points the special character of English renderings of sexual behaviour.

v. *Nature's changing course:* Shakespeare's *Sonnets*

Shakespeare's *Sonnets* at once engage human life in a natural counterchange of growth and decline:

> From fairest creatures we desire increase,
> That thereby beauty's rose might never die,
> But as the riper should by time decrease,
> His tender heir might bear his memory

Sonnet 1

The rose of beauty holds its perfection only for a moment, however it may renew itself by offspring in its own decay; infancy crawls to maturity, yet the glory of that crown is instantly eclipsed and confounded by time, even 'Consumed with that which it was nourished by' (73). We are caught up by our nature in a continual mutation which allows us no stay in our own state:

> As fast as thou shalt wane, so fast thou grow'st
> In one of thine, from that which thou departest:
> And that fresh blood which youngly thou bestow'st
> Thou mayst call thine when thou from youth convertest.
> Herein lives wisdom, beauty and increase;
> Without this, folly, age and cold decay

11

The common metaphors of the advancing season of age and passing day of life seem here to be re-experienced, so that they give substance to a deeply felt sense of the implication of human nature in the processes of natural life and husbandry:

> That time of year thou mayst in me behold
> When yellow leaves, or none, or few, do hang
> Upon those boughs which shake against the cold,
> Bare ruin'd choirs, where late the sweet birds sang.

73

Love itself is taken to express an organic need which the lover experiences in his senses as a fever, a craving, an unnatural barrenness:

> How like a winter hath my absence been
> From thee, the pleasure of the fleeting year!
> What freezings have I felt, what dark days seen!
> What old December's bareness everywhere!
> And yet this time remov'd was summer's time,
> The teeming autumn, big with rich increase,
> Bearing the wanton burden of the prime,
> Like widowed wombs after their lord's decease;
> Yet this abundant issue seem'd to me
> But hope of orphans, and unfathered fruit

97

These ravishingly beautiful evocations of seasonal change are poignant with disquiets which seem to be felt in the very apprehension of love:

> Then of thy beauty do I question make,
> That thou among the wastes of time must go

12

The lover's intuition of time's wastes puts in question a love and beauty which may be just the functions of a process that 'feeds on the rarities of nature's truth' (60). He must seek some mode of permanence within organic change itself, as by

> summer's distillation left
> A liquid prisoner pent in walls of glass

5

His struggle to perpetuate a conceit of perfection keeps him painfully alert to the distance between idea and actuality, reason and passion, will and desire. He sometimes writes as if his bodily organs take on a disposition of their own:

> For thou betraying me, I do betray
> My nobler part to my gross body's treason;
> My soul doth tell my body that he may
> Triumph in love; flesh stays no farther reason,
> But, rising at thy name, doth point out thee
> As his triumphant prize. Proud of this pride,
> He is contented thy poor drudge to be,
> To stand in thy affairs, fall by thy side.

151

The blunt witness that beauty itself may be no more than a passing state, which holds only for the little moment of mature flowering, tells against the dream that we are moved to love by some absolute quality beyond change. Time tans and imperceptibly wastes sacred beauty:

> Ah, yet doth beauty, like a dial-hand,
> Steal from his figure, and no pace perceived

104

The ironic insight of the *Sonnets* is that the lover's very incitements commit him to time, change, decay. Change itself powerfully excites his love just because it is a condition of beauty; for the momentariness of what moves us quickens our desire to possess it:

> Then the conceit of this inconstant stay
> Sets you most rich in youth before my sight

15

The compulsion of the need itself mars the possession when we recognise its cause:

> This thought is as a death, which cannot choose
> But weep to have that which it fears to lose.

64

Nothing in these poems is more majestically invoked than the prospect of mortality which love itself opens to the lover:

> Since brass, nor stone, nor earth, nor boundless sea,
> But sad mortality o'er-sways their power,
> How with this rage shall beauty hold a plea
> Whose action is no stronger than a flower?
>
> 65

Time's thievish progress towards eternity becomes an apocalypse which imperceptibly engulfs in oblivion not only men's lives and doings but all the elements of our globe. The lover's will and judgment simply stand at the mercy of the 'million'd accidents' of time which blindly work such powerful changes. Even his conceits of love are no more than offspring of circumstances which may come to gestation and fruition, but are just as likely to inhearse themselves in his brain stillborn as if 'Making their tomb the womb wherein they grew' (86).

The need to give human qualities a defence against the very force which fostered them gives the *Sonnets* their despairing urgency:

> where, alack,
> Shall Time's best jewel from Time's chest lie hid?
> Or what strong hand can hold his swift foot back?
> Or who his spoil of beauty can forbid?
>
> 65

The impassioned grandeur of the vision makes a universal drama of that desperate struggle to preserve our 'better part' (74) against the mortal promptings which leave us prey to time. Yet this lover cannot find his eternity in a spiritual conquest of the flesh, or a turn from the creature to the creator. Nor does his constitutional urge to distil the perfection of a moment from the mutations of the destructible organism confront him with a moral choice. Love simply makes him feel the ironic contradictions of our ardour to preserve some quality of our own being.

Shakespeare's passionate absoluteness seems so bravely poignant because the poet's assurances of permanence are always proclaimed in the face of general ruin. He will make no appeal to a condition beyond nature itself:

> And nothing 'gainst Time's scythe can make defence
> Save breed, to brave him when he takes thee hence.
>
> 12

We have the hope of renewing our lives and perpetuating our prime in our posterity. Or the very power of the celebration might lift the consummate moment of beauty and of love to a fame beyond dusty oblivion:

> 'Gainst death and all-oblivious enmity
> Shall you pace forth; your praise shall still find room,
> Even in the eyes of all posterity
> That wear this world out to the ending doom.
>
> 55

Then love itself may stand as 'an ever-fixed mark', when the marriage of true minds makes an absolute union which need not be the fool of time:

> Love alters not with his brief hours and weeks
> But bears it out even to the edge of doom.
>
> 116

Yet all these brave recourses only ward off the piercing recognition that we can never be truly sure of more than the present moment:

> Alas, why, fearing of Time's tyranny,
> Might I not then say 'Now I love you best'
> When I was certain o'er incertainty,
> Crowning the present, doubting of the rest?
>
> 115

A quality of present being is the irreducible glory of our lives:

> The summer's flower is to the summer sweet
> Though to itself it only live and die
>
> 94

The writing rings so true to experience because it engages us in a radical debate with ourselves, in which no commitment can be final.

The sequence evolves by a kind of self-realisation, as if the lover's mind struggles to follow out a direction of his whole being which is not in the management of his understanding. His turn from the beautiful youth to the dark lady confirms a more drastic experience of love, which now presents itself to him as a sheer craving of sense in disregard of his judgment. The contrast with Michelangelo's turn from Cavalieri to Vittoria Colonna could scarcely be more ironic. This compulsion is pointedly not moved by beauty, either of body or of mind, but submits him to a sexual enslavement which falsifies his faculties and feelings:

Why of eyes' falsehood hast thou forged hooks,
Whereto the judgment of my heart is tied?

137

These sonnets to the dark lady register the anguish of an ambiguous will and self such as leave the lover in an Augustinian state of self-frustration. They open a contradiction which puts him in bondage to his own depravity:

Only my plague thus far I count my gain,
That she that makes me sin awards me pain.

141

The stripping down of love to the bare erotic compulsion starkly proves the dilemma of the lover who feels himself ensnared in his own nature. He experiences love itself as a betrayal, a surrender to time and change of his yearning for the absolute, an exposure of allurement to its own corrupting power:

Lilies that fester smell far worse than weeds.

94

The very urge to union corrupts itself, not only delivering our nobler part to the gross body's treason (151) but seeking its own death (147). The lover finds himself a victim of uncontrollable drives, and incomprehensible revulsions:

Enjoy'd no sooner but despised straight;
Past reason hunted, and, no sooner had,
Past reason hated, as a swallowed bait,
On purpose laid to make the taker mad

129

He discovers in humiliating experience how arbitrarily his life is moved by compulsions which serve organic needs. Sonnet 129 has its classical antecedents:

Foeda est in coitu et brevis voluptas
et taedet Veneris statim peractae.

Petronius Arbiter

Yet it emerges with such force here because it confirms so many scattered apprehensions of the possessive power of appetite, and defines a condition which holds for more than sexual craving:

Mad in pursuit, and in possession so;
Had, having, and in quest to have, extreme;
A bliss in proof, and proved, a very woe;
Before, a joy proposed; behind, a dream.

129

The cycle seems desperate enough. Extreme begets opposite extreme, craving desire turns at once to nauseated revulsion, the anticipated bliss proves a painful awakening from illusion which does not abate the need to go on seeking it. Shame, remorse, self-disgust accompany the debasement of his will. The sense that his enthralment to love opens him to the unintelligible hazards of his own nature seems to be the most disquieting accompaniment of this expense of spirit.

Scarcely less unsettling is the moral dislocation wrought by such feeling proof that his understanding is the fool of his desire:

> Oh me, what eyes hath love put in my head
> Which have no correspondence with true sight!
>
> 148

Painful experience compels his bewildered acknowledgment that he is irremediably at odds with himself. What he calls love is a craving which works counter to reason, and quite brutally contradicts platonic expectations:

> Who taught thee how to make me love thee more,
> The more I see and hear just cause of hate?
>
> 150

These sonnets prove a radical experience of love which leaves the lover with the dilemma of our double nature. We are animal beings who aspire to unchanging perfection. In a world of relative gratifications the absolute claims of lovers stand to be mocked from within.

3

Body and Soul

It would appear that in most cases soul neither acts nor is acted upon apart from the body ... Thought, if anything, would seem to be peculiar to the soul. Yet if thought is a sort of imagination, or not independent of imagination, it will follow that even thought cannot be independent of body ... So, too, the attributes of the soul appear to be all conjoined with body: such attributes, viz., as anger, mildness, fear, pity, courage; also joy, love and hate; all of which are attended by some particular affection of the body ... those are right who regard the soul as not independent of body and yet at the same time as not itself a species of body. It is not body, but something belonging to body, and therefore resides in body, what is more, in such and such a body ... For the actuality of each thing comes naturally to be developed in the potentiality of each thing: in other words, in the appropriate matter.

> Aristotle, *De Anima* I, I, 403a, 5–19 and II,
> 2, 414a, 19–20, 25–7, ed. R. D. Hicks, pp. 7 and 59

And surely syth experyence teacheth us that the soule whych is of yt selfe a spyrytuall substaunce, god hath of his hygh wysedome and power founden the meane so to put it in a bodye and so to knyt yt therto, that not onely by fyre or frosen water putte aboute yt, but also wythoute any outwarde thynge put unto yt, by the onely boylynge of the distempered humours wythin yt selfe, ye soule is in such gryef, payne and torment, that it wold be as fayne out of the body as the bodye wold be rydde of it: syth we fynde this thus, I dowte nothynge at all but that god can by no meanes then men can thynke or imagyne, so bynde the spyrytuall soule to the fyre, that he shall fele the fervour of yt fyre as he nowe feleth the hete of his ague here 024 and yet shall not the fyre and he be made one person as the soule and the body be now.

> Sir Thomas More, *The Confutation of*
> *Tyndale's Answer*, Book I, *The Complete Works*
> *of St Thomas More*, ed. L. A. Schuster and
> others, New Haven and London, 1973, VIII,
> part I, p. 103

It is intire man that God hath care of, and not the soule alone; therefore his first worke was the body, and the last work shall bee the glorification thereof.

> Donne, *Pseudo-Martyr*, 1610, p. 17.

You (I think) and I am much of one sect in the philosophy of love; which though it be directed upon the mind, doth inhere in the body, and find pretty[1] entertainment there.

> Donne, letter to Sir H. Wotton, Amiens,
> February 1612

i. *Unchanging union:* Donne's *The Ecstasy*

Donne's poem 'The Ecstasy' shows us as if in dramatic retrospect the bodies of mutual lovers which have been arrested in incomplete union, and now wait upon a colloquy of souls before they can fulfil themselves as bodies:

> Where, like a pillow on a bed,
>   A pregnant bank swelled up, to rest
> The violet's reclining head,
>   Sat we two, one another's best;
>
> Our hands were firmly cemented
>   With a fast balm, which thence did spring,
> Our eye-beams twisted, and did thread
>   Our eyes, upon one double string;
>
> So t'intergraft our hands, as yet
>   Was all our means to make us one,
> And pictures in our eyes to get
>   Was all our propagation.
>
> As 'twixt two equal armies, Fate
>   Suspends uncertain victory,
> Our souls, (which to advance their state,
>   Were gone out), hung 'twixt her, and me.
>
> And whilst our souls negotiate there,
>   We like sepulchral statues lay;
> All day, the same our postures were,
>   And we said nothing, all the day.

The description is divertingly pitched between literal force and emblematic, setting the tone of the poem as the poet–lover speaks it, so that we at once take the effect of his resolved calmness, and alert ourselves to the temper of a man who is never far from being amused at his own gravity. The image of ecstasy, which controls the argument, is effectively equivocal. It figures the process by which the two separate souls arrive at an understanding between themselves, like negotiating generals who mysteriously both stand to gain ground by the terms of their parley; and it also describes an awareness granted to the souls thus raised beyond their bodies, and united. What they gain is nothing short of a truth about their own condition, a new understanding of their mutualness in union; but this marvel is none the less a mystery and miracle because they here apprehend it for themselves, without supernatural intervention.

Donne's bold and brilliant conceit, all but comically bold, is to use that figure of mystical experience for a self-recognition of lovers. This ecstasy of love claims kinship with that state in which a privileged soul leaves its body to communicate with spirits, and have divine mysteries revealed to it. Yet Donne actually gives us the souls of two lovers, which go out from their sense-bound bodies to become one, and simply comprehend their new condition. He shows them growing to a revelation of their shared love, such as transforms their lives. We may see what a gain Donne makes upon the simple sensuousness of a classical conceit:

> Qualis nox fuit illa, di deaeque,
> quam mollis torus. haesimus calentes
> et transfudimus hinc et hinc labellis
> errantes animas. valete, curae
> mortales.

> Ascribed to Petronius Arbiter

Donne's device may be audacious but it is certainly not cold. He immensely enlivens and sharpens it by his ingenious dramatic realisation, and especially by the supposititious introduction of a privileged bystander, the adept in love who may now learn the heart of love's mystery from the utterance of these souls in bliss. When he characterises this apprentice-lover as one who has become all mind by the refining power of good love Donne is not proposing that a full love must be all mind; he means that you have to be made all mind by good love before you can get any further in love's mystery, and understand the language of souls. The poem is not for people who are content to love at a lesser rate. The deadpan comedy of the poet–lover who takes his own conceit with such nice literalness alerts us to the precise wit of this diction. 'Within convenient distance stood': an overhearer who happened to stand within discreet distance[2] might take a new concoction[3] and 'part far purer than he came'. This new spiritual influence upon one who has already grown all mind will advance him to a still higher state of being by giving him a better understanding of love.

The mystery itself is revealed in the speech the poet voices for the two souls, which takes up the rest of the poem, as if all that follows is uttered by the lovers in unison. We follow their realisation of what it is they love, and learn as it were with them that they had not previously recognised the moving impulse of their attachment. They now find that they are drawn together by a love beyond difference of sex, which so interinanimates their souls that it makes one being of them; love remingles those already mixed spiritual entities, in a union which is superior to their former state because either soul now supplies the defects of the other. Their immediate gain by this miraculous transformation, and union, is the new clearsightedness which lets them see that such a fusion of souls is beyond change. Simply in coming to recognise the essence of their love, and grasping its real nature, they can also confirm its depth and firmness.

The poem discloses itself as the testimony of a mutual love which commits the lovers wholly and finally to each other, and does not depend upon sense, whatever their need of physical coupling to confirm the union of their whole beings. It marks the development of lovers towards that self-awareness which is also mutual reassurance, as if they find at last that their love needs to know its own quality before they can be confident of themselves and of each other. Because such a discovery must be made together the poem speaks not just from the man's point of view, or in the voice of one lover only, but for both of them, defining and acclaiming that special union to which they both assent. Like 'The Good-Morrow', 'The Canonisation', 'The Anniversary', 'The Sun Rising', it offers itself as a joint testimony rather than a self-expression, their common avowal which will gratify the partner for whom the poet–lover speaks, simply as it meets her own mind with his.

The long episode of parleying which resolves the nature of this firm love is closed with authoritative finality when that understanding is reached:

> For th'atomies of which we grow
> Are souls, whom no change can invade.

So the urgent reopening of the argument does take the reader by surprise:

> But O alas, so long, so far
> Our bodies why do we forbear?

Yet the need to prescribe for a further stage of love is implicit in the gain they have already made. For the interinanimated souls are said to have the further advantage over souls in their single state that their love is made active, as a transplanted violet not only ceases to be 'poor and scant' but

> Redoubles still, and multiplies.

That finely impassioned turn from souls to bodies was prepared in the account of their spiritual fusion, and is necessary to a full realisation of love. What the lovers now go on to urge upon themselves is that their love may be in essence a union of souls, and yet need their bodies as well for its full, active, fruitful expression. The tone of their outcry speaks of a grievous deprivation while their bodies remain inactive, and gives some urgency to the nice process of distinguishing and defining which brings out the relation of spiritual to bodily love:

> They are ours, though they are not we, we are
>   The intelligences, they the sphere.
> We owe them thanks, because they thus,
>   Did us, to us, at first convey,
> Yielded their forces, sense, to us,
>   Nor are dross to us, but allay.

lines 51–6

'Air and Angels', following Leone Ebreo, beautifully proposes that intelligence cannot operate without its sphere; and it is not wholly joke that the lovers owe their bodies thanks for conveying them to each other in the first place since the bodies must activate their love, and their senses must mediate between them, before they can know each other at all. But now the very antithesis between soul and body begins to lose its absoluteness with the claim that the bodies are not dross to them but alloy; which presumably means that the flesh is no more wholly corrupt than the soul is pure spiritual essence. Moreover, the conjoined bodies do not impede the union of souls:

> On man heaven's influence works not so,
>   But that it first imprints the air,
> So soul into the soul may flow,
>   Though it to body first repair.

57–60

The analogy with the operation of angels seems particularly bold in the way it controverts an orthodox assumption with a superior spiritual case. As heaven itself uses a less pure medium so that it may exert its influence on man, so soul may flow into soul even though it first 'repair' to the body. The example suggests that bodily intercourse might even be necessary to confirm the union of souls.

A further quite compelling analogy at once reinforces that understanding, implying categorically that it is just the subtly knitted conjunction of soul and body that makes us human at all:

> As our blood labours to beget
>   Spirits, as like souls as it can,
> Because such fingers need to knit
>   That subtle knot, which makes us man:

61–4

As some mediating element between sense and spirit subtly knits soul and body to make human nature, so affections and faculties unite the lovers' souls and senses in impulses of love:

> Else a great prince in prison lies.

68

In itself the mediaeval physiology is unimportant. What matters is the appeal to the worth of human nature as we find it, so trenchantly urged in this decisive revision of the old ascetic presumption that the soul is a prisoner of the body. In Donne's figure our human nature is no pure spiritual essence which is damnably impeded by a base contingent element, but essentially a subtle knot of body and spirit. The human soul, however truly spirit, would be impotent without the agency of sense because it would not then act upon the outside world or have any palpable effect at all.

These spiritual lovers must turn to their bodies because the soul needs the body, if only so that it may show and realise its own nature; and it works through the senses precisely by the means of affections and faculties, which have the nature of spirit though they are engendered in sense. Far from clogging or corrupting the soul the body is its necessary partner, and the means by which our humanity fulfils itself.

We must take it for a witty parallel which is not just joke that 'weak men' might fail to recognise love if it were not revealed in bodily acts of love; as though the body is the book which displays the mysteries that grow in the soul. These conceits bring us to the marrow of the argument for an embodied love. Donne follows out a particular understanding of the nature of a sacrament when he speaks of a truth which lies altogether beyond sense, and yet needs the body to reveal it in the world and give it effect there. 'The Ecstasy' draws its understanding of love from the persuasion that spiritual essence may be co-present with physical events in the world, disclosing the absolute and eternal order in the passing contingency and relativeness of man's affairs. Weak men to whom a union of souls is revealed in physical acts of love already witness a spiritual and unchanging condition in our sensible and timebound state.

The last phase of the poem comes with a very adroit reversion to the apt overhearer, who now seems to be ourselves, and with the promise of a return to the bodies:

And if some lover, such as we,
Have heard this dialogue of one,
Let him still mark us, he shall see
Small change, when we'are to bodies gone.

73–6

Such a resolution as the new soul has reached produces immediate consequences for its hosts. The lovers' bodies, left still in frigid contemplation of each other, are now to be repossessed by a superior entity which will reveal and activate its mystery through them; the joining of bodies will follow the marriage of souls, and make fruitful that spiritual union. The change must be small, presumably because the resort to bodies does not alter the nature of their bond, but activates a love which now needs only to be shown in its consequences.

'The Ecstasy' lets its lovers see how intelligence and sense interwork in their love, why people who love each other at so rare a rate will hate physical separation yet may endure it:

Dull sublunary lovers' love
(Whose soul is sense) cannot admit
Absence, because it doth remove
Those things which elemented it.

But we by a love, so much refined,
That our selves know not what it is,
Inter-assured of the mind,
Care less, eyes, lips, and hands to miss.

'A Valediction: forbidding Mourning', 13–20

Donne makes a living issue of a scholastic crux, showing us lovers who imperatively need to make sense of their own experience before they can bring it to fruition. The poem flaunts its neoplatonic properties, the lovers' raptness of gaze, the souls' abandonment of the bodies for a revelation of truth, the suspension of bodily life, the elevation beyond nature. But the disembodied colloquy of souls yields no transcendent vision. It simply shows the lovers to themselves.

It seems that for Donne love is an active state of mutual regard which needs to know itself, if only by what it is not, so that the lovers may understand and follow out what they have already proved in experience. 'The Ecstasy' is far from urging lovers towards a pure contemplative stasis. Two lovers seek as one to make clear to themselves something that had perplexed them, not because they wish to contemplate an idea of beauty, but so that they may realise their mutual love. Observing the truth of their condition as it is, they assure themselves of their fidelity to one another and their oneness beyond alteration; and they reassure themselves how much they depend upon their senses in such an entire love. But this is knowledge from which action follows. In the end the ecstatic revelation justifies their bodily union by the union of souls itself; and succeeding poets took that to be the *coup de grâce* for neoplatonic love.

> I was that silly thing that once was wrought
>   To practise this thin love;
> I climbed from sex to soul, from soul to thought
>   But thinking there to move,
> Headlong I rowled from thought to soul, and then,
> From soul I lighted at the sex agen.

Cartwright, 'No Platonique Love'

In his love poetry, as elsewhere, Donne's instinct was to bring down to earth the higher flown pieties of the day with the witness of hard actuality. He takes his own course, though it had been well prepared for him, when he has his lovers persuade themselves that their bodily desire is not an impediment to right love but may even be essential to it. In the poems, that persuasion is gained out of the experience of an achieved relationship which he is always looking for ways of bringing home to the participants, whether by scholastic means or conceited. The play of wit continually has in view the nature of the bond itself:

> But, now the sun is just above our head,
>   We do those shadows tread;
>   And to brave clearness all things are reduced . . .
> Except our loves at this noon stay,
> We shall new shadows make the other way.

'A Lecture upon the Shadow'

Donne imposes no scheme upon experience. Such a poem seems to move as it were from the inside of an existing relationship, by a dramatic fiction which simply offers the lovers a way of realising what their love means. The truth the poet aims at is objective and precise, as if the sensation of being in love, and the vehemence of his affections, are only to his purpose as far as they sharpen his understanding of the constitution of this particular bond, by which it must survive or fail. Understanding the laws of love seems to be a matter of knowing ourselves, generalising our sense of a thousand past experiences into a grasp of the way the world goes, and then perhaps acknowledging the miracle of an attachment which escapes the way of the world. This is wisdom of a kind which is quite alien to idealist philosophy.

'The Ecstasy' is one of the most extraordinary of European love poems, not least because it celebrates a mutual love by both recreating and precisely defining the bond between the lovers. To come to it from the neo-aristotelean theorising of the Italian *dialoghisti*, such as represents the most advanced thinking about love in sixteenth-century Europe, is to be impressed afresh by the vitality of Donne's poetic intelligence which so imaginatively transforms theoretical possibility into lived experience, and realises in the movement and language itself the process of arriving at a new self-awareness. Donne's utterly distinctive voice, and radical aptness of invention, bring the lovers of 'The Ecstasy' before us as living people who may still speak for us. There is nothing here of the self-entanglements of 'Farewell to Love'. The slow, patient, incisive movement, and lucid unfolding of the syntax, show us people who are in the act of making a momentous self-discovery intelligible to themselves, and confirming a tender regard which does not at all dull their alertness to a sceptical world. Grierson was surely right to speak of Donne's metaphysics of love.[4] Contemporary discussions of love undoubtedly sharpen our sense of what Donne is about in such a poem. But their terms are never more than a means by which the poet creates and comprehends a living relationship of love, and seeks to resolve the perpetual dilemma of beings who hunger for absolutes in a world of contingency. Without denying the momentariness of the impulses of sense, 'The Ecstasy' enacts a pattern of sexual love which can yet survive the sating of desire, and stand beyond casualty and time.

ii. *Proving the hermaphrodite:* aristotelean theorists of love

How purposeful is Donne's thinking about love? His love poems do not show us a Dante or a Michelangelo, yet they would scarcely warrant our taking their author for a mere sexual adventurer with a gift for yoking heterogeneous ideas. It is no surprise to find Donne himself speaking of his formal allegiance in the philosophy of love. The poems show him consciously formalising his experience in a precise scholastic way which undercuts idealist thinking. The terms of his remark to Wotton are specific: 'Love . . . though it be directed upon the mind, doth inhere in the body.' His poems give point to the understanding, which clearly mattered at least as much to Donne as it would matter to Hobbes, that human nature realises itself in the body.[5]

Many people in Renaissance Europe shared Donne's interest in the nature of love, and contributed to a debate which went on through the decades. Discourses of love loomed large among the moral dialogues which became popular in the sixteenth-century Courts, and ranged from the elegantly courtly to the strenuously scholastic, and the divertingly down-to-earth. Castiglione and Bembo soon yielded place to disputants of a very different temper.

Few of these debates actually turn on idealist arguments at all. The accounts of love which they develop are by no means all of a neo-platonic piece. Florentine disciples of Ficino were first countered and then infected by the earthy naturalism of aristotelean Padua; and a syncretic work became the great source of ideas about love for theorists of all complexions, the *Dialoghi d'Amore* of the Spanish-born Jew, Leone Ebreo. Between the rival schools, if they merit so categorical a disposition, there was a good deal of common ground; and they differ precisely in the degree of importance they assign to the body in love.

The set dialogues of the Counter-Reformation Academies stand on different ground from the courtesy books of the High Renaissance Courts. Their participants seem disinclined to admit that sharp separation of soul from body which follows the supposal that spirit and flesh are of opposed qualities and ends. They are more concerned to debate such practical aspects of love as the differences between the several kinds of sexual attachment. We find an emerging presumption that body and soul are actively interdependent elements in a human nature which is essentially whole, and one. In these literary encounters neo-aristotelean naturalism is not pressed through to the point where Plato's vision of love gets flatly denied, but it simply leaves no place for a loving transcendence of sense. Interest has shifted so far from the idealising admiration of beauty that by the middle of the sixteenth century in Italy Dante himself has lost favour, and Michelangelo's private platonising earns him sceptical scoffs. The enlightened men and women who so earnestly dissect love in the dialogues occupy themselves with the quality of a human relationship, and the means of fostering a mutual regard.

Some of them are specially concerned with the place of physical coupling in the union of lovers. They proffer leading questions for debate in the characteristic manner of these interlocutors of love. Is physical pleasure a licit part of love? How may we know true love from mere carnal desire? What happens to love when desire is sated? Can lovers ever find peace and permanence in a condition which is inherently unstable? Might people love God in loving each other?

All the theorists are agreed that love may be of several kinds, which are quite diverse in their working and effects. Ficinians tend to deny love altogether to such gross and bestial natures as care for the body only, and to admit only lovers who strive to contemplate pure beauty of soul as a means to the enjoyment of the Divine Beauty. Some writers allow a mixed condition, that of lovers who try to love both body and soul; some even find two further refinements, making five kinds of love in all. The Florentine Court orator Varchi, who had first brought Michelangelo's poems before the public,[6] distinguishes between mixed kinds of love. He gives highest place to 'courteous' or 'virtuous' love, when both body and soul are loved but the soul is loved more than the body, and only the senses of sight and hearing are active. Next comes 'human or civil' love, when the lovers pass to the other, less spiritual senses as well. Lastly comes 'plebeian or vulgar' love, when both body and soul are loved but the body is loved more than the soul.[7] Avowed aristoteleans tended to restrict themselves to two broad categories. They distinguish between vulgar love, whose end is simply the enjoyment of the body, and what Tullia d'Aragona calls honest love.

which is proper to noble men, that is those who have a gentle and virtuous soul, whether they are poor or rich; and which is not generated in desire, as the other, but by the reason.[8]

Nonetheless the several schools generally agreed on the nature of each kind of love.

The characteristic commonly ascribed to the vulgar love is instability. 'All the things that delight our material sentiments, of their nature, when they are possessed are sooner abhorred than loved' declared Leone Ebreo.[9] Tullia tells us that past reason hunted and then past reason hated is the order of the lower love, for desire destroys itself when the satisfaction of sense is the whole end:

I say, that the carnal desire gratified, there is no one who does not instantly lose that will and appetite which so tormented and devoured him . . . not only does it put an end to love, but turns to hate.[10]

There can be no permanency or fidelity when revulsion immediately follows upon attainment. Yet in higher conditions of love, in which appetite is regulated by reason, the satisfaction of physical desire may actually increase affection:

> if the appetite of the lover is quite sated with the copulative union, and that desire, or properly appetite, continently ceases, in no way is cordial love thereby diminished, rather is the possible union bound the closer.[11]

Some writers, Tullia d'Aragona among them, held that in good love physical appetite itself may increase by what it feeds on, seeking bodily union all the more ardently for the pleasure once proved.

It was commonly held that in higher kinds of human love the souls of the two lovers conjoin in perfect union. Love itself is frequently defined as a 'desire to unite oneself with the thing esteemed good', which 'would be the soul of the beloved'.[12] The Paduan academician Speroni put it neatly when he said that lovers in a perfect love are joined so completely that they lose their own semblance and become a strange third species, which is neither male nor female but resembles a hermaphrodite.[13] The orthodox conceit was that the souls of such lovers, compounded by a kind of miracle, become 'one soul in two bodies';[14] and as Tasso put it in his youth, 'the lovers are not two, but one and four'.[15] This manner of arithmetical paradox-juggling comes from Ficino's commentary on the *Symposium* and is elaborately cultivated by neoplatonists. It means no more than that two souls are made one when by love they are 'transformed together, the one into the other',[16] while each soul at the same time becomes two, having another soul added to it; and so there are four souls in all. When this crude sophistry is more than mere conceit-spinning it prescribes for a joining of souls so perfect that 'they are united together in every part, and become mixed and intermingled'.[17]

Such a union of souls cannot be consummated in a normal state; nor may the lovers who achieve it remain as they had been in their singleness. It requires what Leone Ebreo calls 'the ecstasy, or else alienation, produced by amorous meditation'.[18] Cattani says that this love-ecstasy is to be brought on above all when 'we direct our eyes in the face and in the eyes of the person who so much pleases us', which so affects us that 'for the marvel of it we become as persons stupefied'. He adds that the spirit, 'as it were fomented by the continued power of the fixed cogitation, is no sooner affected by that effluence than it all but changes itself into the nature of the other'.[19]

The state of 'privation of sense and movement' thus induced permits an ecstatic contemplation of each other in which the soul leaves its body and remains 'outside the self, in that which it contemplates and desires':

> For when the lover is in ecstasy, contemplating that which he loves, he has no care or memory of himself, nor does he perform any work in his own benefit, whether natural, sensitive, motive, or else rational. Rather is he quite alien to himself, and belongs to the object of his love and contemplation, into which he is totally converted.[20]

We are presented with an analogy which is often openly avowed, and precisely made, between this secular state and the ecstasy of divine contemplation, 'when as the Servants of God were taken up in spirit, separate as it were from the body, and out of the body, that they might see some heavenly mysteries, revealed unto them'.[21]

As the outcome of that 'divine vision' which temporarily unites the soul with the great Fount of Truth is that 'all things are seen most perfectly',[22] so a suitably humbler revelation follows the ecstasy of love. Sometimes the gain in knowledge is material. Following Ficino, writers describe a general exchange and mixing of the beauties of bodies and souls in which love 'levels every inequality and reduces them to parity, in order to unite them perfectly and make not union but unity';[23] or better still, the commingling produces a third thing which is 'finer than they had been separately made', as sometimes comes about in 'a compounding of the voice with the lute, of perfume with perfume'.[24] The virtuous lover, knowing that 'love raises souls to high things',[25] might indeed deliberately seek this condition so as 'to make himself more perfect in the union with the soul of the beloved'; for 'always the lover desires to be made participant in that which he lacks, and knows or believes to abound in the beloved'.[26] Yet some writers speak of a higher illumination which is produced 'when the superior loves the inferior in all the first semicircle, from God down to the prime material'.[27] Again the necessary step to fruition is the intercourse of loving souls. 'There is no perfection or beauty that does not increase when it is communicated, for the fruitful growth is always more handsome than the sterile' said Leone Ebreo, who finds the essence of ecstatic communion in a mystical sharing of the divine beauty and wisdom:

> And so it happens of man with woman; that knowing her in examplary fashion he loves and desires her, and from love passes to the unitive cognition, which is the

end of desire ... This great love and desire causes us to be abstracted in such contemplation that our intellect is raised up; and in such a way, that illuminated by a singular divine grace, it comes to know things above human power and speculation; as happens in such union and copulation with the Highest God.

Moreover, the lovers who achieve such an exalted state are double blessed in that their love is proof against decline; for 'without end is the perfect desire, which is to enjoy union with the loved person'.[28]

Much of this theorising covers common ground. Some account is needed of the proper place of the senses in love, and of the relation of the body's part to the soul's part. There are few writers on love who steadily discount the body. Ficino is one. For him the soul is the essential man and the body its poor drudge or clog. This was a rare severity, yet the Florentine assumption that active love calls for the vital linking of two quite different elements was widely shared at first. Florentine commentators took up from Aquinas the notion that the agent which ties the 'knot between the soul and elemental body'[29] is the 'spirit',[30] which Ficino describes as 'a certain extremely subtle and lucid vapour, generated by the heat of the heart from the most subtle part of the blood'.[31] This 'spirit' at once 'transfuses the life' from the soul to the body, and, 'being spread through all the members, takes the *virtù* of the soul and communicates it to the body'. Conversely the spirit 'takes again, by the instruments of the senses, the images of outside bodies', which the soul is not gross enough to know directly, and presents them to the soul 'as in a mirror', for judgment.[32]

These spirits are necessary mediators between the soul and each sense and faculty. The purer Ficinians drew no corollary which might diminish the essential independence of soul. They conceded only that 'a powerful alteration of the one' element might 'make its way to the other'.[33] But as Aristotle came back into favour in sixteenth-century Italy writers followed the strong example of Leone Ebreo, and tended to be syncretic. Even professing neoplatonists came to disregard Ficino's strict division of our nature. Leone's own view was eccentrically non-Christian. He took up the common idea that the soul is 'mixed of elements, or else principles, discontinuous and separate the one from the other',[34] and declared that the mixture consists of elements of intellect and body, which fitted it to mediate between the two. The soul takes the place of the spirits as mediator between sense and intelligence.

Christian aristoteleans had Aquinas behind them. Thomists

denied that the body is dross precisely because Aristotle had affirmed that all the elements of our nature are absolutely interdependent.[35] Man is not 'a combination of two unlike substances, but a complex substance which owes its substantiality to one only of its two consecutive principles'. An intellect without a body would be impotent, lacking access to the sensible world; and in order to communicate with matter, mind must 'descend, so to speak, into the material plane'. For these aristotelean intellects Aquinas substitutes immortal souls, whose inescapable need of the co-operation of sense-organs he thus affirms:

in order to obtain this co-operation they actualise matter; it is due wholly to them that this matter is a body; and yet they are not themselves save in a body; the man, therefore, is neither his body, since the body subsists only by the soul, or his soul, since this would remain destitute without the body: he is the unity of a soul which substantialises his body and of the body in which this soul subsists.[36]

To see the effect of this teaching on sixteenth-century theorists of love we need not go to zealots such as Bruno, who flatly denied that the body and soul are contraries,[37] or even to the ardent Tullia's affirmation that self-evidently 'all the compound, that is the soul and the body together, is more noble and perfect than the soul alone'.[38] Equicola, a standard courtly authority, noted 'the great friendship and union which is seen between the body and the soul, and found the bond to be so close that 'while this organic member is in one being, we cannot think of the action of the soul apart from the body, much less separate them; nor can the action of the body be considered without the soul'.[39] Aristotelean Padua naturally stood for an indivisible integration of the hypostatic union which guaranteed the status of the flesh. 'I say then' wrote its pundit Speroni,

that our soul, in understanding, has already used the organs of the external and internal sentiments, nor may it understand without those; but those serve it in understanding, supplying it with the species, without which it does not understand. And therefore it is said, and truly, that the man understands and not the soul.[40]

It is still more impressive that writers in the other camp should have concurred to the extent of accepting this crude empiricism, even if it was 'as philosophers and not as Christians'. Varchi starts from just Speroni's position that soul depends upon body, 'our soul being incapable of understanding anything without the sense'; and his conclusion would have won Locke's approval:

all those things which sense cannot feel and apprehend, the intellect cannot treat of or understand, for there is never anything at all in the intellect which has not first been in sense.[41]

The part neoplatonists assigned to the body in love is conveyed in the celebrated figure of the steps. The lover ascends by stages from the lowest kind of love to the highest, at each stage seeking the appropriate form of union with the object of his love. His pleasure in the physical beauty of his mistress leads him to the contemplation of her true beauty, that of her soul; and this prospect draws him ultimately to the ecstatic vision of the eternal beauty. Every step transcends the previous one, which is then left behind. The satisfaction of the body is the lowest step, and only beasts and vulgar lovers go no higher; nonetheless a lover still needs it at first as 'prospect of truth',[42] because physical beauty may at least shadow forth the beauty of the soul. This spendidly impossible view was influential, but in Italian writing it could not long remain undiluted or uncontradicted. Petrarchans, whose idealising manner predisposed them to the sublimated love which the neoplatonists described, yet commonly admitted that in love 'one does not love the soul alone', though they might save their allegiance with a due qualification, 'but principally; and more the soul than the body'.[43] Torquato Tasso himself maintained as a youth the vanity of the opinion that a man might love the soul, or virtue, alone; and in sober age he tempered this view only so far as to allow that if bodily intercourse is not actually necessary to the mingling of souls, then at least it may be desired as an accessory and sign of that union.[44]

There was authority as considerable as Ficino's for quite another view than his. Leone Ebreo owed more to a tradition that took in Ibn Hazm than to celibate schoolmen, or courtly decorum; and he had provided an account of love which satisfied less rarefied demands. While he does not concede that physical union might ever be the end of right love, he emphasises that it is for a number of reasons to be sought. Amorous acts bind the knot faster. They are signs that the love is truly mutual. They allow the fulfilment of the union, which is not complete with the fusion of souls but requires the coupling of bodies 'to the end that no diversity may remain'. Above all, the spiritual condition itself lacks something until the bodies are united, for

with the correspondence of the bodily union, the spiritual love is augmented and made more perfect, just as the understanding of prudence is perfected when it is answered with due works.[45]

This was not the first time that the physical coupling of bodies had been recognised as a means to a higher union. The great Bembo himself, as Castiglione represented him, had remarked that a kiss has power to draw forth souls by the lips, and in chaste love, to join them.[46] Yet public attitudes have altered when the best respected of all contemporary authorities on love justifies lovers whose 'every love is desire, and every desire is love'[47] with an account of the body's part which holds good for the common state of secular love. Ficino had seemed to find no connection between love and the procreation of kind, and looked on human affections as a means of attaining mystical states. If later writers had followed him they would never have thought of praising love for its work in drawing men to temperate coitus, as even Betussi did,[48] or of adding with Equicola that abstention from coitus is actually bad for men, and still worse for women.[49] Leone's argument gained more than the ballast of a little practical sense. Writers who followed him were deliberately rejecting Ficino when they proclaimed that a lover who seeks spiritual union will desire the union of bodies as well, so that he may 'make himself, to the limit of his power, one selfsame thing with the beloved'.[50] Aristotle now supplanted Plotinus as the philosopher in vogue. It would become a reproof of Leone himself that he 'said many things which were not peripatetic'.[51]

Aristoteleans soon drew out the effect of Leone's naturalism and taught as a matter of course that souls cannot love perfectly unless the bodies also couple in love. Equicola found the entire philosophy of 'that prince of philosophers Aristotle' in the presumption that the man is soul and body together; from which he concludes that the actions of soul and body are indivisible in love as in all else. To love truly is of necessity to love the whole being, for 'Love is of soul and body, and the operations of the soul depend upon the body.' It follows that 'the one ministers to the other in voluptuousness, and to delight the one without the other is impossible'.[52] Such a view was bound to recommend itself beyond the debating halls of Padua and Ferrara. Nothing better shows the syncretism of later writers than that a Florentine platonist should commend bodily union before his own *Accademia* in expounding Petrarch, though without altogether denying his birthright. Varchi's refined analysis of the several kinds of love permits him to declare that it is just the human sort, 'when some man loves some woman again in good love', which may not be perfected unless the union is total and entire, 'that is, if as one first conjoins the souls, one does not conjoin the bodies also'. Yet his reason for this argument scarcely admits practical distinction. It is that body and soul are so united while we live that no entity may be more one.[53]

When Speroni takes up the figure of the stairs he uses it to confute the spurners of the body. He allows that our senses provide us with a 'star and path' to the reason, but insists that all the senses benefit us so and not just sight and hearing. Moreover, sense is a step that you have to take every time you wish to fulfil intelligence:

> Whoever is such a fool in love that he has no care of his appetite, but as simple disembodied intelligence seeks solely to satisfy his mind, can be compared to him who, gulping his food without touching it or masticating it, more harms than nourishes himself.

Human beings in love are 'centaurs' in whom reason and desire are inextricably mixed.[54] Love's hermaphrodite, that ultimate perfection of human lovers, will not be made with souls, or minds, alone.

Ebreo decisively revised the Florentine metaphysics of love in another respect which is scarcely less striking. For him a onesided passion merits some other name than love; and the mutual love between man and wife is nothing less than a pattern of universal love, a copy of the 'sacred and divine marriage of the supremely beautiful with the highest beauty, from which the entire universe takes its origin'.[55] Such love requires embodiment. As spiritual intelligences love and move their spheres in order that God's universal design may be realised, so the spiritual intelligence of man unites with the frail human body so as 'to execute the divine plan for the coherence and unity of the entire universe'. The love for one another which embodied intelligences enact binds the universe in one and earns divine love and grace, even furthering our union with God. The love which moves the sun and the other stars is no other than that active affection and union which mutual lovers propose for their desired bliss, and ultimate end.

iii. *No man is a contradiction:* Donne on self-slaughter

There can be no doubt of the pertinacity of Donne's poetic searching of the relation of body to spirit in love. We do not know when he wrote 'The Ecstasy', or what personal circumstances may have prompted 'Air and Angels', 'Love's Progress', and 'A Valediction:

forbidding Mourning'. But he plays tellingly upon 'the soul's, and body's knot' in the *Metempsychosis*, 1601;

> Another part became the well of sense,
> The tender well-armed feeling brain, from whence,
> Those sinewy strings which do our bodies tie,
> Are ravelled out, and fast there by one end,
> Did this soul limbs, these limbs a soul attend,
> And now they joined.

lines 501–6

Then the notorious shaping hyperbole of *The First Anniversary* works precisely to demonstrate that a contraction of bodily powers is a spiritual diminution:

> we'are not retired, but damped;
> And as our bodies, so our minds are cramped:
> 'Tis shrinking, not close weaving that hath thus,
> In mind and body both bedwarfed us.

151–4

The best known conceit in *The Second Anniversary* celebrates a state of innocent purity in which sense and spirit work as one:

> her pure and eloquent blood
> Spoke in her cheeks, and so distinctly wrought,
> That one might almost say, her body thought.

244–6

In the prose writings a reader must be struck by the way Donne will come back to the liaison between soul and body at the critical point of an argument. It seems that some of his most characteristic thinking about differences of doctrine, and the nature of a Church, grows out of a particular conception of the working of the human constitution:

All our growth and vegetation flowes from our head, Christ. And ... he hath chosen to himselfe for the perfection of his body, limmes proportionall thereunto, and ... as a soule through all the body, so this care must live, and dwell in every part, that it be ever ready to doe his proper function, and also to succour those other parts, for whose reliefe or sustentation it is framed, and planted in the body.

Biathanatos, 1648, p. 179.

Love is indivisible when it starts in a due regard for the integrity of human nature itself. An undue contempt for the life of the body in the world may have dangerous, even monstrous consequences. This is the drift of *Biathanatos* and *Pseudo-Martyr*, two polemical tracts which were probably written quite close together in 1608–9. These occasional essays have been reputed outrageous, or taken for documents in neurosis. Attentively read, they smack more of paradox than self-hatred. *Biathanatos* comes before us as a professed paradox (*1648* titlepage, and p. 217) in that serio-satiric mode which Helen Peters's edition of the *Paradoxes and Problems* has helped us to understand, whose effect is a calculated provocation of waters long grown stagnant. Yet this treatise puts a good case, even a just one, which is argued in a manner that impresses by its reasonableness and shrewd commonsense. Donne's sceptical appraisal of the world shows up strikingly in his way of playing off conflicting imperatives so that little more remains to justify them than some common human impulse, and in the balance he discovers between the good and ill consequences of any action, as if our judgment of events in time may have relative validity at best. What he expressly does not attempt is a general defence of suicide, and we quite reverse his drift if we attribute that intention to him. He is at pains to limit strictly the circumstances in which a man may be justified in seeking his own death, as it were allowing that the case for self-slaughter has just so much reason in it; and he links this argument closely with the reasoning advanced in *Pseudo-Martyr* against the pursuit of martyrdom for its own sake.

In *Biathanatos* Donne proposes no more than that it may sometimes be licit, in certain situations, to prefer death to life. He has in view only those occasions when a man must choose between ease in the world and the possibility of eternal life; and he is no less precise in his positive aim of re-encouraging men to a just contempt of this life, and restoring them to their natural state, 'which is a desire of supreame happiness in the next life by the loss of this' (*Biathanatos*, p. 216). Samson brought about his own destruction not principally, as an end in itself, but accidentally in the accomplishment of a greater purpose. St Paul himself welcomed death just so that he might be with Christ, as Calvin allowed:

this may be done onely when the honour of God may be promoted by that way, and no other.

Biathanatos, p. 200.

The muster of powerful examples serves to remind us that Christians have always proved themselves by their willingness to put another end before mere survival and well-being in the world. Circumstances will recur in which a man better testifies to God's glory, and ensures eternal life, by inviting his own death or even killing himself. Donne professes to seek no more than the confirmation of a Christian truism which has dropped out of common reckoning when he persuades us that we should think more favourably of gaining eternal life than of losing this life. But he characteristically tries out this proposal where it will most disturb our settled preconceptions, in the tricky case of people who have deliberately brought on their own death in God's cause.

It is fundamental to Donne's general design that the case for self-destruction has force while it is limited to the martyrs who chose to die rather than deny Christ. So much must be allowed in justice to people who claim the right to pawn their own lives in a cause. Yet no such dire alternative confronts the recusants and Jesuits who now court martyrdom by refusing to subscribe to an Oath of Allegiance. They are required to deny no more than the right of the Pope to depose their lawful king. Donne concedes as much as he does so that he may deny the more categorically all that falls beyond the limit he sets. In a Christian state a man may not justly claim the right to flout the law in the name of an alien Church. His allegiance to a spiritual authority cannot override his obligation to obey the civil power.

The Jesuitical absoluteness which provoked both these tracts is undermined by Donne's very conduct of a legal discussion, in which instances are played off one against another in tacit witness that man's moral stances must be judged in relation to their circumstances. Donne puts two substantive reasons why a spiritual authority may not license its adherents to set themselves beyond the just laws of a Christian country. His essential objection to a spiritual absolutism is that no single human institution has a monopoly of truth. He proposes quite the contrary understanding, that however the sects may vary in the corruptness of their doctrines yet they are all parcels of the universal Church which we shall make up hereafter, if only hereafter; and 'as long as they goe towards peace, that is Truth, it is no matter which way' (*Biathanatos*, p. 20).

let us follow the truth in love, and in all things grow up into him, which is the head, that is Christ, till we are all met together, unto a perfect man. By which we receive the honour to be one body with Christ our head.

Biathanatos, pp. 178–9

Polemic passes into principle, and we recognise Donne's larger engagement with this bitter issue of the day. It is much more than a debating point with him that although human institutions have but

relative worth at best, they may nonetheless embody a vital part of
the whole truth, as it were accommodating to the relative capacities
of their charges such spiritual stock as they conserve:

[It is a] sound true opinion, that in all Christian professions there is way to
salvation ... As some bodies are as wholesomly nourished as ours, with Akornes,
and endure nakedness, both which would be dangerous to us, if we for them
should leave our former habits, though theirs were the Primitive diet and
custome; so are many souls well fed with such formes, and dressings of Religion,
as would distemper and misbecome us, and make us corrupt towards God, if any
humane circumstance moved it, and in the opinion of men, though none. You
shall seldome see a Coyne, upon which the stamp were removed, though to
imprint it better, but it looks awry and squint. And so, for the most part, do
mindes which have received divers impressions. I will not, nor need to you,
compare the Religions. The channels of Gods mercies run through both fields;
and they are sister teats of his graces, yet both diseased and infected, but not both
alike.

Letter to Goodyer, ? April 1615[56]

Donne's second argument against the Roman usurpation of
spiritual sovereignty takes him still more deeply into the make-up of
our nature. His specific counter to the case for the subversive
'Missions of the Pope' is that the separation of authority into secular
power and spiritual power is invalid in itself. In a just common
wealth the civil and the spiritual authorities may not be separated
though they ought to be distinct, for they take several ways to one
and the same end, which is fully realised only when the law of the
land follows out the law of God. The oneness of State and Church is
assured when the authority of both institutions is vested in the same
sacred office, and the conduct of policy takes a spiritual direction, for
'no man can rightly governe earthly matters, except he know also
how to handle Divine' (*Pseudo-Martyr*, 1610, p. 20). Such a fusion of
the offices of priest and king supposes the close interworking of the
spiritual and secular powers; and this mutual support of distinct
elements is argued directly from the right functioning of the human
constitution, in which body and spirit work not as incompatible
entities but as complementary parts of one whole nature:

It is intire man that God hath care of, and not the soule alone; therefore his first
worke was the body, and the last work shall bee the glorification thereof. He hath
not delivered us over to a Prince onely, as to a Physitian, and to a Lawyer, to looke
to our bodies and estates; and to the Priest onely, as to a Confessor, to looke to,
and examine our soules, but the Priest must aswel endevour, that we live vertu-
ously and innocently in this life for society here; as the Prince, by his lawes keepes
us in the way to heaven: for thus they accomplish a Regale Sacerdotium, when

No man is a contradiction

both do both; for we are sheepe to them both, and they in divers relations sheepe to one another.

Pseudo-Martyr, p. 17

The idea that our own nature proves the interfusion of temporal and eternal being controls the argument of *Pseudo-Martyr*, and gives the tract an interest which Donne's best champions have not always allowed.[57] In *Pseudo-Martyr* Donne singles out for reprehension as a dangerous error the 'usurped and detorted' use of 'the Comparisons of *Soule* and *Body*, and of *Golde* and *Leade*' (p. 20). He determinedly refers erroneous versions of authority to the false assumption that body and spirit are separate or even contradictory entities (p. 20).

The much noted uses of his own disposition in both *Biathanatos* and *Pseudo-Martyr* are carefully placed at the outset of the argument, where they may draw a reader into a sympathetic complicity with a man's wish to end his sufferings, while showing him the bars to his attempting it:

I have often such a sickely inclination. And, whether it be, because I had my first breeding and conversation with men of a suppressed and afflicted Religion, accustomed to the despite of death, and hungry of an imagin'd Martyrdome; Or that the common Enemie find that doore worst locked against him in mee; Or that there bee a perplexitie and flexibility in the doctrine it selfe; Or because my Conscience ever assures me, that no rebellious grudging at Gods gifts, nor other sinfull concurrence accompanies these thoughts in me, or that a brave scorn, or that a faint cowardlinesse beget it, whensoever any affliction assailes me, mee thinks I have the keyes of my prison in mine owne hand, and no remedy presents it selfe so soone to my heart, as mine own sword. Often Meditation of this hath wonne me to a charitable interpretation of their action, who dy so: and provoked me a little to watch and exagitate their reasons, which pronounce so peremptory judgements upon them.

Biathanatos, Preface, pp. 17–18

In allowing just so much substance in his adversaries' case Donne intimates that the slight human urge has been petrified into an inhuman principle. We need not doubt that his testimony is authentic; yet it does clear the ground for an impartially reasoned discrimination between true martyrdom and false:

And for my selfe ... I most humbly beseech him ... to beleeve, that I have a just and Christianly estimation, and reverence, of that devout and acceptable Sacrifice of our lifes, for the glory of our blessed Saviour. For, as my fortune hath never beene so flattering nor abundant, as should make this present life sweet and precious to me, as I am a Moral man: so, as I am a Christian, I have beene ever kept awake in a meditation of Martyrdome, by being derived from such a stocke and race, as I beleeve, no family (which is not of farre larger extent, and greater branches,)

209

hath endured and suffered more in their persons and fortunes, for obeying the Teachers of Romane Doctrine, then it hath done. I did not therefore enter into this, as a carnall or over-indulgènt favourer of this life, but out of such reasons, as may arise to his knowledge, who shall be pleased to read the whole worke.

Pseudo-Martyr, An Advertisement to the
Reader, A5^{r–v}

The circumstance he brings home to a just reader from the first is that his family tradition and history, and his own upbringing, would point him to an opposite belief from his present conviction. We understand him to take his position now by his own reason, in judicious disregard of these strong ties of sympathy. Still, such moments of personal candour are undoubtedly more than a polemical manoeuvre. We are invited to see in them a deliberate, and even agonising refusal to submit his reason to family loyalties and the constraints of his nurture. This Advertisement intimates that the argument which follows it judiciously reasons out an Anglican ecumenism, and justifies a wise election of it.

There is no doubt that Donne's intricate management of his intellectual middle course opens him to misunderstanding. He is particularly subtle in his way of sifting from opposite extremes what seems reasonable in them, as if to show that opinions turn vicious just at the point where they become prescriptive, and take on an absoluteness which is alien to our condition. Much of what has been taken for his residual Romanism, as by Mrs Simpson in her edition of *The Courtier's Library* (1930, pp. 12–21), is really no more than a confirmed refusal to allow even his own Church's title to a corner in the truth:

> To adore, or scorn an image, or protest
> May all be bad; doubt wisely.

Satire 3, 76–7

No less than the *Satires, Pseudo-Martyr* and *Biathanatos* express Donne's enduring abhorrence of power gained by the pretence to a unique possession of the saving truth:

> So perish souls, which more choose men's unjust
> Power from God claimed, than God himself to trust.

Satire 3, 109–10

Yet Donne's Christian scepticism is always humanely grounded, and positive in its scope. His readiness to find truth in the teachings of all the Christian sects, more corrupted or less but never whole in itself, follows out his profound conviction that the sectaries and non-sectaries alike have a place in Christ's Church:

> Sir, not only a mathematic point, which is the most indivisible and unique thing which art can present, flows into every line which is derived from the centre, but our soul which is but one, hath swallowed up a negative and feeling soul, which was in the body before it came, and exercises those faculties yet; and God Himself, who only is One, seems to have been eternally delighted with a disunion of persons. They whose active function it is, must endeavour this unity in religion; and we at our lay altars (which are our tables, or bedside, or stools, wheresoever we dare prostrate ourselves to God in prayer) must beg it of Him; but we must take heed of making misconclusions upon the want of it; for, whether the mayor and aldermen fall out (as with us and the Puritans; bishops against priests) or the commoners' voices differ who is mayor and who aldermen, or what their jurisdiction (as with the Bishop of Rome, or whosoever), yet it is still one corporation.
>
> Letter to Goodyer, c. 1609[58]

The argument from the oneness of the human constitution carries him further, to the oneness of human kind:

> as we are all sheep of one fold, so in many cases, we are all shepherds of one another, and owe one another this dutie, of giving our temporall lives, for anothers spirituall advantage; yea, for his temporall.
>
> *Biathanatos*, p. 186

We must take it for more than political opportunism when we find him defining the Church itself as a spiritual direction of the just common wealth, even a common wealth of savages. In *Pseudo-Martyr*, in 1609, he may well have had the American Indians in mind when he spoke of the civilising power which their own humanity must have upon 'a companie of Savages', if only that company might be brought to consent and concur to a civil manner of living, and so produce magistracy and superiority:

> So also, if this Companie, thus growen to a *Common-wealth*, should receive further light, and passe, through understanding the Law written in all hearts, and in the Booke of creatures, and by relation of some instructers, arrive to a saving knowledge, and Faith in our blessed Saviours Passion, they should also bee a *Church*, and amongst themselves would arise up, lawfull Ministers for Ecclesiastique function, though not derived from any other mother Church, and though different from all the divers Hierarchies established in other Churches: and in this State, both Authorities might bee truely said to bee from God.
>
> *Pseudo-Martyr*, pp. 83–4

Donne's resonant proclamation that our common human nature inescapably involves us one with another is well enough known:

> The church is *Catholike, universall*, so are all her *Actions*; All that she does, belongs to *all*. When she *baptizes a child*, that concernes mee; for that child is thereby connected to that *Head* which is my *Head* too, and engraffed into that *body*, whereof I

am a *member*. And when she *buries* a *Man*, that action concernes mee; All *mankinde* is of one *Author*, and is one *volume* ... who bends not his *eare* to any *bell*, which upon any occasion rings? but who can remove it from that bell, which is passing a *peece of himselfe* out of this *world*? No Man is an *Iland*, intire of it selfe; every man is a peece of the *Continent*, a part of the *maine*; if a *Clod* bee washed away by the *Sea*, *Europe* is the lesse, as well as if a *Promontorie* were, as well as if a *Mannor* or thy *friends*, or *thine owne* were; Any Mans *death* diminishes *me*, because I am involved in Mankind.

Devotions Upon Emergent Occasions[59]

His resoluteness in carrying this powerful vision through may be less well appreciated:

we are debters to all, because all are our Neighbours. *Proximus tuus est antequam Christianus est*: A man is thy Neighbour, by his Humanity, not by his Divinity; by his Nature, not by his Religion: a Virginian is thy Neighbour, as well as a Londoner; and all men are in every good mans Diocess, and Parish. *Irrides adorantem lapides*, says that Father; Thou seest a man worship an Image, and thou laughest him to scorn; assist him, direct him if thou canst, but scorn him not.

Sermons, IV, 3, p. 110 (Easter Monday 1622)

'A Virginian is thy Neighbour, as well as a Londoner'. Moelwyn Merchant has well shown us how steadfastly Donne's persuasion that the primitive Virginian natives are also part of humanity stood up to the news of the massacre in the settlement only weeks after he delivered that sermon.[60] When Donne preached at a banquet of the Virginia Company itself later in the year he simply disregarded the clamour for the Indians to be put down like beasts, and urged our duty to our fellow men in whatever condition we find them. He spoke with an impassioned eloquence which does justice to the largeness of his vision:

Before the ende of the worlde come, before this mortality shall put on immortalitie, before the Creature shall be delivered of the bondage of corruption under which it groanes, before the Martyrs under the Altar shalbe silenc'd, before all things shal be subdued to Christ, his kingdome perfited, and the last Enemy Death destroied, the Gospell must be preached to those men to whom ye send; to all men.

Sermons, IV, 10, p. 280 (13 November 1622)

We must carry to the Indians as to our immediate fellow-citizens such love, truth, civility, justice as we possess because we thereby further and hasten 'this blessed, this joyfull, this glorious consummation of all, and happie reunion of all bodies to their Soules'. No man is an island, or a contradiction of his own humanity. We are no more pure spirits in contempt of our bodies than we may arrogate the truth to ourselves, or deny our commitment to our kind – 'to all men'. In furthering a happy reunion of all bodies to their souls we hasten the consummation of love.

iv. *The subtle knot:* Donne's testament of human nature

Donne's intellectual attitudes are not subject to the reversals of his career. The understanding of love which he opened in 'The Ecstasy' needed no drastic renunciation when he took holy orders. On the contrary, a series of sermons which span his preaching ministry, many of them delivered on Easter Day, affirm the mutual dependence of soul and body as it is assured by Christ's taking flesh for pure love, and by the indivisibility of the human and the divine elements in Christ's own manhood. In this conviction Donne never wavered. It affords him his counterthrust against death and dissolution, as if he proves the scope of providential love in his own awareness of the inseparable interworking of mind and senses:

Never therefore dispute against thine own happiness; never say, God asks the heart, that is, the soule, and therefore rewards the soule, or punishes the soule, and hath no respect to the body ... Never go about to separate the thoughts of the heart, from the colledge, from the fellowship of the body ... All that the soule does, it does in, and with, and by the body ... The body is washed in baptisme, but it is that the soule might be made cleane ... In all unctions, whether that which was then in use in Baptisme, or that which was in use at our transmigration, and passage out of this world, the body was anointed, that the soule might be consecrated ... The body is signed with the Crosse, that the soule might be armed against tentations ... My body received the body of Christ, that my soule might partake of his merits ... These two, Body, and Soule, cannot be separated for ever, which, whilst they are together, concurre in all that either of them doe. Never thinke it presumption ... To hope for that in thy selfe, which God admitted, when he tooke thy nature upon him. And God hath made it ... more easie then so, for thee, to beleeve it, because not onely did Christ himselfe, but such men, as thou art, did rise at the Resurrection of Christ. And therefore when our bodies are dissolved and liquefied in the Sea, putrified in the earth, resolv'd to ashes in the fire, macerated in the ayre ... make account that all the world is Gods cabinet, and water, and earth, and fire, and ayre, are the proper boxes, in which God laies up our bodies, for the Resurrection.

Sermons, IV, 14, pp. 358–9 (Easter Day 1623)

The ideas which Donne so sublimely draws together just at the mid-point of his ministry shape his contemplation of mortality from the first extant sermons to *Deaths Duell* itself. He is far from the mortifier of rebellious flesh we are too quick to see in the selected highlights. His prepossession with death might be better explained as a horror like Adam's when he contemplates the ruin of so noble a work as mankind:

> But have I now seen death? Is this the way
> I must return to native dust? O sight
> Of terror, foul and ugly to behold,
> Horrid to think, how horrible to feel!
>
> *Paradise Lost* xi, 462–5

Donne's return upon the prospect of inevitable wreck always fulfils an impassioned urge to outbrave, even transform into glory, the worst that our mortality may inflict upon us. We must put him with Shakespeare and Milton in that high estimation of the body which distinguishes the seventeenth-century English writers from ascetics and idealists alike:

That this clod of earth, this body of ours should be carried up to the highest heaven, placed in the eye of God, sat down at the right hand of God, *Miramini hoc*, wonder at this; That God, all Spirit, served with Spirits, associated to Spirits, should have such an affection, such a love to this body, this earthly body, this deserves this wonder. The Father was pleased to breathe into this body, at first, in the Creation; the Son was pleased to assume this body himself, after, in the Redemption; The Holy Ghost is pleased to consecrate this body, and make it his Temple, by his sanctification; In that *Faciamus hominem*, Let us, all us, make man, that consultation of the whole Trinity in making man, is exercised even upon the lower part of man, the dignifying of his body.

Sermons, VI, 13, pp. 265–6 (Easter Day 1625)

Such an appraisal of our nature is precisely grounded. Donne justifies human worth, and the dignity of the body itself, in the coupling of body and soul which makes us man, and the mingling of physical and spiritual elements in our make-up:

In the constitution and making of a natural man, the body is not the man, nor the soul is not the man, but the union of these two makes up the man; the spirits in a man which are the thin and active part of the blood, and so are of a kind of middle nature, between soul and body, those spirits are able to doe, and they doe the office, to unite and apply the faculties of the soul to the organs of the body, and so there is a man: so in a regenerate man, a Christian man, his being born of Christian Parents, that gives him a body, that makes him of the body of the Covenant ... and then in his baptism, that Sacrament gives him a soul, a spiritual soul, *jus in re*, an actual possession of Grace; but yet, as there are spirits in us, which unite body and soul, so there must be subsequent acts, and works of the blessed spirit, that must unite and confirm all, and make up this spiritual man in the way of sanctification; for without that his body, that is, his being born within the Covenant, and his soul, that is, his having received Grace in baptism, do not make him up.

Sermons, II, 12, pp. 261–2 (preached at Heidelberg on 16 June 1619)[61]

Christ himself offers final confirmation that our nature is essentially mixed, and needs the effective union of soul and body, for he shared our manhood just so long as he united body and spirit, human element and divine. When Christ lay in the grave he relinquished his humanity, though his godhead never left him, because 'the Humane soule was departed' from 'the Carcasse':

But yet for al this powerful *embalming*, this *hypostaticall union* of both natures, we see *Christ* did *dye*; and for all this *union* which made him *God* and *Man*, hee became no man (for the *union* of the *body* and *soule* makes the man, and hee whose soule and body are separated by death, (as long as that state lasts) is properly no man).

> *Sermons*, x, 11 (*Deaths Duell*), p. 237
> (preached 25 February 1631)[62]

Christ's mixed nature effectively seals the marriage of our flesh to divine being and unites 'heaven, and earth, Jerusalem and Babylon together':[63]

As our flesh is in him, by his participation thereof, so his flesh is in us, by our communication thereof; and so is his divinity in us, by making us partakers of his divine nature, and by making us one spirit with himself . . . for this is an union, in which Christ in his purpose hath married himself to our souls, inseparably, and *Sine solutione vinculi*, Without any intention of divorce on his part.

> *Sermons*, IX, 10, p. 248 (preached on
> Whitsunday ?1630)

Eternal being perpetually interpenetrates the world of sense, as in a union of love, countervailing change and death:

In this kisse, where *Righteousness and peace have kissed each other*, In this person, where the Divine and the humane nature have kissed each other, In this Christian Church, where Grace and Sacraments, visible and invisible meanes of salvation, have kissed each other, *Love is as strong as death*; my soul is united to my Saviour, now in my life, as in death, and I am already made *one spirit with him*: and whatsoever death can doe, this kisse, this union can doe, that is, give me a present, an immediate possession of the kingdome of heaven.

> *Sermons*, III, 15, pp. 320–1 (?Trinity Term 1621).

The dignifying of our flesh by its union with spirit in Christ vouchsafes a glorious resurrection of the body itself, which shall repair 'in an inseparable re-union'[64] the divorce between body and soul made by sin:

such a gladnesse shall my soul have, that this flesh, (which she will no longer call her prison, nor her tempter, but her friend, her companion, her wife) that this flesh, that is, I, in the re-union, and redintegration of both parts, shall see God; for then, one principall clause in her rejoycing, and acclamation, shall be, that this flesh is her flesh; *In carne meâ, in my flesh I shall see God* ... As my meat is assimilated to my flesh, and made one flesh with it; as my soul is assimilated to my God, and *made partaker of the divine nature*, and *Idem Spiritus*, the same Spirit with it; so, there my flesh shall be assimilated to the flesh of my Saviour, and made the same flesh with him too. *Verbum caro factum, ut caro resurgeret*; Therefore the Word was made flesh, therefore God was made man, that that union might exalt the flesh of man to the right hand of God ... when *after my skinne worms shall destroy my body, I shall see God*, I shall see him in my flesh, which shall be mine as inseparably, (in the *effect*, though not in the *manner*) as the *Hypostaticall union* of God, and man, in Christ, makes our nature and the Godhead one person in him. My flesh shall be no more of mine, then Christ shall not be man, as well as God.

Sermons, III, 3, pp. 112–13 (preached in the
Easter Term 1620)

In the grave God transforms 'a piece of Copper money' into 'a Talent of Gold' and fits it for eternal life, which was always the true destiny of the body.[65] Even our final beatitude will not be complete until both parts of our nature are reunited, for the soul itself 'is not perfectly well, not fully satisfied, till it be reunited to that body againe'.[66] At that 'redintegration', which is also 'an indissoluble marriage to him, who, for the salvation of both, assumed both',[67] we shall know a bliss of body and soul together such as the angels themselves cannot share. As God married body and soul together in the Creation, so he 'shall at last crowne thy body and soule together in the Resurrection':[68]

The Angels shall feed and rejoyce at my resurrection, when they shall see me in my soul, to have all that they have, and in my body, to have that that they have not.

Sermons, V, 11, p. 230 (undated)

When Donne so insists upon the effective integrity of sense and spirit even in fallen human nature, his imperative care is to justify the resurrection of the whole being. Yet he also puts at issue the final value of our experience in this temporal world. His formal concern is the nature of a sacrament.

Flux and stability make the opposing terms of Donne's poetic self-debate from the first. 'Good Friday 1613. Riding Westward' is our evidence that before he took orders Donne had reached his own understanding of the consequence of events in the world:

> Let man's soul be a sphere, and then, in this,
> The intelligence that moves, devotion is,

216

And as the other spheres, by being grown
Subject to foreign motions, lose their own,
And being by others hurried every day,
Scarce in a year their natural form obey:
Pleasure or business, so, our souls admit
For their first mover, and are whirled by it.
Hence is't, that I am carried towards the west
This day, when my soul's form bends towards the east.
There I should see a sun, by rising set,
And by that setting endless day beget . . .
Could I behold those hands which span the poles,
And turn all spheres at once, pierced with those holes?
Could I behold that endless height which is
Zenith to us, and to'our antipodes,
Humbled below us?

A casual journey westward from Polesworth to Montgomery over
Easter 1613 substantiates eternal truth. Donne's pursuit of his
sociable pleasures at such a time confirms a general aberration of
fallen nature, yet nonetheless discovers to the mind the event
which fuses the momentary with the final order and fulfils God's
loving providence in the contingents of the world. We must take
the poem for the attempt itself to see the world in that radical
way, to discover absolute being in the circumstances of time and
sense.

For Donne such attempts become a discovery of providential
design in the very casualties of the body:

I joy, that in these straits, I see my west;
For, though their currents yield return to none,
What shall my west hurt me? As west and east
In all flat maps (and I am one) are one,
So death doth touch the resurrection . . .

We think that Paradise and Calvary
Christ's Cross, and Adam's tree, stood in one place;
Look Lord, and find both Adams met in me;
As the first Adam's sweat surrounds my face,
May the last Adam's blood my soul embrace.

So, in his purple wrapped receive me Lord,
By these his thorns give me his other crown;
And as to others' souls I preached thy word,
Be this my text, my sermon to mine own,
Therefore that he may raise the Lord throws down.

'A Hymn to God my God, in my Sickness'

The bold yoking of terms so seemingly unlike invites us to take the straits of mortal illness for a passage to bliss. In the sweat, pangs, flush of the fever he endures for himself the blood and thorns which pledge Christ's loving dominion over the random decays of the world, and promise a glorious resurrection. The real presence of Christ does not wait upon the bread and wine at the High Altar. It manifests itself in the fabric of daily events themselves, as if the life of the senses sacramentally realises pure spiritual love.

The transformation of fortuity into timelessness is most forcibly enacted where we should least expect to find it, in Stone's marble effigy of Donne's enshrouded body in St Paul's. This extraordinary revision of the Droeshout engraving which shows Donne's corpse decaying in its winding-sheet invites us to set against that flat map of death a reconstituted figure, who soars up from the urn in restored flesh and trim. The body is sleep-enshrouded still, and has not even drawn itself fully erect; moreover it pointedly renews Donne's lineaments, in nice contrast with those idealised torsos which burst from the tomb of self in Michelangelo's versions of resurrection.[69] It seems that the effigy presents Donne's body in its interim state, when it has been restored from dust though not yet reanimated in a final union with its soul; and we would expect to find it placed as Donne posed for it early in Lent 1631, 'purposely turned towards the East, from whence he expected the second coming of his and our Saviour'.[70] The body's form itself now 'bends towards the east', anticipating that ultimate Easter Day which will annul time and seal an eternal union of humanity and godhead. *Hic Licet In Occiduo Cinere Aspicit Eum Cuius Nome Est Oriens.* The funeral epitaph Donne devised for himself succinctly points the conjunction of meanings which make up one truth. Nigel Foxell aptly remarks that in the ultimate stroke of wit which his marble effigy enacts Donne 'charged the Now and the Here of a single statement with maximum meaning'.[71]

Such conceits draw their power if not their oddity from a peculiarly intimate apprehension of the bond between sense and spirit. Donne's direct self-embodiment of spiritual truth makes a startling contrast with the traditional understanding of a spiritual epiphany, based in Plato and Augustine, such as Caxton follows when he takes the dew and manna from heaven for a shadowy figure of the Atonement, and of the sacrament of the Mass:

That other was gyven to them in a shadowe and ombre but this was gyven in
trouthe now ye shal understonde this that was in ye shadow ... [He glosses the
scriptural anecdote]. All tho thynges ther wer don in figure/for to give know-
leche of thynges more grete and more notable/. It is moche gretter thyng of
the lyght/than of the shadow/semblably of verite/than it is of fygure.

The Golden Legend, 1483, f. xxxii^v

'And the Word was made flesh, and dwelt among us.' The Word
beyond a word gives us quite a different picture of the world from
the Word within a word. 'Wee all know, what differences have been
raysed in the *Church*, in that one poynt of the Sacrament, by these
three Prepositions, *Trans, Con,* and *Sub*' (Donne, *Sermons*, VI, 12, p.
247, 3 April 1625). After the arguments about the Real Presence
from Luther to the Council of Trent we find some of the subtlest
intelligences in England turning from barren controversy to make a
sacrament of everyday life. Yet they had their English pedigree. By
whatever ironic accord they followed out the vision of a Catholic
martyr who happened to be Donne's own forebear. Sir Thomas
More's view of the Church, as R. C. Marius summarises it, quite
strikingly anticipates the Anglican thinking which struggled to
define itself at the Hampton Court Conference in 1604:

it is the nature of the sacramental idea itself which is most germane to his doctrine
of the church. A sacrament is both physical and spiritual; it possesses at once both
a visible and a secret quality. A sacrament comes into being when the Word of
God is joined to the physical elements ... Just how this transfer of spiritual grace
is effected by physical means remains a mystery. It is the same sort of mystery that
we encounter in the union of body and soul or in the way physical fire can torment
the spiritual souls of the dead in purgatory or the damned in hell ... For More
God always chooses this mingling of the corporeal and the incorporeal as a means
of revealing Himself to man and granting grace. He probably would say to us that
man is a creature of soul and body and that God must work with us in a way which
is harmonious to our nature.[72]

This 'incarnational theology' seems to have been 'the well-spring of
More's being', as it was of Donne's:

Unlike his polemical opponents – Tyndale especially – More could never reject
the material world as merely physical. He believed, fundamentally, in the unity of
body and soul. He saw man as a complex entity in whom, ultimately, body and
soul must work together. The spiritual life should be mixed with the public life.
Each drew strength from the other and man's proper condition was the mingled
state, farious, multifarious, harmonious. The vision was not less than noble.[73]

'It is the very body of Cryste, wherewyth hys holy soule is
coupled, and hys almyghty godhed ioyned/from whych fro ye fyrst
assumpcyon therof it was never severyd'.[74] When Donne, Andrewes

219

and their successors wittily discover the ingenious working of providence in our most casual circumstances they bring home to the understanding not only a coherence in the creation, but the interfusion of matter with mind by which eternal love manifests itself in time. Their testimony that sense and intelligence interinanimate each other in a full human nature gives us reason to approve their unified sensibility, even if we have something other than Eliot's meaning in view.

4

Among the Wastes of Time:
seventeenth-century love poetry,
and the failure of love

We step and do not step into the same rivers; we are and are not.

Heraclitus of Ephesus, Fragment 81

Desire, and Love, are the same thing; save that by Desire, we alwayes signifie the Absence of the Object; by Love, most commonly the Presence of the same. So also by Aversion, we signifie the Absence; and by Hate, the Presence of the Object . . . And because the constitution of a mans Body, is in continuall mutation; it is impossible that all the same things should alwayes cause in him the same Appetites, and Aversions: much lesse can all men consent, in the Desire of almost any one and the same Object.

But whatsoever is the object of any mans Appetite or Desire; that is it, which he for his part calleth *Good*: And the object of his Hate, and Aversion, *Evill*; And of his Contempt, *Vile* and *Inconsiderable*. For these words of Good, Evill, and Contemptible, are ever used with relation to the person that useth them: There being nothing simply and absolutely so; nor any common Rule of Good and Evill, to be taken from the nature of the objects themselves; but from the Person of the man

Hobbes, Leviathan 1, 6

The love poetry written in England after Donne's death confirms the decadence of a long European tradition of lyric verse which did not outlast the seventeenth century. It is easy to picture the Caroline love poets cooing wittily round Court and Town while the serious issues of the day were contested elsewhere, whether in Westminster and the shires, or at Horton, Bemerton, and Little Gidding. Carew and Stanley may seem pitifully small fry as the heirs of Cavalcanti and Tasso, or as revellers in the wake of mighty causes. Yet this Stuart love poetry is not negligible. It has its own voice and character, and something quite distinctive to say; and its appraisal of love is shrewd enough to illustrate its times and a small area of general experience. No other European poets use their wit to pose the predicament of beings who see that their love is an appetite of nature, and yet yearn to find spiritual value in it.

By the 1640s European rhetoricians who had never heard of

Donne were analysing wit and classifying witty poetry.[1] A historian of ideas, had there been one, might have traced a long preoccupation with wit in the Italian Courts and Academies. Donne extended the scope of wit in a way which has no parallel outside Britain. An incidental interest of the British poets who wrote of love after 1633 is that they show us what he really stood for in his own time and place.

The mark of Caroline lyric poetry is its vividly articulated dramatic syntax:

> Go search the valleys; pluck up every rose,
> You'll find a scent, a blush of her in those;
> Fish, fish for pearl or coral, there you'll see
> How oriental all her colours be;
> Go, call the echoes to your aid, and cry
> Chloris! Chloris! for that's her name for whom I die.
>
> Anon., 'Tell me, you wandering spirits of the air'

The fluent immediacy with which the slight witty hyperbole is urged to excited life makes the rhetoric of Tudor song seem stately, as if earlier writers were more concerned to heighten the ceremonial blazon than to simulate impassioned thinking:

> Hark! did ye ever hear so sweet a singing?
> They sing young Love to waken.
> The nymphs unto the woods their Queen are bringing.
> There was a note well taken!
> O good! O most divinely dittied!
> A Queen and song most excellently fitted.
> I never saw a fairer,
> I never heard a rarer.
> Then sung the nymphs and shepherds of Diana:
> Long live fair Oriana.
>
> Thomas Hunt, 1601

Caroline love poetry does not move like this. Its particular impulse calls for subtlety in the formal management of quite complex syntactical units:

> What though I spend my hapless days
> In finding entertainments out,
> Careless of what I go about,
> Or seek my peace in skilful ways,
> Applying to my eyes new rays
> Of beauty, and another flame
> Unto my heart, my heart is still the same.
>
> Godolphin, 'To Chloris'

We feel the virtuosity of these taut dramatic modulations, which are yet so suavely subdued to the easy flow that gives the stanza the excitement of spontaneous self-discovery.

The unpredictable mental life of such writing as this shows us how far lyric poets have moved on from a rhetoric of celebration and lament. Donne and Jonson brought about a general advance in intellectual control, which even the poetic minnows display in their lucid exactness and restraint, and their resolved grasp of quite intricate ideas:

> Though poorer in desert I make
> My selfe whilst I admyre,
> The fuell which from hope I take
> I give to my desire.
>
> Godolphin, 'Song: Noe more unto my
> thoughts appeare'

Often a lyric civilly flaunts its lineage in nice metaphysical discriminations:

> Love, like that angel that shall call
> Our bodies from the silent grave,
> Unto one age doth raise us all,
> None too much, none too little, have;
> Nay, that the difference may be none,
> He makes two, not alike, but one.
>
> Cartwright, 'To Chloe, who wished herself
> young enough for me'

The ironic play of wit gives the best of these Caroline poets an intellectual vitality which is quite unlike the ingenious hyperbolising of a Serafino d'Aquila, or a Gongora, in the way it tempers ardour with intelligence. Their wit keeps them wary of the prescribed professions of love, so that passion is always guarded by an awareness of the frailty of our commitments and our lives:

> *Celia:* Then thus my willing armes I winde
>   About thee, and am so
> Thy pris'ner; for my selfe I bind,
>   Untill I let thee goe.
> *Cleon:* Happy that slave, whom the faire foe
>   Tyes in so soft a chaine.
> *Celia:* Farre happier I, but that I know
>   Thou wilt breake loose againe.
> *Cleon:* By thy immortall beauties never.
> *Celia:*   Fraile as thy love's thine oath.
> *Cleon:* Though beauties fade, my faith lasts ever.
> *Celia:*   Time will destroy them both.
>
> Carew, 'A Pastorall Dialogue'

The writing gets its life from the way it challenges the accepted categories of love, as well as love poetry. A quite minor poet, such as Stanley, persistently undercuts his own praises on precise philosophical grounds:

> Though when I lov'd thee thou wert fair,
>   Thou art no longer so;
> Those glories all the pride they wear
>   Unto opinion owe

'The Deposition'

The touch of a sceptical logic keeps poetic exuberance cool:

> Beauties, like stars, in borrow'd lustre shine;
> And 'twas my love that gave thee thine.

With quiet reasonableness the conceited argument turns back upon itself the old hyperbole that a woman is a star, proposing a more accurate relation between the terms of the comparison which draws the mind on to ponder the relativeness of beauty. There is a pungent economy of wit in the way a qualifying aside will transform the sense:

> The flames that dwelt within thine eye
> Do now, with mine, expire

The slight parenthesis demolishes the old troubadour account of the way love moves us, and gives poignancy to the lovers' assumption that their love is wholly relative to their state of desire. Stanley's diction frequently arrests us so, persuading us that a mind is coolly at work in the heat of the passion, and had better be attended to:

> Since by thy scorn thou dost restore
> The wealth my love bestow'd

That unexpected 'wealth' confirms the paradox, quietly suggesting a more basic sense in which a lover's desire lends his mistress her attractive power.

Stanley's poems move by a riddling logic, and with contentious independence. 'The Idolater' draws support from a familiar strictness when it proposes that the worship of a mistress is idolatry; but then it leaves this old bogy behind in favour of the subtler argument that the true idolatry is to worship disdain in the shrine of love, which is what a man does when he continues to love a woman who rejects him. The petrarchan manner is ironically assumed, for the poem mocks the familiar complaint against a mistress's

unkindness in a patronising display of solicitude, which shows the
lover his fate and warns him off it by dethroning the lady:

> Since thou (Love's votary before
> Whilst he was kind) dost him no more,
> But, in his shrine, Disdain adore,
> Nor will this fire (the gods prepare
> To punish scorn) that cruel Fair,
> (Though now from flames exempted) spare

Stanley's analytic manner may be cultivated, but it is not all sham.
His qualifications do sharpen the ironies, they have place in a structure of argument as well as witty spirit. The elaborate syntax controls a tense syllogistic movement, so delicately articulating the
stages of consecutive reasoning that the pattern of the stanza itself
points the wit.

The point of Stanley's logic is another matter. In this poem the
logical processes are always subordinate to the smooth resolution of
the syntax, which his elaborate discriminations do not threaten to
disturb. The wit may be sceptical but it scarcely makes Donne's
impact. It moves with elegant point and neat antithesis, and
Stanley's cavilling relativism does not finally challenge the conventions of love. Donne looks outward to the way people actually
behave, and his wit quite radically sifts the world about it; Stanley's
poem simply re-orders the conventions of a game of love, inviting us
to admire the neat dexterity of the performance.

Yet these Caroline love lyrics are more than mere jewels whose
beauty is sufficient to itself. They resonate with the impulses of an
imaginative engagement that goes beyond the play of conceit. A
simple setting from natural life will quite disturbingly involve the
senses in the spirit of the scene:

> The Lark now leaves his watry Nest
> And climbing, shakes his dewy Wings . . .
> Awake, awake, the Morn will never rise,
> Till she can dress her Beauty at your Eies.
>
> Davenant, 'Song'

Such devices persistently invite us to relate the promptings of desire
to the vitality and decay of nature. In Habington's 'To Roses in the
bosome of Castara' the lover supposes that his mistress's breasts are
a nunnery, in which the flowers she places between them are virgin
nuns, who will prosper there in saintly sweetness, exempt from the

world's contagion, until they at last fade into a hallowed demise and
find an appropriate monument in that marble place:

> In those white cloysters live secure
> From the rude blasts of wanton breath,
> Each houre more innocent and pure,
> Till you shall wither into death.

The slight conceited compliment, so delicately turned, plays out a
drama of innocence and corruption in which the lover's part is
uneasily ambiguous. Caught between desire and admiration, he
fosters the mortal contagion which rages everywhere in the world
while celebrating the one condition which can avert it. Her virgin
innocence is sacred to him because it sustains the natural life which
his own heat would blast; she hallows the flowers only while she
remains impervious to her lover's persuasions. The lover's dilemma
nicely brings out a self-frustrating contrariness in love itself as we
experience it now. Herbert's 'Life' might be a response to such a use
of natural innocence, turning on the frailty of gathered flowers as so
many of these mid-century lyric poems do – 'they/By noone most
cunningly did steal away/And withered in my hand'. The affinity
here of two such different vocations at least shows us how deeply
their own involvement in natural processes disturbed the seventeenth-century poets.

Townshend finds a different way of setting amorous desire against
innocence when he makes his mistress's breasts at once a saving
distraction, such as might have averted the Fall, and a temptation
which would have served Satan's purpose better than the apple:

> Yett had hee ledd mee to thy brest,
>> That waye was best
> To have seduct mee from thy lipp.
> Those apples tempt mee most; They bee
>> Fruit of that Tree,
> That made our first forefathers slipp.
> I dare not touch them least I dye
> The death thou threatnest with thyne Eye.
>
> 'Pure Simple Love'

In Caroline love poetry the Garden of Eden tends to replace the
Golden Age and the state of nature as the condition of a sexual
well-being we have lost. Lovelace's version of original innocence
teasingly echoes Tasso's 'bell'età dell'oro':

> When cursed No stained no maid's bliss
> And all discourse was summed in Yes.
> And naught forbad, but to forbid.
> Love, then unstinted, love did sip,
> And cherries plucked fresh from the lip,
> On cheeks and roses free he fed;
> Lasses like autumn plums did drop,
> And lads indifferently did crop
> A flower and a maidenhead.

'Love made in the first age'

Carew's Elysium is simply a place where the frustrations of lovers are appeased, and our restrictive codes of sexual conduct do not hold:

> All things are lawfull there, that may delight
> Nature, or unrestrained Appetite.

A Rapture, 111–12

The Court love poets, are always ironically aware of their dilemma when they propose that unassuaged desire is at once the cause and the measure of our distance from bliss.

These slight love lyrics keep coming back to the frailty of our desires and our lives. Stanley's 'On a Violet in her Breast' involves the lover's senses in the drooping and revival of a flower, as if he feels that his own virility is subject to the same processes of revival and decay. The terms in which he praises the lady are understandably plaintive, assuming as they do that beauty must wilfully squander itself in the moment of its proud fruition:

> this violet, which before
> Hung sullenly her drooping head,
> As angry at the ground that bore
> The purple treasure which she spread

The examples of Herbert and Vaughan are there to remind us that there may be more than conceit in the discovery of moral tendencies in the processes of nature. 'She swells with pride ... Yet weeps that dew which kissed her last.' The involvement of human lovers in the moral vitality of a flower gives peculiar irony to that imitative 'swell and turn' of the stanza which Saintsbury noted,[2] whose effect is a sudden rearing up from a dropping cadence:

> Doth smilingly erected grow,
> Transplanted to those hills of snow.

The prospect of that delicious transplantation finally and fatally distinguishes flower and lover. The purity which gives new life to the plant arouses his blasting lust.

Stanley's little poem is true to its time and place, not least because it has more in it than courtly hyperbole. Its particular character comes out if we put it by Marino's 'Fiori, stelle d'Aprile', which Praz says 'supplied both motif and conceits for "On a Violet in her Breast"':[3]

> Fiori, stelle d'Aprile,
> Che'l vostro ciel terreno
> Cangiaste col bel seno,
> Or cangerete e qualitate e stile.
> Tra le nevi viveste,
> Di quel petto celeste.
> Non so giá se vivrete entro l'ardore
> Di questo acceso core.

Marino's elegant antithesis between the sustaining snows of her breast and the destructive fire of his ardent heart says something quite different about love, and simply belongs to another world.

Their concern for the processes of organic life leads seventeenth-century love poets to try human passions in a prospect of universal flux, and to disturb the intimacies of lovers with the witness of lust turned to dust by its own heat:

> *Castara*, see that dust, the sportive wind
> So wantons with. 'Tis happ'ly all you'le finde
> Left of some beauty: and how still it flies,
> To trouble, as it did in life, our eyes.
>
> Habington, 'To *Castara*: Upon Beautie'

Carew sets off a woman's beauty against a whole cosmos in constant evanescence, which he depicts in vivid touches as a pageant of momentary splendours forever vanishing; and he typically discovers the universal condition in particular yearnings of sense:

> Aske me no more whether doth stray,
> The golden Atomes of the day
>
> 'A Song'

The fervent repetitions insistently question our standing in the universe, and the fixity of the universal order itself; as if the stars 'That downwarde fall in dead of night' are resplendent chiefly in their dying interruption of the dark. The haunting cosmic image, so casually thrown off, delicately hints that when she has accumulated all these transitory glories she herself will prove only another such beauty of a moment. Yet the recognition that beauty is an effect of transitoriness no more provokes metaphysical distress than it allows us to rest easy with a hyperbole of praise; nor does it open the old invitation to use our youth while we have it – 'Gather the rose of love.' Carew's exquisitely balanced phrasing finely weighs the loss with the glory:

> Aske me no more where Jove bestowes,
> When June is past, the fading rose:
> For in your beauties orient deepe,
> These flowers as in their causes, sleepe.

The parenthetical falling cadence isolates and lingers out that last main verb, as if to surprise us with the promise of so fine a dissolution; dying itself becomes not so much an end as a quiet turning back to the source of vitality and beauty, even a fresh recruitment of life.

A powerful myth of death and resurrection is conceitedly entertained without losing all its power to console. Carew wrote when Donne's celebration of dead innocence might well have been taken for literal truth. Yet in this poem we feel the poise of a mind that responds to quite opposite qualities in a woman's beauty, and keeps them both in play behind the rich lyric celebration, constantly trying the effect of the powers it appraises. The poem holds a fine balance between conflicting impulses, celebrating this life the more keenly for the impermanence of all our attachments of sense, and yet giving scope to the yearning for some absolute quality in the splendours we admire.

These poets understand what they take on when they commit themselves to love in a universe which may have no stability, and no meaning. Hall's 'An Epicurean Ode' lightly tries the assurance of a lover against the prospect of a chance world of flux, questioning love's absoluteness without subsiding into hedonism or despair:

> Since that this thing we call the world
> By chance on Atomes is begot,
> Which though in dayly motions hurld
>   Yet weary not,
>   How doth it prove
> Thou art so fair and I in Love?

The honour paid to beauty and love does not at all gainsay the possibility that we are 'but pasted up of Earth', and not cradled in the skies; indeed Hall is true to the Caroline mode in celebrating his love while questioning the very point and dignity of our existence, and nicely holding such opposite dispositions in balance.

The seventeenth-century English poets are certainly not alone in finding a metaphysical dilemma in love. Dante and the Florentine neoplatonists were at least as much concerned as any later writers to discover some final value in a human attachment. Yet these Caroline songsters are haunted by a fear that the sexual impulse itself may negate or threaten love, as if lovers bring on change and death when they re-enact the concupiscence of Adam and Eve. They take love to be an affection of nature, which is subject to all the uncertainties of sense in a universe that does not favour us. The insecurity of lovers may be heightened by the alarms of the times, as it seems to be in Jordan's 'A Cavalier's Lullaby for his Mistress', which might serve for the Audenism of the 1640s:

> Sweet! sleep; lie still, my dear!
> Dangers be strangers
> For ever, unto thy eye or ear

Invoking love's peace in the midst of war, the poet only localises the imperative attempt to find stability in a universe of unrest. The urgency of such writing is well accounted for by Hall's vision of a fugitive liaison, which his plea seeks to stabilise:

> *Romira*, stay,
> And run not thus like a young Roe away

> 'The Call'

In this poem too the lovers' first need is to find an assured place for their love in the midst of wars, and the perturbations wars arouse:

> No enemie
> Pursues thee (foolish girle) tis onely I,
> I'le keep off harms,
> If thou'l be pleas'd to garrison mine arms;
> What dost thou fear
> I'le turn a Traitour?

But their attempt only confirms the incongruity of love with our lapsed condition:

> Here on this plain
> Wee'l talk *Narcissus* to a flour again

Lying down on the grass to spin legends of 'Love Martyrs' they try all human beings may do to arrest their fate, while beyond them the sinking sun marks the hostility of time to lovers.

These poets buy at a price the imaginative detachment that allows them to invest with a strange beauty even a sense of our inability to master such accidents as love and death:

Pilgrime: Whose soile is this that such sweet Pasture yields?
Or who art thou whose Foot stand never still?
Or where am I?
Time: In love.
Pilgrime: His Lordship lies above.
Time: Yes and below, and round about
Where in all sorts of flow'rs are growing
Which as the early Spring puts out,
Time fals as fast a mowing.

Townshend, 'A Dialogue betwixt Time and a Pilgrime'

Quite disturbingly evocative so far; yet all Townshend can find to ease his dreamlike bewilderment at last is a trite choral praise of growing old together, which leaves us with the thought that they are happy whose threads Fate entwines as one 'and yet draws hers the longer'. This is a typical let-down, for few of these poems make much of the big questions they pose. Some Caroline love poets, caught between delight and unease, show no wish to do more with their conflicting urges than to hold them in nice equipoise, mellowing exhilaration with wistfulness as Herrick does, or striking a low-keyed witty poignancy which may have its own beauty:

Go lovely Rose,
Tell her that wastes her time and me

Waller

Repeatedly some deeply felt self-frustration will be betrayed by a trivial resolution, or the plain evidence that the poet does not know what to make of his own insight. Stanley can manage no more with his revitalised violet than a conceited praise of the lady's breasts, as feeble in wit as in erotic vigour, whose snipsnap antithesis quite belies the rich suggestiveness of his earlier contemplation of the flower:

Since thou from them dost borrow scent,
And they to thee lend ornament.

Hall's peremptory summons to Romira leaves the lovers with nothing but a platitude to affirm when they have made their truce with time:

Nay, thou maist prove
That mans most Noble Passion is to Love.

231

Sentience dwindles to ingenuity, conceit remains conceit. Carew proposes no effective way in which a lady's eyes really might have the power to preserve the light of fallen stars, or her voice might incubate the song of the wintering nightingale; and he winds up his poem with the elaborate fancy that the phoenix itself flies to the lady's fragrant bosom to die. For all their promises, these poems finish up cleverly toying with love. Vaughan's early songs to his Amoret make a striking case in point. They are full of the hermetic ideas which would inform the myth of *Silex Scintillans* but here just work as conceits, limply sustaining the routine moves of the game:

> If Creatures then that have no sence,
> But the loose tye of influence,
> (Though fate, and time each day remove
> Those things that element their love)
> At such vast distance can agree,
> Why, Amoret, why should not wee.

> 'To Amoret gone from him'

We might ask how far these Caroline love poems show purposeful intelligence, or genuinely reason anything out at all. Few of them even seek to sustain an argument through the poem; frequently the sense is complete in the first stanza, and can only be elaborated or varied thereafter. The test case must be Stanley, a poet who repeatedly leaves us feeling that the poem has somehow slipped through our fingers and left no trace. He disputes, qualifies, sharply distinguishes; but little of substance emerges:

> Waters, plants, and stones know this:
> That they love; not what Love is.

> 'The Magnet'

There is a real distinction made here, but nothing in the poem turns on it and it leads nowhere; Stanley simply tips his cap to Donne. Repeatedly we catch the poet slipping away from a real revision of ideas about love to seize some adventitious excitement, which may be quite at odds with his argument:

> Let us twine like amorous trees,
> And like rivers melt in one.

The anatomising of passion quite abruptly gives way to a straight invitation to embrace; Stanley is imagining erotic play at this point, rather than resolving anything about love or marriage. He leaves us wondering if his movement of proof is really more than a clever gloss upon the persuasion to love, or whether the apparatus of his logic itself may be simply too mechanical to hold what he really wants to say. 'The Tomb' quite starkly shows up the world of difference between Stanley's wit and Donne's:

> When, cruel fair one, I am slain
> By thy disdain,
> And, as a trophy of thy scorn
> To some old tomb am borne

The forceful speech-rhythms of 'The Apparition' are a long way from this. Donne's savage mockery has been dissipated in a chattering lyric neatness, a trite diction, and a mechanical chime. Where Donne cuts deep in his searching of erotic life, Stanley's verse slips easily along without resisting the mind because it is not effectively engaged with sexual behaviour at all.

The show of intellectual bravura may be challenging but it is really an effect of art, a clever deployment of the processes of logic rather than purposeful thinking. Stanley would have scorned comparison with Cleveland, whose verse gets its life from a knockabout ingenuity:

> Since 'tis my Doom, Love's under-Shreive,
> Why this Repreive?
> Why doth my She-Advowson flie
> Incumbency?

Yet the two poets only play different versions of the old game of conceited wit, which leads nowhere and says nothing new of love. Stanley studiously maintains his witty argument at the level of an urbane performance, cultivating a civilised anonymity and an impersonal intellectual grace. He may well have felt a need to do more than this, for his writing often displays a quality of mind and force of imagination such as have little scope in these neat witty movements. We might judge him to be reducing vital issues to the small compass of his art rather than simply playing with the common counters of petrarchism, as his Italian counterparts do. Nonetheless the outcome is a highly refined feat of poetic equilibrium, which preserves its fine composure by determinedly fencing out such forces of life as it cannot easily assimilate or order. It seems a trivial art by definition.

Not all mid-seventeenth-century love poets so resolutely set themselves to perfect an art of wit, and to admit only as much of

living experience as might be controlled and impersonalised within
its terms. Yet the writing of even the best of them often stirs with
disquiets which seem to find no adequate focus in the categories of
amorous poetry. Vaughan was only one poet who came to think that
a commitment to sexual love is enough in itself to insulate poets
from the truth of their condition. Nevertheless Dante, Petrarch, and
Michelangelo had admitted all the universe to their love poetry, and
even made love a way to final reality. After Donne the love of
another human being turns back upon itself, and the poets who write
of love are caught up in a different kind of activity from that of the
poets who struggle to bring home to themselves their own desperate
need of grace, or solitarily face up to a degenerating creation.
In mid-seventeenth-century Britain sexual love had become
categorically distinct from the love that moves the sun and the other
stars. A choice now compelled itself between a fashionable amor-
ousness and the imperative search for truth.

If Caroline poetry was a backwater, that need not be because the
poets were reactionaries who followed the King in wanting to do
without politics altogether, as Miss C. V. Wedgwood argued.[4] It
seems that sexual love no longer offered a proving-ground for the
issues which really confronted people. The roll-call of poets who
had some part in the civic events of the 1640s is impressive enough:
Lovelace, Montrose, Newcastle, Godolphin, Davenant, Waller. Yet
their work seems curiously remote from their public career. No
doubt some of them were not much more than 'gentlemen who
wrote with ease'.[5] Love was the courtly fashion, as ever; and there
are Caroline wits enough who stand at the fag end of the long
tradition of court jongleurs, still plying the old prescriptions of
lyric love long after they were played out.

Yet Carew, and Suckling, and Rochester later, are not like their
courtly forebears in England or in Europe. The special character of
their work reflects a distinctive understanding of our nature; and the
distance between them and the Tudor songwriters may be a real
index of change. The best of these Stuart love poets show us that
something quite drastic was happening to society and sexual manners in seventeenth-century England. Their feeling for the life of
their own time and place is sharp enough to make the comparison
with earlier love poetry illuminating. They mark a decisive shift in
attitudes to love over the century that followed Queen Elizabeth's
death, and the shift partly defines us too.

Their poetry witnesses the temper of its own society vividly enough. It seeks strong erotic excitements, celebrating a lady's beauty by figuring the poet's wish to undress her as she walks before him (Suckling, 'Upon my Lady Carlile's walking in Hampton Court Garden'), and finding a dozen ingeniously indirect ways of fancying a mistress's pudenda, or relishing acts of penetration. We are invited to savour the special allure of a lady not yet enjoyed by her husband, of a mistress who is being bled by the surgeons, of plump beauty, of beauty in rags or in chains:

> But if too rough, too hard they presse,
> Oh they but closely, closely kisse.
>
> Lovelace, 'A Guiltlesse Lady imprisoned;
> after penanced'

Carew makes no bones about the motives of lovers when he resolves the argument for singleness in love with the image of a wolf which starves because it cannot decide between two sheep before it ('Incommunicabilitie of Love'). But if these poets assume that love is a concentrating of appetite they well understand how social life must inhibit the predator's scope; and much of their art goes in refining erotic provocation, or tricking out desire:

> and with amorous Charmes
> Mixt with thie flood of Frozen snowe
> In Crimson streames Ile force the redd Sea flowe.
>
> Carew, 'On the Green Sickness'

The focus of such displays of a decadent sensibility is not in question. This image of the penetration of a virgin occurs in a celebration of England as a new Paphos where 'Whatever pleaseth lawfull is' (Carew, 'To the Queene'), and Henrietta Maria queens it over a Court of Love. 'S'egli piace è lice', as Tasso wrote, but the indulgent law holds here only for that improved Golden Age which is the Queen's decorous economy of love. The new style of Court hyperbole extols the Queen's power to order the wild lusts unleashed by the King's godlike virility; and the new version of chivalry values a woman's capacity to hold a man by concentrating his errant fancies:

> He, only can wilde lust provoke,
> Thou, those impurer flames canst choke;
> And where he scatters looser fires,
> Thou turn'st them into chast desires . . .
> Which makes the rude Male satisfied
> With one faire Female by his side
>
> Carew, 'To the Queene'

Just such a civilising harmony of sexual powers is figured in Carew's Court masque *Coelum Britannicum*, which elaborately enlarges chivalric ceremony into a universal play of virile energies, so that knightly valour becomes sexual puissance, and beauty is the power to satisfy it:

> Pace forth thou mighty British Hercules,
> With thy choyce band, for onely thou, and these,
> May revell here, in Loves Hesperides.

So nice a fusion of Tasso and Donne, with its Jonsonian refinement of texture, suggests that Carew does not feel called upon to innovate in such work. The writing is distinguished from earlier love poetry, as from the classical poems Carew reworked,[6] by the way it expresses a particular society. Charles's Court was not like the great Renaissance Courts. It had its own myth of state and its own style, which the Queen's school of love helped to confirm. In particular it seems to have settled for a naturalistic understanding of sexual behaviour which Donne had worked out privately in his verse, as though Donne's example lent authority to that newly congenial way of understanding our own nature. No doubt Donne spoke for his time, and people fastened on him because he showed them to themselves. Certainly there could have been no place for a Spenser or a Sidney in a court whose elaborate rituals of love are styled by their celebrants platonic,[7] though they proceed on assumptions as ironically remote from Plato's as from the transcendentalism of Dante and Ficino. This Caroline love poetry has more of the spirit of Horner than Diotima in it. Times have moved on when a quiet country parson can turn Jonson's sensuous mythologising to cheerful erotic fantasy –

> I dream'd this mortal part of mine
> Was Metamorphoz'd to a Vine;
> Which crawling one and every way
> Enthrall'd my dainty *Lucia*

> Herrick, 'The Vine'

– or when the distinguished translator of a prime text of neoplatonic love emerges in his own poetry as a thoroughgoing relativist, who locates a woman's beauty in her power to arouse male desire.[8]

The new understanding of love gets such coherence as it has from its realisation of the manners of a close social circle, in which an ethic of honour and style makes a brilliant ritual of the natural urge to satisfy desire. The favoured conceits of this court coterie tend to set in play a few basic motives which may be checked in their scope by each other, but are chiefly regulated by the fact that they cannot be realised outside civilised society; so that sexual prowess must be reconciled with the requirements of good manners, and the satisfactions which civil life itself offers. None of these motives operates simply, for the assumption that our nature is common to our kind, and that human beings are alike in their desires and appetites, undercuts both social rank and the conventions that prescribe women's conduct. The rivalry between women and men becomes at bottom a struggle for advantage in which both parties desire like ends, and either sex has a power the other envies. A woman's attractions and fame only mirror men's desire for her, which they seek to satisfy when they celebrate her. Carew candidly undertakes to praise a lady on condition that she give herself to him for their mutual pleasure; he will spend his treasure if she will unlock hers – 'so we each other blesse' ('To a lady that desired I would love her'). Waller's 'The Story of Phoebus and Daphne, Applied' is a mythic embroidering of this bargaining game, which falls so flaccidly at last because it finds an easy way out:

> He catched at love, and filled his arms with bays.

In this poem the struggle between lover and mistress comes down to a simple trial between desire and chastity; and the fame that accrues to both of them is just the unlooked-for product of the lover's poetical pursuit, which he contemplates with equal self-satisfaction.

Carew's poetry in particular mythologises a civil order which is founded in the mutual accommodation of natural drives:

> Plant in their Martiall hands, Warr's seat,
>   Your peacefull pledges of warme snow,
> And, if a speaking touch, repeat
>   In Loves knowne language, tales of woe;
> Say, in soft whispers of the Palme,
> As Eyes shoot darts, so Lips shed Balme.
> For though you seeme like Captives, led
>   In triumph by the Foe away,
> Yet on the Conqu'rers necke you tread,
>   And the fierce Victor proves your prey.
> What heart is then secure from you,
> That can, though vanquish'd, yet subdue?

> *Coelum Britannicum*, 1036–47

Such a nice equipoise of conflicting impulses is precariously regulated by wit, which is all that may give men and women mastery over themselves or the civic jungle. The drastic naturalism of a Donne and a Jonson impels the moves of a coterie game.

In the 1630s this was the Court game of love. The writings of Carew, and Suckling, and Lovelace, always keep us aware of their close society and the strains it imposes, which are outwardly domesticated in urbane manners. 'If it pleases it is lawful' pulls against 'If it is lawful then it will please.' The draconian regimen of a Virgin Queen has long been left behind. A highly guarded ritual of bargaining for advantage follows out the presumption that we are all moved by like natural impulses, which require at once outlet and regulation. A woman's celebrity now depends upon her power to excite, and accrues to her as the reward of her skill in exploiting a man's desire without denying it.

The refined preoccupations of a self-centred Court limit poetic art to a witty image of the manners of a coterie, whose first concern is to bring its more disruptive urges into urbane control. Style is one way by which a man may assert his self-possession, as we see by the common affectation of elegant rakishness, and the deriding of impassioned servitude in favour of a cool detachment. Yet style will not resolve a real clash of interests. Carew is a superior artist because he admits contrary impulses to his poems and holds them in tense balance, when his associates are happy to fall back upon cliches of sentiment or party loyalties.

Carew's best lyrics invoke familiar attitudes only to confound them totally:

> Then shalt thou weepe, entreat, complaine
> To Love, as I did once to thee

'Song: To my inconstant Mistris'

'To my inconstant Mistris' promises a revenge, not because the suitor has been spurned in his attempt upon invincible chastity, but because his mistress has been unfaithful to her established lover. The poem assumes that she was once obdurate, yielded, swore oaths of fidelity to her lover, and then betrayed him; so that it is he who now rejects her for the promise of a surer bliss with another mistress, 'Which my strong faith shall purchase me'. The confrontation of lover and mistress is no trial of high principles but a comedy of social intrigue, in which faithful sentiment counters errant appetite.

Carew's wit is sharp and subtle, but it cuts nothing like so deep as Donne's. Carew is sceptical and relative only far enough to quicken the spirit of a song, for his poems do not commit the lover to the jungle they evoke, in which momentary appetites masquerade under the styles of morality. They find an accommodation with contrarious circumstance, and their measured coolness tempers the clashing motives into mannerly composure. 'Ingratefull beauty threatned' redresses old odds by trying the real balance of power between a lover and his mistress, weighing her pride against his capacity to give her beauty its fame, and urging that her fatal attractions are nothing without her lover's response to them:

> That killing power is none of thine,
> I gave it to thy voyce, and eyes:
> Thy sweets, thy graces, all are mine

The manner of amused condescension is beautifully created; and the point has substance. To argue that her attractions would not have any power but for the fame which he has given her is to do a little more than wittily play for advantage, or deny the mystery of love:

> Thou art my starre, shin'st in my skies

The suave possessive pronoun marks the distance between Carew and those idealising poets for whom the lady is truly a star – 'Un'alta stella di nova bellezza/che del sol ci to' l'ombra la sua luce' (Dino Frescobaldi, c. 1300). It suggests that the beauty we attribute to a woman is partly a projection of our own desire for her, and partly a reflection of the celebrity we give her; she is distinguished not by her inherent beauty of spirit but by the heat she kindles in her lovers.

Carew devastatingly puts down presumptuous beauty by reminding her that what really distinguishes her from the common herd is not her inherent quality at all:

> Thou hadst, in the forgotten crowd
> Of common beauties, liv'd unknowne

His unruffled sanity mocks the excesses of lovers with its insistence that love is no more than an accommodation of our sexual urges to the needs of civil life. We feel his intelligence in his exact discrimination of words and phrasing, his nice articulation of a quite complex vision of civil manners, the deflating play of his scepticism upon any extreme claim. If his poems do not move with Donne's unpredictable force they nonetheless create their own poise, offering the civilised pleasure of disharmony resolved, disproportion redressed. The precise patterning of 'To my inconstant Mistris' has moral symmetry in itself in the way it works out opposite fates from contrary causes; though the activity of mind is of a different order from the suddenness which startles us in 'Womans Constancy'. Carew's elegant mode of wit does not call for shock or richly charged diction; he aims for coolheaded lucidity, and the balanced articulation of his reasoning realises an order in which justice is exactly achieved:

> If the quick spirits in your eye
> Now languish, and anon must dye;
> If every sweet, and every grace,
> Must fly from that forsaken face:
>> Then (Celia) let us reape our joyes,
>> E're time such goodly fruit destroyes.
>
> Or, if that golden fleece must grow
> For ever, free from aged snow;
> If those bright Suns must know no shade,
> Nor your fresh beauties ever fade:
>> Then feare not (Celia) to bestow,
>> What still being gather'd, still must grow.
>> Thus, either Time his Sickle brings
>> In vaine, or else in vaine his wings.

'Song: Perswasions to enjoy'

His lyrics typically advance by producing a like sanction from opposite causes, or by challenging some orthodox pose of love and then sharply drawing out the consequences either way, so as to open his adversary to the exact finishing stroke. This power to make a drama of a complicated chain of argument does give his stanzas the feel of spontaneous reasoning; though they move to complete a pattern rather than to search out shocking truth.

Carew's wit realises itself through his mastery of a rhetoric, that elegant yet subtle modulation of the sense across the elaborate stanza pattern. We feel the fine temper of his mind in his infinitely delicate counterposing of ideas, nice control of tone and nuance, subtle varying of the tension between syntax and formal pattern so as to point, edge, inflect. Such finished artistry plainly did not flow; much of the 'trouble and pain' Suckling twitted him with in 'A Session of the Poets' must have gone to suggest an intelligence in tight self-control, so that each stanza seems to unfold the resolved order of a complex thought which is held whole and taut in the mind. There is a civilising spirit akin to Marvell's at work in the cool suppleness of the poise, the weighing of opposite possibilities, the colloquial ease which yet preserves the ardour of song.

Suckling himself was a hedonist who scorned such artistic pains, yet saw as clearly as Rochester what scope love now offered its more drastic devotees. His poetry endorses a life centred in a style, which tempers the zeal for pleasure with a lively scepticism. Love is a flame, which rarely burns just at the right height but 'would die, Held down or up too high' ('Song: No, no, fair heretic'); or it is a clock that strikes 'Strange blisses/And what you like best' at quite unpredictable moments ('That none beguiled be'). The precariousness of these blisses only confirms the arbitrariness of attachments which are founded in the need to satisfy involuntary appetite, or fancy:

> I am confirm'd a woman can
> Love this, or that, or any other man
>
> 'Verses'

In Suckling's poetry love always disappoints, for the reality never can come up to the imagined expectation. Women may keep their hold on men only by holding off fulfilment:

> Fruition adds no new wealth, but destroys,
> And while it pleaseth much the palate, cloys
>
> 'Against Fruition'

A man will free himself of his bondage to women just by putting down rebellious flesh:

> A quick corse, methinks, I spy
> In ev'ry woman . . .
> They mortify, not heighten me
>
> 'Farewell to Love'

Lovers operate in an area of total uncertainty where will is at the mercy of chance and occasion, as well as vanity pretending to be scruple – 'I hate a fool that starves her love/Only to feed her pride' ("Tis now, since I sate down before'). They are fools of their own appetites:

> For thou and I, like clocks, are wound
> Up to the height, and must move round
>
> 'To His Rival'

The writing quite pointedly suggests that the hazards of love only instance the uncertainties of our lives altogether in the arbitrary universe we inhabit.

Love in Suckling's poetry, as it never becomes in Donne's, is a predatory sport which we indulge because we can find no better way of fulfilling our nature. But he is no mere cynical seducer. His poems define a social activity, and their self-mocking manner prescribes men's attitudes to women in polite society, unsentimentally intimating the kind of bargains they must make with themselves as well as their desirable adversaries – 'I offer'd forty crowns/To lie with her a night or so ...' ('Proffer'd Love Rejected'). While Milton was meditating the apotheosis of artificial style, 'natural easy Suckling' sought a way of refining in lyric verse the casual civility of coffee house and salon:

> I prithee spare me, gentle boy,
> Press me no more for that slight toy,
> That foolish trifle of an heart

Suckling's affectation of negligent indifference to love, his bland mockery of his former follies, proclaim that he is his own man and not the humiliated slave of a woman or his importunate senses:

> Then hang me, ladies, at your door,
> If e'er I dote upon you more.
>
> 'Verses: I am confirm'd a woman can'

Love must be kept in its place among the affairs of a man of the world and the Town:

> When I am hungry, I do eat,
> And cut no fingers 'stead of meat ...
> I visit, talk, do business, play,
> And for a need laugh out a day
>
> 'The Careless Lover'

The studied elegance serves to distinguish a gentleman from 'th'unhallow'd sort of men' ('Against Fruition'), however little difference there may be in their sexual natures, and their fallen condition. This Caroline mode makes a gentlemanly ritual of conviviality, coupling love with tippling as if we show our mettle in the style of our pleasures.

A witty style at least gave an opening to intelligence, as Johnson observed of the metaphysical poets; and in Charles's court the wit that served to heighten erotic excitements soon turned to question its own ends. Lovelace was a bold poetical voluptuary, who nonetheless sought in poetry a way of posing choices which seemed to confront loyal gentlemen in the 1630s and 1640s. He wittily sets against each other the claims on a man's devotion, settling the conflict of loyalties with a flourish which cannot be gainsaid:

> I could not love thee (Deare) so much,
> Lov'd I not Honour more.
>
> 'Song: To Lucasta, Going to the Warres'

Love or arms, the boudoir or the camp? The old dilemma is quite succintly pointed, even if the appeal to honour seems little more than a generous vaunt. Lovelace does not show how his honour may genuinely reconcile the rival modes of manliness; he simply makes a profession which will placate both sides, flaunts the talisman that all must approve.

Lovelace's liveliest love poems characteristically invite us to ponder a wittily posed debate between conflicting loyalties. 'To Althea, From Prison' ('When Love, with unconfined wings') paradoxically opts for physical captivity rather than the bondage of love, because confinement in a just interest is the only freedom worth having:

> When flowing cups run swiftly round
> With no allaying Thames,
> Our careless heads with roses bound,
> · Our hearts with loyal flames;
> When thirsty grief in wine we steep,
> When healths and draughts go free,
> Fishes, that tipple in the deep,
> Know no such liberty.

But then honourable love itself becomes a liberating constraint when it confirms a man's allegiance to a cause which is distinguished by its gallant style. Love, loyal pledges, devotion to the King, freedom, are the unimpeachable articles of Lovelace's chivalric creed, and he can do little more than declaim them with spirit while keeping up the show of proving them, as if our intelligence really might have something to work upon. All the poem really yields us is a lively image of its times, albeit warmed by that generous assurance of devotion.

The brittleness of a faith founded in loyal enthusiasm shows up in a poem which does try to face hard circumstances, 'To Lucasta, From Prison'. This time Lovelace soon slips aside from his witty play upon the several modes of bondage to ask himself seriously what freedom of soul is now possible. He uses the momentary liberty imprisonment gives him to try his loving allegiance around

243

the various causes which offered for it in the late 1640s, rejecting each claimant in turn as unworthy, or no longer accessible in the circumstances: peace, war, religion, Parliament, liberty, property, political reform, the public faith. At last he falls back on the one absolute loyalty:

> What then remains but th'only spring
> Of all our loves and joyes?   The KING

Yet he celebrates the King's power and right very forlornly when he sees that 'now an universall mist/Of Error is spread or'e each breast'; and the poem finishes with a bewildered plea to the King – or it might be God – for light to see 'How to serve you, and you trust me'. The cavalier temper at the limit of its resource looks to personal loyalty in a way which gives weight to Miss Wedgwood's claim that the political irrelevance of these poets shows us why the King's cause was bound to fail.[9] With the King gone too, the mist would soon envelop Lovelace and his kind.

Lovelace miserably endured the ruin of his cause, and his poems offer evidence enough of the way the Court culture crumbled under the stress of civil war. Carew died just before war broke out; and Suckling fled to France in 1641 after failing to rescue Strafford, only to die by his own hand, or by horrible accident, a year later. Vaughan's abandonment of his Amoret in pursuit of lost innocence and countries beyond the stars, his sudden persuasion that a man could do no more in the impending cataclysm than seek to save himself, measures the shock Royalists sustained by the events of 1648–9; and we see how little love poetry mattered to them then.

When the Cavalier voice makes itself heard again there is a difference:

> I have been in love, and in debt, and in drink,
> This many and many a year

Booze, women, and debt: this is Brome, comically hitting off a character (he calls the poem 'The Mad Lover'), in which vein he is readily represented as the voice of a fagged out Royalism.[10] Rochester confirms the altered style:

> While each brave *Greek* embrac'd his Punk,
> Lull'd her asleep, and then grew drunk.

> 'Grecian Kindness: A Song'

The heroic struggle for Troy finishes up in the common human solaces, cynically coarsened by the diction.

Brome in one way, as Rochester in another, does reveal the poverty of love poets as the seventeenth century wore on. On the continent love dwindles to a clever–pretty arcadianism; in England people are still desperately trying to say something real, and saying something desperate. To write of love at all was to search for something stable to hold on to, some vestige of the humane culture of the Renaissance Courts. Christopher Hill argues that the Stuarts precipitated a flight of Court gentry to their country estates.[11] For this or whatever reason, the poetry often looks to country patrons and rural activities. Ben Jonson's celebrations of the great country houses propose a version of civil culture,[12] just as Fanshawe's famous ode of 1630 glorifies the attempt to order English society about the great country properties:

> Beleeve me Ladies you will finde
> In that sweet life, more solid joyes,
> More true contentment to the minde,
> Than all Town-toyes.
>
> *An Ode Upon . . . His Majesties Proclamation . . .*
> *Commanding the Gentry to reside upon their*
> *Estates in the Country*

This is the contentment of innocence, which shows up the guilty discontents of political life:

> 'Tis innocence in the sweet blood
> Of Cherryes, Apricocks and Plummes
> To be imbru'd.

Here, while fortune lasted, was a prospect of Eden to hold on to. The choice between country retirement and an involvement in affairs became a moral dilemma. The love poets who wrote after the war suggest, however exaggeratedly, that there was a social crisis here too in the dwindling of the satisfactions of civil life to the point where sex and style preoccupied their art. They seek in sexual pleasure something that will give life a savour when the order which sustained poetic love is dissolving about them. Love poetry no longer rehearses a metaphysical quest, or a moral trial, but dwindles to the chronicle of a coterie pursuit, a ritual of search and momentary satisfactions centred on St James, Covent Garden, and 'the Fields of Lincolns Inn'.

The love poetry that follows the Restoration offers a changed style of love. Etherege, Sedley, and Buckhurst are not so much urbane as knowing, not detached but eagerly ribald. The fine composure is lost, and there seems nothing but the chase and its outcome to order men's manners:

> Cuffley! whose beauty warms the age,
> And fills our youth with love and rage,
> Who like fierce wolves pursue the game,
> . While secretly the lecherous dame
> With some choice gallant takes her flight
> And in a corner fucks all night.
>
> Etherege, 'Mr Etherege's Answer'

These lyrics and verse letters of the Restoration rakes shift the focus of fashionable fellowship to the Town, ousting Court manners in favour of sexual adventury in the Holborn streets. They are witty chiefly in the way they temper a lively engagement in the sport with sharp self-appraisal, and a devastating candour about sexual motives:

> Against the Charmes our *Ballocks* have,
> How weak all humane skill is?
> Since they can make a *Man* a *Slave*,
> To such a *Bitch* as *Phillis*.
>
> Rochester, 'Song'

The put down could scarcely be deadlier, or funnier. Love, already made contingent upon whim by the conceit that beauty is the lover's gift, comes down at last to the genital urge which draws us to a woman in spite of ourselves and her sheer disagreeableness. Far from preserving our independence, the new naturalism makes us abject slaves of our own cravings.

In these poems the wanton vagaries of our common nature mock social rank: .

> Thus she who Princes had deny'd,
>   With all their Pomp and Train,
> Was, in the lucky Minute try'd,
>   And yielded to a Swain.
>
> Rochester, 'A Song: As *Cloris* full of
> harmless thoughts'

Fidelity is a sin against nature:

> 'Tis not that I'm weary grown
> Of being yours, and yours alone:
> But with what Face can I incline,
> To damn you to be only mine?
>
> Rochester, 'Upon his Leaving his Mistress'

The failure of love

The actuality of women's desires demolishes courtly myth:

> That much she fears, (but more she loves,)
> Her Vassal should undo her.
>
> Rochester, 'To Corinna: A Song'

Pastoral idyll comes down to the sexual feats of Strephon, Phillis and Coridon under a tattered blanket in Lincoln's Inn Fields (Rochester, 'Song'), or to the undoing of Cloris in a pigsty:

> Now pierced is her Virgin Zone
> She feels the Foe within it;
> She hears a broken amorous Groan,
> The panting Lover's fainting moan,
> Just in the happy Minute.
>
> Rochester, 'A Song: To Chloris'

A casual scepticism, following out Donne to the candid limit, collapses the entire metaphysic of beauty:

> This shows Love's chiefest magic lies
> In women's cunts, not in their eyes
>
> Etherege, 'Mr Etherege's Answer'

Such verses spiritedly and derisively define their little world. They ritualise the manners of a coterie, and are themselves coterie performances, like tippling, which keep up the fellowship of the game. Drinking, drabbing, and gaming, so wittily turned into art of a kind, impose their own terms on poets who seek no other recourse than stylish wit to give them some mastery over chance and their own nature.

When the local style of young English aristocrats sets the poetic mode, and the pastimes of moneyed youth come to determine the moral temper of art, then nobility itself has shifted its value. 'Al cor gentil ripara sempre amore.' The noble idealism of a Guinizelli or a Sidney is no longer in sight, and the sport of the Town becomes a faith. Love poets no more expect the attachments of sex to carry their minds beyond the world of sense than they search a woman's beauty for a ray of the Divine Essence, or take women themselves for miracle-working stars. The very idea that the lover may progress up a scale of qualities towards a realm of pure spirit loses its meaning in a universe ordered by quantitative laws, in which love is a mere glow upon the blind biological urge.

Neoplatonism has gone out of the window with pseudo-Dionysius, and taken with it the assumption that sense and spirit pull in opposite directions. The metaphysical pretensions of love poetry have quietly lost their credit, and Rochester, Etherege, Sedley, Buckhurst and their peers are left to seek such assurance as they may find in sexual prowess carried off with verve, the dregs of chivalric errantry. If the young bloods and rakes now take over love poetry this is no mere modish annexation but a mark of what love has come to mean, and perhaps even a portent of what life no longer means. When we next encounter a considerable body of love poetry in English it will be more notable for feeling than for intellectual grasp.

The Restoration wits decisively brought love down to earth when they made a way of life of the hunt for sexual satisfaction, and allowed men only the release of a dwindling into sentiment and marriage. They found no need to look beyond nature for the cause of a woman's power over men, and saw a jungle of natural appetites at work behind the artificial manners of polite society. Their cult of witty virility left them little but a ritual of manhood to hold on to when the chase lost its zest, and appetite palled. In their verses love itself becomes nothing more than a dulling debility of taste:

> Love a Women! you're an Ass
> 'Tis a most insipid Passion;
>
> Rochester, 'Song'

Rochester took the ingenious pursuit of pleasure further than his fellows, and asked more of it. He is always struggling to wring a faith from our errant devotions:

> Lest once more wand'ring from that Heav'n,
> I fall on some base heart unblest;
> Faithless to thee, False, unforgiv'n
> And lose my Everlasting rest.
>
> 'A Song: Absent from thee I languish still'

> Let the Porter, and the Groom,
> Things design'd for dirty Slaves,
> Drudge in fair *Aurelia's* Womb,
> To get Supplies for Age and Graves.
>
> 'Song'

It is characteristic of him to imply a search for a saving grace when he turns in distaste from pleasures which so unbecomingly level gentleman with drudge, and prefers witty talk over a bottle instead.

Rochester's poetry shows an extreme determination to make love a mere puppet of sexual pleasure; yet it also expresses the anguish of an existence which is devoid of metaphysical sense, and racked by arbitrary discontents. Rochester confirms the proven shortcomings of our experience by his awareness of what life might be:

> How blest was the Created State
> Of Man and Woman, e're they fell,
> Compar'd to our unhappy Fate,
> We need not fear another hell!

'The Fall: A Song' follows Donne in ironically measuring our distance from the innocent state by our loss of sexual pleasure, and inadequate sexual performance:

> Naked, beneath cool Shades, they lay,
> Enjoyment waited on Desire:
> Each Member did their Wills obey,
> Nor could a Wish set Pleasure higher.

Our sad decline from this blissful condition becomes a symptom of a present existence in which the descendants of Adam and Eve are no more than 'poor Slaves to Hope and Fear', who can never have a secure hold on their joys:

> They lessen still as they draw near,
> And none but dull Delights endure.

'The Fall' runs true to its age in its easy way of entertaining universal inquietudes. Yet Rochester's throwaway close is no mere drollery of wit:

> Then, Cloris, while I Duty pay,
> The Nobler Tribute of my Heart,
> Be not You so severe to say,
> You love me for a frailer Part.

The irony is disturbing as well as frank. She is to keep up the pretence of a sentimental loyalty, though they both know that the reality is frailer, because their illusion of satisfaction and permanence is all they may have to console them.

Rochester finds in sexual life a telling instance of the precariousness of our condition. He shares with his associates a dedication to the momentary bliss of union, but he will not profess their brave relish for the brevity of our attachments. His 'Love and Life' is no such offspring of Donne's naturalism as Suckling's 'No such constant Lover' or Etherege's 'To a Lady, Asking Him How Long He Would Love Her'. With the past already lost, and the future not yet his, then 'The present Moment's all my Lot', which he dedicates 'as fast as it is got' to his mistress. This fragile reassurance is as much as we may give or expect:

> Then talk not of Inconstancy,
>   False Hearts, and broken Vows:
> If I, by Miracle can be
> This live-long Minute true to thee,
>   'Tis all that Heav'n allows.

It scarcely seems ironic that an article of a rake's creed should so readily become a judgment of life, and even threaten our sense of identity and permanence. The poet must be taking his scepticism seriously when he discerns behind the relativeness of our assurances a universal condition which gives us no hold on our fleeting experience, or our own being. Like other poems of the day, 'Love and Life' brings home to us through love the little time we have, and the vanity of our striving for permanence. As earlier European lyrics, the song takes love to epitomise the life of sense, pointing the insecurity of our condition. What makes it distinctive and disturbing is Rochester's profession of a faith which has been won by miracle out of a chaos of change and delusion, yet still may never be sure of itself for more than the present moment. The poem quite poignantly sets off sceptical self-candour with yearning, and catches the dilemma of beings who cannot reconcile their rage for the immutable with the actuality of their state. There seems to be more in question than a tradition of love poetry when the present rapport becomes our only certitude, and frail sense governs our lives. The slight love lyric intimates that not only poetic love but a mind has come to the end of its resource.

Rochester writes of love as we find it now, at this stage of our degeneration from an original state of bliss. Yet he takes no account of sin or grace. The Fall he laments is no more than the loss of a golden age of love, which comes home to a man most intimately in the untimely decline of his member, that humiliating evidence of the way our powers come short of our appetite and will. The part sex played in Adam's ruin gives him some warrant for this ribald limiting of the consequences of the Fall to the inadequacy of our sexual powers. But the paradox of Rochester's poetry is that it restricts life to secular experience, and even to present sensation, while sharpening our sense of the way in which we fall ever further short of what we might be. Rochester still looks to a falling away from that right state to account for the way life fails us, and to show us why our affairs never go as they might. Whether he is gambling with despair or simply seeking a faith he poses the dilemma of all these seventeenth-century love poets, who so often fail their own insights because love itself can no longer sustain what they want to make of it. In the compacts they make with their frail fellow-creatures they find neither coherence nor certitude. They never get beyond the self-frustrating sense that their own desire at once brings home to them and accounts for the way life disappoints us, offering us splendours which fade and fail, and promises which always fall short.

Seventeenth-century love poets differ from their predecessors in that they no longer find in love a choice between sense and spirit, or a proof that sense is inherently depraved and the sensible world a delusion. They assume that our degeneration from the created state will be made good not when we renounce or transcend our human capacities, but when we recover them and realise them fully. A yearning for lost innocence resonates through seventeenth-century lyric poetry, expressing itself most poignantly in praises of young girls, whose natural charms stir wistful guilt in the worldly admirer. Comparing girls with shortlived flowers is one way of confronting innocence with blasting lust; another way is to recall a harmless affection which has disturbingly matured into desire:

> Ah! Chloris! that I now could sit
> As unconcerned as when
> Your infant beauty could beget
> No pleasure, nor no pain.
>
> Sedley, 'To Chloris'

Versions of the intimacies between a young girl and her older admirer range from the delicate to the perverse, from Bold's warnings of the power innocent beauty has over men ('Chloris, forbear a while') to Rochester's 'A Song of a Young Lady to her Ancient Lover'. They mingle celebration with regret in a curious manner of elegaic poignancy, as if our very hankering after innocence sadly confirms the fatal ambiguity of our state, reminding us that we cannot now love innocently.

The disjuncture of love which undoes Milton's Adam comes to seem too simply represented as a separation of sense from innocence.

Among the Wastes of Time

Seventeenth-century love poets do not even find themselves torn between their devotion to a woman and the love they owe to God; rather, they are caught in the fatal ambiguity of a condition which perverts their very yearning for the condition of the first lovers into impulses of corruption and death. Love offers scant moral choice to lovers who cannot alter their own condition, or disregard their own nature. For them, sexual love simply brings out the contradictoriness of the world and our present being when it leaves us so vulnerable to the opposite impulses we find in ourselves. To be conscious of that divided heart which Marvell spoke of ('A Dialogue between the Soul and Body')[13] is to balance against each other the extreme claims the world makes upon us. The man who wishes to get on reasonable terms with life in the world has no alternative but to reach an accommodation with himself and his fellows, so that he may gain what he can without relinquishing too much:

> *Mirabell:* Well, have I liberty to offer conditions – that when you are dwindled into a wife, I may not be beyond measure enlarged into a husband?
>
> Congreve, *The Way of the World,*
> IV, 5, 206–8

In the seventeenth century few poets act in the faith that the love of another human being might have absolute spiritual worth, and fewer still take sexual love to be anything other than a natural affection, which shares the decay of nature since the Fall. Love quite intimately brings home to us our present condition at this stage of man's decline from the first state of nature, though it does not offer us a way of bettering it. Love poetry ceases to stage a moral drama and turns to lyric reflection, plangently drawing out the way things are with us, and pointing the irony of a craving which so disturbingly accompanies its expectations with the certainty of disillusion. It is a haunted art, because it sets off the promise of fulfilment against the sad actuality, and holds both states in prospect by way of making us more disquietingly aware how far love is prey to time.

The election that confronted these poets was nonetheless imperative. Their very awareness of what it means to be a creature of time, and need to understand what sin has wrought upon us as time runs on, effectively turned them away from the idealism they sometimes professed and committed them to sense. They looked to organic processes to show them how our circumstances distinguish us from the created life around us, tacitly acknowledging that all natural existence is subject to the same laws. Such differences as we may pose between sensible being and spiritual being are in any case less critical than the contrast between fallen and unfallen nature; and other creatures may not have wholly shared our own lapse. Reading the creation aright we may still glimpse the original state in the present decay. In the seventeenth century the effort to see things as they really are readily became a search for the condition of the Eden we have lost.

The question that oppressed categorical spirits was how men who acknowledge their distance from the just state may yet remain part of a corrupt social order at all. For them, the one choice which mattered was that between some sort of accommodation with the degenerating world, and abandonment of it, whether a man should make such terms as he might with his unregenerate self and his fellows, or commit himself wholly in the one cause that really matters. The heroic motive in seventeenth-century poetry was the lonely resolve to master our fallen condition so that a man might remake himself nearer the first state. After Donne, sexual love offered no way of furthering such a radical end as that.

5

Through Nature to Eternity:
Vaughan's *Silex Scintillans*

And forthwith the Word of God leapt up from the downward-tending
elements of nature to the pure body which had been made, and was united
with Mind the Maker; for the Word was of one substance with that Mind.
And the downward-tending elements of nature were left devoid of reason, so
as to be mere matter.

Pimander, Lib. 10

Until the day break, and the shadows flee away, I will get me to the mountain
of myrrh, and to the hill of frankincense ... Thy plants are an orchard of
pomegranates, with pleasant fruits; camphire, with spikenard, Spikenard and
saffron; calamus and cinamon, with all trees of frankincense; myrrh and aloes,
with all the chief spices: A fountain of gardens, a well of living waters, and
streams from Lebanon. Awake, O north-wind; and come, thou south; blow
upon my garden, that the spices thereof may flow out. Let my beloved come
into his garden, and eat his pleasant fruits ... Set me as a seal upon thine
heart, as a seal upon thine arm: for love is strong as death; jealousy is cruel as
the grave.

The Song of Solomon 4:6, 4:13–16, 8:6

i. *In search of the quickening spirit*

Henry Vaughan's *Silex Scintillans* figures a spiritual crisis,
expressing a man's attempts to make his life anew when his world
had collapsed about him. Vaughan's writing has the excited
urgency of a running attempt to come to terms with brutal and
scarcely intelligible events, with pain and afflictions which the
poet represents not merely as his private misfortunes but the stuff
of life as it unalterably is. From poem to poem there is a struggle
to comprehend experiences which are too intensely realised to be
patient of easy resolution:

> Sure thou didst flourish once! and many Springs,
> Many bright mornings, much dew, many showers.
> Past ore thy head: many light *Hearts* and *Wings*
> Which now are dead, lodg'd in thy living bowers.
>
> 'The Timber'

The perception is quite movingly articulated. Vaughan's opening stanzas can catch so much in themselves, hold so many different elements of a thought in the impassioned cadences of a taut lyric pattern, that the rest of the poem may seem to have no way of sustaining that sudden apprehension. Within a few lines it is the poem itself which has died, though it labours its ingenuities for some fourteen stanzas more:

> So murthered man, when lovely life is done,
> And his blood freez'd, keeps in the Center still
> Some secret sense, which makes the dead blood run
> At his approach, that did the body kill.
>
> And is there any murth'rer worse then sin?
> Or any storms more foul then a lewd life?
> Or what *Resentient* can work more within,
> Then true remorse, when with past sins at strife?

Vaughan's uncertain grasp of his own poetic impulse is plain for all to see in the lyrics by which he is best known. Encountered in poem after poem as we read through the sequence there is something that needs accounting for in the unpredictable falterings of power, whose effects are such as we might expect in a less considerable poet. A. Alvarez reinforces a common impression when he remarks that Vaughan was by the standard of Donne and Herbert a non-thinker who 'never shows any real power of analysis', and whose commitment to single moments of intense sensation makes him 'at one moment vivid, profound and original, and at the next, dull, prosaic and derivative'.[1] Yet a reader who follows Vaughan out in his metaphysical extremity may not be so ready to account him a poet of sensation rather than thought, or to suppose that the unevenness of his poems betrays a lack of analytic power. The easy moralisings, facile compromises, unearned resolutions, sudden losses of intensity, speak of an endeavour which is quite unusually precarious in its power to engage the mind.

Such lapses may seem incidental to an honest rendering of so critical a trial of a man's being, the price his understanding must pay for the sheer intractable force with which his disquiets present themselves. Possibly the poet endured for the sake of his successes such moments of lost insight as he recognised; and we must ask ourselves why such moments are more obvious in Vaughan's poems than they might be in Donne's poetry or Marvell's. Yet there is no doubting the surge of ardour when he finds his way to reconcile sensibility and understanding, and his burden momentarily lifts:

> O, is! but give wings to my fire,
> And hatch my soul, untill it fly
> Up where thou art, amongst thy tire
> Of Stars, above Infirmity

'Disorder and frailty'

Read cursorily or in snippets *Silex Scintillans* may impress more by its sudden glories than by a coherent pattern. But it invites us to see it as a whole, a continuing struggle to make sense of some terrible derangement of the poet's state so that he may build anew. As a record of the effect upon Anglican consciousness of the public events following 1648 the two parts together make a telling document in dislocation; then domestic misfortune seems to have accompanied the ruin of party and Church, and left Vaughan with the sense that a general cataclysm was upon us in which a man could but seek to save himself as best he might.

Vaughan is a poet of extreme commitments, fierce rage as well as intense joy. The savagery of his attacks on his times, and the factions that dominated them, answers his yearning for serenity:

> What thunders shall those men arraign
> Who cannot count those they have slain,
> Who bath not in a shallow flood,
> But in a deep, wide sea of blood?

'Abels blood'

Silex Scintillans is shadowed by a gloom which comes near despair, an engrossment with death and dissolution. Yet it also figures a man's efforts to live in prospect of a quite different order of being from our present condition, which may nullify corruption with its own regenerative vitality. The passion kindles in the unremitting effort to comprehend cold mortality in the universal working of love.

The Vaughan everyone knows is the poet of sudden splendours, those ejaculatory visions which stop us in our tracks when we come on them in the anthologies with their simple assurance of a serenity beyond our world:

> My Soul, there is a Countrie
> Far beyond the stars
> Where stands a winged Centrie
> All skilfull in the wars

'Peace'

They are all gone into the world of light!

O thou that lovest a pure and whitend soul!
That feedst among the Lillies, 'till the day
Break, and the shadows flee

'Dressing'

I saw Eternity the other night
Like a great *Ring* of pure and endless light,
All calm as it was bright

'The World'

These anthology-gems give a just impression of the poet as far as they
go, for the ecstasies and the luminous images of an order which
transfigures ours are important in his travail, though they are far
from all that is there. But Vaughan's other-worldliness must not be
misunderstood. In quite essential ways it is the reverse of otherworldly. What distinguishes his poetry is that he apprehends that
other state so keenly while keeping it in habitual tension with our
natural lives.

The poems themselves show that far from abandoning the natural
order of things in favour of some disembodied state in the sky he was
the more deeply committed to the life of nature by his intuition of a
world disintegrating about him, and his sense that such disorder
could not be final. Vaughan took the right state for man to be the
first order of nature as God created it, which is not everywhere
decayed even at this distance from the Fall; and he supposed with
Donne that spiritual regeneration comes by way of our solitary
efforts to get back to that equilibrium:

Since then our businesse is, to rectifie
Nature, to what she was . . .

Donne, To Sir Edward Herbert, at Julyers,
lines 33–4

For some people in the seventeenth century, among them
Vaughan's twin brother, rectifying nature meant alchemical
attempts to transmute the qualities of matter. Such an enterprise
stands upon a quite particular understanding of the spiritual
potentiality of matter, as Boehme shows when he parallels the
emergence of gold from brute earth with the resurrection of the new
purified spirit in God's image from the 'gross, deformed, bestial
dead husk of fallen man'.[2] Thomas Vaughan himself speaks of his
practice of an art which unites a particular spirit with universal
being by drawing upon the 'chain or subordinate propinquity of

complexions between visibles and invisibles ... by which the superior spiritual essences descend and converse here below with the matter'.[3] Henry Vaughan took the still more discomforting way of grappling with the frailties of our human understanding itself. He set himself to find in the very conditions of our life in the fallen world the evidences of the final order of things. This resolve is plain to see in the poems themselves, and has moral courage in a high degree. His purpose is to search fallen nature rather than rise above it, to confront the symptoms of our mortality, even come to terms with them, while truth may be discovered in the dust. Vaughan would not be half the poet he is if he did not keep alert his sense that physical being and spiritual being are finally one, as if he wills to be a creature of eternity even while he inhabits a world of sense and death. It is the imperative need to elect his natural course with his whole being which gives his apprehensions of transfigured life their luminous urgency.

In the late 1640s choice was scarcely an intellectual luxury. Vaughan's Royalist partisanship seems to have changed his life. In the collapse of the Anglican cause which followed the overthrow of the King he abandoned such secular hopes as were expressed in his early training in law, and his fashionable versifying. His retirement to rural Breconshire seems to have been a retreat from a de-generating world towards the country of his innocence, and the pristine wisdom of its aboriginal inhabitants. HENRICUS VAUGHAN. SILURIS M.D. reads his tombstone in the churchyard of Llansantffraed. We cannot authenticate the medical training; but his translations of hermetic treatises tell us what kind of medicine Vaughan must have practised in his long rural ministry, while his twin brother was quite independently seeking to perfect himself through spiritual alchemy.[4] Henry Vaughan outlived his brother by some thirty years, but he published only one more collection of poems after *Silex Scintillans*, II, the *Thalia Rediviva* of 1675, which simply gathered verses he had not found place for in earlier collec-tions. The thirty-five years without poetry only brings out the con-sequence of the spiritual crisis which made him a great poet for a few years in the early 1650s.

The spiritual travail so powerfully sustained in *Silex Scintillans* shows the division of seventeenth-century Britain in the way it resists the intellectual currents of the 1650s and 1660s. Vaughan's poems attempt nothing less than the defiant grounding of a new life in a myth of sacred love, which accounts for the vitality of the entire universe in terms of a 'continuous commerce' between creatures and their creator, in R. A. Durr's phrase.[5] In essence Vaughan simply tries to live out the doctrine of love drawn from St Augustine by St Bernard, St Bonaventura and the Victorines, which had helped shape Dante's *Divina Commedia*; and he shares some fundamental assumptions with the Milton who issued his own blast against the trend of the times in 1667, under the challenging title of *Paradise Lost*. Vaughan and Milton have in common an understanding of love which sets them against transcendental metaphysicians on the one hand, and empirical scientists on the other.

This spiritual manifesto which shapes up defiantly in the middle of the century quite categorically denies the premises of the new thought that was then gaining ground, and would soon take over intellectual life. It reads less like the rearguard action S. L. Bethell describes[6] than the triumphant proclamation of a state such as only the mind informed by love may realise. The natural creation of *Silex Scintillans*, as of *Paradise Lost*, is not the universe assumed in mathematical physics, and it controverts the idea of a geometry of nature. To Vaughan, Lockeian empiricists and Cartesian rationalists are alike just dealers in vanity, in as far as they deny that created things have part in an organism of love:

> my volumes sed
> They were all dull, and dead,
> They judg'd them senslesse, and their state
> Wholly Inanimate.
> Go, go; Seal up thy looks,
> And burn thy books.   'And do they so?'

We shall not wish to draw the battle lines altogether hard and fast when we recollect what part alchemical experiment and hermetic speculation played in the thinking of the founders of natural philosophy.[7] Yet Vaughan's poetry allows no compromise between the quantitative materialism of the new physics and his own understanding that creation is a sentient organism which love animates, sustains, and orders by degrees of spiritual ardour. The conflict between a mechanistic and a providential understanding of natural processes agitates seventeenth-century writing from Donne's poetry on, and becomes urgent in *Paradise Lost*. Vaughan wrote *Silex Scintillans* partly out of his need to assert the working of providential love within the order of nature, alienating himself not only from a Hobbes but from such pious rationalists as Mersenne, Descartes, and the Anglican divines who would soon express the times, Barrow, Tillotson, South and their like. For Vaughan, the universe of natural philosophy and the universe of rational theology are alike empires of death, a whirl of random atoms.

The universe Vaughan inhabits is the antithesis of Newton's because he conceives that it is not inert but essentially alive, not neutral but purposefully animated by loving joy, and providentially disposed for our good. S. L. Bethell well remarks that in Vaughan's poetry 'Nature is sacramentally interpreted as both signifying and actually embodying the mysterious operations of the Holy Spirit.'[8] So Vaughan seizes on the vitality of the natural creation as the principle of its moral life, attempting repeatedly to render it in images of energy, light, concentrated power, sympathetic attraction. To be open to those powers which work around us is to recover as much as we now can of the condition of the early men who held familiar commerce with God's agents, as the Old Testament reminds us when it shows 'An Angell talking with a man' ('Religion'). Announcing himself on the title-page of the first *Silex Scintillans* as 'Henry Vaughan *Silurist*' the poet marks together his local allegiance, and his moral progress, which is effectively a retrieval of time. But at this distance from the Fall, even the man who has made his life anew must find what universal truth he can in the evidence of its origin which each creature affords in its fulfilment of its own purpose; and Vaughan looks for these signs in the distinctive activities of nature which surround him:

> All things here shew him heaven; *Waters* that fall
> Chide, and fly up; *Mists* of corruptest fome
> Quit their first beds and mount; trees, herbs, flowres, all
> Strive upwards stil.
>
> 'The Tempest'

What denies the vital coherence of the universe, or masks it from us, cannot itself be a force of life. Vaughan consistently speaks of sin as a disintegration into dust, or a self-blinding with that cloud of mortality which is all we corrupted beings see when we look at our world now, and accept it for our only reality:

> O knit me, that am crumbled dust! ...
> Come, and releive
> And tame, and keepe downe with thy light
> Dust that would rise, and dimme my sight.
>
> 'Distraction'

To share that condition of random distractions and dispersals is to define ourselves as dust even before our bodily death.

The poet of *Silex Scintillans* seeks a part in the continual interchange of love which sustains our creation and makes it one. Like Milton, Vaughan supposes that we inhabit a universe which was created when the Holy Spirit 'hatch'd all with his quick'ning love', and subsists as a living extension of God's love:

> Thou cloath'st thy self with light, as with a robe,
>   And the high, glorious heav'ns thy mighty hand
> Doth spread like curtains round about this globe
>   Of Air, and Sea, and Land.
>
> The beams of thy bright Chambers thou dost lay
>   In the deep waters, which no eye can find;
> The clouds thy chariots are, and thy path-way
>   The wings of the swift wind.
>
> In thy celestiall, gladsome messages
>   Dispatch'd to holy souls, sick with desire
> And love of thee, each willing Angel is
>   Thy minister in fire.
>
> Thy arm unmoveable for ever laid
>   And founded the firm earth; then with the deep
> As with a vail thou hidst it, thy floods plaid
>   Above the mountains steep . . .
>
> And as thy care bounds these, so thy rich love
>   Doth broach the earth, and lesser brooks lets forth . . .
>
> Thou send'st thy spirit forth, and they revive,
>   The frozen earths dead face thou dost renew.
> Thus thou thy glory through the world dost drive,
>   And to thy works art true.
>
> Thine eyes behold the earth, and the whole stage
>   Is mov'd and trembles, the hills melt and smoke
> With thy least touch: lightnings and winds that rage
>   At thy rebuke are broke.

> 'Psalme 104'

Vaughan takes love for a cohesive force of sympathy, a kind of animated magnetism such as della Porta described, and Gilbert himself spoke of,[9] which holds the universe in harmonious order and preserves it from decay. When love is withheld things relapse at once towards the primal disorder which is true death – 'they to dust return' ('Psalme 104'). Yet love is far from seeking to draw everything to itself and make the many return to the One. On the contrary, it shows itself in that spirit of difference which gives creatures their distinct 'signature' and life, and sustains each created kind in a characteristic mode of vitality that is directed to some quite particular end:

> Father of lights! what Sunnie seed,
> What glance of day hast thou confin'd
> Into this bird? To all the breed
> This busie Ray thou hast assign'd;
> Their magnetisme works all night,
> And dreams of Paradise and light.

'Cock-crowing'

The point of such poems is precisely that the activity is not one-sided. Love depends for its effects upon the return of love, not only in creatures sensible of benefit but throughout the processes of nature, which sustain each other by a natural interchange of virtue. In this vital reciprocity of being, organic life itself is nothing other than an exchange of love; so that the fruitful sympathy between earth and heaven makes one order with the communion of angels, who are 'sick with desire/And love of thee' ('Psalme 104'), and with the saving response of all 'Love-sick souls' to Christ's glance of love:

> Sure, *holyness* the *Magnet* is,
> and *Love* the *Lure*, that woos thee down

'The Queer'

Christ's Atonement becomes the supreme demonstration of life-giving love because it revives decayed man with the powerful sap and moisture of God's own blood, though only when he has prepared himself with his tears to let love work upon him:

> My dear, bright Lord! my Morning-star!
> Shed this live-dew on fields which far
> From hence long for it! shed it there,
> Where the starv'd earth groans for one tear!

> This land, though with thy hearts blest extract fed,
> Will nothing yield but thorns to wound thy head.

'Jesus Weeping' 1

Some of the best known poems in *Silex Scintillans* convey the anguish of the conviction that we alienate ourselves further from this lifegiving reciprocity of creation as we grow more remote from

Through Nature to Eternity

our first state. Vaughan supposes that our former part in the harmony of love around us gave us direct and familiar 'conference' with
heaven ('Religion'), and drew our minds thither as naturally 'as first
love draws strongest' ('Corruption'):

> Nor was Heav'n cold unto him; for each day
>   The vally, or the Mountain
> Afforded visits, and still *Paradise* lay
>   In some green shade, or fountain.
> Angels lay *Leiger* here; Each Bush, and Cel,
>   Each Oke, and high-way knew them,
> Walk but the fields, or sit down at some *wel*,
>   And he was sure to view them.

Now, instead, as time runs on, we find ourselves alone and desolate,
lacking all hope:

> Almighty *Love*! where art thou now? mad man
>   Sits down, and freezeth on,
> He raves, and swears to stir nor fire, nor fan,
>   But bids the thread be spun.

'Corruption'

Yet the conceit which shapes the poetry is that our self-separation
from that created order was not a physical banishment. On the
contrary, Vaughan yearns for an Eden such as he has known in his
own life, and still lies all about us; but his own experience gives
proof that men cut themselves off from their bliss as they grow older
by their preoccupation with the world they make for themselves, in
wilful opposition to true life:

> The world
> Is full of voices; Man is call'd, and hurl'd
>   By each, he answers all,
>   Knows ev'ry note, and call,
>   Hence, still
> Fresh dotage tempts, or old usurps his will.

'Distraction'

Vaughan's present sense that he simultaneously inhabits unlike
orders of being comes out in the harsh and frequent contrasts he
draws, even within the same poem, between a condition of luminous
equipoise and the state of the world as we find it:

> Fair, order'd lights (whose motion without noise
>   Resembles those true Joys
> Whose spring is on that hil where you do grow
> And we here tast sometimes below,)

> With what exact obedience do you move
>   Now beneath, and now above,
> And in your vast progressions overlook
>   The darkest night, and closest nook! . . .
> But here Commission'd by a black self-wil
>   The sons the father kil,
> The Children Chase the mother, and would heal
>   The wounds they give, by crying, zeale . . .
> Thus by our lusts disorder'd into wars
>   Our guides prove wandring stars,
> Which for these mists, and black days were reserv'd,
>   What time we from our first love swerv'd.

'The Constellation'

No one who recollects Henry King's account of his own sufferings under the Commonwealth will doubt the authenticity of Vaughan's characterisation of the times.[10] Vaughan's complaints of the hatred visited upon the lost cause he shared with King set off those celebrated evocations of 'those early dayes' of 'Angell-infancy' when we directly apprehended pure love:

> When yet I had not walkt above
> A mile, or two, from my first love,
> And looking back (at that short space,)
> Could see a glimpse of his bright-face;
> When on some *gilded Cloud*, or *flowre*
> My gazing soul would dwell an houre,
> And in those weaker glories spy
> Some shadows of eternity

'The Retreate'

Such powerful impulses pointedly reverse our assumption that experience of the world is the way to wisdom. They affirm just the contrary, that the means to know the truth of creation is the 'narrow way' of self-undoing which takes us back to '*Nature* in her simplicity',[11] and our own infant innocence:

> An age of mysteries! which he
> Must live twice, that would Gods face see;
> Which *Angels* guard, and with it play,
> Angels! which foul men drive away.

'Childe-hood'

W. A. L. Bettany writes quite strikingly beside the point when he remarks that in 'Childe-hood' Vaughan 'calmly repudiates the orthodox Christian doctrine of original sin, and, in a beautiful fallacy, transfers to the childhood of the individual man that innocence which elsewhere he has predicated of the childhood of the race'.[12] Innocence is innocence, and the yearning to return to that state need no more deny original sin than it lands a man in a fallacy. Vaughan's wished retreat simply calls for an unmaking of his worldly self:

> O how I long to travell back
> And tread again that ancient track!
> That I might once more reach that plaine,
> Where first I left my glorious traine,
> From whence th'Inlightned spirit sees
> That shady City of Palme trees;
> But (ah!) my soul with too much stay
> Is drunk, and staggers in the way.
> Some men a forward motion love,
> But I by backward steps would move,
> And when this dust falls to the urn
> In that state I came return.
>
> 'The Retreate'

Vaughan assumes that beings who regenerate themselves by willingly turning away from a corrupting world to seek the sources of life are still capable of experiencing the true joy of oneness with creation, and of having intimations of the original state. No one will doubt the intensity of his attempts to realise that condition in which we feel ourselves to be native to another element than our familiar world of pain and loss:

> I see them walking in an Air of glory,
>   Whose light doth trample on my days:
> My days, which are at best but dull and hoary,
>   Meer glimering and decays.
> O holy hope! and high humility,
>   High as the Heavens above!
> These are your walks, and you have shew'd them me
>   To kindle my cold love,
>
> 'They are all gone into the world of light!'

Like the Odes of Vaughan's mentor Casimire,[13] the poems insist upon the circumstances in which men might directly see the light of heaven, talk with angels, share in the universal interchange of sympathy, walk the fields of Bethany, experience vital joy:

> O Joyes! Infinite sweetnes! with what flowres,
> And shoots of glory, my soul breakes, and buds!
>   All the long houres
>   Of night, and Rest

Through the still shrouds
Of sleep, and Clouds,
This Dew fell on my Breast;
O how it Blouds,
And *Spirits* all my Earth! heark! In what Rings,
And *Hymning Circulations* the quick world
Awakes, and sings;
The rising winds,
And falling springs,
Birds, beasts, all things
Adore him in their kinds.
Thus all is hurl'd
In sacred *Hymnes* and *Order*, The great *Chime*
And *Symphony* of nature.

'The Morning-watch'

Some writings directly present attempts at innocent apprehension, enacting occasions when time, place, circumstance are transformed into a condition beyond time, and our existence momentarily becomes what it was. Vaughan represents these promptings to himself as intimations of our right state just because they make a sacrament of natural being, and momentarily bring us into one with the rest of creation. They prove the working of love, whether they come to us in 'brighter dreams' and 'strange thoughts' ('They are all gone into the world of light'), in pondering the Old Testament ('Religion'), or as most of them seem to, in the festivals and offices of the Church, whose symbolic meanings Durandus had drawn out:[14]

Bright shadows of true Rest! some shoots of blisse,
Heaven once a week;
The next worlds gladnes prepossest in this;
A day to seek
Eternity in time; the steps by which
We Climb above all ages; Lamps that light
Man through his heap of dark days; and the rich,
And full redemption of the whole weeks flight.

'Son-dayes'

Man's alien state becomes the harder to support if we suppose that it is our lot alone:

I would I were a stone, or tree,
Or flowre by pedigree,
Or some poor high-way herb, or Spring
To flow, or bird to sing!
Then should I (tyed to one sure state,)

All day expect my date;
But I am sadly loose, and stray
A giddy blast each way;
O let me not thus range!
Thou canst not change.

'And do they so?'

How far the rest of the natural creation shared in man's fall had been matter for debate. Vaughan decisively prefers the view that Campanella as vehemently rejects.[15] In his version of our forfeiture of Eden the Fall fatally separated mankind from all other creatures, who are 'guided by God to their right ends':

Weighing the stedfastness and state
Of some mean things which here below reside,
Where birds like watchful Clocks the noiseless date
    And Intercourse of times divide,
Where Bees at night get home and hive, and flowrs
        Early, aswel as late,
Rise with the Sun, and set in the same bowrs;

2

I would (said I) my God would give
The staidness of these things to man! for these
To his divine appointments ever cleave,
    And no new business breaks their peace;
The birds nor sow, nor reap, yet sup and dine,
        The flowres without clothes live
Yet *Solomon* was never drest so fine.

3

Man hath stil either toyes, or Care,
He hath no root, nor to one place is ty'd,
But ever restless and Irregular
    About this Earth doth run and ride,
He knows he hath a home, but scarce knows where,
        He sayes it is so far
That he hath quite forgot how to go there.

4

He knocks at all doors, strays and roams,
Nay hath not so much wit as some stones have
Which in the darkest nights point to their homes,
    By some hid sense their Maker gave;
Man is the shuttle, to whose winding quest
        And passage through these looms
God order'd motion, but ordain'd no rest.

'Man'

We are at odds with all those things about us which by their nature observe 'That busy commerce kept between/God and his creatures, though unseen' ('The Stone'). Other created things show a pious steadfastness of sympathy and an inerrancy in their office; we see love fulfilling itself in the way that herbs sleep towards the east, flowers strain towards heaven, birds herald the return of light:

> Their eyes watch for the morning hue,
> Their little grain expelling night
> So shines and sings, as if it knew
> The path unto the house of light.
> It seems their candle, howe'r done,
> Was tinn'd and lighted at the sunne.
>
> 'Cock-crowing'

Man alone has grown indifferent to the prompting of nature which he once felt:

> But hearts are not so kind:
>
> 'Sure, there's a tye of Bodyes'

Indeed the proof of our alienation is not just that we are constantly distracted by our errant faculties and passions, and by the mind's itch for material knowledge. Much more intimately grieving is the way that our affections cool and die, so that we fail to sustain our most precious personal bonds:

> Sure, there's a tye of Bodyes! and as they
> Dissolve (with it,) to Clay,
> Love languisheth, and memory doth rust
> O'r-cast with that cold dust

Here is the evidence of corruption in our inward experience. Loyalties grow cold, even memory fades with the dissolving of the physical bond in death; and then the false, short flattering delights of the world soon carry us 'Wide of a faithful grave'. *Silex Scintillans* expresses the paradoxical need to keep alive a sense of creaturely companionship by a due occupation with loss, death, the grave itself:

> Dear, beauteous death! the Jewel of the Just,
> Shining nowhere, but in the dark;
> What mysteries do lie beyond thy dust;
> Could man outlook that mark!
>
> 'They are all gone into the world of light!'

Cooled ardour must be rekindled, the shock of death kept fresh, grief itself perpetuated by a continual return to the thought of its object, and revival of the pain of deprivation:

So o'r fled minutes I retreat
Unto that hour
Which shew'd thee last, but did defeat
Thy light, and pow'r,
I search, and rack my soul to see
Those beams again,
But nothing but the snuff to me
Appeareth plain;
That dark, and dead sleeps in its known,
And common urn,
But those fled to their Makers throne,
There shine, and burn;
O could I track them! but souls must
Track one the other,
And now the spirit, not the dust
Must be thy brother.

'Silence, and stealth of days!'

The poems linked by a pilcrow-sign in *Silex Scintillans* catch the bitterest irony of loss, the guilty sense that our very habituation to the death betrays disloyalty to the dead person. But they also enlarge our perception of deadness in the world altogether.

Such an intimate drama of last things needs no Satan or formal hell. The poetry realises a universe in which love is a force of life, and continually works to resist an inert decomposition into dust. Our final wellbeing may depend upon the force with which we bring it home to ourselves that existence in the world not only dissipates our resources of sympathy but literally undoes us in the end, so that our final physical dissolution only confirms our spiritual state:

O how in this thy Quire of Souls I stand
(Propt by thy hand)
A heap of sand!
Which busie thoughts (like winds) would scatter quite
And put to flight,
But for thy might;
Thy hand alone doth tame
Those blasts, and knit my frame.

'Church-Service'

Vaughan foreruns Simone Weil in making a moral drama of St Augustine's conceit that love is gravity.[16] Moral life becomes a continual contention between the dissipating pull of worldliness and the single impulse towards God:

> only *Earth*,
> And *Man* (like *Issachar*) in lodes delight,
> Water's refin'd to *Motion*, Aire to *Light*,
> Fire to all three, but man hath no such mirth.
>
> *Plants* in the *root* with Earth do most Comply,
> Their *Leafs* with water, and humiditie,
> The *Flowres* to air draw neer, and subtiltie,
> And *seeds* a kinred fire have with the sky.
>
> All have their *keyes*, and set *ascents*; but man
> Though he knows these, and hath more of his own,
> Sleeps at the ladders foot; alas! what can
> These new discoveries do, except they drown?
>
> Thus groveling in the shade, and darkness, he
> Sinks to a dead oblivion

'The Tempest'

We lose our prospect of life by yielding to the world's voices just because we then make our bodies no more than 'dust and stones' ('Church-Service') in a universe of death, soon to be lost in a random dispersal of atoms:

> Peace, peace! I blush to hear thee; when thou art
> A dusty story
> A speechlesse heap, and in the midst my heart
> In the same livery drest
> Lyes tame as all the rest;
> When six years thence digg'd up, some youthfull Eie
> Seeks there for Symmetry
> But finding none, shal leave thee to the wind,
> Or the next foot to Crush,
> Scatt'ring thy kind
> And humble dust, tell then dear flesh
> Where is thy glory?

'The Check'

Or still worse, we quite deliberately 'overflow/And drown' our eyes ('The Match') with the rubbish of a universe of dead matter, in our desperate lust for knowledge of 'The skinne, and shell of things' ('The Search'). Love will not disclose itself to us in such searches as that:

> To rack old Elements,
> or Dust
> and say
> Sure here he must
> needs stay
> Is not the way,
> nor just.

'The Search'

> O foolish man! how has thou lost thy sight?
>   How is it that the Sun to thee alone
>   Is grown thick darkness, and thy bread, a stone?
> Hath flesh no softness now? mid-day no light?

'The Tempest'

Our very apprehension that so many things we once felt for are now no more than dust, such as we too must become, will oppress us when it leaves us with a sense of futility, and clouds our eyes to the prospect of renewed life:

> Then let not dust your eyes obscure,
> But lift them up, where still alive,
> Though fled from you, their spirits hive.

Vaughan weighs these dire effects of the world against such contrary signs as he discerns, taking them for a real temptation to the mind. Man's preoccupation with matter seems to offer a reading of the universe which is plausible enough in itself to call for a very resolute countering faith, and a certain spiritual heroism:

> Storm'd thus; I straight perceiv'd my spring
>   Meere stage, and show,
> My walke a monstrous, mountain'd thing
>   Rough-cast with Rocks, and snow;
>   And as a Pilgrims Eye
>   Far from reliefe,
> Measures the melancholy skye
>   Then drops, and rains for griefe,
>   So sigh'd I upwards still, at last
>   'Twixt steps, and falls
>   I reach'd the pinacle

'Regeneration'

In effect *Silex Scintillans* attempts to stage a quite immediate confrontation between love and death; and the fear that life may be no more than a random whirl of dead matter gives vehemence to the images of a sacred vitality which works against the gravitation of dust. Love and its effects become vital processes of life because nothing else can so intimately unite 'the spiritual and physical, the infinite and finite',[17] and counter the dead drift into the void – 'for *Love*/Is only stronger far than death' ('The Incarnation, and Passion'):

When first thou didst even from the grave
And womb of darknes becken out
My brutish soul, and to thy slave
Becam'st thy self, both guide, and Scout;
   Even from that hour
Thou gotst my heart; And though here tost
  By winds, and bit with frost
    I pine, and shrink
    Breaking the link
'Twixt thee, and me; And oftimes creep
Into th' old silence, and dead sleep,
   Quitting thy way
   All the long day,
Yet, sure, my God! I love thee most.
   Alas, thy love!

           'Disorder *and* frailty'

Christ's care for us holds us up by an unseen 'love-twist' when we are on the 'very brink/And edge of all' ('Retirement'); it lures us to bliss as a magnet ('The Queer'); it bears us aloft as by fire or wings against the inert weight of sin and earth ('Disorder *and* frailty'; 'The Knot'); it pulls us into one body as God's Church:

Tell me, O tell who did thee bring
And here, without my knowledge, plac'd,
till thou didst grow and get a wing,
A wing with eyes, and eyes that taste?

Sure, *holyness* the *Magnet* is,
And *Love* the *Lure*, that woos thee down

           'The Queer'

Thou art the true Loves-knot; by thee
   God is made our Allie,
And mans inferior Essence he
  With his did dignifie.

For Coalescent by that Band
  We are his body grown,
Nourished with favors from his hand
  Whom for our head we own.

           'The Knot'

Love is stronger than death just because it has organic virtue. Christ's blood not only revitalises those who prepare their hearts to receive it but reanimates their dust in the grave, as it were magically restoring what had seemed lost forever:

But going hence, and knowing wel what woes
    Might his friends discompose,
To shew whàt strange love he had to our good
    He gave his sacred bloud
By wil our sap, and Cordial; now in this
    Lies such a heav'n of bliss,
That, who but truly tasts it, no decay
    Can touch him any way,
Such secret life, and vertue in it lies
    It wil exalt and rise
And actuate such spirits as are shed
    Or ready to be dead,
And bring new too.

'The Sap'

Beza's Commentary on St Paul's Epistle to the Romans, which
Vaughan found so apt to his conceit of a creation in travail for
Christ's return, makes the Atonement itself the ground of spiritual
magic as the supreme act of restoration by love:

that vertue of the quickning Spirit which is so weake in us, is most perfect and
most mightie in Christ, and being imputed unto us which beleeve causeth us to be
so accompted of, as though there were no reliques of corruption and death in us
... For our sinnes are defaced by the bloude of Christ, and the guiltines of our
corruption is covered with the imputation of Christes obedience: and the corruption it selfe (which the Apostle calleth sinful sin) is healed in us by litle and litle,
by the gift of sanctification, but yet lacketh besides that, another remedy to wit,
the perfit sanctification of Christs own flesh, which also is to us imputed.[18]

The Christ of both the Vaughan brothers is the great hermetic
alchemist, whose providence oversees the process which ensures
that 'Dissolution is not death' but 'only the separation of things
which were combined', such as 'undergo dissolution, not to perish
but to be made new'.[19]

Thou art the same, faithfull, and just
        In life, or Dust;
    Though then (thus crumm'd) I stray
        In blasts,
Or Exhalations, and wasts
        Beyond all Eyes
        Yet thy love spies
    That Change, and knows thy Clay.

The world's thy boxe: how then (there tost,)
    Can I be lost?

'Buriall'

The final reckoning itself becomes no Day of Wrath but a show of provident care, which will quicken into fresh being the long-forgotten dead, just as it makes the lost flower bloom again from 'the bare root / Hid underground' ('Disorder *and* frailty'):

> O day of life, of light, of love!
> The onely day dealt from above!
> A day so fresh, so bright, so brave
> Twill shew us each forgotten grave,
> And make the dead, like flowers, arise,
> Youthful and fair to see new skies.

> 'The day of Judgement'

S. L. Bethell finely marks how Vaughan addresses the instrument of love, the Blessed Sacrament itself, as a 'medicine of immortality', and 'effects a wonderful interpenetration of the Sacrament, the human soul, and the natural order':[20]

> O drink and bread
> Which strikes death dead,
> The food of mans immortal being! ...
>
>   O quickning showers
> Of my Lords blood
> You make rocks bud
> And crown dry hils with wells and flowers!

> 'The Feast'

Love transmutes into new life the very images of death and dust, making the clay grow gold in its secret maturation:

> So let thy grace now make the way
> Even for thy love; for by that means
> We, who are nothing but foul clay,
> Shal be fine gold, which thou didst cleanse.
>
> O come! refine us with thy fire!
> Refine us! we are at a loss.
> Let not thy stars for *Balaams* hire
> Dissolve into the common dross!

> 'White Sunday'

The emblems of mortality which most oppress us in the world, the graves of our dead forerunners, become our best pledge of life when we see deeper into their quiet assumption of Christ's own care with the eye of retired understanding:

> There dust that out of doors might fill
> Thy eies, and blind thee still,
> Is fast asleep;

Up then, and keep
Within those doors, (my doors) dost hear? *I will.*

'Retirement'

Thus Vaughan converts Herbert's magnificent metaphor of our fellowship in dust ('Church-monuments') into a figure of an occult incubation, which justifies his own turn from the world to seek the hidden signatures of life in their holy hiding places. If the vision is benign in the end, it is also uncompromisingly exclusive.

A right acceptance of death is a condition of that full exchange of love for love with Christ upon which our spiritual vitality depends:

Thy love claims highest thanks, my sin
The lowest pitch:
But if he pays, who *loves much*, then
Thou hast made beggers rich.

'Tears'

Silex Scintillans displays a man who stakes his well-being on the irradiation of understanding by love, to the point where he supposes that the quality of our bond with the rest of creation is enough to settle here and now the issue of spiritual life and death, which the final judgment will confirm:

'Twas so, I saw thy birth: That drowsie Lake
From her faint bosome breath'd thee, the disease
Of her sick waters, and Infectious Ease.
But, now at Even
Too grosse for heaven,
Thou fall'st in teares, and weep'st for thy mistake.

Ah! it is so with me; oft have I prest
Heaven with a lazie breath, but fruitles this
Peirc'd not; Love only can with quick accesse
Unlock the way,
When all else stray
The smoke, and Exhalations of the brest.

'The Showre'

Many of these poems must be taken for urgent spiritual endeavours, kindlings and shows of love. The fine ejaculatory suddenness of their openings assails the poet's own dullness. We hear the voice of a man who is speaking to himself as much as to God, determinedly seeking to rouse himself from deadly spiritual torpor and surprise himself into sentience:

O knit me, that am crumbled dust!

'Distraction'

Come, come, what doe I here?

Peace, peace! I know 'twas brave,

'Content'

Come my heart! come my head
In sighes, and teares!

'The Call'

My Soul, there is a Countrie

'Peace'

This seems far from mindless enthusiasm or visionary rapture. In fact it is precisely the lapse of intelligence we remark when we occasionally catch the poet using his considerable resources of rhetoric to whip up his own fervour:

> Iesus, my life! how shall I truly love thee?
> O that thy Spirit would so strongly move me,
> That thou wert pleas'd to shed thy grace so farr
> As to make man all pure love, flesh a star! . . .
>   O come and rend,
> Or bow the heavens! Lord bow them and descend,
> And at thy presence make these mountains flow,
> These mountains of cold Ice in me! Thou art
> Refining fire, O then refine my heart,
> My foul, foul heart!

'Love-sick'

No doubt the impulse is the more vehement because the poet conceives that his solitary ardour has so much to overcome if the flint is to yield any spark, the veil upon the mind to be shattered. The teachings of the Catholic reformer Juan de Valdes (c. 1500–41), which so interested mid-seventeenth-century Anglicans, had been controverted by the Council of Trent precisely because de Valdes and his followers set such store by sheer faith and right feeling: 'he that by his faith feeleth not the marvellous effects [of spiritual rebirth] . . . which the inspired faith doth in a Christian man, let him know that he hath not yet the true Christian faith'.[21]

Yet the positive source of Vaughan's poetic peremptoriness may be discerned in the free imaginative vitality of his expectation of a realm of love, which will also be a condition of light:

Then I that here saw darkly in a glasse
But mists, and shadows passe,
And, by their owne weake *Shine*, did search the springs
And Course of things
Shall with Inlightned Rayes
Peirce all their wayes;
And as thou saw'st, I in a thought could goe
To heav'n, or Earth below
To reade some *Starre*, or *Min'rall*, and in State
There often sate,
So shalt thou then with me
(Both wing'd, and free,)
Rove in that mighty, and eternall light
Where no rude shade, or night
Shall dare approach us

'Resurrection and Immortality'

The sudden ardour expresses the intense will to believe that reality is there in the natural manifestation, just beyond dust-clouded eyes, to be won by the force of a spiritual resolve and take one aback with a momentary gleam of its naked splendour. This scarcely seems a matter of the emotional re-experiencing of some commonplace and orthodox ideas which E. C. Pettet describes.[22] Rather, 'thought was with him an emotion', as Edith Sichel finely remarked of Vaughan some eighteen years before Eliot found this character in Donne.[23] Vaughan commits himself to visual projections in a way that no other metaphysical poet does because he conceived that reality is accessible to us as something immediately seen, a momentary piercing of the dust and dark. What makes him a metaphysical poet, rather than an enthusiast or a visionary, is undoubtedly the 'habit of mind which feels in the created universe the uncreated universe beyond',[24] but also his expectation that right seeing and feeling follow right understanding. The poems are essentially attempts to make hidden truth intelligible to the mind; and Vaughan's declensions into dull banality often mark a failure of interpretative wit. It is a measure of the resoluteness of his assumption that love is as much a quickness of intelligence as of passion that he so rarely becomes shrill or perfervid, and has no rhetoric of sentiment.

He does quite crucially assume that the quickening work of love simply goes on and may still be apprehended, however dulled to its operations we become in our ordinary lives. Vaughan strives intensely to comprehend the life of an organism of love, whose vitality he opposes to the insentient force of a machine. His alertness to natural processes, and capacity to create their life in verse, are surely quite distinctive, however rarely he can carry the vision through; and a poem becomes a spiritual perception in itself when it is the very means of realising the interplay of love in the creation. Vital energy is often quite thrillingly snatched from the void of torpor:

> Oft have I seen, when that renewing breath
> That binds, and loosens death
> Inspir'd a quickning power through the dead
> Creatures a bed,
> Some drowsie silk-worme creepe
> From that long sleepe
> And in weake, infant hummings chime, and knell
> About her silent Cell
> Untill at last full with the vitall Ray
> She wing'd away,
> And proud with life, and sence,
> Heav'ns rich Expence,
> Esteem'd (vaine things!) of two whole Elements
> As meane, and span-extents.
>
> 'Resurrection and Immortality'

If the universe is as Vaughan conceives it then it cannot be indifferent to our attempts to understand it:

> Shall I then thinke such providence will be
> Lesse friend to me?
> Or that he can endure to be unjust
> Who keeps his Covenant even with our dust.
>
> 'Resurrection and Immortality'

Rendering life so vividly in poems must have mattered to the poet as evidence of his capacity for even a momentary sympathy with the spirit which animates creation, and kindles his own endeavour. The poems define themselves in the end as the returns of loving comprehension, momentary dispersals of lethargy and blindness such as the creation itself assists if we temper ourselves to it in sympathy with its own spirit. In the teeth of all contrary appearances they affirm that providential care works upon us still, reconciling us to its own modes of love so that we may respond in kind:

> Poor birds this doctrine sing,
> And herbs which on dry hills do spring
> Or in the howling wilderness
> Do know thy dewy morning-hours,
> And watch all night for mists or showers,
> Then drink and praise thy bounteousness
>
> 'Providence'

The bond of kind is not finally severed with death; love does not fade into forgetful oblivion but may still direct us from above, as by the virtue of a star:

> Gods Saints are shining lights: who stays
> Here long must passe
> O're dark hills, swift streames, and steep ways
> As smooth as glasse;
> But these all night
> Like Candles, shed
> Their beams, and light
> Us into Bed

'Joy of my life!'

The universe we inhabit is neither neutral nor arbitrary in its dealings with our deserts. Those very crosses and afflictions which just men bear in the world only show the working of provident love, being warranted by the pains Christ himself suffered for us:

> And since these biting frosts but kil
> Some tares in me which choke, or spil
> That seed thou sow'st, Blest be thy skil!
>
> Blest be thy Dew, and blest thy frost,
> And happy I to be so crost,
> And cur'd by Crosses at thy cost....
>
> Thus while thy sev'ral mercies plot,
> And work on me now cold, now hot,
> The work goes on, and slacketh not

'Love, and Discipline'

Unjust suffering becomes the seal of love in the world; whereas worldly triumph only marks a severance from true life.

All the more pointed then that one relationship of love gets short shrift. When so much is made of a universal bond of sympathy Vaughan's attack on erotic attraction seems notable. Here is a body of lyric poetry which spiritualises organic fruition itself, and finds grace in the radiance of the stars, while turning clean away from sexual ardour and even from human beauty. Vaughan was not content just to drop his amorous versifying tacitly in the two years between *Olor Iscanus* and *Silex Scintillans*. He makes his renunciation of such fashionable passions emphatically explicit in *Silex Scintillans* itself, and even couples it with his attack on empirical inquiry. Nor does he attempt to distinguish between sensible and intelligible love. In a collection so exclusively devoted to ways of reaching spiritual truth there is no time spent at all in the search for some elevating power in a woman's beauty, no inclination to abstract an intellectual ideal from its sensible embodiment. Vaughan simply opposes the pull of sexual allure to true love, and looks for meaning in the life of creatures as it is:

> Mans favorite sins, those tainting appetites
> Which nature breeds, and some fine clay invites,
> With all their soft, kinde arts and easie strains
> Which strongly operate, though without pains,
> Did not a greater beauty rule mine eyes,
> None would more dote on, nor so soon entice.
> But since these sweets are sowre, and poyson'd here
> Where the impure seeds flourish all the year
> And private Tapers will but help to stray
> Ev'n those, who *by them* would finde out the day,
> I'le seal my eyes up, and to thy commands
> Submit my wilde heart, and restrain my hands;
> I will do nothing, nothing know, nor see
> But what thou bidst, and shew'st, and teachest me.

'The hidden Treasure'

Vaughan well allowed that a credo of love must take account of right sexual union. 'Isaacs Marriage' sets out at length the absolute difference between holy marriage in the patriarchal age of mankind and sexual commerce in our degenerate state:

> happy those
> White dayes, that durst no impious mirth expose!
> When Conscience by lew'd use had not lost sense,
> Nor bold-fac'd custome banish'd Innocence;
> Thou hadst no pompous train, nor *Antick* crowd
> Of young, gay swearers, with their needlesse, lowd
> Retinue; All was here smooth as thy bride
> And calm like her, or that mild Evening-tide;
> Yet, hadst thou nobler guests: Angels did wind
> And rove about thee, guardians of thy minde,
> These fetch'd thee home thy bride, and all the way
> Advis'd thy servant what to do, and say;
> These taught him at the *well*, and thither brought
> The Chast, and lovely object of thy thought

Isaac's spiritual union comes to fruition in the universal reciprocity of love just because it follows out the right order of nature:

And now thou knewest her coming, It was time
To get thee wings on, and devoutly climbe
Unto thy God, for Marriage of all states
Makes most unhappy, or most fortunates;
This brought thee forth, where now thou didst undress
Thy soul, and with new pinions refresh
Her wearied wings, which so restor'd did flye
Above the stars, a track unknown, and high,
And in her piercing flight perfum'd the ayer
Scatt'ring the *Myrrhe*, and incense of thy pray'r.
So from *Lahai-roi's* Well some spicie cloud
Woo'd by the Sun swels up to be his shrowd,
And from his moist wombe weeps a fragrant showre,
Which, scatter'd in a thousand pearls, each flowre
And herb partakes, where having stood awhile
And something coold the parch'd, and thirstie Isle,
The thankful Earth unlocks her self, and blends,
A thousand odours, which (all mixt,) she sends
Up in one cloud, and so returns the skies
That dew they lent, a breathing sacrifice.

The 'her' of these lines soon merges with Isaac's own soul, which must disburden and renew itself by pious devotion for its celestial venture of love. Even patriarchal liaisons seem to have much the same moral status as Donne allows women themselves:

They were to good ends, and they are so still,
But accessory, and principal in ill.

The First Anniversary, lines 103–4

To put Vaughan against the Florentine followers of Plato is to see how radically unplatonic is the metaphysics of love which shapes the poetry of *Silex Scintillans*. Like them he believes that we inhabit a world of illusion, and must seek the true reality in another state. But he does not look to a transcendental order of ideal forms, abstracted from their material being, or separate spiritual from sensible existence in its effects. His controlling conviction is that the life of spirit interfuses with the life of sense. Created things attain their highest state of love not as they approach the condition of the source of love but in the fulfilment of their individual being, the performance of their own right function. Spiritual truth is to be sought in the distinctive life of things, which may be an activity of the body. Ross Garner was clearly right to insist on 'a central core of experience as the principle of organisation in Vaughan's religious poetry',[25] and to find the shaping impulse of this experience in Vaughan's sense that the life of the spirit cannot be separated from the life of the body.[26] R. A. Durr adds that the urge which unifies body and spirit is love.[27] Donne expresses just Vaughan's understanding of the Incarnation:

since he came in the flesh, hee is now made man; And, that God and Man, are so met, is a signe to mee, that God and I, shall never be parted.

Donne, Sermons, VI, 8, p. 179, Christmas Day
1624

If *Silex Scintillans* discovers no primary way to truth through sexual love, whether embodied or ideal, it is just because Vaughan holds out still less hope of a mutual fruition of right love in our fallen state than we find in *Paradise Lost* xi, or in *Samson Agonistes*:

> Praying! and to be married? It was rare,
> But now 'tis monstrous

'Isaacs Marriage'

For him there is no good to be drawn from the world at all while we ourselves are spiritually dead, and behave as if the creation may be no more than a chance conjunction of atoms. What we see then is all idleness, 'queint follies, sugred sin', mere shadows and cobwebs, and worse:

> Blind, desp'rate *fits*, that study how
> To dresse, and trim our shame,
> That gild rank poyson, and allow
> Vice in a fairer name;
> The *Purles* of youthfull bloud, and bowles,
> Lust in the Robes of Love,
> The idle talk of feav'rish souls
> Sick with a scarf, or glove

'Idle Verse'

Such false wit as would dress lust in the robes of love well matches our false attempts to know the universe; vain passions suit with vanity of spirit:

> I beg'd here long, and gron'd to know
> Who gave the Clouds so brave a bow,
> Who bent the spheres, and circled in
> Corruption with this glorious Ring,
> What is his name, and how I might
> Descry some part of his great light.
> I summon'd nature: peirc'd through all her store,
> Broke up some seales, which none had touch'd before,
> Her wombe, her bosome, and her head

> Where all her secrets lay a bed
> I rifled quite

'Vanity of Spirit'

Our only right course is to abandon such impostures altogether in favour of true understanding and love, such as we must be born again to attain. We must remake our lives and affections in the world:

> Therefore, those loose delights and lusts, which here
>   Men call good chear,
>   I will close girt and tyed
> For mourning sack-cloth wear, all mortified . . .
> Besides, those Kerchiefs sometimes shed
>   To make me brave,
> I cannot finde, but where thy head
> Was once laid for me in thy grave.
> Thy grave! To which my thoughts shal move
> Like Bees in storms unto their Hive,
> That from the murd'ring worlds false love
> Thy death may keep my soul alive.

'The Obsequies'

In the moral extremity which *Silex Scintillans* enacts unredeemed sexuality has only destructive power; and Vaughan follows out as a reform close to home the conversion of erotic passion into redemptive love. St Mary Magdalen's decays of sin are renewed by the 'Divine Restorative' of Christ's blood, which transform into 'fixed stars' her 'loose and tempting spies', and convert into true love a false art of attraction:

> Dear *Soul*! thou knew'st, flowers here on earth
> At their Lords foot-stool have their birth;
> Therefore thy wither'd self in haste
> Beneath his blest feet thou didst cast,
> That at the root of this green tree
> Thy great decays restor'd might be . . .
> Cheap, mighty Art! her Art of love,
> Who lov'd much and much more could move

'St Mary Magdalen'

The poet takes for an authentic spiritual alchemy the effect on his own career of the Holy Bible, whose quickening touch of solicitude has refined into true desire his wild pursuit of vanity:

> By this milde art of love at length
> Thou overcam'st my sinful strength,
> And having brought me home, didst there

284

> Shew me that pearl I sought elsewhere.
> Gladness, and peace, and hope, and love,
> The secret favors of the Dove,
> Her quickning kindness, smiles and kisses,
> Exalted pleasures, crowning blisses,
> Fruition, union, glory, life
> Thou didst lead to, and still all strife.

'To the Holy Bible'

Where then may we really encounter the active life of love in the universe about us? Vaughan assumes that it is everywhere to be realised, not in cold abstractions of any kind but by our own sympathetic involvement in the living processes of creation. Such evidences of spontaneous love as creatures do offer to the quickened intelligence inhere in their fulfilment of their roles, and may no more be discovered in supposed laws of matter than in mere outward appearances. They present themselves to the mind in intelligible images, spiritual hieroglyphs of the uncorrupted state such as only unclouded faculties may grasp:

> O that man could do so! that he would hear
> The world read to him! all the vast expence
> In the Creation shed, and slav'd to sence
> Makes up but lectures for his eie, and ear.
> Sure, mighty love foreseeing the discent
> Of this poor Creature, by a gracious art
> Hid in these low things snares to gain his heart,
> And layd surprizes in each Element.

'The Tempest'

Vaughan wrote at a time when the Egyptian hieroglyphs brought to light in the anthology of Horapollo were still taken to enshrine a secret wisdom, as the language of men who were nature's priests because they lived so much nearer the original human state:[28]

Egyptian characters were used by the first people of the world before such hieroglyphics came into common employment among men ... Together with the sciences, and the names of things, they were discovered and taught by Adam our first parent. Nonetheless the animals, in which were to be found the particular likenesses of divine secrets, served solely for the observances of priests and not for the common ends of writing ... From these animals they dug out allegories of divine secrets, according to the use of the religion of those times.[29]

A latter-day Silurean had good metaphysical authority for believing that nature's truths revealed themselves in occult signs, which have been deliberately left for our erected wit to interpret, rather than in abstract laws:

Nature is the sculptor: she endows everything with the form which is also the essence, and thus the form reveals the essence.

There is nothing that nature has not signed in such a way that man may discover its essence ... The art of signs teaches us to give each man his true name in accordance with his innate nature ... Since nothing is so secret or hidden that it cannot be revealed, everything depends on the discovery of those things which manifest the hidden.[30]

Over and again Vaughan attempts his own application of such ideas:

> Each *tree, herb, flowre*
> Are shadows of his *wisedome*, and his Pow'r.

'Rules *and* Lessons'

He persuades himself that the love whose gracious art devised such subtle means of ensnaring our hearts must work for an answering motion of love; when a man so opens himself to the creatures that they in loving kindness fall open to him, then he at least strikes sparks from the flint of a hardened heart:

> What ever 'tis, whose beauty here below
> Attracts thee thus & makes thee stream & flow,
>   And wind and curle, and wink and smile,
>   Shifting thy gate and guile ...
>
> Yet, seeing all things that subsist and be,
> Have their Commissions from Divinitie,
>   And teach us duty, I will see
>   What man may learn from thee.

'The Starre'

Love and sacred wit are in the end the same endeavour; and they are not to be appreciated, much less replaced, by the cold abstracting intellect of mere meddlers in the working of the universe. Vaughan's flat opposition to the assumptions of empirical science made his occultism defiant.

Silex Scintillans has the curious distinction of making great poetry out of ideas about the physical universe which we take to be crackbrained in Vaughan's alchemical brother, and aberrant in Newton. How far can Vaughan carry off his faith that the natural hieroglyphs he discovers hold truths which are quite lost to us in the decays of time since the Fall? We cannot doubt that for Vaughan the act of writing a poem may itself be a way to truth, when the poet seeks to reach and understand the qualities which actually inhere in creatures in virtue of their retaining so much more than we do of their original purity of purpose:

Romans 8:19

Etenim res Creatae exerto Capite observantes expectant revelationem Filiorum Dei.

> And do they so? have they a Sense
> Of ought but Influence?
> Can they their heads lift, and expect,
> And grone too? why th'Elect
> Can do no more: my volumes sed
> They were all dull, and dead,
> They judg'd them senslesse, and their state
> Wholly Inanimate.
> Go, go; Seal up thy looks,
> And burn thy books

The insights do not seem equally arresting. A poet who is so prone to slip into homely moralising could not have found it easy to tell a spiritual illumination from a moral example. But then what kind of enlightenment does Vaughan actually seek in such natural effects as a shower of rain, or a waterfall?

> With what deep murmurs through times silent stealth
> Doth thy transparent, cool and watry wealth
> Here flowing fall,
> And chide, and call,
> As if his liquid, loose Retinue staid
> Lingring, and were of this steep place afraid,
> The common pass
> Where, clear as glass,
> All must descend
> Not to an end:
> But quickned by this deep and rocky grave,
> Rise to a longer course more bright and brave.
> Dear stream! dear bank, where often I
> Have sate, and pleas'd my pensive eye,
> Why, since each drop of thy quick store
> Runs thither, whence it flow'd before,
> Should poor souls fear a shade or night,
> Who came (sure) from a sea of light?
> Or since those drops are all sent back
> So sure to thee, that none doth lack
> Why should frail flesh doubt any more
> That what God takes, hee'l not restore?
> O useful Element and clear!
> My sacred wash and cleanser here,
> My first consigner unto those
> Fountains of life, where the Lamb goes?
> What sublime truths, and wholesome themes,
> Lodge in thy mystical, deep streams!

Such as dull man can never finde
Unless that Spirit lead his minde,
Which first upon thy face did move,
And hatch'd all with his quickning love.
As this loud brooks incessant fall
In streaming rings restagnates all,
Which reach by course the bank, and then
Are no more seen, just so pass men.
O my invisible estate,
My glorious liberty, still late!
Thou art the Channel my soul seeks,
Not this with Cataracts and Creeks.

'The Water-fall'

A waterfall may seem to be factitiously taken for a hieroglyph of man's spiritual life, and of the course of creation; and sheer verbal dexterity helps point the conceit. We are told that the waters come from a sea of light, pass fearfully through a deep and rocky grave with their 'liquid, loose Retinue', then rise to 'a longer course more bright and brave'; and that just in perceiving this progress so, the purified spirit may reassure itself of the transitoriness of its fears and glooms here, and of a glorious transformation thereafter. It is because the waterfall brings it home to the understander that such a process is natural to creatures in the order of which we are part that it is praised for the 'sublime truths, and wholesome themes' which 'Lodge in thy mystical, deep streams'; in spontaneously fulfilling its necessary functions of purification and refreshment it shows the understander how such salutary vitality may also enable his own aspiring spirit to reach the 'Fountains of life, where the Lamb goes'. Yet the poem boldly claims to be an enterprise for an initiate wit, assuring us that the mystic sense of the waterfall-hieroglyph cannot be grasped by dull man unless the same spirit leads his mind as first moved upon the water, hatching 'all with his quickning love'. We must take this quickening love at once for the spirit which impregnated matter in the first place, and the impulse that prompts man's sluggish mind to apprehend the signatures of love in the creation now. Love kindles dull brute matter to self-apprehending life, and warmth of sympathy. It seems that the very animation of wit, that sharpening of ingenuity which allows the mind to construe such hieroglyphs as this, must be taken for a clearing of spiritual vision towards a reconciliation with God's providence. The poem itself tells us that the waterfall discloses its nature to the initiate not merely for his moral edification, but as a living instance of natural processes in which he may discern for himself the order of an economy of love.

The emblematic application of mere artifacts might seem more patently arbitrary, however ingeniously it is carried through:

Eternal God! maker of all
That have liv'd here, since the mans fall;
The Rock of ages! in whose shade
They live unseen, when here they fade.

Thou knew'st this *papyr*, when it was
Meer *seed*, and after that but *grass*;
Before 'twas *drest* or *spun*, and when
Made *linen*, who did *wear* it then:
What were their lifes, their thoughts & deeds
Whither good *corn*, or fruitless *weeds*.

Thou knew'st this *Tree*, when a green *shade*
Cover'd it, since a *Cover* made,
And where it flourish'd, grew and spread,
As if it never should be dead.

Thou knew'st this harmless *beast*, when he
Did live and feed by thy decree
On each green thing; then slept (well fed)
Cloath'd with this *skin*, which now lies spred
A *Covering* o're this aged book,
Which makes me wisely weep and look
On my own dust; meer dust it is,
But not so dry and clean as this.
Thou knew'st and saw'st them all and though
Now scatter'd thus, dost know them so.

O knowing, glorious spirit! when
Thou shalt restore trees, beasts and men,
When thou shalt make all new again,
Destroying onely death and pain,
Give him amongst thy works a place,
Who in them mov'd and sought thy face!

'The Book'

In Vaughan's moving vision of the course of all life this book surely becomes a very telling emblem of death, dispersal and recovery. The figure works the more powerfully because it really is made to show us how the scattered elements, which once had their own natural organic life, are artificially reassembled in the arbitrary form of dead learning. The recovery and resurrection of those *disjecta membra* will be an unmaking of the book and a reconstitution of the living organisms; the book reveals to the quickened eye, quite counter to our worldly wisdom, nothing less than the working of provident love.

Vaughan's poems authenticate his vision, the poetry is the thinking. Vaughan was undoubtedly one of those spiritual pilgrims to whom 'the miseries of the world/Are miseries, and will not let them rest'. But he had the temper of his time and place in that he yearned for a final pattern in temporal events which often seemed to deny it. It was the search for such a pattern, and the attempt to realise it in a whole impulse of the spirit, which makes his poems so much more than the exercises in subconscious association that E. C. Pettet describes:

> many of his lyrics, including most of the best ones, evolve not so much through the logical connected development from thought to thought as by way of association, sometimes rather oblique in nature, and by the spontaneous proliferating of some unifying complex of imagery . . .
>
> *Silex Scintillans* is quite remarkable for the way in which its numerous recurrent image-clusters, besides inspiring so many poems, come together without the writer's conscious ordering. Time and again one constituent of a compound image will call up the rest of it through what can only have been some process of subconscious association.[31]

R. A. Durr well shows how Vaughan's images work as '*signs* bearing a conventionally defined meaning', and yet 'transcend their semiotic significance as they function in the context of the total network of interrelations'.[32] The play of mind one encounters in *Silex Scintillans* as a whole seems better characterised as purposeful poetic thinking than as subliminal association, or mystical intuition, or just a discharge of emotion. We are the losers if we sell such poetry so short that we no longer see how Vaughan, with whatever difference from Herbert, speaks to our condition. By the 1650s, in England, it was not intellectually easy to savour the anguish of life in a universe without meaning and yet affirm that natural being is sacred, or to experience the pain and injustice of the world and still apprehend so intensely the life of a loving providence in the creation. *Silex Scintillans* wages the struggle, which engages intelligence no less than feeling, to make sense of our existence in a metaphysics of sacred love and live out that resolve.

ii. *Appraising the world*

In canto xxvii of the *Paradiso* Dante and Beatrice ascend to the Crystalline Sphere of heaven, marking as they go our world of lust and pride – 'this threshing-floor' – which now turns far away below them. At this

outer limit of natural being Beatrice appropriately defines for the
pilgrim the relation of eternity to time, of absolute love and providence to contingent events, 'smiling so happily that God appeared
to joy in her face':

> La natura del mondo, che quieta
>   il mezzo e tutto l'altro intorno move,
>   quinci comincia come da sua meta;
> e questo cielo non ha altro dove
>   che la mente divina, in che s'accende
>   l'amor che il volge e la virtù ch'ei piove.
> Luce ed amor d'un cerchio lui comprende,
>   sì come questo li altri; e quel precinto
>   colui che 'l cinge solamente intende.
> Non è suo moto per altro distinto;
>   ma li altri son misurati da questo,
>   sì come diece da mezzo e da quinto.
> E come il tempo tegna in cotal testo
>   le sue radici e ne li altri le fronde,
>   omai a te può esser manifesto.

The nature of the universe which holds its centre still and moves all else about it
begins here as from its hub; and this heaven has no other seat but the divine mind,
in which is kindled both the love that turns it and the virtue which it rains down.

Light and love comprehend it in one circle, as it comprehends the other
spheres; and that girdle is moved solely by him who makes it.

Its motion is not set apart from all else; rather, the others take their measure
from it, just as ten is made up of a half and a fifth.

And how time may have its roots in that pot and its leaves in the other [spheres]
may now be plain to you.

Paradiso xxvii, 106–20

Time has its roots in eternity, temporal being is sustained by the
virtue of eternal light and love; whatever has identity in the world is
a mode of that eternal light and love. Beatrice's words offer us the
image of a universal reciprocity of love in which natural creatures,
no less than the seraphim and cherubim, receive that lifegiving
power to the extent that they will to return it. When Beatrice at once
bursts out to condemn cupidity –

> Oh cupidigia che i mortali affonde
>   sì sotto te, che nessuno ha podere
>   di trarre li occhi fuor delle tue onde!

– we understand that 'cupidigia' is so damnable precisely because it
completely overwhelms mortal beings who, once they have succum-
bed to it, lose the power to 'lift their eyes above your waves'. Such a

love of self, or greed for self, works directly counter to the universal
disposition of a loving providence and denies the very principle of
God's creation.

Dante's conceit of a creation vitalised by love given and returned
is illuminatingly akin to Vaughan's. So it is scarcely a surprise when
a commentator on the *Paradiso* discovers 'a notable parallel with
these lines' in Vaughan's 'The World', a poem which he thinks 'was
written, probably, with no reference to Dante, but drawing from the
same tradition'.[33] He points the parallel from the first stanza and the
last two lines of 'The World'.

'The World' is one of the few poems in which Vaughan confronts
the ordinary activities of secular men. It is a revealing piece, not least
in its intermittent imaginative power:

'The World'

I saw Eternity the other night
Like a great *Ring* of pure and endless light,
   All calm, as it was bright,
And round beneath it, Time in hours, days, years
    Driv'n by the spheres
Like a vast shadow mov'd, In which the world
   And all her train were hurl'd;
The doting Lover in his queintest strain
    Did their Complain,
Neer him, his Lute, his fancy, and his flights,
    Wits sour delights,
With gloves, and knots the silly snares of pleasure
    Yet his dear Treasure
All scatter'd lay, while he his eys did pour
    Upon a flowr.

2

The darksome States-man hung with weights and woe
Like a thick midnight-fog mov'd there so slow
   He did nor stay, nor go;
Condemning thoughts (like sad Ecclipses) scowl
    Upon his soul,
And Clouds of crying witnesses without
   Pursued him with one shout.
Yet dig'd the Mole, and lest his ways be found
    Workt under ground,
Where he did Clutch his prey, but one did see
    That policie,
Churches and altars fed him, Perjuries
    Were gnats and flies,
It rain'd about him bloud and tears, but he
    Drank them as free.

3

The fearfull miser on a heap of rust
Sate pining all his life there, did scarce trust
   His own hands with the dust,
Yet would not place one peece above, but lives
   In feare of theeves.
Thousands there were as frantick as himself
   And hug'd each one his pelf,
The down-right Epicure plac'd heav'n in sense
   And scornd pretence
While others slipt into a wide Excesse
   Said little lesse;
The weaker sort slight, triviall wares Inslave
   Who think them brave,
And poor, despised truth sate Counting by
   Their victory.

4

Yet some, who all this while did weep and sing,
And sing, and weep, soar'd up into the *Ring*,
   But most would use no wing.
O fools (said I,) thus to prefer dark night
   Before true light,
To live in grots, and caves, and hate the day
   Because it shews the way,
The way which from this dead and dark abode
   Leads up to God,
A way where you might tread the Sun, and be
   More bright than he.
But as I did their madnes so discusse
   One whisper'd thus,
This Ring the Bride-groome did for none provide
   But for his bride.

John 2:16 and 17
*All that is in the world, the lust of the flesh, the lust of the Eys, and the pride of life, is not
of the father, but is of the world.*
   *And the world passeth away, and the lusts thereof, but he that doth the will of God
abideth for ever.*

If Vaughan does not always seem to know the vision from the
banal moralising it may be because his grasp of moral life is less sure
than Donne's or Herbert's or Marvell's. Certainly he attributes less
than they do to the power of man's will, and lacks their keen sense of
moral peril. You do not find him posing that immediate choice
which gives Herbert's poems their terrible directness:

My throat, my soul is hoarse;
My heart is wither'd like a ground
Which thou dost curse.
My thoughts turn round,
And make me giddie; Lord, I fall,
Yet call.

'Longing'

For Vaughan moral life is not so much a conflict as a wooing, a matter of a man's response to the force that holds the whole creation in the magnetic power of its love. He sees himself more as inadequate lover than as agonist:

I long, and grone, and grieve for thee,
For thee my words, my tears do gush,
O that I were but where I see!
Is all the note within my Bush.

'The Pilgrimage'

Hardly less noticeable throughout *Silex Scintillans* is the poet's inclination to cope with mundane designs by dissevering himself from them. Vaughan's contempt of the world becomes a party alignment. For him 'the world' is simply that part of human activity (and human kind as well) which stands outside the pale of regenerate life, and hence beyond the scope of Christ's saving love. This indeed is the stark presumption which 'The World' sets out to try. The subject of this slight lyric poem is nothing less than the relation of time and the world to eternity, the real value of worldly activities and motives. That a man should turn so naturally to lyric poetry when he has these imperative metaphysical questions to pose to himself is remarkable enough, and it is just the kind of sudden raid upon the eternal which distinguishes English poetry in the brief era between Donne and Rochester. To find anything like it you would have to go back to Cavalcanti and Dante; and the difference between that Florentine poetry and the English metaphysical lyrics marks a drastic shift in European consciousness over some three centuries.

'The World' is a vivid poem, full of life and sudden surprises, but it does not engage us in the dynamic process of a tough argument, as though the mind must there and then fight its way to a new truth. On the contrary, it puts the resolved state of things in a few vivid images and simply spells out their purport, by way of bringing home to the poet and us the true condition of human existence in our lapsed creation. So the poem presents an encounter of opposites, but a clear and simple one which arises out of our instantaneous perception of the contrast between the image of eternity and the image of time. The attributes of eternal being – calm stability, refulgent beauty, permanence and the like – stand point-by-point against the condition of the dark, distracted, insubstantial time-hurled world. Vaughan has something of Milton's cosmic grandeur of imagination. But the breathtaking casualness of his opening announcement here, and the irresistible onward sweep of the vision, all but distract us from the point of the juxtaposition which is the absolute opposition between the two parts of the conceit.

Vaughan amplifies the second part first, with his emblems of such representative activities of the world as love, statecraft, money-grubbing, sensual pleasure-seeking, riotous living, lightminded triviality. This part of the poem gives substance to an argument which by stanza four he is ready to develop; and he takes it further in that simple but powerful return to the opening contrast. The two images, as we now vividly see, do not wholly exclude each other after all for some few souls escape the world and make the perilous transference from time to eternity, impelled by motives to which Vaughan's images give spatial amplitude. Plainly it is the difference we feel between that elevating virtue and the supineness of the rest which allows him to sweep in so superbly, and moralise the division between the few and the many:

> O fools (said I,) thus to prefer dark night
> Before true light

This time there will be no dismal lapse into platitude at the climax of his argument. Logical necessity and lyric fervour coincide to elevate the mood of the assault on the benighted worldlings, which brings out what their worldliness really entails. Carried up so into lofty denunciation the voice is ready to spring that last dramatic surprise, the sudden shift into an exalted whisper which resolves at a stroke both the play of images in the poem and the implicit opposition they set up between the worldly and the eternal conditions. The pure circle of eternity becomes the ring of marriage; and all further argument is stopped short, for only the bride of Christ can make the transference in any case, and gain this ring:

> *This Ring the Bride-groome did for none provide*
> *But for his bride*

The *sotto voce* simplicity of that conclusion is convincing, and might even strike us with a sense of relief if we are accustomed to Vaughan's mode of virtuoso tightrope walking. More than any other great seventeenth-century poet (and he may be most characteristically Welsh in this) he lives by his momentary excitements, and by the fortunate coming together in his imagination of elements not obviously at one, vivid visual apprehensions, adroit effects of wit, lyric passion. It does not always happen that his first imaginative impulse can extend itself into a tightly sustained argument, or even maintain its lyric impetus. Donne, Herbert, Marvell are of stabler poetic temper than Vaughan. Without fervour he is nowhere.

The closure of 'The World' has its difficulties if Vaughan meant it to answer the questions he has raised. What can it really mean to say that the bridegroom provided the ring for none but his bride? Vaughan is undoubtedly thinking of a choice rather than a predestination, and the voice announces that the ring is reserved for those few who are willing to make themselves the brides of Christ by detaching themselves altogether from the love of worldly objects. The poem categorically (and curiously) distinguishes between their activities and the worldly concerns of all the rest. For them there will be no sexual love, policy, money, sensual delights, or anything but weeping and singing. Penitence and praise oddly become the means to salvation, while all else is damning distraction.

This is uncompromising enough, but we must assume that Vaughan means it. He is not the man to be seduced by a poetic flourish into a sense he would not stand by elsewhere; and in any case this is a critical moment in *Silex Scintillans*. We seem no longer to be countenancing a society in which Christian activity has place and grace. In Vaughan's poem the world claims its own as they choose it, and simply holds them down; the ring is not for them. All that matters, or can matter, is that we detach ourselves from this world so that we make the crossing spontaneously. We must live our eternity here and now.

This is not the kind of detachment from the world which follows out a resolve to live the life of spirit, rather than the life of sense. It is the proof of a moral exclusiveness which separates a few regenerate beings from most of human kind. Vaughan is not so much attacking a character he shares with all other men in virtue of our common humanity, as condemning those men who cut themselves off from the truth he sees. The poem mounts no general assault on our moral nature, or drama of the moral will. Vaughan does not involve himself in the human activities he condemns, or admit himself a citizen of that world at all.

Elsewhere in *Silex Scintillans* Vaughan's denunciations of 'the world' may prompt us to ask what it is in common life that merits such categorical dismissal. No doubt he needed to confirm his will in a renunciation which was not wholly easy to him, as Donne turns his keenest raillery on the life of affairs he had involuntarily lost. But Donne knew just what he was mocking, and partly mocked his own attachment to that teeming life. The evidence of 'The World' is that in contrast with Donne's enforced rustication Vaughan's was a self-chosen retirement, which sustained itself by moral isolation and wholesale contempt. On the one hand stands the regenerate poet, with a very few such solitary strivers towards original innocence; on the other hand there is the world of ordinary men, unregenerate and perhaps unredeemable. It is not unlike the view of the depraved Old Testament world which Adam sees from the high mount:

> anon
> Grey-headed men and grave, with Warriours mixt,
> Assemble, and Harangues are heard, but soon
> In factious opposition, till at last
> Of middle Age one rising, eminent
> In wise deport, spake much of Right and Wrong,
> Of Justice, of Religion, Truth and Peace,
> And Judgement from above: him old and young
> Exploded, and had seis'd with violent hands,
> Had not a Cloud descending snatcht him thence
> Unseen amid the throng: so Violence
> Proceeded, and Oppression, and Sword-Law
> Through all the Plain, and refuge none was found.
>
> *Paradise Lost* xi, 661–73

Vaughan regularly assumes such a view of his own situation but rarely exposes the sense of the world in which it is founded, or shows what his grasp of human motives really amounts to. Our interest in the matter cannot be just that it is we who are being condemned. There is no doubt that it was the attempt to define his own predicament in the critical years around 1650 which fired his imagination; and the sources of his power, as the reasons for his lapses, must concern us. 'The World' has no such awful flats as some of the poems submit us to but the part of the poem which rehearses the activities of us worldings, though lively enough, scarcely operates at the level of the rest. So often in Vaughan the imaginative vitality comes and goes quite abruptly, and here we may see where mere adroitness takes over.

After the casual splendour of his opening vision Vaughan's representative worldlings seem a farcical lot whom the poet himself cannot take in earnest. His lover is a comic stereotype, silly rather than sinful and lacking even the dignity of lust; Vaughan characterises him as a foppish fool who scarcely knows what he is after, and asks no more than to dote on his mistress's beauty. Even Spenser's lustful monsters have more force than this, for at least they answer to something brutish in sensual nature. The miser is no better, a stock figure who hardly bears upon the monetary realities of Vaughan's or anybody else's day, and has little force even as a picture of covetousness. The dangerous world needs a better representative than this terrified accumulator of dust, whose self-destructive obsession with material things scarcely mirrors a human reality. Vaughan is not thinking concretely of the life around him at this point, as we see when we come to the epicures and lightminded people, about whose corrupting activities he cannot find anything specific to say at all.

The statesman is a different matter when his comportment is rendered with such Shelleyan savagery, which at least evinces some grasp of a real moral character, and of the baneful effects of politic schemings. Here Vaughan does show concern for civic action, and an awareness that life in the world may merit moral appraisal:

> but one did see
> That policie

To impute to the divine judge even that much concern for the unregenerate world is something. Vaughan more often writes as though God has simply withdrawn himself from that part of mankind which has turned its back upon him – 'Ah! he is fled!' ('The British Church'). But he seems here to be writing of events which he knows too well to reduce or dismiss, and which merit their condemnation – 'And Clouds of crying witnesses without/Pursued him ... Churches and altars fed him ... It rain'd about him bloud and tears ...' The writing at least shows up the flimsiness of the emblematic caricature he goes in for elsewhere, which simply evades the need to take civic life seriously.

The luminous beauty of the vision recommends the contrasting account of regenerate life:

> Yet some, who all this while did weep and sing,
> And sing, and weep, soar'd up into the *Ring*,
> But most would use no wing.

That 'soar'd up' lights the whole conceit, with its miming of a sudden marvellous release into universal grace from the drudgery of those earthbound pieties:

> weep and s̄īng, / and s̄īng, and w̄eep, *soar'd* . . .

Away they go quite suddenly, as though launched by a power they had stored up in that laborious alternation of lament and hymning, by which they showed their preference for true light while the rest of us lived in grots and caves, and hated the day. That heavy ritual of devotion is recompensed by the bold flight which it makes possible:

> Because it shews the way,
> The way which from this dead and dark abode
> Leads up to God

Yet it seems strange that so many people should hate the day, and knowingly refuse the way to God. In Vaughan's terms their continuance in worldly enterprises is madness, for he simply does not allow that what they do may be useful and offer as much moral scope as singleminded devotion. As he represents it, sexual love no less than politics merits only stark condemnation and dismissal, since it is manifestly halfwitted to prefer such foolery to eternal life. He leaves us to ask why only lives devoted to penitence and praise should earn an eternal world.

To question the poem so is to resist that splendid sweep of the unfolding impulse with a cavil which does not trouble Vaughan. His whole concern is to display the gap between mere worldly bustle and vital life; and expressions of sheer vitality of spirit excited his imagination, whereas moral behaviour challenged his wit. He renders the activity of the creation with a vividness which persuades us of its spiritual life:

> stars nod and sleepe,
> And through the dark aire spin a firie thread
> Such as doth gild the lazie glow-worms bed.

> 'The Lampe'

How far do intelligence and imagination come together in the resolution of 'The World'? That sudden drop of the voice at the end is expressive, and the echo of Herbert lends authority to the last simple words. This cannot be God or Christ who speaks however, and it is evidently not one of the fools in his madness. We must take it for the voice of truth sounding through space, which settles rather than resolves the conflict of values the poem has opened. The poet's vision, thus dramatically completed, carries its own assurance that it is pointless for him to dispute with the fools, or seek to relieve their frenzy, since none of them can make the vital leap anyway. Only those who love Christ rather than the world will be gathered into the pure and endless light of divine love.

Vaughan's conceit puts an unbridgeable distance between the bride and the lovers of the world. Yet he seems to mean nothing more severe than that there is no easy way of finding the path which leads to God, or of learning to tread the sun:

> and be
> More bright than he.

A man must divorce himself from the world before he may betroth himself to Christ, for a life in the world can only distract him from the true end of love. The point of the whole movement, which the figure of the ring now completes with an emblematic quibble, seems to be that the way is there all right but worldly men cannot take it even if they would. Here there can be no doubting Vaughan's drift. He means that we fix ourselves in our eternal attitude here and now in our present existence, either as distracted dust or as singleminded lovers. When we put our worldly concerns behind us and betroth ourselves to Christ we leave the world while still physically existing in it, and move spontaneously and inevitably towards the ring. 'The World' turns out to be a celebration of love from its opening image to its final words, marking the distance between those who fit themselves to love, and those who fail to love aright.

The poem intimates that the greater part of mankind will not be saved, but that the few who attain the ring, and the many who cannot reach it, alike will their condition; we save ourselves by our resolute choice of Christ rather than the world. If his antithesis between Christ and 'the world' is valid then eternal being and our human activities in the world simply exclude each other, and the election of one or other is enough in itself to settle all merely moral issues. Once we make our choice then the frailties of human nature remain with the worldlings, and the elect must simply seek to avoid the occasions of frailty; as though the battle with the self is then over and people can do no more than confirm themselves in their chosen course, hastening their own dissolution in a myriad of worldly pursuits, or heightening the fervour of their aspiration towards that country beyond the stars. Such conflict as remains must thereafter be fought out not within the self but between two camps; though what Vaughan anticipates is not a conflict but an implacable mutual disdain.

Like Dante, Vaughan offers us an image of the spheres from an emblem of love. Yet Vaughan's device quite disjoins time from eternity, directly opposing the activities of the fallen world to the ardours that gain us Christ's love and the ring of espousal. Dante's shaping conceit of the continuity, or interpenetration, of the orders of being is crucially modified in this poem by Vaughan's conviction that men must recover their innocence before they may rise from earth to light. 'The World' offers us at best a heroic leap across the gulf, and tells us that for most men there will be no crossing at all. We need not look for a Beatrice to mediate the espousals of *Silex Scintillans*.

Vaughan's self-isolation from the public life of his day after the debacle of 1648–9 made a bogy of every distraction from regenerative love. The arch-adversaries of the poet of *Silex Scintillans* are not the forces of hell, or even the sins that make him unreceptive to grace, but the world itself, and death. It is what he makes of our encounters with these corruptions that proves him. No other seventeenth-century poet who concerns us, not even Traherne, believes anything like this. Vaughan's radical attack on worldly life gives him more in common with Bunyan than with Herbert; indeed his supposed discipleship to Herbert must be called in question when the two men took such different views of their spiritual situation, and of themselves. To see *Silex Scintillans* as a visionary version of *The Temple* is to harm Vaughan with a false expectation, for the two works use devotional poetry to quite different ends. Yet Vaughan is no spiritual sport; on the contrary, he gives imaginative authenticity to some of the most powerful ideas which were running in the seventeenth century, and part of the excitement of his writing comes from his perception of a wholeness in those ideas which he took for final truth.

Vaughan is unlike other seventeenth-century devotional poets in that he does not undertake to speak for all men. A man may have no thought of publication when he writes out of his own solitary circumstances, and yet suppose himself to stand in the same predicament as all other human beings; so that his own spiritual wrestlings have a common substance. Donne's *Holy Sonnets*, written for himself and a few friends, express the general dilemma of fallen men who must seek God's grace before they can move to save themselves. Yet Vaughan's concern extends no further than the 'some' of the present poem; and we might ask how far his devotional attitudes as such could have drawn in anyone beyond that small circle even in his own day, when their tendency is so exclusive. But then even his 'some' expresses a notional allegiance, for one of the idiosyncrasies of *Silex Scintillans* is that it conveys no effective sense of community with living men at all, or of a communion with that regenerate few. Vaughan's relationship with his God, as with the countryside in which he lived, is regulated by the sheer force of his own apprehensions and ardours. The common sympathy he feels and most movingly expresses is with the dead, and with those living processes of nature which intimated to him a spiritual renewal beyond the grave, or a possible rebirth into our lost innocence. In his poems he stands alone amidst the natural creation, seeking his own rehabilitation in the order of love:

> I will not fear what man,
> With all his plots and power can;
> Bags that wax old may plundered be,
> But none can sequester or let
> A state that with the Sun doth set
> And comes next morning fresh as he

'Providence'

After the civil wars many men, and not only Royalists, must have felt themselves to be lone survivors in a dangerous world. But Vaughan has far more than historical testimony to offer us. He is one of those artists who strive to live out their vision; and for all our cavils, it was no mean prospect of love that he fashioned for himself out of the great legacy of Christian metaphysics. *Silex Scintillans* is the attempt of a man reborn from corruption to see the universe anew, and aright, by the sheer force of his purged imagination. Small wonder if his glimpses of glory isolated him from the ruinous world he saw around him, and were not readily reducible to lessons for life.

iii. *Love in the dust*

The death of Vaughan's younger brother William in 1648, at twenty or so, appears to have been one of the desolating events that transformed into vision the innocently modish wit of *Poems* and *Olor*

Iscanus, and helped make a poet of a versifier. The evidence that a close personal loss affected Vaughan so deeply is to be found in *Silex Scintillans* itself, which is haunted by death as *In Memoriam* is haunted. Vaughan's anguished preoccupation with last things has its focus in a series of untitled poems running through both parts of the gathering, 1650 and 1655, which respond to the quite recent death of a young brother. When Miss Gwenllian Morgan hit on the evidence of burial she put it beyond much doubt that these poems refer to William Vaughan.[34] Our attempt to grasp the pattern of a very strange literary career brings us back to them as the proving-place of Vaughan's quarrel with himself, and with the condition of man's life in the world. He seems to have taken the man's death for one of those absolute events which put our human existence on trial; and he encountered it with a humanity as sensitive as any we shall find expressed in seventeenth-century writing.

He does not spare himself or our kind. Feeling man's vulner-ableness so keenly, he questions our assurance that we have some special standing among created things. Shocked realisation that even the pain of his loss fades into acceptance brings home to him the most bitterly ironic of human frailties, the inability of love itself to stand up to the simple inexistence of its object; and it shows him how fatally eager our minds are to gloss over the harsh reality of death. A more immediate sense of guilt, which indicates that Vaughan may have felt some responsibility for the disaster, only makes the death of an innocent youth seem still more outrageous, even more difficult to reconcile with the working of a just and benevolent providence. Vaughan's painful self-questioning resolves itself into a struggle to make such a death intelligible by a better understanding of love.

In the heat of this crucible Vaughan's distinctive vision takes shape. His poetic preoccupations in these years appear in recurrent images which dramatise a private myth, and express the heroic will of a vital creation to resist a world of dead dust: the candle in the cave, the pearl of Christ's life in the world, the gleam of lost childhood, the sympathetic virtue of the stars. A man's struggle to find sense in his existence may deny the facile assurances of our conventional consolations without making successful poems. There is much in these mourning lyrics to bear out Alvarez's judgment that Vaughan had not the power of analytic thought which we find in Donne and Herbert, and is so wholly committed to moments of intense sensation that he is 'at one moment vivid, profound and original, and at the next, dull, prosaic and derivative' (*The School of Donne*, 1961, pp. 89–90). The sinkings and uncertainties are distressingly real. But they may strike us as the vulnerable areas of a heroic unwillingness to accept experience at too easy a rate, or settle for unearned reassurance.

The moving poem that begins 'As time one day by me did pass' is the evidence that by 1655, when it was published, Vaughan had come to terms with the event and the universe in which it could occur, partly because time had transmuted death's horror. But the climax comes much earlier in a piece which approaches the death indirectly and allows a perspective that a direct confrontation might not admit, the untitled poem which opens 'I walkt the other day':

1

I walkt the other day (to spend my hour)
    Into a field
Where I sometimes had seen the soil to yield
    A gallant flowre,
But Winter now had ruffled all the bowre
    And curious store
    I knew there heretofore.

2

Yet I whose search lov'd not to peep and peer
    I'th' face of things
Thought with my self, there might be other springs
    Besides this here
Which, like cold friends, sees us but once a year,
    And so the flowre
    Might have some other bowre.

3

Then taking up what I could neerest spie
    I digg'd about
That place where I had seen him to grow out,
    And by and by
I saw the warm Recluse alone to lie
    Where fresh and green
    He lived of us unseen.

4

Many a question Intricate and rare
    Did I there strow,
But all I could extort was, that he now
    Did there repair
Such losses as befel him in this air
    And would e'r long
    Come forth most fair and young.

5

This past, I threw the Clothes quite o'r his head,
    And stung with fear
Of my own frailty dropt down many a tear
    Upon his bed,
Then sighing whisper'd, *Happy are the dead!*
    What peace doth now
    Rock him asleep below?

6

And yet, how few believe such doctrine springs
    From a poor root
Which all the Winter sleeps here under foot
    And hath no wings
To raise it to the truth and light of things,
    But is stil trod
    By ev'ry wandring clod.

7

O thou! whose spirit did at first inflame
    And warm the dead,
And by a sacred Incubation fed
    With life this frame
Which once had neither being, forme, nor name,
    Grant I may so
    Thy steps track here below.

8

That in these Masques and shadows I may see
    Thy sacred way,
And by those hid ascents climb to that day
    Which breaks from thee
Who art in all things, though invisibly;
    Shew me thy peace,
    Thy mercy, love, and ease.

9

And from this Care, where dreams and sorrows raign
    Lead me above
Where Light, Joy, Leisure, and true Comforts move
    Without all pain,
There, hid in thee, shew me his life again
    At whose dumbe urn
    Thus all the year I mourn.

The simple opening of the poem suggests the heedless well-being of a man who does not suspect what is in store for him; but 'A gallant flowre' is ominously picked out, and 'Winter', 'ruffled', 'bowre', already bring in a note of menace. 'Curious store' seems an arrestingly odd term to use of the various kinds of flowers he had formerly noticed in the field, putting them before us on a par with the passing ornaments which divert us in the world, and reminding us that our passing pleasures will not stand up to the harsh proof of a winter which is not followed by spring. Breconshire in the aftermath of civil war seems a long way from the Europe of the great neoclassical poets who had pondered upon the brevity of life by the example of flowers – 'Collige, virgo, rosas . . .'.

The second stanza is almost as simple in its syntax, and becomes childlike at the end when the poet reports his unsuspecting thoughts. The poem quite artfully shifts its times as the poet brings us through his disquiets of spirit to the new understanding he has gained, or must still petition for. Within its brief course, it plots the drastic mutations of an inner life which has been altogether discomposed by the recognition it enacts in the figure of the lost flower.

The self-communing over the vanished flower which is recalled in stanza 2 suggests a quite habitual search for a hidden reality beyond the 'face of things', almost a profession of occultism; and the odd syntax of lines 3–5 gives the idea point. It is not only the flower that 'sees us but once a year' but 'this here', the spring we know. Beyond our present awareness may there be a different order of seasons, or some different kind of renewal? Here in our present state of being spring comes as a grudging alien, promising new life but doing nothing to arrest the change which moves us towards death. If we take a flower's 'springs' to refer also to its sources of life, the very principle of its life and growth, then the lines do indeed seem to be raising the possibility of other fountains of life and other seasons of rejuvenation than the spring that visits the world only once every year, and comes to us all just once in our lifespan.

The brusque switch from reflection to action in stanza 3 brings a new if obscure urgency, like Christian's nameless fear in the face of the coming wrath. The poem quietly imposes its own mode of meaning on us, so that the mere absence of verbal subtlety in 'what I could neerest spie' suggests the utter unwariness of the state of mind, as does the way of saying a thing in childlike particularity – 'That place where I had seen him to grow out'. Vaughan's thinking is vividly dramatic, as we see in the way the curious stanza pattern is made to bring out the working of the mind. The poem really does move forward as if it is being spontaneously thought through, and everything must be searched out anew; nothing may be imposed for form's sake. The short line itself is no ritual tag but has varied life of

its own, now controlling an interval of time, and now arresting the
flow to let a vital idea work:

> Where fresh and green
> He lived of us unseen.

What we are offered in this disinterment is nothing less than a
revelation, the sudden disclosure of a realm of recrudescent life
whose existence we do not dream of if we look only at the face of
things. Something which to all common appearances was dead and
gone for good turns out to be living still in another dimension, and
even preparing a new existence in that secret incubation.

The rarefied questioning this discovery prompts suggests that
the process is so far removed from our normal awareness that our
limited reason cannot cope with it. But even if the apparition
bewilders the poet, coming upon him as a kind of miracle which
makes nonsense of our usual categories of understanding, the fact
is plain to see, and its testimony to something more than just
survival needs no gloss:

> he now
> Did there repair
> Such losses as befel him in this air.

'This air' is the common life above ground, and also our existence
in a world of corruption whose inevitable losses will thus be made
good. It is typical of the way the mid-seventeenth-century English
poets use an example from organic life that by this time the figure
and the thing figured are one. We see that it is not enough here to
speak of emblem and its meaning, figurative and literal sense. The
untimely blasting of the flower is more than a figure of the death of
an innocent young man, and the arbitrary breaking of a bond of
love. It instances a general process to which flowers and human
lives are alike subject; and the poem moves forward by making us
compare the two events, and continually review our responses to
them.

When Vaughan asks us to take the search for the lost flower as a
shocking confrontation with death he is not just dramatising a
common emblem. We must suppose that he explores the one event
through the other, reliving a spiritual encounter which has
changed his life. The climax of this drama comes with that abrupt
gesture in stanza 5, in language that suddenly exposes the nerve:

This past, I threw the Clothes quite o'r his head

The lineaments of a human deathbed starkly materialise from the comforting terms of the natural example; and our minds are prompted to make the grim link between the moment of a man's death and the graveside rite of throwing earth upon the coffin. Image of lost flower and image of dead man are separated out again and weighed against each other; though only in our arbitrary response to them.

There are impulses at work here that scarcely admit detachment, and seem supportable only because they have been transferred to the device of the search for the flower, which allows the poet to contemplate what he might find too distressing to confront. The alarmed reburial of the flower mimes a painfully complex response, in which his remorse that he could have believed the flower lost for good sets off his continuing fear of death, which still puts our survival in question. He envies as well as celebrates the root's warm hidden safety from the world, and its certainty of a marvellous renewal. Yet in one active sense we cannot help distinguishing this opening of the earth from the opening of a grave, for what is here discovered is very different from what we expect. The poem works to assure us that such old expectations are false. By his ingeniously indirect means Vaughan encounters and exorcises the physical horror of burial. What he uncovers is not after all a mouldering corpse, ghastly in its mockery of its former humanity, but the seed of a new and transformed beauty.

The poem has moved from simple thoughtlessness to a complex response to a death, in which words and images work quite ambiguously. A man might throw the earth back over the root so as to leave the organic processes undisturbed. But coming with such an abrupt pang of alarm the image calls up a death scene, and is carried through so in the account of the tears, the bed, the benediction. The story of the uncovering of the root is made to elicit an unguarded response to a death, which heightens the shock with a cruel self-recognition. His own mortality is brought home to him; and his longing to emulate the dead struggles with his horror of coming to the same condition.

At this deathbed which is also a renewal it is himself he mistrusts:

> stung with fear
> Of my own frailty

The arrangement of the lines and the syntax allows us to remind ourselves in passing why such a sudden disclosure of death might well be enough in itself to sting a man with fear. The sight makes him afraid because he too must die, being frail, and because his own prospect of new life in death may be blighted by the frailty of sin. But the sense which carries forward is that he now sees what frailty it was to grieve for someone who has all this time been at peace, and in prospect of new glory. His tears are for himself as well as for the death; and now they are not only tears of mourning.

That culminating whisper gathers all his jarring disquiets into one intense affirmation, which has as much in it of yearning as discovery:

> *Happy are the dead!*
> *What peace doth now*
> *Rock him asleep below?*

The incantatory sway of the voice imitates the work of some reconciling force, which has healed the brawls of the world in this quiet incubation of life. We see that the dead man has become a pattern for the poet's own self-imposed sequestration from the world, which prepares a fresh awakening.

The moralising style of stanza 6 brings us down with a bump. Doctrine here seems impertinent to what has been happening in the poem, reducing a universal experience to a mere emblem which needs its gloss, and shifting the emphasis of the metaphor quite jarringly back to the roots in the earth. Vaughan seems to be betrayed into this particular bathos partly by his persuasion that he is expounding occult mysteries for a few regenerates. Yet what he says here has point, for it is not obvious that a poor root may have such a triumph after it has fallen so low among creatures that it must sleep under foot all winter, wholly lacking the means to truth which are open to higher forms of being, and trodden down by 'ev'ry wandring clod'. In denying the ignominy of death Vaughan quite reverses our common expectation of spiritual worth. What we tread down for dead truly lives; what we deem most alive may be mere dead clod.

The root challenges our values still more directly in that we must learn wisdom from a thing which lacks our powers of intellect, reason, or sentience to raise it to the truth. Nonetheless it knows what we do not know, has a truth we seek; the few who are prepared to attend to what it tells us do not assume man's superior place in the natural creation, but recognise that the life around us may yield us epiphanies we cannot now discover in ourselves, and must gather from other creatures. The humblest life may express a rightness of aspiration denied to beings who have 'wings' to truth, but use them only to evade it.

The dramatic shift to apostrophe and petition, which take up the rest of the poem, powerfully follows out the consequences of a radical spiritual revelation:

> O thou! whose spirit did at first inflame
> And warm the dead

The familiar address itself comes as a shock after the wistful third person of the earlier anecdote – 'Rock him asleep below' – which so poignantly marked the dead person as an object abruptly cut off from the poet, and put beyond his reach. God can be discoursed with, even if the loved dead are gone beyond colloquy. Addressing God so familiarly as a 'thou' whose spirit 'at first' inflamed and warmed the dead, he opposes to the neutrality of dead matter a personal solicitude, and shows the same love at work in universal processes as in intimate relationships. 'At first' takes in the Holy Spirit's sacred incubation of life in the first place, which gave chaos a form and name, warmed the cloddish clay, animated the frame of the universe as well as the human body; but the phrase also distinguishes the original life of the flower from the new existence we are now promised. A process is confirmed. The life and identity which death seemed to deny were bestowed by God's love in the act of generation, and are preserved by it now; the hidden recruitment after death is no singular event but a repetition of the first gift of life, the continuance of the sacred work of creation.

Vaughan's metaphysical extremity authenticates his Christian hermeticism. God has brought life from chaos, and goes on bringing life from the chaos of this world; what we call death is change and growth and not, as we had supposed, final ruin. The conceit of the vanished flower not only draws death within the scope of God's providence, but makes it part of an economy of life which fosters the individual identity of creatures. It is not so much a miracle we are afforded here, as an understanding of life and death which shows that no miracle is needed. We are invited to recognise that death does not deny life, and the two states are not even separate. The body undergoes its sacred renewal in the grave, just as matter underwent a sacred transformation once the Holy Spirit had impregnated it with life and spirit in the first place.

If this death is indeed such a providential incubation then the dead man becomes one with all those things which await new life in retreat, whose pledge is Christ's body in the tomb. Yet men cannot assume their part in the processes of creation. On the contrary, we must earn new life by a right understanding of the life we already have in our own retreat from the world, and need divine grace to acquire it. The appeal to Christ's example follows the implicit invoking of his resurrection:

> Grant I may so
> Thy steps track here below.

The break between stanzas allows us to pause here, and read the words as a plea that the poet might so far be helped to follow out Christ's progress in his own life that he may arise from the grave in glory; and we then take a still more pointed meaning as the syntax is completed:

> That in these Masques and shadows I may see
> Thy sacred way

When he asks for guidance in so tracking Christ's steps here below that he may see God's sacred way in these 'Masques and shadows' Vaughan is once more seeking to encounter the world aright, willing a better way of seeing. He asks that such masks and shadows as the lost flower, and death itself, might show him the working of God's providence – 'Thy sacred way'. But he is also pleading that the traces of Christ's steps while Christ shared our humanity might yet serve a man to see, and follow, his sacred way through the frivolities and insubstantial pageants of this world.

The poem itself seeks to realise one of 'those hid ascents', uncovering a hidden intimation of loving providence which may teach us to recognise ourselves beyond the masking appearance, and so rise out of the grave into true day. But 'those' also looks back to 'Thy steps', Christ's ways as he proved them when he walked in the world, and now shows them again in the rebirth of this flower. If these ascents are everywhere hidden from us, it is because our own corruptness blinds us to the true life of creation, and the world itself throws dust in our eyes; but when we do clear our vision enough to discover them they are rungs to resurrection and true day, showing us the way out of the grave of present error and the world itself:

> 'till the day
> Break, and the shadows flee   'Dressing'

Vaughan's conceit makes one general illusion of the grave, this world, and our secular knowledge altogether, bundling them into a single order as the prime masques and shadows, and finally dismissing them as clouds which we must burst through into the light, wraiths which a brilliant dawn will dispel. But it no more overlooks events in the world than it underrates death itself; it simply promises us that despite all appearances these hazards too are part of a divine disposition. God's purposes and presence are hidden from us in our present lives, though they may be discerned by just such a search as the poem itself figures. The progress that makes up the poem is not finally an indulgence of private grief; it is justified to all who will it by the idea of a hidden providence, which has care of the righteous dead as of the sufferings of the righteous in the world, and also heeds the attempts of regenerate men to discern the truth.

The prayer for illumination culminates in a request which does not generate much poetic life:

> Shew me thy peace,
> Thy mercy, love, and ease.

When he prays to be led beyond the world through the grave, Vaughan opposes to the true life of heaven an existence in which our miseries follow upon our blindness to the truth of things; all our strife is with shadows and illusions. It is our inadequate understanding of death that makes us grieve at the loss of people we love, and the prospect of our own decease. Vaughan's effective response to the world of illusion, whose pain he has rendered so palpably, is simply to dismiss it altogether in favour of a wholly unrealised condition of light, joy, absence of grief. In a poem so vividly experienced, so purposeful in its mental life, words which do as little work as these tell of a mind not wholly engaged by its ideas at this point. The banal round-up of the benefits of life in heaven merely counters the shortcomings of a world which itself remains unrealised in the poet's mind as a general condition of ill. *Silex Scintillans* figures a spiritual life which seems as little engaged with heaven and hell as it is with a personal adversary, or with living well among our fellows. In these poems nothing matters so much as that a man should see how to escape the grave by Christ's love, and avoid the damnation of being abandoned forever in nameless dust.

The re-emergence of private entreaty resolves quite movingly at the end the disquiets which have been troubling the poem all through:

> There, hid in thee, shew me his life again
> At whose dumbe urn
> Thus all the year I mourn.

The vanished life, rediscovered in the earth, is in the end hidden in God; the search for hidden truth has been justified by God's own pledge of love. The poet has the hope of finding his brother's life again, as he was shown the flower's life again, and as men met and meet with Christ's life again. If he is nonetheless still committed to this present life, and to mourning the dead, it is because the 'dumbe urn' does not in itself proclaim the doctrine of a secret rebirth, or promise a revival. For all the testimony of the buried life the urn remains unopened. We must continue to occupy ourselves with the face of things rather than the hidden reality; mourning is still our lot here. The figure of the dumb urn finally comes between the dead man and the dead flower. We ourselves have no such direct intimation of a rebirth as the root promises, and are thrown back on mingled grief and hope, faith rather than evidence. The Fall and our sin cut us off from the natural creation, and make our death seem final. A dead man's life will not re-emerge exactly as the life of a dead flower, if only because we may not see it here; the urn does not speak, our grief has real point. Final consolation must wait; for his life is 'hid in thee', not in the ground or the urn, and can only be regained when the poet himself is finally led above and grief itself abolished.

Vaughan's brief lyric poem is no simple rendering of a mood but a powerful piece of thinking, which draws us on through a full movement of the mind and spirit. It works its way forward with the dramatic unpredictableness of a living experience, as if to find its own shape and end. We cannot doubt that something momentous is in question in this slight piece about a casual stroll in the country which shockingly confronts a man with death, and brings him to a better acceptance of our mortality, even a partial acquiescence in a grievous human lot. Intensely felt as it is, the poem conveys more than the pain of a scarcely supportable loss. It is an attempt to make untimely death intelligible, a rite by which a man seeks to reconcile will and reason to such occurrences in our lives as most violently outrage our expectation of justice and love. No consolations or reassurances may diminish the arbitrary horror of a young man's death and dissolution; we can come to no fitter response in our present life than perpetual mourning, and faith. But we feel the closing of a circle of love which fulfils all the yearnings of the poem in the return upon the life hidden in God, and the dumb urn.

iv. *Love restored*

The poem which opens 'As Time one day by me did pass' appears for the first time in the 1655 edition of *Silex Scintillans* and represents an attempt after some years, when time allows the poet a healing perspective, to reconcile his mind finally to what still seems the wanton ruin of love and innocence:

> As Time one day by me did pass
>   Through a large dusky glasse
>   He held, I chanc'd to look
>   And spyed his curious book
> Of past days, where sad Heav'n did shed
> A mourning light upon the dead.
>
> Many disordered lives I saw
>   And foul records which thaw
>   My kinde eyes still, but in
>   A fair, white page of thin
> And ev'n, smooth lines, like the Suns rays,
> Thy name was writ, and all thy days.
>
> O bright and happy Kalendar!
>   Where youth shines like a star
>   All pearl'd with tears, and may
>   Teach age, *The Holy way*;
> Where through thick pangs, high agonies
> Faith into life breaks, and death dies.
>
> As some meek *night-piece* which day quails,
>   To candle-light unveils:
>   So by one beamy line
>   From thy bright lamp did shine,
> In the same page thy humble grave
> Set with green herbs, glad hopes and brave.
>
> Here slept my thoughts dear mark! which dust
>   Seem'd to devour, like rust;
>   But dust (I did observe)
>   By hiding doth preserve,
> As we for long and sure recruits,
> Candy with sugar our choice fruits.

Love restored

O calm and sacred bed where lies
  In deaths dark mysteries
  A beauty far more bright
  Then the noons cloudless light
For whose dry dust green branches bud
And robes are bleach'd in the *Lambs* blood.

Sleep happy ashes! (blessed sleep!)
  While haplesse I still weep;
  Weep that I have out-liv'd
  My life, and unreliev'd
Must (soul-lesse shadow!) so live on,
Though life be dead, and my joys gone.

The argument is quite movingly modulated, drawing us through the stages of an intense little spiritual drama to a quietude which is very different from the opening calm. The syntax controls an advance of consciousness, and expressively shapes each inflection of thought and feeling. When Vaughan's poems are working well they seem to realise a whole inner experience. In the present poem the casual passage of time is quite suddenly interrupted by a chance revelation, the return upon the mind of an ordeal which time has transformed but not obscured; and the poet's awed celebration of that distant event leads him to a new acceptance of it, and a new understanding of life and death which is also a desolating self-awareness. To speak of a revelation here is no more than to take the experience as the poem offers it. But we need to be clear that what is revealed to the poet was actually there all the time, and now suddenly appears in its true light; the vision he sees, far from transcending natural life, discloses the life of things as it really is.

The poem arrests us with its brusque invoking of that elaborate personification of time, which figures a still more insistent intrusion upon the poet's casual life than the chance encounter he spoke of in 'I walkt the other day'. This time the prompting must come from within his own mind, and plainly we may take the apparition that goes by him for an emblem of memory, which allows him to snatch back a moment from time by a means time itself affords. The poem presents itself as the poet's response to what he sees in Time's book, through Time's dusky glass, by the mourning light which sad heaven sheds upon the dead: 'In tal parte della memoria ...' (*Vita Nuova* 1). He is speaking, then, of something that happened long enough ago for him to have buried it in his mind and lost the pain of it, though that proof of love is itself a cause of disquiet when the grief re-emerges now. We feel in the poem the shock of the unexpected trick of consciousness which has restored to him, albeit at a distance, something seemingly lost, and suddenly brings on his private need to settle with the event and with the years.

Yet passing time with its book and perspective glass cannot be just an emblem of memory, for it figures processes which take place around us, and are imperfectly seen by our clouded eyes rather than imperfectly recalled at a distance. Sad heaven sheds a mourning light not only upon the lives the dead once lived but upon the abiding residue and consequence of their existence in time, as time's book records it. The book enshrines the quality of those existences, separating the 'disordered lives' and 'foul records' from the lucent hieroglyphs of the virtuous. This is no mere list of names the poet reviews but the value of the lives themselves, which is set down here now as it resolved itself in the world. His passing pang over the foul entries laments the lives and their outcome together, affectingly catching both his pity for old acquaintances whom he now sees self-judged, and a qualm for the self-ruin of the nature he shares. Presumably it takes so many epithets and a simile to describe the contrasting entry, 'Thy name ... and all thy days', because these are the qualities of a well-ordered life in the world that make it a positive force, give it a power or virtue like Christ's which is not extinguished in death. The sudden slip into direct address some twelve lines on in the poem does not really suggest that the poet has been addressing the dead man all the time, though it quite movingly brings out his own sense of the sudden felt presence of a being long dead. It is just this movement forward by such disconcerting shifts of address and attack that renders so powerfully the working of an inner life.

When he breaks out at once in impassioned celebration of the brief existence he confirms a revaluing of the young man's life, and holy death, which needs the present tense. The example remains, and works, even though men lose sight of it in the world; such exemplary lives themselves are not lost but shine forever as stars, however obscure they may become to our darkened eyes. Something seemingly dead has been won back from the shrouding dark, and found to live more intensely than before. But the sudden change of tense and mood tells us that we are occupied now with a continuing condition as much as with that past event. The outburst is a yearning elegy for lost youth and innocence altogether, which is quite beautifully centred in the image of the star pearled with tears. He looks back through tears upon his own childhood, and sees it in the splendour it had; regret for lost happiness, always strong in Vaughan's poems, reinforces his desolating awareness that men outlive their wise innocence and live on in complacent corruption. Yet he celebrates at the same time a transformed purity of being which is not dimmed by time and death, but shines the more vitally for the sufferings it has endured here, and for our grief at them.

It is wholly typical of Vaughan's poetic thinking that a private event should gather in the portents of a universal myth without ever ceasing to be heeded for its own sake. But the several dispositions which are celebrated here are not distinct; rather, the images powerfully make one 'Holy way' of the means by which good men gain life and clear sight:

> Where through thick pangs, high agonies
> Faith into life breaks, and death dies

The pangs and agonies of early death are transformed into the positive travail of a heroic conquest over our resisting mortality. What matters is not survival in the world but the transforming of our nature and condition, so that they show themselves again in their native purity and glory.

The poem returns to the account of his vision through that elaborate analogy of the 'meek *night-piece*'. The *OED* quotes these lines when it defines *night-piece* as 'A painting or picture representing a night-scene', which appears to be Webster's meaning in *White Devil* v. 6. But Vaughan is surely thinking of a trick effect, in which something we cannot make out when we look at it in the flat light of day shows up in clear relief as a candle-beam catches it at night. When he says that 'one beamy line' from the 'bright lamp' displays the humble grave, though day has 'quailed' it, he means that his memory has been drawn back to a neglected event by some prompting beyond himself; but we also take it that he could not truly understand the young man's death until he looked back at the grave through the dim light of time with the help of this one beam. The meaning of such a crisis could not be grasped at the time, or in the mourning aftermath, or at any time in the world's distracting daylight; nor could he grasp it now if the star of youth had not continued to guide and influence him, even though he was unaware of its working:

> Gods Saints are shining lights: who stays
> Here long must passe

> O're dark hills, swift streames, and steep ways
> As smooth as glasse;
> But these all night
> Like Candles, shed
> Their beams, and light
> Us into Bed.

'Joy of my life!'

There is a brilliant transformation, years on, when he confronts the grave now and contemplates again the 'green herbs, glad hopes and brave' which bestrew it. Those sad emblems of the death of youth, and of the consigning to dust of hopeful prospects, become the promises of resurrection, intimations of the glad prospects and brave assurances of new life. Vaughan keeps opposite impulses finely balanced by such equivocal images, suggesting that grief and celebration cannot be contraries.

But above all he seeks to make peace with himself for the dulling of his pain, and neglect of the death:

> Here slept my thoughts dear mark! which dust
> Seem'd to devour, like rust

How much more grievous then if his mind had wholly yielded to time and dust such a 'dear mark' of his thought, had fallen short in this absolute trial of his love by letting love cool in the absence of its object! Yet even the dust of death turns out now to be other than it seems; time's thickening film over the memory does not annihilate but preserves. The lines remind us of the trick of the mind figured in that casual glance back, and sudden arrest, which had led him to relive the death. The lost life was hidden to his frail eyes, but it has emerged again at length in undiminished power and a clearer light.

We need not doubt that these lines figure a retrieval of the most grievous of human frailties, the failure of love. So the banal analogy which supports them does damage the sense, suggesting that reassurance may be too easily come by when it can be so slickly confirmed:

> As we for long and sure recruits,
> Candy with sugar our choice fruits.

The preserving powers of dust scarcely seem equal to the task Vaughan requires of them, which is to make the very agent of our mortality the means of a secret recruitment. Then the thought falls into bathos when 'preserve' takes him on to the candying of the choicest fruit with sugar, which preserves it by sweetly hiding it when it is barely ripe. Vaughan offers a hostage to a Johnsonian idea of metaphysical poetry when he allows himself to think that the dust of the grave, and the obscuring passage of time, can be fitly represented by candied sugar; though he fails here for lack of ingenuity rather than excess of it. But then his wit must have cut deep when we take a flimsy conceit to betray an over-readiness to find providence in even so human a lapse.

What follows is pure assurance. Again the flow of the narrative is halted so that we contemplate an image picked out of time, and set before us in a timeless present. But glorious vitality has passed into luminous peace, and the grave itself is transformed:

> O calm and sacred bed

Seeing things clearly is always important in Vaughan, but his vision is a way of making something intelligible. The images in this poem pass before the eye as if casually in an album, offering themselves for chance spots of brightness salvaged from the murk of time and consciousness. Here the flow of experience itself is stilled and ordered. The deathbed-grave has not been caught up in time and made alms for oblivion. It remains a fixed and final mark which shows how little time matters; as even our best states in the world are not to be compared with this refulgent peace. The quiet return to the present tense catches anew the sense of an equipoise won out of turbulence.

The transmuting of horror into beauty is most pointedly implied in the final images of the stanza, though it is not made explicit in the lines themselves:

> For whose dry dust green branches bud
> And robes are bleach'd in the *Lambs* blood.

He writes 'For whose ...' not 'From whose ...' and evidently has in mind the sealing of the servants of God in Revelation 7:

After this, I beheld, and lo, a great multitude, which no man could number, of all nations, and kindreds, and people, and tongues, stood before the throne, and before the Lamb, clothed with white robes, and palms in their hands ... These are they which came out of great tribulation, and have washed their robes and made them white in the blood of the Lamb ... They shall hunger no more, neither thirst any more, neither shall the sun light on them, nor any heat. For the Lamb which is in the midst of the throne, shall feed them, and shall lead them into living fountains of water; and God shall wipe away all tears from their eyes.

Vaughan's pointed recruitment of his dead brother to this select number need not mean that the death was violent, though the passage must have had more point for him if the young man had died bloodily in great tribulation. The lines tell of a transfiguration that is already in process and may soon be fulfilled, for even while the body moulders to dust in its loathsome grave the branches are in bud which it will hold in glory before Christ's throne, and its robes are being bleached white by the innocent blood Christ shed in his own thick pangs and high agonies. The quiet allusion to the final triumph of the just, and to the Lamb's particular care of those who died like him, crowns the rich play of wit. Christ authenticates in his own example all that has been promised for the dead.

The benediction over the grave most movingly completes the poem by reversing the condition of mourner and mourned. The ashes are happy in their secure sleep; the poet is left desolate:

> Sleep happy ashes! (blessed sleep!)
> While haplesse I still weep;
> Weep that I have out-liv'd
> My life

Vaughan's wit can be quite unlike Donne's wit or Herbert's. This turn on 'weep' is typical of the way he will read further into an attitude, or urge some natural intimation, as though he uncovers new levels of meaning in the creation itself. The survivor grieves, though the object of his sorrow is in bliss, because we cannot see beyond the temporal loss; it is our own frailty we mourn for. Then the impulse returns upon itself. His tears are justified after all, though not by his brother's death, or his own mortality, or even the cooling of love. He must weep just because he still lives. Private desolation and the sense of a general doom come together in the lines. The chance recollection which took him back through the years to reckon with an old grief has brought him in the end to know himself, and revalue his life. That re-emergence from the dust of the 'dear mark' moves him to recognise not only that his life is empty now that his brother is no longer part of it, but that when he out-lived his innocence he himself became the true corpse:

> when thou know'st this,
> Thou know'st how wan a ghost this our world is
> Donne, *The First Anniversary*, lines 369–70

Time has shown him that his brother took the holy way of love which Christ opened to the heroic few; and though his own way must be far worse, it is something that he prepares to encounter it in a true understanding of what it means to live. The poem confirms him in an understanding which has wholly changed his own being.

The perfect closure of cadence and complex sense marks the conclusion of a long engagement with the monstrous injustice of innocent death. The obliterating passage of time itself falls into true perspective; time is put in its place. His brother's life is not dimmed by the passing of years, and would not be lost if all remembrance of it faded; on the contrary, it is just our own understanding of such an existence which is frail. Starting out to mourn the death, he has found more bitter cause to grieve in the way time dims the shock and even the memory of it; and he finishes now by lamenting his own survival, which leaves him still caught up in time and vulnerable to its effects. Our image of time is turned, a no less disturbing prospect replaces the discomforting vision of the waning of love. Such uncorrupted lives remain and shine as an absolute mark of men's cleared thought; it is we survivors who move on in oblivious unreality.

The elaborate device of passing time which frames the poem is no mere sport of wit. On the contrary it distinguishes what is essentially prey to time and death from what is not, without requiring us to divide one part of our nature from another. The only distinction which matters is that between uncorrupted and corrupted life, between the heroic few whose mortal ashes will be transfigured in glory, and the rest who disperse themselves into dusty oblivion in a long self-ruin, 'Carico d'anni e di peccato pieno' (Michelangelo, *Rime*, no. 293). The developed conceit quite precisely controls our understanding of our lives and deaths in time. It tells us that we are creatures of time and death to the extent that we lose our first state, and that we must seek to put off corruption not by mortifying the body, or rising above it, but by remaking ourselves altogether.

Vaughan does not often integrate imaginative and intellectual life so finely, but 'As Time one day' scarcely bears out the judgment that by the standards of Donne and Herbert he was unable to think at all. If Vaughan did not think like his mentors (as they did not think like each other) it is partly because he was responding to the pressures of his particular time and circumstances with his own distinctive apprehension of the universe we live and die in. *Silex Scintillans* articulates a man's struggle to reach an acceptance, which the rest of his long life seems to have sustained. But to think of that resolved retirement as a calm won out of passion is to recognise that such poetry as Vaughan's is not born of emotion recollected in tranquillity. On the contrary, it is itself active experience, an engagement of the whole consciousness such as properly deserves the name of thought. The difference between a religious poetry conceived as immediate experience, and poetry which recollects or reflects upon experience, is the difference between a Vaughan and a Keble.

6

Humanity Vindicated:
Milton's pattern of heroic love

Our Saviour Christ by His nativity took upon Him the shape of man; by His circumcision He took upon Him and submitted Himself to the degree of a servant. By the first He made Himself in case, and able to perform the work of our redemption; by the second He entered bound for the performing of it. All was to this end, that He might restore the work of God to his original perfection. In the bringing of which to pass it was decreed by God in the beginning as a thing necessary, that the head of the serpent, by whose means it was violated and defaced, should be bruised ... where he suffered in His body hunger, in His soul temptation: what is it else but a proclaiming of His great love towards us? As if He should exulting say, What is it that shall separate Me from the Love of men?

Lancelot Andrewes, Sermon 1 of *Seven
Sermons upon the Temptation in the Wilderness*
(1592), *Sermons*, Oxford, 1841–3, V,
pp. 479–81

there should be no such difficulty to shake our faith, as once to imagine to fetch CHRIST from Heaven for the *remission* of our *sinnes* ... because CHRIST (to whom alone this Commission was originally granted) having *ordained Himselfe a body*, would worke by bodily things, and having *taken the nature of man upon Him*, would honour the nature He had so taken.

Lancelot Andrewes, *A Sermon Preached at
Whitehall upon the Sunday after Easter*, 1600,
XCVI Sermons, 1629, *Certain Sermons*, p. 56

Paradise Lost xi and xii make it plain that the world Rochester and Vaughan inhabit is the world into which Adam and Eve are turned out in the last lines of the poem. This is a degenerate and degenerating estate of nature. Milton does not fudge the depravation of manners in the fallen world. Michael compellingly brings home to Adam the corruption of love, the perversion of right and justice, the degrading of the human form, the forfeiture of the divine part of man's nature. Adam and Eve go hand in hand to encounter our condition; yet their embraces now promise no recovery of Paradise, or saving grace.

Still their case is not hopeless, for the world they enter has not lapsed beyond redemption. God still inhabits it for a start:

> and of his presence many a signe
> Still following thee, still compassing thee round
> With goodness and paternal Love, his Face
> Express, and of his steps the track Divine.

Paradise Lost xi, 351–4

God's presence continually weighs against bad in the world, 'supernal grace contending/With sinfulness of Men' (xi, 359–60), and works to bring good out of evil by the supporting agency of the Holy Ghost

> who shall dwell
> His Spirit within them, and the Law of Faith
> Working through love, upon thir hearts shall write,
> To guide them in all truth, and also arme
> With spiritual Armour

xii, 487–91

Confirming God's continued care for his creatures, and central to all man's hopes, is the promise that a descendant of Eve will bring about the overthrow of Satan and the dissolution of his empire. Adam's lapse is to be redeemed by a second Adam, who will himself raise a new order 'Founded in Righteousness and Peace and Love' (xii, 550) out of the purging conflagration which abolishes the old state. Adam must share with Eve the pledge that humanity will be redeemed by one who inherits our nature:

> The great deliverance by her Seed to come
> (For by the Womans Seed) on all Mankind

xii, 600–1

The exchanges between Adam and Michael (xii, 552–87), set out the terms of man's right comportment in the fallen world, to which love is the key, 'By name to come calld Charitie, the soul/Of all the rest' (xii, 583–5). Love is uniquely necessary to the wellbeing of humankind because it makes us one with Christ by restoring our lapsed humanity. God so loved the world ... The timeless enters time not in a mysterious conjunction of unlike natures but by the perfecting of human nature. *Paradise Lost* keeps before us from the opening lines the assurance that Christ will fulfil his love for his own kind by renewing our degenerate humanity, and that Eden has been lost to us only 'till one greater Man/Restore us' (i, 4–5). One greater *man*. Heavenly love is to outdo hellish hate; yet it asks a testimony in kind, and will triumph in Milton's rendering precisely as a supreme proof of pure selfless human compassion.

324

The Christ of *Paradise Regained* is no alien visitant but the human embodiment of God's solicitude, the realisation in human nature of divine wisdom and charity. The fusion in him of divine nature and human nature marks the absolute union of spirit and flesh in love. There is no prospect now of the fulfilment of human nature in the paradise of one another's arms. Christ's human love is manifested in his being a man, encountering the fallen world and suffering its injustice, taking on Satan. He is still the 'Most perfect *Heroe*' of Milton's early poem 'The Passion', the new Hercules whose supreme feat is to assume human nature and endure death. Yet his heroism here simply enlarges his quiet observance of the bond of kind, which Milton brings out in his filial regard for Mary, care for his disciples, fellow-feeling with all sufferers for Adam's sin.

Commentators on *Paradise Regained* have well recognised that Christ's defeat of Satan is effected wholly within the scope of his human nature, 'By Humiliation and strong Sufferance ... weakness ... consummat vertue' (*Paradise Regained* i, 160–7). Satan's tempting bids are brought before us quite pointedly as attempts to nullify the efficacy of Christ's atoning incarnation by provoking him into a wrong use of love, such as would be demonstrated by a resort to powers beyond humanity. Christ counters with human resources the temptations Satan proffers, which seem calculated to appeal at the several levels of our being, sensual, moral, intellectual. Generous human love is enough in itself to rebut Satan's commendations of the attributes which pass for goods in the world, whose appeal is partial and exclusive. Our humanity cannot fulfil itself in ends which satisfy one part of our nature only, even the godlike part:

> Who therefore seeks in these
> True wisdom, finds her not, or by delusion
> Farr worse, her false resemblance onely meets,
> An empty cloud.

Paradise Regained iv, 318–21

On the contrary, 'wisdom eminent' (*Paradise Regained* iii, 91) lies in our tempering flesh, intellect and spirit in one harmonious entity by love.

Milton's attention to the human essence of Christ's incarnation and atonement expresses more than a doctrinal idiosyncrasy. Its warrant must be sought in his insistent care that his Christ should indeed come before us as very man and very God, yet accomplish the defeat of Satan and recovery of man's lapse in the unaided being of very man. Christ routs Satan in his human nature, by such powers as we ourselves may embody if we only amend our corruptions. Indeed Christ's incarnation stands at the opposite remove from the self-aggrandising exploitation of human character for superhuman ends which intimidates us in the gods of antiquity. His selfless identification with our humanity neither limits his godhead nor condescends to an inferior condition; it is no more a metamorphosis of god into man than of man's nature into god. We must take it for proof of the divinity of perfected human nature, the vindication of God's continued love for mankind. Milton's poetic testimony of universal love makes a telling contrast with Dante's. The poet of the *Commedia* moves through love to a clear intelligible vision of the love that sustains the universe; the ultimate proof of love is that it draws the poet up to itself, impelling him by the lure of beauty to transcend his humanity altogether in pure illumination of spirit. Milton simply moves the opposite way, to the unsparing embodiment of love in the fallen world. The ultimate proof of the divine love he posits is that it incarnates itself to prove the worth of our human nature.

When Milton's human originals leave the Garden they do not wholly lose their expectation of a sacramental presence in natural events, or quit the ground of a metaphysics of sexual love. By 1667 they would have needed to share the isolation of a Vaughan or a Traherne, or of Milton himself, to sustain such a double vision of the world they lived in. What remains to love poets when that vision fades is a language of witty compliment, which has lost the vitality to sustain the life of the mind in love. Love itself becomes the hostage of moralists and men of sentiment. The vivacity of a Burns or a Byron owes more to the poet's command of a rhetoric of personal feeling than to the play of his intelligence in proof of love. When Byron evokes *Paradise Lost* iv (as well as *Inferno* v) to set off the childlike abandon of Haidee and Don Juan he invests the state of innocent sexuality with the poignancy of a doomed idyll of youth:

> Alas! they were so young, so beautiful,
> So lonely, loving, helpless, and the hour
> Was that in which the heart is always full,
> And, having o'er itself no further power,
> Prompts deeds eternity cannot annul,
> But pays off moments in an endless shower
> Of hell-fire – all prepared for people giving
> Pleasure or pain to one another living . . .

Mix'd in each other's arms, and heart in heart,
    Why did they not then die? – they had lived too long
Should an hour come to bid them breathe apart;
    Years could but bring them cruel things or wrong;
The world was not for them, nor the world's art
    For beings passionate as Sappho's song;
Love was born *with* them, *in* them, so intense,
It was their very spirit – not a sense.

Don Juan 2, cxcii and 4, xxvii

Byron's nice tempering of the heart's imperatives with the way of
the world is witty in a manner which could not admit the radical
intelligence of a Donne or a Marvell. That he and Browning write
our most alert love poetry since the seventeenth century only
witnesses the contraction of the scope of love.

Notes

Preamble: The Lineage of Love

1 My *Literary Love* (Arnold, 1983) extends to dramatic writing the scope of the present inquiry.
2 Plato, *Symposium*, translated Michael Joyce, 1938. Given in *The Symposium and Other Dialogues*, ed. J. Warrington, 1964, p. 46. All quotations from *The Symposium* are given in Joyce's translation.
3 Aristotle, *De Anima*, ed. R. D. Hicks, Amsterdam, 1965, p. 63.
4 St Augustine, *Confessions*, translated W. Watts (1631), 1931, II, p. 147.

1. Sense and Innocence

1 *The Sermons of John Donne*, ed. E. M. Simpson and G. R. Potter, Berkeley: University of California Press, 1953–62. Volume III of this edition was published in 1957.
2 F. Sansovino, *Dante Con Lespositione di Cristoforo Landino et di Alessandro Vellutello*, Venice, 1564, 32ʳ. Landino's commentary was first published in 1481.
3 Benevenuti de Rambaldis da Imola, *Comentum Super Dantis Aldigherii Comoediam* (c. 1373–80), Florence, 1887, I, p. 206. G. B. Gelli, *Letture Edite e Inedite ... Sopra La Commedia di Dante* (1553/4), ed. C. Negroni, Florence, 1887, I, p. 346.
4 *La Comedia di Dante Aligieri con la nova espositione di Alessandro Vellutello*, Venice, 1544, C viʲ⁻ʳ.
5 *La Divina Comĩedia di Dante Alighieri Postillata da Torquato Tasso* (Tasso's notes c. 1570), Pisa, 1830, I, p. 92.
6 Renato Poggioli argues otherwise in his commentary on this episode, 'Tragedy or Romance? A Reading of the Paolo and Francesca Episode in Dante's Inferno', *PMLA*, 1957, pp. 313–58.
7 da Imola, *Comentum*, I, p. 208.
8 Gelli, *Letture*, I, pp. 337–8; though Gelli also says that Dante lets the woman talk 'because the poet wishes to show how much more easily a woman gives away secrets than a man', I, p. 346.
9 Boccaccio, *Il Comento ... Sopra La Divina Commedia di Dante Alighieri*, Florence, 1846, II, p. 82; *Esposizioni sopra la Comedia di Dante*, ed. Giorgio Padoan, in *Tutte le Opere*, VI, Milan, 1965, pp. 313–25; Gelli, *Letture*, I, p. 351.
10 Boccaccio, *Trattatello In Laude Di Dante*, ed. P. G. Ricci, in *Tutte Le Opere*, ed. V. Branca, Verona, 1974, III, p. 480; da Imola, *Comentum*, I, pp. 212–13 and 216; *Vellutello*, 1544, C viiiʲ; *Landino*, 1564, 34ᵛ–35ᵛ; *Dante con l'espositione di M. Bernardino Daniello da Lucca*, Venice, 1568, p. 40.
11 da Imola, *Comentum*, I, p. 211.

12 *Landino*, 1564, 32ʳ.

13 Paget Toynbee, 'Dante and the Lancelot Romance', *Dante Studies and Researches*, 1902, pp. 1–37. I do not accept the argument now in fashion that the discrepancies between the two episodes are as much to the point as the correspondences.

14 St Augustine, *Confessions*, VIII, xii. This telling parody was pointed out by T. K. Swing, *The Fragile Leaves of the Sybil: Dante's Master Plan*, Westminster, Md, 1962, p. 299.

15 Boethius, *De Cons. Phil.*, II, iv.

16 *Henry Crabb Robinson on Books and Their Writers*, ed. E. J. Morley, 1938, I, p. 330.

17 *Corso Torinese Sopra Dante*, Lezione Ventesima, 1854–5; expanded into *Francesca da Rimini secondo i critici e secondo l'arte*, *Nuova Antologia*, 1869. Both versions are given in *Lezioni e Saggi Su Dante*, ed. S. Romagnoli, Turin, 1967, pp. 205–15 and 635–52 (*Opere di Francesco de Sanctis*, ed. C. Muscetta, vol. v).

18 *Commentarium* (c. 1340), Florence, 1845, p. 89. See D. W. Robertson, *A Preface to Chaucer: Studies in Mediaeval Perspectives*, Princeton, N. J., 1962, p. 89.

19 *Landino*, 1564, 35ʳ.

20 *Vellutello*, 1544, C viiiᵛ.

21 C viᵛ.

22 Gelli, *Letture*, I, p. 338.

23 *Ibid.*, II, p. 351.

24 Dante, *Comento*, Florence, 1844, II, pp. 46–59 and 80–3.

25 *Chartularium Universitatis Parisiensis Sub Auspiciis Consili Generalis Facultatum Parisiensum*, I, *1200–86 AD*, ed. H. Denifle and A. Chatelain, Paris, 1889, pp. 543–58. The terms of Tempier's condemnation of Averroism are discussed by P. F. Mandonnet, *Siger de Brabant et l'Averroism latin ou XIIIᵉ siècle*, Fribourg, 1899, I, chs. V and VII, and by M. Grabman, 'Das Werk De Amore Des Andreas Capellanus Und Das Verurteilungsdehiret Des Bischofs Stephan Tempier Von Paris Vom 7 March 1277', *Speculum*, 1932, VII, pp. 75–9.

26 *Chartularium Universitatis Parisiensis*, I, p. 553.

27 Translated as *The Ring and the Dove* by A. J. Arberry, 1953.

28 *Ibid.*, pp. 26, 58, 189–90, 195.

29 *Ibid.*, pp. 238, 57–9.

30 *Ibid.*, pp. 230–84.

31 M. Valency, *In Praise of Love*, New York, 1961, pp. 144ff.

32 *Comento del Magnifico Lorenzo de' Medici sopra alcuni de' suoi sonetti*, in *Opere*, ed. A. Simioni, Bari, 1913, I, p. 16.

33 Tullia d'Aragona, *Della Infinità D'Amore*, in *Trattati D'Amore Del Cinquecento*, ed. G. Zonta, Bari, 1968, p. 216.

34 G. P. Capriano, *Della Vera Poetica*, Venice, 1555, F2ʳ.

35 M. Equicola, *De natura d'amore*, Venice, 1526, 10ʳ.

36 Calanson's poem is given in *Chrestomathie Provencale*, ed. K. Bartsch, Eberfeld, 1868, cols. 161–4. Riquier's poem is given in *Die Werke der Troubadours, in Provenzalischer Sprache*, ed. V. S. G. Mahn, Berlin and Paris, 1853, v (ed. S. L. H. Pfaff), pp. 210–33. I am indebted to the commentary on the two poems in J. Anglade, *Le Troubadour Giraut Riquier*, Bordeaux and Paris, 1905, pp. 254–6, and to the elucidatory observations of my

colleague Dr T. O. Jones. There is a commentary on Calanson's poem in O. Damman, *Die allegorische Canzone des Guiraut de Calanso*, Breslau, 1891, pp. 67–9.

37 Anglade thinks that the first door is desire itself (p. 255).

38 Texts of Guinizelli, Cavalcanti, Lapo Gianni, and of 'Poi che saziar non posso' by Cino da Pistoia from *Poeti del duecento*, II, ed. G. Contini, Milan and Naples, 1960. Texts of Frescobaldi and of lines from 'Li Vostri occhi gentili' by Cino da Pistoia, from *I Rimatori del Dolce Stil Novo*, ed. G. R. Ceriello, Milan, 1950. Text of Dante's Odes from *The Odes of Dante*, ed. H. S. Vere-Hodge, Oxford, 1963.

39 I have benefited by discussion of this curious stage of the poet's pilgrimage in the work of a number of modern commentators, notably Charles Singleton, *Journey to Paradise*, Cambridge, Mass., 1958, chs. IX–XIV, pp. 141–287; R. Poggioli, 'Dante Poco Tempo Silvano: Or a "Pastoral Oasis" in the *Commedia*', *80th Annual Report of the Dante Society*, 1962, pp. 1–20; A. B. Giamatti, *The Earthly Paradise and the Renaissance Epic*, Princeton, N. J., 1966, pp. 94–119; R. Hollander, *Allegory in Dante's Commedia*, Princeton, N. J., 1969, pp. 150–9.

40 *Tutte Le Opere*, ed. E. Moore, Oxford, 1894, pp. 375–6.

41 Dante, *Convivio*, ed. G. Busnelli and G. Vandelli, Florence, 1964, II, pp. 350 and 353.

42 See his discussion of the question whether the body may be saved, *De Civitate Dei* xiii, 1–24.

43 *Convivio* iii, ii, 8–iii, iii, 12, ed. Busnelli and Vandelli, I, pp. 270–86.

44 St Bernard of Clairvaux (1090–1153), *Sermones in Cantica Canticorum* lxxxiv, Migne P.L. clxxxiii, col. 1186.

45 *Ibid.*, lxxxiv, Migne P.L. clxxxiii, col. 1886.

46 *Ibid.*, xviii, Migne P.L. clxxxiii, col. 862.

47 *Ibid.*, xxvii, Migne P.L. clxxxiii, col. 919.

48 St Bernard of Clairvaux, *Liber De Diligendo Deo* ch. xv, Migne P.L. clxxxii, col. 998.

49 Richard of St Victor (d. 1173), *Benjamin Minor* xii, Migne P.L. cxvi, col. 8.

50 Given in *Yorkshire Writers: Richard Rolle of Hampole*, ed. C. Horstman, 1895, I, p. 165. Also in *Deonise hid Divinite*, ed. P. Hodgson (1955), 1958, p. 22. There is a modernised version of H. Pepwell's text, 1521, in *The Cell of Self-Knowledge*, ed. E. G. Gardner, 1910.

51 Richard of St Victor, *Benjamin Minor* v, Migne P.L. cxcvi, cols. 4–5.

52 *Ibid.*, lxxxi, Migne, P.L. cxcvi, col. 57.

53 References are to St Bonaventura (1221–74), *Opera Omnia*, Quaracchi, 1882–1902. Some of the writings of St Bonaventura were also issued in a compendious two-volume edition, Quaracchi, 1900–11, referred to here as ed.min.

54 *Breviloquium*, Prologus 4, vol. v, pp. 205–6; ed.min. pp. 20–3. *In Hexaemeron* ii, 15–18 and xiii, 11–33, vol. v, pp. 338–9 and 389–92. *De reductione artium ad Theologiam*, 5, vol. v, p. 321; ed.min. pp. 372–3.

55 *In Hexaem.* xxiii, 22–33, vol. v, pp. 391–2; II *Sententarium* xiii, ii, ii, Conclusio; xiii, iii, iii Conclusio; xiv, ii, ii, i and Conclusio; xiv, ii, ii, ii and Conclusio; xiv, ii, ii, iii: vol. II, pp. 321–2, 327–9, 358–61.

56 *Stimulo Divini Amoris*, translated by B. Lewis as *The Goade of Divine Love*, Douai, 1642, The Translator to the Reader, unpaginated.

57 II *Sentent.* Proem. ii.i; xxx, ii, i fund. ivm: vol. II, pp. 4–6, 22–4, 537–8,

721–2. *Breviloquium* ii, xi; ii, xii; iii, iii, ii: vol. V, pp. 229, 230, 232–3. Ed.min. pp. 91, 94, 101–2. *In Hexaem.* xiii, 12, vol. V, pp. 389–90.

58 *In Hexaem.* xiii, 12, vol. V, p. 390. *Breviloquium* ii, xii, vol. V, p. 230; ed.min. p. 94. *Itinerarium* I, 1; I, 2; I, 7; 4, 2: vol. V, pp. 296–8, 306; ed.min. pp. 294, 295, 297, 324.

59 *In Hexaem.* ii, 27, vol. V, p. 340.

60 *De Triplici Via*, Additamentum iii, vol. VIII, pp. 19–23. *De Donis Spiritus Sancti* iii, 5, vol. V, p. 469. *Breviloquium* ii, xii, and v, i, vol. V, pp. 230, 252–3; ed.min. pp. 94, 164, 166. *Itinerarium* iii, 1–2, vol. V, pp. 303–4; ed.min. p. 314. *II Sentent.* xxvi, i, iii and Conclusio, and xxvi, i, iv and Conclusio, vol. II, pp. 638–41.

61 *Quaestiones disputatae* vol. V, pp. 117–20. *De Triplici Via* vol. VIII, pp. 3–27. *In Hexaem.* xxii, 24–40, vol. V, pp. 441–3. *Itinerarium* ii, 11–13; iii, 3; iv, 1: vol. V, pp. 302–3, 304, 306; ed.min. pp. 312–13, 316–19, 324. *De perfectione vitae*, i, 3, vol. XIII, p. 108.

62 *De Triplici Via* vol. VIII, pp. 3–27 (esp. section iii, pp. 11–18).

63 *Breviloquium* ii, xi; iii, iii: vol. V, pp. 229, 232–3; ed.min. pp. 91, 101–2. *In Hexaem.* i, 17; xix, 4; xxii, 35: vol. V, pp. 332, 420, 442. *II Sentent.* Proem; xxx, ii, i, fund. ivm: vol. II, pp. 5, 721.

64 *In Hexaem.* ii, 32; ii, 29: vol. V, pp. 341, 342. *Itinerarium* vii, 4, vol. V, p. 312; ed.min. p. 346. *De Triplici Via* iii, 13, vol. VIII, p. 17; ed.min. p. 42. *Vitis Mystica* xxvii, 91, vol. VIII, p. 203.

65 *De Triplici Via* 3, 16; 4, 6: vol. VIII, pp. 7, 14; and *passim* in *Vitis Mystica.*

66 *De Diligendo Deo*, chs. XI and XV, Migne, P.L. clxxxii.

67 *Joannes Coletus Super opera Dionysii*, ed. J. H. Lupton, 1869, p. 21.

68 St Augustine, *De Trinitate* x, i, 3, Migne P.L. xlii, col. 973, and ed. W. J. Mountain and F. Glorie, Turnhout, 1968, pp. 314–15 (in *Aureli Augustini, Opera*, Part xvi, i, Corpus Christianorum, Series Latina L); *St Thomas Aquinas: Summa Theologia*, 1964, la. 2ae. 3, 4.

69 *De Trinitate* x, i, 3 and Migne, P.L., xlii, col. 474.

70 Dante, *Convivio* iii, ii, 5–19, 11, pp. 266–79.

71 *Convivio* iii, ii, 8–10, 11, pp. 270–1.

72 *Vellutello*, 1544, AI viiiʳ.

73 *Dante con l'espositione di M. Bernardino Daniello da Lucca*, p. 426.

74 Giovanni di Gherardo da Prato, *Filomena*, 1389–1432, book 2, canto iii, stanzas 24–5 and 33. Given in *Poesie di Mille Autori Intorno a Dante Alighieri*, ed. C. del Balzo, Rome, 1891, III, pp. 311–412.

75 The symbolism of the *Commedia* is illuminatingly studied in H. F. Dunbar, *Symbolism in Mediaeval Thought and its Consummation in the Divine Comedy*, New Haven, 1929, pp. 284–310; Charles Singleton, 'Commedia: Elements of Structure', *Dante Studies* 1, Cambridge, Mass., 1954, pp. 8–98 and 'Journey to Beatrice', *Dante Studies* 2, Cambridge, Mass, 1958, pp. 184–201; E. Auerbach, 'Figura', *Scenes from the Drama of European Literature*, New York, 1959, pp. 62–76, and *Dante, poet of the secular world*, Chicago, 1961, sections IV and V, pp. 101–73; A. C. Charity, *Events and their Afterlife: the Dialectics of Christian Typology in the Bible and Dante*, Cambridge, 1966, esp. pp. 167–261; R. Hollander, *Allegory in Dante's Commedia, passim*. J. A. Mazzeo well shows how Dante's conception of love shapes the *Commedia* in 'Dante's Conception of Love', *Journal of the History of Ideas*, XVIII, 2, 1957, pp. 147–60, and in *Structure and Thought in the Paradiso*, Ithaca, N.Y., 1958, *passim*.

76 See ch. 5 above.
77 Aristotle, *Ethics* vi, i–ii, and *Metaphysics*, θ, ν; *Albertus Magnus, Metaphysica* 11, 2, 6, *Opera Omnia*, Westphalia, 1964, xvi, ii, p. 490, and 11, 1, 9, pp. 471–3, and 11, 2, 15, pp. 501–2. See also Aquinas, *Summa Theol.* 1², q.85, a.1 and 1⁴, q.75, a.6.
78 *Epistle to Can Grande della Scala* in *Tutte Le Opere di Dante Alighieri*, ed. E. Moore, Oxford, 1897, 111, p. 255 (3rd edn, 1904, p. 417).
79 *Il comento al primo canto dell'Inferno pubblicato e annotato da Giuseppe Gugnoni*, Città di Castello, 1896, *prefatio*, pp. 27–8.
80 *Vellutello*, 1544, C vi⁵.
81 *Landino*, 1564, f.32⁵.
82 *Summa Theol.* la. 2ae. 3, 4.
83 Aquinas discusses the whole matter of angelic knowledge and love in *Summa Theol.* la.54, 1–60, 5. He raises the question of the relative work of knowledge and of desire (appetite, love) in many places in the *Summa Theol.*, for example: la.27, 1–5; la.16, 4 ad 1; la.14, 4 and 8; la.16, 5; la.19, 1, 1 and 4; la.26, 2; la.79, 1; la.80, 2; la 2ae, 26–34; la.2ae. 29, 5; 3.27, 1, 4 and 13. See the excellent discussion of this point in Appendix 10 of vol. 1 of the Blackfriars edition of the *Summa Theologiae*, 'The Dialectic of Love in the Summa', pp. 124–31.
84 *Joannes Coletus Super opera Dionysii*, p. 20. See E. G. Gardner, *Dante's Ten Heavens*, 1904, pp. 228–9.
85 The subtitle of Vallgornera's *Mystica Theologia Divi Thomae*, 1662, describes Aquinas as the Prince of both theologies, scholastical and mystical. The editor of the first volume of the Blackfriars edition of the *Summa* justly points out that this opens a division not found in the *Summa. Summa Theol.* 1, p. 131.
86 *Sermones de Diversis*, Sermo xxi, 2, Migne P.L. clxxxiii, col. 594; *In Nativitate Domini*, Sermo 1, 5, Migne P.L. clxxxiii col. 117; *Epistola* cviii, 2, Migne P.L. clxxxii, col. 250.
87 Dom David Knowles, *The Evolution of Mediaeval Thought*, 1962, pp. 146–8.
88 Migne P.L. clxxvi, cols. 954–6.
89 Richard of St Victor, *Benjamin Minor* v and xii, Migne P.L. cxcvi, cols. 4–5 and 8–9.
90 *The Goade of Divine Love*, translated by B. Lewis, Douai, 1642, The Translator to the Reader, unpaginated.
91 J. Mediolanensis, *Stimulus Amoris*, Claras Aquas, 1905, esp. Prologue and chs. xiv and xvii, pp. 3–7, 37–41, 68–75, 102–5.
92 Latin text in *Opuscula Sancti Patris Francisci Assisiensis*, Claras Aquas, 1904, p. 125.
93 *Speculum Perfectionis*, ch. lxix, in St Francis of Assisi, *Writings and Early Biographies*, ed. M. A. Habig, 1973, pp. 1197–8.
94 *Scripta Leonis, Rufini, et Angeli*, ed. R. B. Brooke, Oxford, 1970, p. 214.
95 Italian text in *Le Laude*, ed. L. Fallacara, Florence, 1955.
96 St Catherine of Siena, *Libro della Divina Dottrina (Dialogo della Divina Providenza)*, ch. li, ed. M. Fiorilli, Bari, 1928, p. 98.
97 *Le Lettere de S. Caterina da Siena*, ed. N. Tommaseo, Florence, 1860, Letter cii, ii, p. 200.
98 Walter Hilton, *The Scale of Perfection* ii, 33–5, ed. E. Underhill (1923), 1948, pp. 378–89.
99 Walter Hilton, *Of Angels' song*, c. 1390, in *Richard Rolle of Hampole ... and his Followers*, ed. C. Horstman, 1895, 1, p. 182.

100 *A Book of Showings to the Anchoress Julian of Norwich*, c. 1393, ch. LXXXVI, Revelation 16, ed. E. Colledge and J. Walsh, Toronto, 1978, pp. 733–4.
101 *Incendium Amoris*, ch. XLI. Latin text in *The Incendium Amoris of Richard Rolle of Hampole*, ed. M. Deanesley, Manchester, 1915, p. 275.
102 *Ibid.*, ch. V, p. 160.
103 St John of the Cross, *El Cantico Espiritual*, ed. M. M. Burgos, Madrid, 1944, p. 292.
104 St John of the Cross, *Noche Oscura*, ch. XIX, in *Vida y Obras Completas*, ed. P. Crisogono, P. Matia de Nino, P. Lucinio, Madrid, 1960, pp. 712–17.
105 St John of the Cross, *El Cantico Espiritual*, p. 174.
106 St John of the Cross, *Llama de Amor Viva* in *Vida y Obras Completas*, pp. 999–1000.
107 In *La Poesia*, ed. J. L. L. Aranguren, Madrid, 1973, p. 129.
108 Marsilio Ficino develops an account of love by way of commentary on Plato's *Symposium* in his *In Convivium Platonis De Amore, Commentarium*, which was written in 1469 and first printed in 1484. My references are to the text in Ficino, *Opera Omnia*, Basileae, 1576, II, pp. 1320–61. Ficino's own Italian version of this commentary was published as *M. Ficino sopra lo Amore*, Florence, 1544, and I add references to this edition. There is a modern edition, with a translation into French, by R. Marcel, *Commentaire sur le Banquet de Platon*, Paris, 1956.
    Pico della Mirandola's understanding of love emerges most fully in his commentary on some poems by G. Benivieni, which was written about 1490 and first published with his works in 1495. My references are to the first separate publication of this commentary, *Commento del Illustrissimo Conte Johanni Pico Mirandulano sopra una Canzone de Amore composta da Hieronymo Benivieni Cittadino Fiorentino secondo la mente e opinione de Platonici*, Florence, ?1519.
109 Ficino discusses the relationship between sense and mind in his *Theologica Platonicae, Opera Omnia*, 1576, I, especially pp. 99–424; in the *Epistolarum, Opera Omnia*, I, especially pp. 633–753; and in the *Praedicationes, Opera Omnia*, I, especially pp. 473–89.
110 Ficino, *Theologica Platonicae*, p. 306.
111 Ficino, *De Amore*, II, p. 1352; *Sopra lo Amore*, p. 190.
112 *De Amore*, pp. 1354–5; *Sopra lo Amore*, p. 202.
113 *De Amore*, p. 1328; *Sopra lo Amore*, p. 49.
114 *De Amore*, p. 1356; *Sopra lo Amore*, p. 207.
115 Pico della Mirandola, *Commento*, ?1519, f.32^v.
116 *Ibid.*, f.36^r.
117 *Ibid.*
118 Ficino, *De Amore*, p. 1354; *Sopra lo Amore*, pp. 192–3.
119 *De Amore*, p. 1352; *Sopra lo Amore*, p. 190.
120 Pico della Mirandola, *Commento* f.60^r.
121 *Ibid.*, ff.59^r–60^r.
122 *Ibid.*, f.33^r.
123 *Ibid.*, f.12^r.
124 Ficino, *De Amore*, p. 1328; *Sopra lo Amore*, p. 49.
125 *De Amore*, p. 1362; *Sopra lo Amore*, p. 246.
126 *De Amore*, p. 1328; *Sopra lo Amore*, pp. 49–50.
127 *De Amore*, p. 1328; *Sopra lo Amore*, p. 47.
128 *De Amore*, p. 1353; *Sopra lo Amore*, p. 193.

129 *De Amore*, p. 1353; *Sopra lo Amore*, p. 193.
130 *De Amore*, p. 1355; *Sopra lo Amore*, p. 203.
131 *De Amore*, p. 1323; *Sopra lo Amore*, p. 18.
132 *De Amore*, p. 1323; *Sopra lo Amore*, p. 18.
133 See the quotation from the *Comento del Magnifico Lorenzo de' Medici* given on p. 38.
134 *Comento del Magnifico Lorenzo de' Medici*, I, p. 139.
135 Ficino, *De Amore*, p. 1326; *Sopra lo Amore*, p. 26.
136 Pico della Mirandola, *De Hominis Dignitate*, ed. E. Garin, Florence, 1942, pp. 104–11.
137 See Richard of St Victor, *Benjamin Minor* lxxviii, Migne, P.L. cxcvi, and *Benjamin Major* xiii, Migne P.L. cxcvi, cols. 122–3.
138 Petrarch, *Familiarum Rerum Libri* iv, i, ed. E. Bianchi, in *Prose*, ed. G. Martelotti, P. G. Ricci, E. Carrara, and E. Bianchi, Milan and Naples, 1955, pp. 830–44.
139 In *J. L. Vives, Opera Omnia*, ed. F. Craneveldius, Valencia, 1783, IV, pp. 3–8.
140 Ficino, *Argumentum*, in *Opera Omnia*, II, p. 1836.
141 D. P. Walker surveys neoplatonic writings on magic in *Spiritual and Demonic Magic from Ficino to Campanella*, 1958. Kitty Scoular studies ideas of natural magic in English poetry from Spenser to Marvell in *Natural Magic*, Oxford, 1965. Keith Thomas marshals the evidence of magical practices in English religious life in *Religion and the Decline of Magic*, 1971.
142 *Pimander*, Libellus xii, 15b, ed. W. Scott, *Hermetica*, Oxford, 1924, pp. 232–3.
143 *Pimander*, Lib. xii, 16, in Scott, *Hermetica*, pp. 234–5.
144 H. C. Agrippa, *De Occulta Philosophia Libri Tres*, 1533, transl. J.F., 1651, p. 337.
145 *Ibid.*, pp. 338–9.
146 *Asclepius* I, 2b–3a, in Scott, *Hermetica*, pp. 288–91.
147 T. Campanella, *Del Senso Delle Cose E Della Magia*, ed. A. Bruers, Bari, 1925, p. 331.
148 *Asclepius* iii, 21, in Scott, *Hermetica*, pp. 334–5.
149 G. B. Della Porta, *Magiae naturalis sive de miraculis rerum naturalium libri iii*, Naples, 1558, translated by T. Young and S. Speed, 1658, pp. 13–14.
150 John of Rupescissa, *De Consideratione quintae essentiae*, quoted in L. Thorndike, *A History of Magic and Experimental Science*, New York, 1934, III, p. 364.
151 William Gilbert, *De Magnete*, 1628, v, v and xii. See E. Zilsel, 'The Origins of William Gilbert's Scientific Method', *JHI*, II, 1, 1941, pp. 61–76.
152 R. Fludd, *Mosaicall Philosophy*, 1659, pp. 169–70.
153 Pliny, *Historia naturalis* vii, Proem, transl. P. Holland, 1601, ed. J. Newsome, Oxford, 1954, p. 46. See also Plutarch, *De amore prolis*, esp. 1–3, in *Moralia* VI, ed. C. Helmbold, 1957, pp. 328–57, and *Gryllus*, esp. 3–10, in *Moralia*, pp. 492–533.
154 Campanella, *Del Senso Delle Cose*, pp. 20–1.
155 Agrippa, *De Occulta Philosophia Libri Tres*, p. 278; see also pp. 459–60 and 468.
156 *Ibid.*, p. 278.
157 Campanella, *Del Senso Delle Cose*, p. 175.
158 *Ibid.*

159 Fludd, *Mosaicall Philosophy*, p. 185.
160 Agrippa, *De Occulta Philosophia Libri Tres*, pp. 337–40.
161 Kepler, *Harmonice Mundi*, 1619, in *Opera*, Linz, 1619, II, titlepage of Book 4, and p. 645.
162 *Anima Magica Abscondita* (1650), in *The Works of Thomas Vaughan*, ed. A. E. Waite, 1919, p. 77.
163 Agrippa, *De Occulta Philosophia Libri Tres*, pp. 389–91.
164 *Pimander* Lib. I, 14–15, in Scott, *Hermetica*, pp. 120–3.
165 Thomas Vaughan, *Anima Magica Abscondita* in *Works* p. 77.
166 Agrippa, *De Occulta Philosophia Libri Tres*, pp. 26–7.
167 Paracelsus, *Astronomia Magna*, in Paracelsus, *Sämtliche Werke*, ed. K. Sudhoff and W. Matthiessen, Munich and Berlin, 1928–38, I, xii, p. 174. Given in *Selected Writings*, ed. J. Jacobi, transl. N. Guterman, 1951, p. 195.
168 Joseph Hall, *The Art of Divine Meditation*, 1606 in *The Works of Joseph Hall*, Oxford, 1836, VI, p. 51.
169 Campanella, *Del Senso Delle Cose*, p. 331.
170 Fludd, *Mosaicall Philosophy*, p. 60.
171 Joseph Hall, *The Art of Divine Meditation*, p. 49.
172 The small anthology of hieroglyphs published by Aldus in 1505 under the name of Horapollo, a Greek grammarian of the fourth century AD, purports to gather and explicate the esoteric sign-language of the priests of ancient Egypt. It was many times reissued and translated, and initiated a European cult of the hieroglyph.
173 Robert Boyle, 'Discourse Touching Occasional Meditations', in *Occasional Reflections upon Several Subjects*, 1665, pp. 13–18, 39–42, 75.
174 *Ori Apollinis Niliaci, De Sacris Aegyptiorum notis, Aegyptiace expressis*, Paris, 1574, ii^r.
175 Luca Contile, *Ragionamento ... Sopra viiii Inventioni E Loro Origine*, Pavia, 1574, p. 2.
176 C. Ripa, *Iconologia*, Siena, 1613, p. 10.
177 Scipione Bargagli, *Dell'Imprese*, Venice, 1589, p. 330.
178 *Pimander*, Lib. I, 15 in Scott, *Hermetica*, p. 123.
179 Agrippa, *De Occulta Philosophia Libri Tres*, p. 460.
180 *Ibid.*
181 Della Porta, *Magiae naturalis*, p. 14.
182 Campanella, *Del Senso Delle Cose*, p. 316.
183 Robert Fludd, *Mosaicall Philosophy*, p. 21; *Gloria Mundi*, in *The Hermetic Museum* (Frankfurt, 1678), translated by A. E. Waite, 1893, II, pp. 180–1.
184 Agrippa, *De Occulta Philosophia Libri Tres*, p. 357.
185 Della Porta, *Magiae naturalis*, p. 15.
186 Fludd, *Mosaicall Philosophy*, p. 21.
187 Thomas Vaughan, *Magia Adamica* (1650), in *Works*, pp. 76–7, 144.
188 Della Porta, *Magiae naturalis*, p. 14. E. M. Butler gives a general account of the European cult of the magus in *The Myth of the Magus*, Cambridge, 1948.
189 Agrippa, *De Occulta Philosophia Libri Tres*, p. 460.
190 *Ibid.*, pp. 559–60.
191 *Ibid.*, Cusanus, *De Docta Ignorantia*, in *Opera*, Paris, 1514, I, Lib. III, f.xxxii^v.
192 *Pimander* Lib. ii, 9, in Scott *Hermetica*, pp. 138–9; Lib. viii, 3–4, in Scott, *Hermetica*, pp. 176–7; Lib. x, 16–20, in Scott, *Hermetica*, pp. 198–201.

193 Cusanus, *De Docta Ignorantia*, I, Lib. III, f. xxx^v–xxxi^r.
194 *Asclepius*, iii, 22b, in Scott, *Hermetica*, p. 337.
195 Agrippa, *De Occulta Philosophia Libri Tres*, p. 460.
196 Henry Vaughan, *The Mount of Olives*, and *Man in Glory*, in *Works*, ed. L. C. Martin, Oxford, 1957, pp. 175–6, and 196.
197 Frances Yates, *Giordano Bruno and the Hermetic Tradition*, 1964, p. 435.
198 Thomas Vaughan accidentally killed himself in 1666 in the course of his work in spiritual alchemy. The intellectual principles on which he based his work have been fully explicated in an unpublished doctoral thesis by Eluned Crawshaw, 'The alchemical ideas of Thomas Vaughan and their relationship to the literary works of Henry Vaughan', University of Wales, 1970. Boyle sent a paper to the Royal Society in 1675/6 telling of his attempts to solve the problem of transmutation, 'by God's blessing'. See L. T. More, 'Boyle as Alchemist', *JHI*, II, I, 1941, pp. 61–76. Newton's hermetic interests are discussed by J. E. McGuire and P. M. Rattansi in 'Newton and the "Pipes of Pan"', *Notes and Records of the Royal Society of London*, XXI, 1966, pp. 108–43; by J. E. McGuire in 'Transmutation and Immutability: Newton's Doctrine of Physical Qualities', *Ambix*, XIV, 2, June 1967, pp. 91 and 94–5; and B. J. T. Dobbs, *The Foundations of Newton's Alchemy*, Cambridge, 1975.
199 Juan de Valdes, *Las Ciento Diez Divinas Consideraciones*, c. 1539, transl. by Nicholas Ferrar, 1638, as *The Hundred and Ten Considerations of Signior John Valdesso*, ed. F. Chapman, 1905. See especially Considerations xix, xl, lxxiii, lxxiv, xcv.
200 S. L. Bethell, 'The Theology of Henry and Thomas Vaughan', *Theology*, LVI, 394, April 1953, pp. 137–43.
201 Milton, *On the Morning of Christ's Nativity*, lines 37–44.
202 A. J. A. Waldock, *Paradise Lost and its Critics*, Cambridge (1947), 1961, p. 83.
203 'Angels and the Poetic Imagination from Donne to Traherne' in *English Renaissance Studies*, ed. J. Carey, Oxford, 1980, p. 168.

2. *Against Mortality*

1 E. H. Wilkins, *The Triumphs of Petrarch*, Chicago, 1962, p. vi.
2 E. H. Wilkins renders 'bel velo' as 'beauty' (*ibid.*, p. 113). The Einaudi editors gloss 'velo' as 'aspetto' (*F. Petrarca: Canzoniere, Trionfi, Rime Varie*, ed. C. Muscetta and D. Ponchiroli, Turin, 1958, p. 547 n. 143). Such reading disguises a point of substance. If 'intera' does indeed hint at a reuniting of soul and body then 'velo' implies that she may at some future time repossess her body, so that heaven will see her entire again in single beauty of body and spirit.
3 Scribbled in Michelangelo's hand on a sketch for *The Fall of Phaeton* in the British Museum. Reproduced in *Drawings by Michelangelo*, the catalogue of the British Museum Exhibition of 1975.
4 Letter of 20 January 1538, *Le Lettere di M. Pietro Aretino*, Paris, 1609, II, p. 10.
5 C. de Tolnay, *Michelangelo*, Princeton (1943–60), 1975, V, pp. 48 and 181, and plates 227–30.
6 The Windsor *Ganymede* is probably a contemporary copy of Michelangelo's original drawing.
7 In his scholarly edition of Michelangelo's poems E. N. Girardi corrected the misreading which led previous editors to assume that the poem was

addressed to Vittoria Colonna. *Michelangiolo Buonarroti: Rime*, Bari, 1960, p. 426.

8 *Esequie Del Divino Michelagnolo Buonarroti*, Florence, 1564, D2ᵛ. Facsimile edition by R. and M. Wittkower as *The Divine Michelangelo: The Florentine Academy's Homage on his Death in 1564*, pp. 100–1 and 148–50.

9 *Esequie* D2ᵛ, facsimile p. 100.

10 L. Tonelli, *L'amore nella poesia e nel pensiero del Rinascimento*, Florence, 1933, p. 107.

11 Girardi, *Michelangiolo*, p. 355.

12 G. R. Ceriello, *Michelangelo Buonarroti: Rime*, Milan, 1954, p. 15.

13 'Qui si fa elmi', *The Sonnets of M. A. Buonarroti and T. Campanella*, translated by J. A. Symonds, 1878.

14 See my essay 'For the death of Cecchino Bracci', *MLR*, LVIII, 3, July 1963, pp. 355–63.

15 *Le Lettere di Michelangelo Buonarroti*, ed. G. Milanesi, Florence, 1873, pp. 462–4. Translated J. A. Symonds in *The Life of Michelangelo Buonarroti*, 1893, ii, pp. 134–5. Michelangelo drafted this letter at least three times before he sent it.

16 Translated Symonds in *Sonnets*.

17 Benedetto Varchi, *Opere*, Milan, 1834, I, pp. 98–114.

18 *Le Lettere di M. Pietro Aretino*, Paris, 1609, II, p. 10. The letter is quoted in translation in Symonds, *Life*, II, pp. 51–5.

19 Giorgio Vasari, *Le vite de' piú eccellenti pittori, scultori, e architetti*, Florence, 1856, XII, p. 276.

20 In her monumental edition of Michelangelo's letters, 1963, E. H. Ramsden admirably rounded up and dismissed some attempts to grub for evidence of sexual impropriety in the epigrams for Cecchino Bracci (II, pp. xxxiv–v). Yet she gave away her own defence by misreading Michelangelo's grim coda to Epigram xix (Girardi no. 197) as a piece of salacious wit; and her reviewers pounced on the opportunity she offered them to proclaim Michelangelo's paederasty.

21 Francisco D'Ollanda, *Quatro Dialogos da Pintura Antigua*, Porto, 1896. D'Ollanda was a Portuguese miniature painter who worked in Rome in 1538. There is a translation of these dialogues in C. Holroyd, *Michael Angelo Buonarroti*, 1903.

22 Ascanio Condivi, *Vita di Michelagnolo Buonarroti*, in *Rime e Lettere di Michelagnolo Buonarroti* ed. G. Saltini, Florence, 1948, p. 147. There is a translation of Condivi's *Life* in Holroyd, *Michael Angelo Buonarroti*.

23 'Forse perchè d'altrui pietà mi vegna'.

24 'Giunto è gia'l corso della vita mia'.

25 'Con tanta servitù, con tanto tedio'.

26 Condivi, *Vita*, p. 151. E. Garin discusses Michelangelo's nurture and his platonising in *The Complete Works of Michelangelo*, Novara, 1965, English version 1966, II, pp. 517–30. E. N. Girardi considers the intellectual temper of Michelangelo's writings and poetry in the same publication, II, pp. 531–56.

27 See Donato Gianotti, *De' giorni che Dante consumò nel cercar l'Inferno e'l Purgatorio*. Given in C. Guasti, *Rime di Michelangelo Buonarroti*, Florence, 1863, pp. xxvi–xxxiv.

28 'Quanta dolcezza al cor per gli occhi porta'.

29 'Per fido esempio alla mia vocazione'.

30 Published in 1498 as the *Regola del ben vivere*, and several times reissued. Quoted in P. Villari, *Life and Times of Girolamo Savonarola*, 1897, p. 741.
31 Loyola, *Spiritual Exercises*, First Week, First Exercise, no. 53, and other places. Despite his antipathy to the rigorous spirit of the Counter Reform movement Michelangelo greatly admired Loyola.
32 J. Tusiani, *The Complete Poems of Michelangelo*, p. 141.

3. Body and Soul

1 Given as 'piety' in the early editions of the letters, 1651 and 1654. Edmund Gosse alters that to 'plenty' (*The Life and Letters of John Donne*, London, 1899, I, p. 291).
2 *OED* 'convenient' 5: morally or ethically suitable; becoming.
3 *OED* 'concoction' 2a: ripening, maturing, or bringing to a state of perfection; also, the state of perfection so produced.
4 H. J. C. Grierson, ed., *The Poems of John Donne*, Oxford, 1912, II, p. 41.
5 Hobbes, *Leviathan* 3, 34; 3, 38; 4, 46.
6 See p. 158.
7 B. Varchi, *Lezzione Sopra L'Amore*, in *Lezioni*, Florence, 1590, pp. 326–7.
8 Tullia d'Aragona, *Della Infinità di Amore*, in G. Zonta, *Trattati d'Amore del Cinquecento*, Bari, 1912, p. 222.
9 Leone Ebreo, *Dialoghi d'Amore*, ed. S. Caramella, Bari, 1921, p. 6.
10 Tullia, *Infinità*, p. 235.
11 Leone Ebreo, *Dialoghi*, p. 49.
12 G. Betussi, *Il Raverta*, in Zonta, *Trattati*, pp. 10–11.
13 Sperone Speroni, *Dialogo di Amore, Opere*, Venice, 1740, I, p. 3.
14 B. Gottifredi, *Lo Specchio d'Amore*, in Zonta, *Trattati*, p. 297.
15 T. Tasso, *Conclusioni Amorose* in *Le Prose Diverse*, ed. C. Guasti, Florence, 1875, II, p. 68.
16 F. Sansovino, *Ragionamento nel quale brevemente s'insegna a' Giovani Uomini la Bella Arte d'Amore*, in Zonta, *Trattati*, p. 180.
17 Betussi, *Raverta*, p. 34.
18 Leone Ebreo, *Dialoghi*, p. 173.
19 F. Cattani, *I Tre Libri d'Amore*, Venice, 1561, pp. 119–20.
20 Leone Ebreo, *Dialoghi*, p. 176.
21 J. Weemes, *A Treatise of the Foure Degenerate Sonnes*, 1636, p. 72.
22 Leone Ebreo, *Dialoghi*, p. 43.
23 T. Tasso, *Le Considerazione sopra Tre Canzoni de M. Gio. Battista Pigna*, in Guasti, *Prose*, II, p. 92.
24 Speroni, *Opere*, I, p. 4.
25 Betussi, *Raverta*, p. 95.
26 *Ibid.*, pp. 23, 24.
27 Leone Ebreo, *Dialoghi*, p. 383.
28 *Ibid.*, p. 51. See also pp. 43 and 384.
29 F. Cattani, *I Tre Libri*, p. 111.
30 Aquinas, *Summa Theol.* 1a. 76, 7. 2.
31 M. Ficino, *Sopra lo Amore*, Lanciano, 1914, p. 92.
32 Cattani, *I Tre Libri*, p. 111.
33 *Ibid.*, p. 112.
34 The phrase is Varchi's, in 'Dell'Anima', *Lezioni*, p. 721.

35 *De Anima*, esp. II, 1, 403a, 2–403b, 19, and II, 2, 414a, 3–414a, 28.
36 I am indebted to M. Etienne Gilson's elucidation of *Summa* 1a. 75–80 in ch. IX of *The Spirit of Mediaeval Philosophy*, 1936, from pp. 186–8 of which the quotations are taken.
37 Bruno, *De Gl'Heroici Furori*, Turin, 1928, p. 89.
38 Tullia, *Infinità*, p. 197.
39 M. Equicola, *Libro di Natura d'Amore*, Venice, 1526, f.110ᵛ.
40 Speroni, *Discorso dell'Anima Umana, Opere*, III, 370.
41 Varchi, *Lezioni*, pp. 371, 612.
42 Betussi, *Raverta*, p. 32.
43 Varchi, *Lezioni*, p. 381.
44 Tasso, *Conclusioni, Considerazioni*, in *Prose*, II, pp. 67, 89.
45 Leone Ebreo, *Dialoghi*, p. 50.
46 B. Castiglione, *Il Libro del Cortegiano*, ed. V. Cian, Florence, 1947, pp. 489–90.
47 Leone Ebreo, *Dialoghi*, p. 213.
48 Betussi; *Raverta*, p. 140.
49 Equicola, *Natura*, f. 111ʳ.
50 Tullia, *Infinità*, p. 223.
51 Tullia, *Infinità*, p. 224.
52 Equicola, *Natura*, f. 197ʳ.
53 Varchi, *Lezioni*, p. 338.
54 Speroni, *Opere*, I, pp. 6, 22–23.
55 Leone Ebreo, *Dialoghi*, p. 425.
56 *John Donne: Selected Prose*, chosen by Evelyn Simpson, ed. Helen Gardner and Timothy Healy, Oxford, 1967, pp. 146–7.
57 'Who but a monomaniac would read *Pseudo-Martyr* through?' A. Jessopp in a private letter to E. M. Simpson, quoted by her in *A Study of the Prose Works of John Donne*, 1924, p. 166 fn. 1. 'The two books [*Biathanatos* and *Pseudo-Martyr*] ... are ... the dullest of Donne's works' (E. M. Simpson, *Prose Works*, p. 166). '*Pseudo-Martyr* is the longest and, without doubt, the least interesting of Donne's early works' (*John Donne: Selected Prose* chosen by Evelyn Simpson, p. 43). 'Most of it now makes dull reading' (Geoffrey Keynes, *A Bibliography of Dr John Donne*, Oxford, 1973, p. 4).
58 *John Donne: Selected Prose*, p. 137.
59 Donne's *Devotions Upon Emergent Occasions* (1624), ed. A. Raspa, 1975, pp. 86–7.
60 Donne's Sermon to the Virginia Company', in *John Donne: Essays in Celebration*, ed. A. J. Smith, 1972, pp. 433–52.
61 See also *Sermons*, I, 3, p. 220 (24 March 1616/17); II, 1, pp. 65–6 (?1616); V, II, p. 230 (undated); VI, 2, p. 75 (Easter Day 1624).
62 See also *Sermons*, IX, 8 (Easter Day 1630).
63 *Sermons*, II, 8, p. 185 (21 February 1618/19). See also *Sermons*, I, 9, p. 309, (19 April 1618); II, 9, p. 209 (Easter Day 1619); VI, 7, pp. 155 and 159–60, (13 June 1624); VI, 8, p. 179, (Christmas Day 1624); X, 4, p. 117, (undated).
64 *Sermons*, VII, 10, pp. 257–8 (preached at the funeral of Sir W. Cokayne, 12 December 1626). See also *Sermons*, IV, 2, p. 75 (Easter Day 1622); V, II, (undated); VI, 2, p. 71 (Easter Day 1624); VI, 13, pp. 265–6 (Easter Day 1625); VII, 13, p. 345, (Candlemas Day 1626/7); VIII, 5, pp. 140–1 (Christmas Day 1627).

65 *Sermons*, VIII, 2, p. 92 (preached in commemoration of Lady Danvers, 1 July 1627).
66 *Sermons*, VII, 12, p. 322 (28 January 1626/7).
67 *Sermons*, VIII, 6, p. 168 (27 January 1627/8).
68 *Sermons*, VIII, 8, p. 203 (5 April 1628).
69 Michelangelo sketched at least fifteen studies for the Resurrection, c. 1532–33, possibly in association with Sebastiano del Piombo. Six of these sketches were on view in the British Museum exhibition *Drawings by Michelangelo*, 1975, and are reproduced in the catalogue of the exhibition, pp. 46–50. Some of the sketches of resurrected figures are reproduced in C. de Tolnay, *Michelangelo*, V, pp. 179–80.
70 Izaak Walton, *Life*, 1670, p. 75. Before it was removed at the destruction of old St Paul's in the Great Fire the effigy seems to have been mounted facing east, against the south east pier of the central tower of the cathedral (Sir W. Dugdale, *The History of St Paul's Cathedral in London*, 1658, pp. 62–3; *The Note-Book and Account Book of Nicholas Stone*, ed. W. L. Spiers, Oxford, Walpole Society, 1919, pp. 64, 90). When it was resited so that it no longer faced east it became a mere macabre curiosity.
71 Nigel Foxell, *A Sermon in Stone*, 1978, p. 22. My argument owes much to Foxell's subtle pursuit of Donne's meaning in this rich device.
72 Introduction in *The Complete Works of St Thomas More*, VII, part 3, p. 1290.
73 *St Thomas More: Action and Contemplation*, ed. R. S. Sylvester, New Haven and London, 1972, pp. 13–14.
74 More, *The Confutation of Tyndale's Answer*, *Complete Works*, VIII, part 1, p. 118.

4. *Among the Wastes of Time*

1 P. F. Minozzi, *Delle Libidini Dell'Ingegno*, Venice, 1636, *Gli Sfogamenti d'Ingegno*, Venice, 1641; M. Pellegrini, *Delle Acutezze*, Genoa, 1639, *I Fonti dell'Ingegno*, Bologna, 1650; B. Gracian, *Agudeza y Arte de Ingenio*, Madrid, 1642; Sforza Pallavicino, *Del Bene*, Rome, 1644, *Considerazioni Sopra l'Arte Delle Stile, e Del Dialogo*, Rome, 1646, *Trattato dello Stile*, Rome, 1662; E. Tesauro, *Il Canocchiale Aristotelico*, Venice, 1654.
2 *Minor Poets of the Caroline Period*, Oxford, 1905, III, p. 105n.
3 Mario Praz, 'Stanley, Sherburne and Ayres as Translators and Imitators of Italian, Spanish and French Poets', *Modern Language Review*, XX, 1925, pp. 280–93.
4 C. V. Wedgwood, 'Poets and Politics in Baroque England', *Penguin New Writing*, XXI, 1944, pp. 123–36.
5 Pope, *The First Epistle of the Second Book of Horace Imitated*, line 108.
6 See K. A. McEwen, *Classical Influences upon the Tribe of Ben*, Cedar Rapids, 1939.
7 See K. M. Lynch, *The Social Mode of Restoration Comedy*, New York, 1926, especially chapters III to V; and F. O. Henderson, 'Traditions of *Précieux* and *Libertin* in Suckling's Poetry', *English Literary History*, IV, 1937, pp. 274–98.
8 Thomas Stanley translated Pico della Mirandola's commentary on a *canzone* of celestial and divine Love by G. Benivieni, as *A Platonick Discourse upon Love*, 1651.

9 Wedgwood, 'Poets and Politics in Baroque England', pp. 12⁻–8.
10 As by C. V. Wedgwood in *Poetry and Politics under the Stuarts*, 1960, pp. 108–14.
11 Christopher Hill, *Intellectual Origins of the English Revolution*, Oxford, 1965, pp. 11–13.
12 See L. C. Knights, 'On the Social Background of Metaphysical Poetry', *Scrutiny*, XIII, 1945, pp. 37–52.
13 See Christopher Hill, 'Society and Andrew Marvell', *Modern Quarterly*, IV, 1956, pp. 6–31, and *Puritanism and Revolution* (1958), 1968, pp. 324–50.

5. *Through Nature to Eternity:*
Vaughan's *Silex Scintillans*

1 A. Alvarez, *The School of Donne*, 1961, pp. 89–90.
2 J. Boheme, *De Signatura Rerum*, 1621, VIII, pp. 47–8. In William Law's translation of the *Works* (1764–81), 1912, p. 89.
3 *Anima Magica Abscondita*, in *The Works of Thomas Vaughan*, ed. A. E. Waite, 1919, p. 77.
4 L. C. Martin gives the texts of two such translations in his *OET* (1914) edition of Vaughan's works, *Hermetical Physick*, 1655, and *The Chymists Key*, 1657, both translated from Latin treatises by Heinrich Nolle.
5 R. A. Durr, *On the Mystical Poetry of Henry Vaughan*, Cambridge, Mass., 1962, p. 144.
6 S. L. Bethell, 'The Theology of Henry and Thomas Vaughan', *Theology*, LVI, 394, April 1953, pp. 137–43.
7 See p. 114, note 198, above.
8 Bethell, 'The Theology of Henry and Thomas Vaughan', p. 141.
9 See p. 105. G. B. della Porta, *Natural Magic*, translated by T. Young and S. Speed, 1658, p. 201; W. Gilbert, *De Magnete*, V, 12.
10 See M. Crum, *The Poems of Henry King*, Oxford, 1965, pp. 19–22.
11 Thomas Vaughan, *Euphrates*, 1655, in *Works*, p. 396.
12 *Silex Scintillans*, an edition, 1905, Introduction, p. xxxi.
13 See M. C. Sarbiewski, *The Odes of Casimire*, transl. G. Hils (1646), Augustan Reprint Society no. 44, Los Angeles, 1953.
14 Durandus, *Rationale Divinorum Officiorum*, c.1286–91.
15 See p. 106.
16 Simone Weil, *Le Pesanteur et la Grace*, 1947 (transl. by Emma Crawford as *Gravity and Grace*, 1952). See also *Cahiers*, Paris, 1953, II, pp. 186 and 276–7 (transl. by A. Wills as *The Notebooks of Simone Weil*, 1956, pp. 262 and 322).
17 Durr, *Mystical Poetry*, p. 159.
18 Beza, *Iesu Christi D. N. Novum Testamentum*, 1574, given in the translation by L. Tomson, 1576, f.246ʳ.
19 *Pimander*, Lib. xii, 15b–16, in Scott, *Hermetica*, I, pp. 233–5. See pp. 3, 103–4, 176–80, above.
20 Bethell, 'The Theology of Henry and Thomas Vaughan', p. 141.
21 A. Paleario, *Del Beneficio di Gesu Christo Crocifisso, Verso I Christiani*, Venice, 1542–3, 32ʳ, transl. E. Courtenay, 1548, as *A Treatise Most Profitable of the Benefit that True Christians Receive by the Death of Jesus Christ*, ed. C. Babbington, 1855, p. 134. This treatise, published anonymously, was

taken to be an apology for Valdes's doctrine of justification, and placed on the first Index of Prohibited Books in 1549. It was repeatedly condemned and denounced thereafter. Paleario was later executed as a heretic, as were several other associates of that celebrated circle of Catholic reformers which met at the Church of San Silvestro al Monte to discuss the ideas of Valdes, and included Reginald Pole, Michelangelo Buonarroti, and Vittoria Colonna among its regular participants. Edward Courtenay, later Earl of Devonshire, had close family ties with Cardinal Pole; he translated this treatise while imprisoned in the tower as a Catholic claimant to the throne.

22 E. C. Pettet, *Of Paradise and Light*, Cambridge, 1960, p. 21.
23 Edith Sichel, 'Henry Vaughan: Silurist', *The Monthly Review*, XI, 112, 113, April 1903, p. 117.
24 Ross Garner, *Henry Vaughan: Experience and Tradition*, Chicago, 1959, p. 162.
25 *Ibid.*, p. 163.
26 *Ibid.*, p. 152 and *passim*.
27 Durr, *Mystical Poetry*, p. 159.
28 See pp. 109–12 above.
29 Luca Contile, *Ragionamento Sopra La Proprieta delle Imprese*, Pavia, 1574, f.27^r.
30 Paracelsus, *Astronomia Magna*, in *Paracelsus. Sämtliche Werke*, ed. K. Sudhoff and W. Matthiessen, Munich and Berlin, 1928–33, I, xii, pp. 174–7. Given in *Paracelsus: Selected Writings*, ed. J. Jacobi, translated by N. Guterman, 1951, pp. 195–6.
31 Pettet, *Of Paradise*, p. 24.
32 Durr, *Mystical Poetry*, p. 142.
33 J. D. Sinclair, *The Divine Comedy of Dante Alighieri*, 1971, III, p. 400.
34 See F. E. Hutchinson, *Henry Vaughan*, 1947, pp. 95–6.

Index

345

Index

Index

Index